# BEYOND GURUS

# BEYOND GURUS

## A Woman of Many Worlds

Nancy Cooke de Herrera

Blue Dolphin Publishing, Inc.
1993

Cover Photo: Tatwala Baba, a revered Indian saint who resided in the Valley of the Saints and was reputed to be approximately 120 years old.

Cover photos by Richard A. Cooke, III

Acknowledgment is gratefully given to the following for use of copyrighted material:
    Charles L. Hillebrand and Ralph A. Johnson, "Vampy Eyes," © 1919, p. xv.
    *Life Magazine*, July 20, 1949, photo: Bob Ebert, p. 32.
    *Look Magazine*, February 6, 1968, p. 232.
    *Saturday Evening Post*, May 4, 1968, p. 233.
    *Sports Illustrated*, November 25, 1957, photo: Robert Riger, p. 401; Margaret Durrance, p. 402.
    *Swedish Life Magazine*, 1957, p. 306.

Published by Blue Dolphin Publishing, Inc.
P.O. Box 1908, Nevada City, CA 95959

ISBN: 0-931892-49-X

Library of Congress Cataloging in Publication Data:

Herrera, Nancy Cooke de, date
    Beyond gurus / Nancy Cooke de Herrera.
    p.  cm.
    ISBN 0-931892-49-X (trade hardcover) : $22.00
    1. Herrera, Nancy Cooke de, date.  2. Religious biography.  I. Title.
BL73.H47A3 1992
291'.092—dc20
[B]                          92-31571
                                       CIP

Printed in the United States of America by
Blue Dolphin Press, Inc., Grass Valley, California

5       4       3       2       1

*In Memory of
Luis*

# Table of Contents

# Acknowledgments

FIRST OF ALL MY FAMILY, my well-educated sons and daughter, gave invaluable input. Rik started the process by accompanying me to various remote places, which he recorded with his camera, and many of the photos appear in this book. Brett researched my letters, extracted details filed away in the past, and assisted me in organizing my material for the manuscript. Starr helped me become a "modern woman" with a fax machine, computer, and such. Last but not least, María Luisa, with her art historian's eye, proved to be the ultimate editor.

If I had not attended Barnaby Conrad's Writer's Workshop in Santa Barbara, I doubt that my manuscript would ever have reached publishable form. Thank you, Barnaby and all the staff, for your expertise and guidance.

Over the years since I started *Beyond Gurus*, certain names float up as helpers in what seemed an unending process: Marshall Lee, an agent and friend in New York; Tom Green and Terry Pearce from Tiburon, California for their unfailing enthusiasm; Mercedes de Chavez, my housekeeper, who protected my time; Arnold Schulman, playwright and neighbor, who is always there to tap into for advice; Pamela Hassell, a new but valuable friend; and Jim and Nancy Strohecker who offered advice and loving support.

Also, the approval of friends such as Marcella Rabwin, Ruth Dillingham Bromfield, Zandrah Ralphs, Iris Schirmer, and Lucy Lamkin, all of whom read the manuscript, helped me maintain my determination to see my story published.

And not to be forgotten is my publisher, Paul Clemens, who first contacted me about my story many years ago. He comes from a spiritual background, so we speak the same language. It has been his enthusiastic support that has brought this project to completion. He publishes "books which help people."

# Introduction

To me, Nancy Cooke de Herrera is an extraordinary personality. Though born in San Francisco with the proverbial silver spoon, she broke away from her conservative background with a zest for living and a thirst to experience all that life might offer. Making her home in Honolulu, Argentina, and India, as a naturally gregarious Aries, she has filled her life with exalted personalities attracted by her graciousness and charm.

However, Nancy's admirers are not confined to the important and the glamorous. Whomever's life she has touched, whether that person be great or small, he or she has been thrilled by her presence. This energetic soul brings a lighter spirit and heart to anyone knowing her. After the tragic death of her husband, she recognized that in each of us is a need for a supportive philosophy, a school of thought, and a desire for enlightenment. She is the rare person who understands that in searching for deeply satisfying answers, one runs the gamut from the practical to concepts of the loftiest spiritual nature.

With Nancy de Herrera one encounters a growth in understanding, an expanding consciousness, and a broadening horizon.

This story follows the unfoldment of a spirit who, while greatly enjoying the mundane pleasures of life, gains knowledge of universal law, and arrives at the certainty of eternal life. Through her search she finds her inner teacher and her own humanity. It will be a real pleasure for the readers, as it has been for me, to join Nancy in her activities and conclusions. I cannot but wonder what will come next in this richly embroidered life.

Carroll Righter
January 1988

*from*

*Family Album*

*Nancy's mother as a young woman in Nebraska*

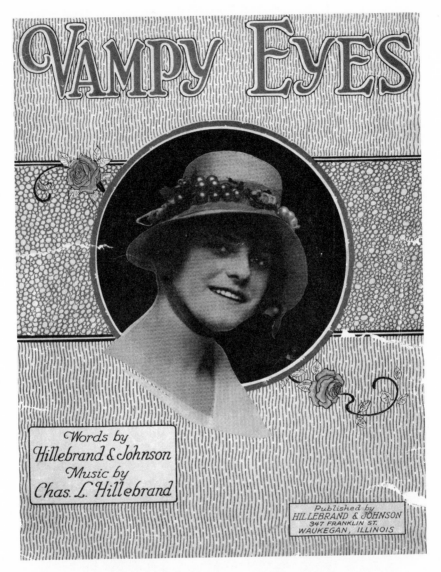

Nancy's mother's face on sheet music
(© 1919 Chas. L. Hillebrand & Ralph A. Johnson)

Nancy and
Ardagh Marie Veitch,
about 2 and 3 years old

Our grandfather,
Richard M. Veitch,
who lived with us until I was 17

Our family home in Piedmont, California

*The three Veitch sisters—Ardagh Marie, Nancy and Doryce
in the early thirties*

*Nancy, Doryce, Ardagh Marie and their mother during the thirties*

*Nancy's mother with dog,
Pumpkin*

*Nancy at sixteen with dog,
Caesar*

*Nancy's favorite photo of her
father, about 1940*

*Nancy's mother, Marie Morledge
Veitch, in the forties*

*The three sisters at Doryce's wedding to Herbert Hills in 1946*

*Newspaper photo of Ardagh Marie, Doryce, Nancy and their mother*
*leaving for Honolulu in 1941*

*Nancy's family with her mother and grandmother*
*on her return from Argentina in 1957*

# PART ONE

## Changing Focus On Life

## 1

# *Welcome to India*

A S THE PLANE DESCENDED OVER THE DELHI TERMINAL on a dark, starless night in March of 1962, I had the deep premonition that this trip would change my life forever. Traveling around the world as a good will personality with the U.S. State Department, I was accustomed to being welcomed by governments as a celebrity with a full agenda of activities awaiting me. On this night, however, I was an unofficial visitor, strictly on my own. I was walking into the unknown. India was a new horizon for me. Not knowing a soul in this ancient and mysterious country, I prayed that my good friend Tom Slick would be there to meet me. Three months had passed since our last communication—would he show up?

When a steward opened the door, an earthy fragrance filled the cabin. A wave of insecurity washed over me as I climbed down the ramp and looked through the airport lights for the customs house. Then as the soft air caressed me, a thrill of anticipation pushed away my insecurities. "I'm finally in India. This is the moment I have been waiting for." Would this mystical land supply me with answers to the questions that had haunted me for the past seven years? After all, India was known as the cradle of spiritual knowledge.

I'd come directly from Teheran where, as a guest of the Shah of Iran, I had presented a fashion show to provide publicity for The New Path Society. This was a group of Iranian women who were attempting to ban the obligatory usage of the *chador* and the facial veil that the women had been wearing for centuries.

I was to meet Tom Slick, Texas oilman and parapsychologist. Our plan was to roam the Himalayan foothills together calling on lamas, swamis and yogis. While Tom was searching for psychic phenomena, levitation, teleportation and materialization, I would follow my own search.

"Where is my natural love of adventure?" I silently asked, prodding myself into a confident air. "No matter what happens, it will be fine. If Tom's not here, I'll check into a hotel and in a few days go on to Bangkok."

We were herded into a low, tin-roofed shed glaring with fluorescent lights. A uniformed Indian reached for my suitcase keys, asking in clipped English, "Have you anything to declare, *Memsahib?*" I shook my head, indicating no, and scanned the crowd teaming in the balmy air around me. Standing nearly six feet tall, I looked out over the crowd but saw nothing familiar. "Oh please, Tom, be here. . . . I have such expectations for this trip."

Emaciated bearers waited by the exit, their somber eyes scrutinizing the passengers. One porter placed three large suitcases on another's head. White-turbanned Sikhs with dark faces and curled up beards milled among brown-skinned women in bright saris—then, finally, a broad, sunburned forehead framed by prematurely gray hair and mystical, silver-blue eyes peered through the congestion and a smile of recognition lighted the face.

"Tom, over here!" I pushed my way past the passengers. "Boy, am I glad to see you. I was wondering what I'd do if you were not here."

Tom gave me a hug and laughed. "Welcome to India," he said. "You look like a rhapsody in blue. And that blonde mane of yours is like a beacon in this place. You were easy to find."

While at Yale, Tom opted for a life of scientific research rather than the world of oil exploration. From the fortune in huge oil deposits discovered by his late father, he had the financial reserves to make such a choice.

He had established several important foundations, but his favorite was The Mind Science Foundation in San Antonio, Texas, and nothing was too unusual for him to consider. Several months before, I went with him looking for Bigfoot (also known as the Yeti, or Abominable Snowman) in the Trinity Alps, a primitive area of northern California.

A well-built five-foot-nine, Tom, intellectually and spiritually, was my soulmate. He challenged my horizons, he excited me with his ideas, and I felt safe with him. Romantically, time would tell. Neither of us was pushing for a commitment, although we had a close relationship. For now, I was thrilled by his presence.

Tom frowned at my four-inch heels. "Let's get you off those stilts and down to my size. From now on you'll be in hiking boots and khaki."

"I'll be delighted to get out of these clothes, but as the U.S. Ambassadress of Fashion, I had to make an elegant departure from Teheran."

"You will find plenty of material here for your next lecture series."

"I've already thought of that. My agent will make a new brochure with the pictures I'll take."

Tom signaled a turbanned porter to secure my bags, and soon we were in an old-fashioned taxi rattling into the night. Little could be seen in the darkness; wooden-wheeled bullock carts passed silently in the opposite direction, their shrouded drivers asleep as the animals patiently plodded along. There was almost no traffic, other than a stray cow or two.

Excitement had pushed away my fatigue. "O.K., I'm here . . . ready to go . . . when do we start?"

"Early tomorrow morning. But the first order of business is to get you to the hotel and to sleep. Later this afternoon, an Indian parapsychologist from Rasjasthan University, Ranjit Ganguli, will join us. He'll bring a Yogi who will demonstrate complete control over his body. While we take his pulse, he will stop his heart beat for minutes; then he'll send blood to any part of his body we indicate."

"It sounds fascinating."

"It could be more than fascinating—it could be *very* practical," he replied with a twinkle in his eye. I ignored his innuendo; my interest was on our travel plans.

"Later you can take a tour of the city, and tonight we go to a ball at the French Embassy."

"And tomorrow, where do we go?"

"To Almora, in the mountains near the Tibetan border. Hopefully, we will find Lama Anagarika Govinda. Govinda is translating Buddhist works into books for Western readers. He's well-known in England where he lectures yearly."

This was particularly interesting to me. Previously, during a period of stress and indecision in my life, I had sought answers in Buddhist literature. However, even though the Buddhist emphasis on compassion attracted me, I found the writings unfathomable. I would need to learn a new language to understand the texts.

Religion had always fascinated me. At times this interest got me into trouble. During the seventh grade, while attending a private convent, I asked so many questions during catechism the nuns finally dismissed me from class and had me take art during that hour instead. Yes, I looked forward to meeting Govinda.

Soon our car turned off Jan Path, Delhi's main shopping thoroughfare, into a driveway lined with stately palm trees that led to the Imperial Oberoi Hotel. A magnificently uniformed Sikh doorman greeted us and led the way into a dark wood-panelled lobby, straight out of the thirties. It was inviting and appropriate. Again I noticed the smell of India. It seemed to impart a mixture of flowers, smoke, and earth.

An hour later, unpacked, bathed and lying on cool sheets, I watched the ceiling fan turn slowly, my thoughts turning with it. "Am I really here resting on a hotel bed in India?" As far away from my family in California as I could be, I wondered what my three sons and daughter were doing. It was yesterday for them, I realized.

A flood of love and gratitude washed over me as I thought of Mother. By living with us, and with the help of our housekeeper, she made it possible for me to follow my career as a global fashion authority. My two sisters also lived nearby, completing this support system.

A year after my husband's death in Argentina, we left our home in Buenos Aires and all the happy memories it contained, and returned to San Francisco. It was a painful but correct decision, and now, seven years later, things were going well; my children were thriving, and I loved my profession, along with the financial stability it provided.

With this contented thought and to the sounds of birds greeting the Indian day, jet lag won out and I fell into a deep sleep.

The next morning, Tom, Ranjit Ganguli—an earnest young Indian—and I set out on our journey in a brand new Dodge, a real luxury in India. Our Sikh driver, Kali, was so proud of his car that every time we came to a bump in the road he made us get out and walk. Then, when the radiator boiled over, we found he didn't know how to open the hood.

*Nancy, Tom Slick and Cathy McLean*
*at the French Ball in New Delhi, Feb. 1962,*
*the night before we headed for the Himalayas*

"I think we're in for trouble," announced Tom. "We would have been smarter to stick to the Indian-made Ambassador; every driver knows how to fix them."

We travelled over rough terrain, across the hot Ganges plain as we headed north. The hours passed rapidly, as everything was a feast for the eyes. Tom was an encyclopedia on India. "The first time I came here I hated it; the next trip I fell in love with it. It's important to meet this country properly." This was his eighth trip, so I knew I was in good hands.

At night while the driver slept in the car, Ranjit, Tom and I shared spartan sleeping quarters, usually a DAK bungalow, a kind of primitive cement hut built by the British for passing travelers. We bathed out of a bucket, and our beds consisted of four posts and a webbed frame over which we spread our bedrolls. Hardly conducive to flaming romance.

For food by day, I lived on hardboiled eggs, fresh oranges, bananas and peanut butter, rather than eat in the dirty places available. "If you stick to Punjabi food straight out of the boiling oil, you will be safe," cautioned Tom, but I treasured my powdered milk and the other staples I'd picked up in Delhi. At night we'd get the DAK bungalow attendant to buy fresh vegetables, which were plentiful, and cook our meal over a small fire in front of us. This way I knew what we were eating—I was taking no chances with dysentery.

Soon snow-capped mountains were visible, but it was slow going. We had just spent a day waiting for a mechanic to come from a far away village to fix the car. Tom had had it with delays; he decided to go on without the troublesome Dodge or its driver. "Kali will go back and we will continue by bus."

The bus was memorable. The windows were so dirty one could hardly see out. A leathery-faced old hillsman sat backwards, cleaning his teeth with a stick and staring at me without interruption.

"You are a one-woman show for him," laughed my companion. "He may never have seen blue eyes before."

The bus driver rarely took his hand off the horn. Women got on with naked babies, and everyone took turns helping the mothers. It didn't matter that the baby would wet the pants of the obliging passenger. Everyone laughed and chatted. I felt as though I were on the "Toonerville Trolley." When we came to villages, we got down to tend to bathroom necessities—it was my introduction to standing on two footblocks and squatting.

It was getting cold as we gained altitude. "Look at that, Tom, I'm impressed! In spite of this chilly weather, those people are bathing. They wash their few rags and then put them on again."

He explained, "It's part of the Hindu religion to bathe daily, even if it means going into a cold river. You rarely smell any body odor amongst the hill people."

There was constant activity in the villages. Everyone seemed to have a job to do. "These people don't seem to be starving, as most Westerners think," I remarked.

"It is all worked out on a barter system. When statistics report that the average Indian lives on only two rupees a day, it's misleading."

Finally we arrived in the hill station of Almora. The imprint of the British Raj still remained in the architecture of what had originally been summer residences. Lama Govinda's home was another five miles of walking—so huffing, puffing, and suffering in the thin, cold air, at six thousand feet, we traversed the final mountain slope astonished by the magnificent scenery around us.

With no means of communication, there was no way to ascertain that the Lama would be there, or that he would receive us. Tom explained the term *lama*, "When a Buddhist monk becomes a teacher and has a following, he earns the title of lama."

Finally, a small stone house came into view. A tall pole stood between us and the building. From its top fluttered long white cloths covered with strange print. Tom explained, "These are Buddhist prayer flags. Each Tibetan family has its own prayer mark; they use it to stamp cloth after cloth until they create a whole grove of flags as evidence of their devotion. As the wind blows, the prayers flutter their way up to heaven." I thought, "What fun to do this at home."

The heavy rough-hewn front door opened and a thin, angular-faced European woman stood on the threshold. With long, flowing robes and her hair tucked into a hood that arched over her dark-rimmed eyes, she could have been from another century. Hardly pausing to study us, she tipped her head to the side with a smile and said, "I am Li Gotami, the lama's wife. My husband is working, but he will be pleased to receive you." We felt such relief at her welcome.

Li Gotami escorted us into a small, bare room. The whitewashed, stone walls bore the scant decoration of mandalas, portraits of monks, and mountain scenes. There was little furniture on the stone floor. *Thangkas*, Tibetan scrolls, hung from the ceiling.

On a carpeted platform, spotlighted by sunshine beaming through a tall window, sat a frail figure. Above his burgundy and saffron robes, the man wore a loose wool cap, which hung below his ears and rose to a point high over his head. This framed a thin face with bushy eyebrows, deep-hollowed blue eyes, and an aquiline nose. A thin white beard hung from the tip of his chin. This was Govinda; born to German parents in Bolivia, he was, at sixty four, the most revered Western-born lama.

I followed Tom's example and greeted him with my hands pressed together in *namaste*, the traditional Indian salutation. Then I ventured, "*Mi querido Padre. Con mucho gusto conocerle.*"

"*Gracias—y yo también, Señora.*"

Govinda inquired about my Spanish and how I happened to have a name like *de Herrera*.

"My late husband was an Uruguayan."

Govinda bobbed his head enthusiastically. "Yes, yes . . . I know that continent well. My grandfather was a comrade in arms to Simón Bolívar, one of the *gran libertadores* of South America." With this, he gestured for us to sit on cushions lying on the floor.

"Your Holiness," Tom said, introducing himself. "I have come to you for help. I am seeking proof of psychic and physical phenomena that can be repeated under scientifically controlled conditions at my Mind Science Foundation in Texas. I believe that if we can demonstrate these abilities in a manner beyond dispute, we will be able to get our foot in the door of the Western mind and open up new realms for exploration."

Govinda's face exhibited little. He drew Tom out, asking him to enlarge on some of his points. Then he seemed to make up his mind; evidently he would trust this stranger's motives and talk freely. I felt relief; I'd been praying for four days that this would not be a false lead.

"To us Buddhists, such attempts to 'prove' extrasensory perception through scientific tests seem crude and laughable. The conditions for these experiments are in themselves the greatest hindrance to any success." Govinda's cheeks flushed. He paused and cleared his throat. "By reaching for objectivity, you exclude the emotional and spiritual elements of the human mind, without which no state of real contemplation can be created."

We were jolted by his concise appraisal. Seeing the expression on my face, Govinda softened his voice. "In Tibet, our concentration and psychic sensibility is greatly increased in the solitude and silence of nature. The mind is not blunted and diverted from itself by the noise and activity of modern life. Rather, it becomes spiritually attuned and can enter into a silent communication with other attuned minds." His eyes shifted back toward Tom as he gently added, "Thus, telepathy is common among Tibetans."

Whether it was the musky incense or the conviction of this uncommon man, I sensed myself slipping into another dimension. Govinda continued, "Whenever the object of concentration comes before the mind, it takes on a greater reality and can then be held and contemplated with full attention. The past is telescoped into the present and the present shows itself not as a dividing line between a past that has died and a future that has yet to be born, but as a single aspect of the co-existence and continuous body of living experience in four dimensions . . ."

"Do you believe in the existence of the fourth dimension?"

"It is amusing, young man, that just two weeks ago a Professor Heisenberg came here to ask me about that subject."

"Heisenberg!" I was astonished. Recently I had read an article about Heisenberg, the discoverer of quantum physics. I almost shouted, "The man who won the Nobel Prize? Do you mean he came all the way here?"

Govinda nodded, "Yes, that is the same man. Apparently, modern mathematicians are reaching such complicated answers that they need to learn about the fourth dimension in order to explain them. They know we understand this dimension." He smiled as he shared this confidence.

Excitedly, Tom pursued the topic and soon the lama was describing one of his own psychic experiences. He related how *lung gumpa*—the Tibetan walking levitation—came over him once in a perilous situation and brought him back to safety . . . he was able to walk across a lake!

Tom concentrated on getting an exact description of the event, but I felt he was ignoring the state of mind which evokes such feats—the physical phenomenon was but the momentary effect of a mental state which could have far greater implication in our lives. Govinda was showing us a path to unlimited possibilities. Casting aside my timidity, I asked, "Your Holiness, if one is interested in seeking spiritual knowledge, how should one begin?"

"First you must practice meditation, my lady. Meditation is essential for the evolution of the soul."

"But how do I learn this?" The cushion on the floor was no longer uncomfortable.

"You will need a teacher. He will teach you . . . there are many forms of meditation. Some use the breath, some a *mantra*, some use colors. . . ."

"What is a *mantra?*"

"It is a sacred sound vibration which awakens and stimulates the intuitive qualities of the mind. But leave this to your guru; he will know what is best for you." His eyes penetrated mine as he said, "Always remember, your guru will be in a mortal body and only be a certain percent divine; so forgive his weaknesses and keep your eye on the divine."

"Your Holiness, do you believe in reincarnation?"

He smiled, "Yes, we believe the soul evolves through many lifetimes. "

Later Tom said that was like asking the lama if he breathed. But I wasn't discouraged; I had to begin somewhere. Ever since my husband's death, I had been looking for assurance that there is justice in the universe. I had already concluded it involved more than one lifetime to work out that justice, so Govinda's words encouraged me.

Later that afternoon as we descended the mountainside, I felt as if I were walking on clouds. I was dizzy and my vision out of focus. The world around me seemed like a Van Gogh painting. I could see swirls spinning in cartwheels against the alpenglow. Everything was in motion.

"Tom, I don't know what's happening—I have such a strange feeling—as if I were drunk."

He laughed, "You have become 'sensitized.' Just by sitting near such a saintly man, you receive his *darshan*, the energy, the good vibrations."

"I feel as though my heart will break open, it's so full of happiness. Boy, if we could ever bottle this, we'd retire for life!"

"Speaking of bottles, is that a bottle of Scotch I see in that store?" We had come into a local center; on both sides of the road were little stall-like shops. This particular shop sold everything from soap to incense—and scotch. The Haig and Haig was dirty but intact. The proprietor said he'd had it for over ten years. "I bet he was getting worried that he'd never sell it," said Tom.

Later we celebrated in the men's waiting room at the railroad station, where we spent the night on benches. There were no hotels, and I refused to stay alone in the women's section. From my knapsack I produced a can of caviar I'd brought from Iran. We had a party while Ranjit looked on with distaste. I don't know whether it was due to our repast, or due to the fact that I, a woman, was in the men's room.

The morning train took us to Dehra Dun, former site of a major British cantonment. After a splendid cup of tea, it was the bus again, this time to Hardwar, the second most holy place in India, located on the banks of the Ganges. As it was my first glimpse of the sacred river, I insisted on running down the *ghat* steps and wading in the water before we started our search for a revered yogi Tom had been told about.

We had a name and no directions, but miraculously we found him sitting on top of a cement temple, his naked body baking in the sun.

After Ranjit convinced him in Hindi, the little dried-up man begrudgingly agreed to talk to us. He asked for a glass of water to illustrate his point. When the glass appeared, we were each requested to touch the water. The yogi then held it quietly, and we watched the liquid turn solid! Ranjit then asked us to touch it again to verify that it was now ice. We were thunderstruck! We had not expected anything like this. The man wore only a loin cloth, had no props, it was a hot day, and we were not hypnotized. The holy man told Ranjit, "Water is made up of so many molecules of hydrogen and oxygen. Ice is the same; all I have done is to change the characteristic of the water by altering the rate of vibration of the molecules." Scowling, he continued, "You are scientists; can you control nature peacefully? You will destroy the world with your science; leave this place and bother us no more, or stay and learn union with God." His eyes shut in dismissal.

Later, in a noisy taxi we debated about what we'd seen. "There is no scientific explanation for what we have just observed." I had majored in chemistry at Stanford; I was scientifically oriented.

"Agreed, but the title yogi is given only after the individual demonstrates his ability to control nature," Tom pointed out. "That old boy sure earned his credentials. If only I'd had a movie camera."

"Someone would insist you'd faked it," I consoled, but I knew we had just witnessed something that was impossible.

Tom was in high spirits . . . now he knew this expedition would make history. "Our next goal is to find a swami named Sivananda who lives in Rishikesh." It was thirteen miles north of Hardwar over a windy road full of pot-holes, which did not slow down our driver for a minute. He roared through the congestion of carts, animals, bicycles, and horse-drawn *tongas*, or buggies, overloaded with passengers. Tom chuckled as I held my breath and prayed. "I don't think it's our karma to be killed on the way to The Valley of the Saints."

"The hell with our karma, what if the driver thinks it's good for his karma to die in such a holy place?"

It's called The Valley of the Saints because of the holy men who live there near the headwaters of the Mother Ganga. The valley is dotted with numerous temples and ashrams, or religious academies. Most of these clustered near the town, perched on the river bank. Sivananda, the most revered of the saints, had the largest ashram in this spiritual center.

The streets were lined with small wooden stalls. Through the car window I could make out piles of vegetables, dried grains, brassware, brightly colored yard goods, religious objects, and crudely made household tools. Men haggled over prices while others gathered around open braziers, where turbanned Sikhs prepared vegetable dishes in wok-like pans filled with spitting hot oil. The enticing scent of curry was everywhere.

Suddenly our driver screeched to a halt. Ahead, like a sea of dirty laundry, swirled an impenetrable confusion of carts and pedestrians. He turned his sweat-beaded brow to Tom and said, "You walk now, *Sahib*."

Tom leaned forward, "How will we find The Divine Life Forest Academy?"

"No problem, *Sahib;* it is very close. " He pointed to a street corner about a hundred yards away, "There turn right, walk down to river embankment and turn left. Ashram easy to find. " His sing-song English was enveloped by the din as Tom opened the door. I put my dark glasses on to ease the glare and keep out the dust. Beggars and hawkers ran up trying to attract our attention and money. Tom grabbed our daybag and pulled me by the hand, ignoring pleas and gestures of 'baksheesh.'

There were no sidewalks, so we zigzagged down the center of the dusty, clay road—retreating to the sides every few steps to avoid rickshaws and carts. Making our way slowly, we encountered a group of lepers sitting on the side of the street. They were horribly disfigured. Some balanced their dented cups between handless limbs; without lips or noses they pleaded for alms. Others held out their walking sticks to bar our passage and force a gift from us. I froze, not wanting to touch anything they had handled.

"Here, take these small coins," Tom said, forcing them into my paralyzed hand, "Put one in each cup and they'll leave you alone."

I did what he said, but tried not to look at the pathetic creatures. It was hard to realize they were human—this thought made me feel guilty. "Oh, Tom, why must people exist in such horrible condition?"

"Yes, I know, but the Indian government does provide a place for lepers to live."

"Can you imagine what those places are like if they'd rather live here and beg? "

We began to walk faster. Just before the corner a rickshaw backed us against the wall; I felt a hand lightly tap my shoulder, *"Baksheesh, Memsahib?"*

I spun around to see a naked man daubed all over with ashes. His black hair was coiled on top of his head and a huge live snake hung from his neck. I gasped and threw my last coins at him.

Tom tugged me around the corner; nothing seemed to faze him. "The driver said to turn here. . . ." The crowd thinned out as we descended towards the swiftly flowing waters of the Ganges. Across the wide river white-washed domes and temples fringed the far bank. All appeared empty except for one huge building, which was entirely covered with ornate printing.

"What's that?" I asked.

"It is the Gita Bhavan. A wealthy and devout Hindu built it to shelter those who want to study the Bhagavad Gita and other scriptures. The decorative printings are Vedic quotes."

Suddenly on our left was a high wall. Crude brick stairs ran up its side and ended in a gated archway. Square black letters surrounded by colored lights announced Sivananda's ashram.

We must have been observed climbing the stairs, for as we crossed the stone courtyard, a gaunt, dark Indian in white robes came out of a room on the far side and walked towards us in greeting.

"I am Chidananda, secretary and disciple to His Holiness Swami Sivananda." When he heard why we had come, he smiled, "You are in luck. His Holiness has just come out of a long meditation and will be giving an audience shortly. But we must hurry."

We followed him into the main building and down a stairway to a basement called the "meeting cave." He seated us on a wooden bench against a cold, damp wall, and excused himself. Other disciples, or *chelas*, of the Swami had already gathered in the room. They sat on pillows strewn about the earthen floor. Their heads were shaven and their white robes bespoke their devotion. Tom and I shifted on our bench, trying to be comfortable without leaning against the wet wall.

Little light came into the cave and many candles were burning. Smoke mingled with the sinuous trails of incense and the sweet aroma of flowers. Potted plants were clustered near a chair at one end of the room. Mildewed and peeling whitewashed walls were heavily decorated with religious paintings depicting blue Krishnas, photographs of *sadhus*, or holy beggars, and figurines of animal-headed gods. Between these hung garlands of dusty artificial flowers. Some of the *chelas* sat in the lotus posture with their eyes closed, their hands cradling a humble offering to their master. Others lounged, talking to their colleagues, glancing at us with interest. There were about twenty in all.

Chidananda reappeared at a door near the chair. Turning and looking expectantly back through the opening, he slowly retreated from the entrance. "The master is coming," he announced quietly. The students jumped to their feet and held out their offerings, making short, shallow bows and uttering low chanting sounds.

A broad, hairless, yellow-brown head floated calmly into the room. *Chelas* threw themselves to the floor to kiss Sivananda's feet. The massive holy man slowly made his way through the commotion, waving blessings to all. He accepted fruit and flowers from those in his path, while others stood behind him, bestrewing his coat with rose petals. Finally, when he stood before his chair, he motioned for everyone to sit and then did so himself.

A disciple picked his way through the crowd and received permission to place a heavy garland of orange targate flowers around the Swami's neck. Sivananda put his feet on a stool, revealing velvet boots. He beamed as he slowly reviewed his congregation. His immense frame was magnified by a camel-hair coat. His brown eyes appeared slightly crossed behind a bulbous nose, but this did not negate a powerful, confident demeanor.

When his gaze came around to us, he called Chidananda to his side. Learning who we were, he welcomed us to his ashram in good English. He instructed his secretary to take the garland from his shoulders and to place it on mine. Everyone turned to look at me; it was an honor, but it was heavy and I felt like a horse that had just won the Derby.

Sivananda intoned to his *chelas*, "Come, let's have one of you rise and tell our guests what you have learned here at the Academy." Not one, but more than half the gathering stood up in turn and told of their gratitude and love for their master, for the wisdom he bestowed on them. Then the Swami began a discourse. He pitched his comments toward Tom, turning to us while describing the achievements of science.

Taking advantage of a pause, Tom asked rhetorically if scientific knowledge was leading to peace. The answer came back, "No, to destruction! In order to generate peaceful vibrations, one must possess individual tranquility, which alone will pave the way to world peace. This requires self-discipline . . . this is what we practice here."

Giving Tom a confident smile, he concluded, "A scientist without discipline is a danger to the world. You should learn to meditate."

My thoughts went back to the irate "ice yogi." Evidently, science was a dirty word in the valley. How differently Lama Govinda had received Tom as a scientist.

Tom was nonplused by the Swami's ardor, but asked, "Your Holiness, could you explain about meditation? What does it offer a scientist?"

"What are the benefits of meditation?" A smile flickered across his face, and he played to the crowd. He talked at length about meditation and its goals. "Meditation helps the mind to rule the senses and the practitioner to control his mind." This quickly led into a description of the path to God-realization, and, prompted by questions from the *chelas*, to comments on the Divine Presence, Advaitic Unity, *sadhana*—Atmic Glory—we were lost. Was he speaking English? The garland got heavier. I was tempted to take it off, but was afraid of insulting some tradition.

When the discourse ended, Sivananda came over and sat between Tom and me, ordering a *chela* to take a picture. An ancient camera was produced which made a flash and a puff of white smoke. Only when he took his leave of us did I notice his wrinkled hands and realize he was a very old man.

As the Swami left, the students chanted and rang small bells . . . they ignited powders and passed around strange things to eat, combinations of seeds, pastes, and dried fruits. Leery of food prepared by unclean hands, I took no chances, and, pretending to eat, dropped what I was given down the front of my blouse.

After Sivananda retired, Chidananda came over and sat next to me. "What did you think of Swamiji?" He used the suffix *-ji* that I had learned was a form of endearment.

There being no point in pretense, I said, "My impressions are somewhat negative. All the ritual and the kissing of feet are simply not for me."

Chidananda's face was compassionate. "Yes, I could see that in your expression. There is much you do not understand." He gestured for Tom to listen and continued. "If Swamiji could have his way, none of this obeisance would take place. When he first came out of the forest where he lived for years in solitude, people fell to the ground to kiss his feet. He had no choice but to let them show their devotion to him in such humble ways, or they felt themselves unworthy."

That seemed rational to me. He then went on to tell us about the Academy and its students, and describe their practice of self-discipline.

He encouraged me to ask questions and later, as he escorted us to the gate, asked me, "Did you ever think of finding a guru for yourself?"

"Yes, I'm looking for a teacher to guide me, but I'm not ready to renounce my worldly life. It's a dilemma for me."

Chidananda's eyes darkened, "Yes, it is hard to renounce . . ." Then he brightened and offered, "Perhaps I can help you. There is a swami with an ashram across the river who appeals to Western students. He teaches the path of the householder, and requires no withdrawal from worldly activity. You might talk with him; his name is Maharishi Mahesh Yogi. Perhaps he will be the teacher for you. If not, do not worry, we have a saying here: 'when the *chela* is ready, the master appears.'"

We bid the friendly holy man goodbye and headed for the river to find the man named Mahesh. Tom was just as curious as I. A barge-like boat was departing for the opposite bank; already overcrowded, the passengers made room for us. Quietly we were stared at by numerous pairs of dark eyes. I tried to pull myself in from being touched by the ash-covered saint sitting next to me. Tom had explained, "The ashes keep him warm."

A small child extended her hand to my hair. Her mother explained, "Please excuse my daughter. She has a doll with hair like yours, and wants to touch it." We laughed and answered her questions as to where we were from and what we were doing there.

"Oh, you are too late. Maharishi has just left for California. It is a pity; he is a very respected teacher."

So we were saved a climb up the hill. Little did I know then how many times I would return to this exact place in the future.

ॐ

# THE YOGA-VEDANTA FOREST ACADEMY

P.O. SIVANANDANAGAR, RISHIKESH
DIST. DEHRA DUN, HIMALAYAS, INDIA.

*Founder*
Sri Swami Sivananda

17.6.62

Sri Nancy Cooke,
California.

Rev.Immortal Self,

        Salutations and adorations. Om Namo Narayanaya.

        I am delighted to go through the contents of your kind letter of the 8th instant.

        Kindly send a copy of the book that you are intending to publish for our library. I am sure your notes and experiences on your trip here with Mr.Slick will prove to be of great inspiration to others in your country and our own students here.

        All your friends are welcome to this abode. Welcome to all of them! I shall attend to them all and serve them. I am sure by your efforts and influence more and more of your countrymen will take interest in the Eastern culture and philosophy and find peace and solace in them.

        May Lord bless you all with fine health, long life, joy, peace and eternal happiness!

        With deep regards,Prem and OM,

Thy own Self,

18113

*Letter from Sivananda*

## 2

# An Offering of Miracles

FOR WEEKS WE TRAVELLED BY RICKSHAW, oxcart, train, taxi, and bus.
Sometimes our quest was in vain, other times successful. Our
bedrolls got grimier by the day, but the soul of India had entered
my heart. I was captivated by this exotic land, and my mind was being
blown open by what I was witnessing.

In Srinagar, capital of Kashmir, we interviewed a young boy with
special ability. By covering his head with a black bag and concentrating
on the whereabouts of a particular person described to him, he would go
into a trance, and tell in detail the location of that individual. By this
method he had helped the police recover the body of a drowned child
after all other attempts had failed. The body was covered by weeds in
Dal Lake.

Near Amritsar, capital of the Punjab, a man read the Brigu Samita,
the book of life, for us. Finding the corresponding palm leaf, marked in
mulberry juice with the correct astrological signs for that day, he told
Tom his past, present, and future; as it turned out, he was accurate about
the past, but way off on the future.

Tom was so hopeful and became exasperated with me when on
occasion I would point out how easily something could have been faked.
After one demonstration I spoke out, "Give me an hour and all those

robes and I bet I could do better. You talk about scientific, controlled conditions—that was a complete con-job!" I was worried that Tom, in his eagerness to find phenomena, would be fooled.

By late March we looked forward to one of the highlights of our expedition—a visit to Dharamsala to see the Dalai Lama, God-King of the Tibetans. We lucked out; a forest ranger lent us his jeep and driver. However, while passing through the Kumon Forest, made famous by Jim Corbett's book on tiger hunting in this region, we got stuck in a river. Night was falling, and our driver became increasingly anxious about man-eating tigers, "See those cliffs ahead, Memsahib; the people are too poor to burn their dead, so they throw the bodies over the cliffs. The tigers are used to man-meat."

This news startled us. Tom remarked, "All we have to protect ourselves are fishing poles; maybe we'd better listen to the driver and spend the night in the temple he insists on going to."

I was so disappointed; I'd been looking forward to the hotel in Dharamsala—especially to the use of a Western toilet. It was a ghastly night, surrounded by sleeping and coughing bodies. Poor people, I'm sure I heard a few give a last agonized gasp. In the morning I insisted on taking a cold bath out of a bucket, "I'm not going to call on a God-King covered with negative vibrations." Tom tolerated my outburst; I'd been a good sport so far.

Dharamsala, where His Holiness resided, is near the Tibetan border at seven thousand feet. As we wound up the mountain, we observed the precautions the Indian Army was taking to protect the revered holy man. At every turn were tanks, guns, and troops. India had granted him political asylum after his spectacular escape from Tibet. For three months after leaving Lhasa, the God-King, and the thousands who followed him into exile, disappeared until he arrived in India. The Chinese planned to kill him and put the Panchen Lama in his place.

Just before reaching the summit, we met a large group of Tibetan children parading down the hill, each carrying a long white scarf. They greeted us with happy faces, cheeks pink from the brisk air. With youthful energy they hailed us, "Jole, where are you from? California, is that in America?"

An older man, who seemed to be in charge, came forward. He wore a Tibetan hat, its crown covered with dusty brocade; the fur-lined ear flaps were turned up like a Dutch girl's cap. His heavy, black padded robe hung below his knees and was thrown off one shoulder and caught in the middle by a wide leather belt. A long turquoise and coral earring hung from one ear only. When he smiled, he showed large, stained teeth. "It is most auspicious that you arrive at this time. His Holiness has just come out of two weeks of silence. Today we are celebrating the second anniversary of his escape from Lhasa. These children were just received by him." He gave us directions and went on his way.

With renewed excitement, we continued up the steep grade. When we came to the gate and the guards protecting the holy residence, we presented the letter we had prepared in advance requesting an audience. Within minutes, a young man with a gaunt, high-cheekboned face approached us from within the official compound. "I am Sonam Kazi, interpreter for His Holiness." He held out his hand in greeting, and shook ours with enthusiasm. "If you will follow me, I will take you to him. He will be very happy to receive you on this special day." We were elated. Kazi's English was excellent.

We followed his long, black-coated figure up the hill to what must have been an old English summer bungalow with green wooden shingles, and leaded glass windows. It was surrounded by pine trees and over-looked a magnificent view of the mountains and Gangetic plains below. I could feel the altitude as we walked up the Lingkor, the holy path which circled the residence in exile. We passed pilgrims making rounds, repeating their *mantras* and spinning their miniature prayer wheels.

We entered a friendly, faded-chintz-covered room. There was the assorted furniture usually found in summer places—what didn't fit somewhere else was sent here. The floor was covered with Tibetan carpets of all sizes; the furniture was large, overstuffed, and comfortable. Little wooden tables, an umbrella stand, *thangkas*, books, magazines—all added to the busy friendliness of the room. Kazi stopped us. "No, you do not need to take off your shoes."

Before we could be seated, a tall young man briskly entered the room from the rear. A spicy scent of incense arrived with him. His face was long and cleanly shaven. He wore eyeglasses which accented his penetrating gaze. We knew him to be in his late twenties.

Kazi stepped forward, "I have the honor of presenting His Holiness, the Dalai Lama." We made the sign of *namaste*. I presented my *khata*, a white ceremonial scarf, and we seated ourselves as directed on the couch. I was thrilled—we were sitting two feet away from a God-King.

The Dalai Lama wore Western men's shoes and trousers; these were covered by a long, wine-colored robe with saffron-colored lining. His

*Nancy presenting* khata *to His Holiness the Dalai Lama in Dharamsala, India in 1962*

*Nancy with Tibetan children at Self-Help Center, Misoorie, India (a hill station above Dehra Dun, created by the British)*

*Nancy with Tibetan woman in Misoorie Self-Help Center*

right hand fingered his prayer beads. As we related, through Kazi, the purpose of our trip, he watched our faces with keen interest. However, he brushed aside the subject of psychic phenomena. "What I want you to hear is about the genocide being practiced against my people by the Chinese. The outside world does not know the truth."

The cruelties he spoke of were almost unbelievable—the killing of thousands of priests, the raping of nuns, the refugees fleeing out over treacherous mountain passes with new stories of their ruthless captors.

"Hundreds of monasteries have been destroyed. These were the centers of our Tibetan culture."

As he told us of the thousands who had lost their lives in attempting to escape, his serious face was filled with sadness. "Instead of bringing their own belongings, they carried out the holy scriptures, the *Kangyur*, printed on palm leaves hundreds of years old and carefully wrapped in cloth." Kazi brought one for us to see. "In order to keep our tradition alive, we must get as many young children out of Tibet as possible. We need money to build schools. Switzerland, Norway, and the United States have been very kind to us. We will get our country back one day, but it may be a hundred years or so—time means nothing to a Tibetan."

Soon the hour we had been allotted had passed. Catching Tom's eye, I signaled it was time. Kazi nodded his head in agreement. Standing up, we expressed our thanks to His Holiness for receiving us, and I added, "You can be sure I will pass on all I have heard to my audiences, and Mr. Slick will help through his education foundation. He has a special affection for Tibetans and Sherpas ever since he organized a group of them and went hunting for the Yeti."

"What do you know about the Yeti?" came in English from His Holiness. It surprised us to hear him speak directly after having spoken through an interpreter for an hour. Now he came forward, took each of us by the arm, and said, "Please stay; my English is poor, but there is much to talk about."

"Do you believe in the existence of the Yeti?" I asked.

"First, tell me what you know about the Yeti."

Luckily, Tom always carried photos of the evidence he had collected to prove the existence of this legendary creature. He dug into his pockets, and minutes later the three of us had our heads together like a group of conspirators. The pictures were of Yeti footprints, a skull, the droppings, and a lair where the creature supposedly gave birth.

As I sat there, I kept reminding myself who this man was. He was so likeable and easygoing. Tom had told me, "For two years after the death of the thirteenth Dalai Lama, the court lamas searched until they found him as a small baby." While a youth he was cloistered from contact with outsiders except on religious occasions, yet at this moment he was like any young man, swapping adventure stories.

Everyone who lived in Dharamsala, and thousands of Tibetan refugees in India, were there only to be near him, the same man who at this point was asking Tom to describe the droppings of the Yeti!

Only after exhausting Tom's information did His Holiness tell us, "Yes, I am convinced of the existence of the Yeti. One of my most respected lamas told me of a creature who would come each day and help him draw water from the well. It was very similar to yours, Mr. Slick."

His face was animated now; it was easy to see this was a subject of great interest to him. "Another lama reported to me that a similar creature would visit his hermitage every week or so to eat the grain he spread out on the frozen ground. He knew when it was approaching by the strong smell that preceded it."

"That is evidently why it got the name of the Abominable Snowman," added Tom. "Was he ever able to tame this creature?"

"No, but it continued its visits for a long period of time—especially during the winter months when food was hard to find. They usually eat the blossoms of the rhododendron trees and wild berries—they are not carnivorous."

All barriers to friendship were soon dissolved when Tom volunteered to raise money for schools. His Holiness then came forward with an offer which electrified us. "I am convinced of your dedication, Mr. Slick. If you will bear all expenses of the project, I will send three of my lamas to your foundation in Texas, and they will exhibit the power of man to levitate, materialize objects, and to pull the load of seven elephants under duress!"

We were stunned—was it possible? Our search was over; Tom had found what he had come to India for. I was elated at having been part of such an important expedition. Plans were made for follow through, and when we finally took leave, we shook hands with the God-King, promising to tell the Western world about the Chinese atrocities.

We floated down the hill to where Ranjit awaited us, as the guards had not allowed him to accompany us. He would be so happy to return home; on many occasions he had asked me, "Are all Americans so full of energy?" He had difficulty in keeping up with us.

Little fat dogs yapped at our feet, and soon a curious crowd gathered around us while we related our experience to our Indian companion. Kazi explained, "Many of them have never seen a European before. They would like you to share tea with them."

Smiling, Tom watched me as I took my first sip.

"Oh my God, what's in this?"

He laughed, "It is tea made with rancid yak butter and salt; it is very good for keeping the body temperature up in cold weather."

The taste was unexpected and nauseating. It prompted my ungracious reply, "The heck with my temperature going up, my problem will be in keeping the tea down!"

---
3
---

# Atomic Death

B Y EUROPEAN STANDARDS THE DHARAMSALA HOTEL could hardly be
called deluxe, but it had electricity. So that night, after a shower,
I settled down to read some Buddhist literature and to think back
on the interview with His Holiness. Feeling chilly, I decided to plug in
the small wall-heater. As I inserted the plug, all the lights went out.
Looking out the window, I could see the whole place was in darkness.
Soon a bearer came with a candle, "So sorry, Memsahib, somebody plug
in heater and blow out all lights. Man come fix tomorrow." So much for
my evening of reading.

The weak candle threw strange images against the walls, but I felt
cozy in my room alone. It was pleasant to let my mind wander back over
the past month. There had been few moments of solitude in which to
do so.

It appeared that Tom had been successful in his quest, but what
about mine? I'd certainly found plenty of lecture material, as well as
colorful, ethnic costumes for my show. That afternoon I'd bought articles
of clothing from the refugees, which would help me illustrate the
dramatic story of the Tibetans. But what about that other dimension—
the spiritual world which was beginning to intrigue me? I had felt such

serenity while sitting at the feet of the holy men we'd called on. It was a serenity I had not felt for years, and I was not going to let it slip away. Had I been guided to India by this inner need? I seemed ripe for the knowledge I was receiving.

After seven years of reading and searching I had come to certain conclusions, but it was here in India that those conclusions were taking form and being expressed back to me in words. These words excited me; they pointed to a path for me to follow. I needed a belief that would serve as an insurance policy, an insulator, against ever again experiencing the terrible grief that had engulfed me after Luis's death.

A deep sadness came into the silence around me as a face drifted into my consciousness—it was the face of a handsome, dark-haired man with golden lights in his brown eyes. His finely-chiseled features were full of intelligence and humor. Everything about him exuded energy and passion. Oh, beloved Luis, what a short time we had together, but what an impact you have had on my life! Yes, he was the love of my life, and what joy we shared—more happiness and excitement than most people would know in a lifetime.

My thoughts went back to our meeting. It was summer 1951—my first trip to Europe. One evening in Paris, my French friend, Huguette Empain, had implored me, "I know you are exhausted by parties, but you must join us, we need you. We have three attractive Americans who drove in Le Mans last week. You won't have to struggle with French; they all speak English. Be a good sport and meet us at eleven at the Plaza Athene." She would not take no for an answer.

Luis told me later that when he saw me in the distance, he thought to himself, "Hope she is the one joining us." He said he liked the way I was dressed, the way I walked, and the way I came up and in a friendly way said, "Hi, I'm Nancy Cooke." Nothing coy, nothing mysterious.

What a night it was! We went to Dinashads, a Russian restaurant specializing in caviar-filled blinis. These were washed down by quantities of champagne. Every time we drank a glass, presented to us on a violin, we emptied it and threw it into the fireplace. Later, while dancing at Jimmy's, Luis led me into a slow tango. Wrapping our bodies together, as is customary with this sensuous dance, he made me terribly aware of the intimacy we shared. I liked the smell of his hair and the feeling of his strong body pressed to mine. I surrendered myself totally to his directions. When the music stopped, he slowly let me go, saying, "I think

I've been searching for you all of my life." I laughed and discounted his words, "Isn't it wonderful what magic champagne creates."

It was 8:30 a.m. when I returned to my hotel. Five hours later I met Luis de Herrera for brunch at the Ritz. I was curious as to how I'd find him by day. I was puzzled by the deep impression he'd made on me. Maybe I'd be disappointed. But he looked even better, in spite of a lack of sleep. When he entered a room, something changed—his vitality radiated to all. Six-foot-three and powerfully built, he had been the amateur golf champion of every South American country. He had played in the British Open just before coming to Le Mans to meet his pal, Briggs Cunningham, the veteran U.S. racing driver. Although born in London, he was actually an Uruguayan citizen living in Buenos Aires, Argentina. Educated both in Spain and France, he'd finished his schooling at Cambridge. All of this I had found out the night before.

Now across the table we discreetly probed to find out more about each other. He took the initiative, "I've known and liked many North Americans, but you are not typical. Huguette said you were in your twenties, but you have a quiet confidence, a worldliness beyond your years. Where does this come from?"

What a question. I laughed, "Two months ago my divorce was finalized, after nine years of marriage in Honolulu. Also, I'm the mother of three little boys who at present are spending their vacation holidays with their father, while their mother takes her first trip to Europe." I made a sweeping gesture. "So there it all is, my life history."

"No, I want to know more. You are very at home in the world and have a natural ease with people. I watched you closely last night, or didn't you notice?" He was persistent. "Tell me more about your background, your family."

"Well, I had a wonderful childhood shared by two look-alike sisters, which made life even more fun. I went to Stanford University for three years before getting married to Richard Cooke, and lived in Honolulu during the war."

"That must have been interesting."

"It was fascinating. As all the military wives were sent home, we local women were in great demand. We became hostesses for the top army and navy officers—we became good friends with Admiral Nimitz and Admiral Halsey especially."

"Was your husband in the military service?"

*Nancy's wedding day to Richard A. Cooke, Jr. in Honolulu*

*Nancy and Dick Cooke with sons Starr, Brett and Rik*
*Christmas 1948, Honolulu*

*Nancy with boys in Honolulu,*          *Nancy in Honolulu, 1949*
*1949*

*Executive's wife, blond Mrs. Richard Cooke, Jr., whose husband is with one of Hawaii's potent "Big Five" companies, berates a longshoreman who tries to crash "We the Women"'s picket line—Life Magazine, July 20, 1949*

Nancy greeting her father with
Ruth Dillingham in Honolulu

Nancy, her mother and Emelyn
Knowland in Honolulu

Nancy as "Crystal" in the play The Women by Claire Booth Luce
(presented by Honolulu Community Theater in 1950
with Kenau Wilder as Sylvia)

*Nancy in Honolulu, 1950*
*with Jimmy and Gloria Stewart*
*and Johnny Gomez*

*Joan Fontaine and new husband,*
*William Dozier, arriving in*
*Honolulu, 1950*
*(also, Ruth Dillingham)*

*"I'm pretty brave to pose with*
*Esther Williams in Honolulu, 1949"*

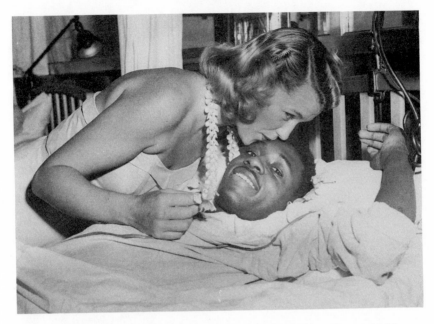

*Nancy working to raise morale of wounded from Korean War in 1950 at
Tripler Hospital in Honolulu. This man was a double amputee.*

"Not before the war. After Pearl Harbor he became a naval officer."

"So it was a command performance when the top boys invited you."

"Yes. As a matter of fact, Admiral Towers, who was head of Naval
Air for the Pacific, included my husband and me at all his functions. He
even sent his aide to teach me how to make a perfect martini."

"I like that man's style."

"It was a unique experience; we were in on everything. Also, I took
part in Community Theater and helped entertain the troops."

He laughed, "My question is well answered."

"Thank you, but now tell me about yourself."

"I'm a banker by profession, on an extended holiday. But this I
talked about last night. I am married and have four children." My heart
registered dismay, but it was just as well. It was best not to get involved
with anyone yet; I needed time to enjoy my newly-won freedom.

Then I heard Luis add, "But I no longer live with my wife. We have
a *separación del cuerpo* (a legal separation), as there is no divorce law in
Argentina." Not so safe after all.

As we talked, something special was happening. So-called experts
have reported that we know these things within ten minutes. His eyes

searched mine and found answers. A part of me quietly suggested caution, things were moving too fast.

We spent several days visiting Versailles, touring the French countryside, and eating in small inns. Luis was full of enthusiasm. His French was fluent, as well as his knowledge of French art and history. I could not have picked a more attractive guide. We ran over with words—we had so much to talk about. Knowing that he was leaving in a few days' time, and that this relationship could go nowhere, I kept him at arms distance—actually I was shy about allowing him into a more intimate relationship—I'd been off the "dating" market for such a long time, and I was unsure of myself.

He mentioned he would be in England at the same time I'd be visiting my friend, Nancy Oakes (well-known to the press because of the notoriety resulting from the grisly murder of her father, Sir Harry Oakes, in Nassau during World War II). I'd given him my London address, and as I said goodbye in Paris, I silently prayed, "Please call me—I do want to see you again." How little I knew; maybe he had a ladyfriend already there waiting for him.

Several days later, arriving at Heathrow, there was Luis waiting for me! I was so surprised—he looked unbelievably handsome. My heart almost burst as he embraced me and kissed me in a very gentle way.

His first words delighted me. "Something came up unexpectedly. Your friend Nancy has gone to Scotland for a few days. I told her I'd meet you and be your guide. She agreed it would be more convenient for her to have you stay at the London Ritz where I am until she returns."

The staff at the Ritz greeted me with great warmth—they had known Luis during his Cambridge days. I was a bit perplexed when we came to a suite of rooms connecting to the public hall through one common door. But my room was on the left and Luis's on the right, so I said nothing.

"Do your unpacking, and then come over to me for a lovely English high tea," invited my handsome guide. (It actually crossed my mind as to how we would keep our bills straight . . . I was so naive.)

Needless to say, once I crossed that hall, I never got back to my room again except to bathe and change clothes.

Luis with great gentleness introduced me to the passion my body was capable of and had never experienced. Until then it had been easy to keep my distance with men—sex was no big thing as far as I knew. Arriving at the altar as a virgin, I found my wedding night a total

*Luis was the amateur golf champion of many South American countries including Argentina, Chile, Brazil and Uruguay*

*A happy couple, Monte Carlo 1951*

*Nancy and Luis in 1951*

*Nancy and Luis in Mexico 1951, just before parting*

*Happy days, visiting in California in May 1953. Left to Right: Luis,*
*Vic Millar, Father, Ardagh Marie Millar, Mother, Herbert Hills.*
*Front: Nancy and Doryce Hills*

*Nancy and Luis with María Luisa at age three months*

disappointment. Why all the hoopla about this painful, messy act? Time didn't seem to help. Dick and I had no "fire" between us and I slowly became a "frigid wife." But now, with an experienced partner, possessing a body chemistry perfectly matched to mine, a whole new world of sensations opened up.

Several days later Luis confessed, "I called Nancy Oakes and told her you would be delayed a week—maybe you'd better give her a ring."

So she had been there all the time! She howled when I explained, and said, "Go off and enjoy yourself, I'll be here all summer."

Luis and I had fallen desperately in love by the time we joined his Australian friend, Peter Reid, and spent a month touring France, Switzerland, and Monaco. It was a story-book trip, one that would make us suffer more when we parted. We could not stay together; there were too many obstacles, but knowing it didn't make it easier.

Luis followed me to New York and then to Los Angeles, delaying our eventual separation. Finally, with despair, we agreed to go our separate ways. He returned to Argentina and his family, and I to Honolulu to bring the boys back to California for school. My enchanted summer was over.

The joy of being reunited with my precious, blond-haired, little sons helped my aching heart, but it was an emotional time for me. I'd closed a nine-year chapter in my life, and would now move away from my circle of supportive friends. We had all been newly-weds and first-time parents together—our roots were deep. My mother-in-law, whom I loved—it was because of her that I stayed married as long as I did—had asked me not to stay in the Islands for Dick's sake.

So, even though I was relieved to have my divorce behind me, I felt both apprehension and hopeful expectations as I returned to the San Francisco Bay area.

Getting my family resettled and moved into a new house kept me so busy that life began to fill in, even though I longed for Luis. Then in October a letter arrived. He wrote, "You are under no obligation to me, but I can't go on as it is. I will get a divorce in Uruguay and Mexico. Only when I am completely free will I appear in your life again. Darling girl, I refuse to envision a future without you!"

I didn't come down from the clouds for days; my happiness wiped away all problems. Everything would be worked out in time. What I knew for now was that it was possible! Six long months later, Luis came to California and formally called on my father to ask for my hand.

Then Dick came for a visit with our sons. While staying at my sister's, he agreed to my taking the boys to Argentina. This was a big relief to me, as I had to have his written permission to take them out of the U.S. (Foolishly, I thought his oral promise was good enough.) It was agreed that I would send the boys to Honolulu for the summer, and go to Argentina, select schools, and so on, and then return for them in September. We would make the trip back to Buenos Aires together.

So with good faith I made my plans. Only when I looked at a map and saw how far away Buenos Aires was did I have butterflies in my stomach. It was as far away from San Francisco as Australia. My family had mixed emotions. They were happy for my joy, but felt sad about my going such a distance. However, I had no choice; Luis's family banking business was there, and this was the source of his income.

On June 26, 1952, one year from the day we met in Paris, I joined my husband-to-be in Chile; from there we traveled to Argentina. The country was in turmoil over the impending death of Evita Perón. All night life was subdued as the people waited, but it hardly affected us. All we needed was each other. Luis would go to the office for an hour, and then return home for lunch to make sure I was not homesick. Luckily, he had a good Scottish manager to run things.

After selecting a fine British school, ordering uniforms, and getting everything ready for the children, Luis and I went to Montevideo, Uruguay, to be married. We were so happy, even though I wished my family could have been there with us.

Then the bomb dropped. Dick wrote saying he would never let the boys come to Argentina. He had waited until I was married and could not change my mind.

It threw me into a complete panic, soon to be replaced by rage. Luis comforted me with plans to return together to the U.S. for Christmas. So began my custody battle with the Cooke family, one that dragged on and on.

On April 12, 1954, my birthday, our daughter, María Luisa, was born—what a heavenly time! It was also a time to make another decision, one the boys begged me to make. So, after trying for two years through lawyers and repeated lengthy stays in California, I took the whole family back to Argentina without the written permission of anybody.

I took enough money with me to support the boys until their father came to his senses. Now my happiness was complete. We all adored the baby, Luis was a supportive and admired step-father, and we bought a large house outside the city near the school. Everything was going beautifully when, six months later, tragedy struck.

On returning from a New Year's Eve party, Luis had been violently sick. He recovered, but didn't feel normal for a couple of weeks, so we decided he should check into the British Hospital for a check-up. As a typical Argentine, he was sure it was something wrong with his liver.

How I remember that dreadful day—every minute is engraved on my heart. It was January 15th, a beautiful summer day. A battery of diagnostic tests were run, and we were waiting in his room for the results.

Finally, Harry Fergusson, Luis's doctor and old golfing friend, came in with a handful of papers and announced, "Well, pal, I'm afraid my suspicions were correct. You have a blood intoxication. It must have been what you ate the night you became so sick."

"That Chilean lobster?" asked Luis.

"Very likely. Anyway, you're not going to get over it immediately. We're going to keep you here and give you regular transfusions until we wash out this reaction." Turning to me, he said, "I guess you'll be staying here for a while, dear Nancy. You'd better move your car into the shade. It's going to be a hot day. Let me walk out with you."

This was strange. I had parked my car in the shade, but I didn't say anything. Evidently, Harry wanted to talk to me alone.

Once out in the corridor, he took my elbow and guided me into a nearby waiting room. His raw-boned, weathered Scots face was sad. "Nancy, Luis is seriously ill."

I don't know why, but a dreaded thought crossed my mind. I asked, "Is it leukemia?"

"Yes." His large features seemed to drop as he sighed.

"Does that mean he is going to . . . to die?" I choked on the word.

"I'm afraid so, unless there is a miracle. It's rare at his age, but the leukemia is acute."

"But he's always been so strong and healthy."

"Yes, but now there will be a crisis. If we can just get him through the next ten days. . . ."

I was sinking into the earth. Harry's voice seemed far away as he continued, "I contacted Dr. Albert Pavlowski, head of the World Blood Society, who is luckily in Buenos Aires. I asked him to check my diagnosis, praying I or the lab made a mistake. The diagnosis is correct."

For a moment my vision expanded. Harry seemed to be standing at the opening of a distant tunnel. As if outside myself, my voice asked, "Will it be a painful death?"

"No, he'll be spared that."

Someone pulled the cork, and my whole life poured out on the floor. I tried to grab hold of myself—not break down. In a matter of minutes, I had to see Luis. Harry settled me back into a chair and asked a passing nurse to bring me a sedative.

He took my hands, "This will be hard. Go back and stay with Luis until Dr. Pavlowski and I return." His grip tightened. "Talk and try to appear as normal as you can. We don't want to arouse his fear. He has only a small chance of surviving this crisis, but if he panics, he won't even have that."

I don't know how I did it, but it is amazing what you can do for someone you love. Harry and I agreed it was best to convince Luis that he was reacting to lobster poisoning. If I broke down, he would guess the truth.

The next hour seemed like a hundred. Sitting on the hospital bed, running my fingers through Luis's fine black hair and chatting with him,

I had to fight back thoughts of the reality crushing in on us. To me, my husband was everything a man could be. His Latin temper was counterpoised by his English heritage. He was tender, affectionate, and bombastic. How he loved to debate, an incessant devil's advocate, taking either side. Never knowing what to expect from him, I was captivated by this electric man. I looked at his strong chest and shoulders, his athletic golfer's hands and legs. He emanated health. I couldn't believe what was happening.

Finally, Harry returned with a small, fair-skinned man whose kind brown eyes looked out of a prematurely lined face. After Dr. Pavlowski examined Luis, he asked me to join him for a cup of coffee in the hospital cafe, leaving Harry and Luis talking golf.

Harry had told Pavlowski that Luis and I had been exposed to an atomic fallout twenty months before. Perhaps there was a connection. He urged me, "Please start at the beginning—don't leave anything out. I need to get the complete picture."

"In May of '53," I began, "we were visiting the Grand Canyon. One evening in a bar, we heard a radio announcement that the atomic test previously scheduled for that day had been canceled because of high winds. Luis commented, 'Those damn fools don't know what they're fooling around with.' Another man at the bar volunteered, 'They're taking tremendous precautions—it won't hurt anyone but a few animals—all roads in and out of the area are closed.' He sounded well-informed, so we dropped the subject, and forgot about it.

"Early the next morning, we left for Zion National Park; I was driving and remember turning off the car radio, as there was no reception in the canyon. We were awestruck by the rugged beauty of the scenery—I don't have any idea exactly how long we were there."

Pavlowski asked me if we knew the bomb had gone off. "No, we'd never thought of it since leaving the hotel." Now I thought back on how stupid we had been.

He interrupted, "What kind of car were you in—were the windows down?"

"Oh yes. It was a station wagon—it was a beautiful, warm day—we had the windows wide open."

"Where were you stopped?" He was making notes.

"We had driven through the towns of Mesquite and St. George, which are in Utah. Shortly after we left St. George, three men in army fatigues signaled us to pull over."

"Were there no signs warning you to stay off the road—anything to that effect? Had you seen any other army personnel?"

"No, we were just driving along, enjoying the beauty of the desert."

"And the soldiers? What then?"

"They were three young corporals. One asked, 'Where have you come from?' When we explained, he said, 'But that road is closed. Don't you know there's been an atomic fallout?' We didn't know a thing. I thought back to the scene. How oblivious we had been. I pointed out that we hadn't seen and couldn't have heard anything.

"One of the soldiers in a uniform one size too big commented, 'There's been a slip-up somewhere; the roads in that area are closed from the Canadian border to Mexico.' They told us to get out of the car so they could do some testing. One of them pulled out an instrument, explaining, 'This geiger counter tests for radioactivity.'

"At his request, I raised my foot while he held the instrument to my moccasin. I saw the red needle go to the top, and asked, 'What does that mean?'

"'It says you're hot, lady.'

"Foolishly, I answered, 'Oh, thank you.'

"Luis reprimanded me, 'This is not funny, Nancy.' Then they tested the car, and pronounced it the hottest one they had seen that day."

"You mean other cars happened through also?" asked the doctor.

"Apparently."

"What about the people who live in those towns you mentioned? Were they evacuated?"

"No. We asked about that. They were warned to keep their windows shut and stay indoors until advised differently."

Dr. Pavlowski sighed. "About what time of day was it?"

"Mid-afternoon. They sent us about a half-hour's drive down the road to what they called a decontamination center. There the car was washed approximately six times and each time retested with the geiger counter."

"What did you and your husband do during this time?"

"Well, Luis was angry. He asked one of the soldiers, 'How do you know if you've received a dangerous dose of this radiation?' The soldier wasn't very tactful. 'Oh, you'll know. You'll get nauseated, your hair will begin to fall out, and you may go blind.'

"'For Christ's sake!' was Luis's response. His Latin blood boiled over. There was a saloon across the street. We went there. Luis ordered a double scotch, only to be told by the bartender, 'Sorry, sir, it's a state election day, and in Nevada we can't serve alcohol 'til after seven.' That's when the you-know-what hit the fan."

Pavlowski's eyes never left my face. "And then what did you do, see a doctor?"

"No. When we returned to the car, we were given a package of soap and told to bathe and wash our hair with it. We were to put our clothes in a laundry bag and send them to the cleaners." So they could contaminate everybody else's, flashed through my mind. "It was suggested we have a blood count taken in about six months, but we really didn't know enough to be worried."

"Yes, go on."

"Well, there's not much more to tell. The road to Overton, Nevada, where we had planned to stay with relatives, was closed. So we went straight to Las Vegas where my aunt and uncle came and met us instead. That night Luis and Uncle Fred drank up practically all the scotch in town."

The doctor was now conversing with himself. "So that makes it about nineteen to twenty months ago—that figures."

"What do you mean?" I held my breath, not wanting to hear the answer.

"Most of the victims of Nagasaki and Hiroshima, who didn't die during the blast, developed this particular acute type of leukemia and died between eighteen months and two years after the fallout."

"Oh, Doctor Pavlowski, do you really think this is the same thing? Isn't there any chance it could be something else?" I was begging for hope.

"My dear, I wish I could tell you differently, but you've asked me to be truthful. I know of no case where a patient has lasted longer than ten months with this illness. And, I've never seen a more virulent case." He went on to describe how the cells looked like little walking canes under the microscope. There could be no mistake. I clenched my fists to my mouth.

"Your husband will have a crisis in ten days. If he lives through that, he can live from two to ten months, allowing that he can tolerate the medication."

He looked directly at me. "You should stay away from X-ray or any form of radiation for the rest of your life." This fell on deaf ears. My only interest then was Luis.

Later I asked more questions. The doctor felt the fact that Luis had had hepatitis shortly before leaving Buenos Aires had made him more vulnerable to the deadly affects of radiation. Also, he was fourteen years older than I. Pavlowski said he would call Dr. John Lawrence at the University of California's Atomic Research Lab with the exact details, to find out if this information could have any bearing on his course of treatment.

"Isn't there anything else we can do? Should we get Luis to the States?"

"I don't think your husband could tolerate a long trip, but there is something we can try. I have been using a new medicine which might help. However, I want to confer with Dr. Lawrence before administering Perinithol."

This presented another hurdle. There was only enough Perinithol in Argentina for two days of treatment; we had to obtain more from the U.S. immediately. I threw myself completely into solving this—the momentary problem helped to stave off thinking of the future, but when I heard Mother's voice on the phone and told her of Luis's illness, I broke down for the first time. It made me realize how far away I was, how alone.

Mother promised to put the Perinithol on the first Pan Am flight, so treatment commenced. Luis responded well; his blood count held up between transfusions, and Harry became optimistic that he would survive the first crisis. We hung on every straw. I took hope. If we could just get him home where we could build up his strength for the second crisis. Two to ten months—anything could happen in that amount of time. I would not allow myself to think otherwise.

I spent every possible hour in Luis's room treasuring each moment, trying to imprint every sound, every touch into my memory. During the periods between headaches and relapses, Luis was especially lively—particularly after the transfusions. Switching from subject to subject and waving his arms for emphasis, he was his animated, handsome and cheerful self. It seemed unbelievable that he could be dying. I watched for signs of the coming crisis. I prayed for a miracle.

Leslie Pepper, an old friend of Luis's, came to the hospital daily to spell me, so that I could dash home to check on our household. Miss Julia, our nine-month-old baby's nurse, was aware of the gravity of Luis's condition, but I said little to the boys, not wanting to alarm them. I'd decided to wait until we got Luis home. On the eighth day, Leslie took me aside and said, "I think we're in for trouble. Luis is hemorrhaging again."

"But Harry said that he was much better."

"He said that yesterday. Now he's worried that the medicine is losing its effect. Nancy, there's just no point in fooling ourselves."

I didn't want to admit it, but I too had noticed how Luis's urine bottles were black with blood. He sneezed blood. His gums were raw. Dr. Pavlowski had predicted he would die of a cerebral hemorrhage. I was terrified. Harry reassured Luis that it was the body just throwing off some blood from the transfusions. I wondered if Luis suspected the truth but was afraid to ask.

Leslie had not given up hope. He said, "Theodore Hicks is in town again. I've arranged for you to meet him."

The previous year, Hicks, an American evangelist, had come to Argentina on a tour of the major South American cities. Quoting the Bible, he affected instantaneous healings before the multitudes who jammed into the theaters and stadiums to hear him. The newspapers were filled with stories of his miraculous cures. Leslie's mongoloid daughter had been helped by her encounter with Hicks. This I had helped to arrange. Now Leslie wanted to do the same in reverse.

"I think you should see him . . . even Perón has told the Catholic Church to put up or shut up. He suggested they demonstrate the same kind of healing that Hicks was doing for hundreds in Buenos Aires every day."

"But of course I'll go to see him—he may be the miracle we've been praying for. Thank you, thank you, my dear friend."

A visit with the faith healer presented a ray of hope. If only my faith were strong enough, God would help.

So the next evening, as I sat in The Continental Hotel lobby waiting to see Hicks, I prayed for strength. Also, "Not Luis, please do not take Luis." I didn't want to face life without him. I promised to atone for any sins I might have committed. I hadn't meant to hurt Dick when

I took the children away—I mentally went through any acts of mine which had caused unhappiness for others.

I made all sorts of promises, if only my husband could be saved. But I felt so alone—then is when a strong faith would have helped me.

Mr. Hicks's secretary found me in the lobby and escorted me upstairs to the evangelist's room. If I had not been led to him, I never would have noticed him. He was a man of medium build with salt-and-pepper gray hair. He wore a baggy suit, but his appearance belied the conviction in his steady, pale blue eyes, which penetrated me as he opened the door.

"Come in, my child. There is help for all who seek it in the house of God." Mr. Hicks's measured tone was smooth and rich. "Your friend told me of your beloved husband's illness. We will speak of that later, but first let us talk about you."

He motioned for me to sit on the couch next to him. "Do you believe that the Almighty Father has unlimited power?"

"Yes."

"Do you pray?"

"Yes, constantly. I talk to God and to Jesus and implore them to heal Luis and to give me strength. My words may sound trite, but God knows what is in my heart and how desperate I feel." The dam broke, and the tears I had been holding back poured out.

"It is better to let the tears come first, my child, " he whispered. "Then we will pray together and ask God to send you strength."

When I regained control, Mr. Hicks asked me to kneel and put my arms around his waist while he stood holding my head in his hands. He intoned a prayer in a loud, firm voice. "Lord God Almighty, we stand here in your presence. . . ."

A soothing calm came over me. I could feel the ringing words of his prayer permeating me, bypassing my comprehension. Mr. Hicks prayed that God would give me strength to pass through my ordeal, that I might have great faith, knowing that only faith would help me in the days to come. He was not praying for Luis, but for me!

I felt better and we made plans for Mr. Hicks to visit Luis the following morning. I also warned, "Luis doesn't know what he has, or the severity of his illness. Have I been wrong in not telling him the truth? The doctor suggested waiting until later."

"No, my child. We all must make decisions. You are doing a kindly thing. You want to save your husband. He will know when it is his time to die." A smile transformed his solemn demeanor.

"As for my call, I will tell him that I am visiting various floors at the hospital and make the whole meeting seem accidental."

When the evangelist dropped in the next day, Luis received him cordially. I left the room so that they could be alone. When I returned, Mr. Hicks had departed, and Luis described a remarkable scene. "The old boy asked me about my life, my beliefs, and whether there was anything burdening my conscience. I told him I hoped I had not caused anybody harm, and if I had, it was not with bad intention." Luis went on, "He then had me put my arms around his waist and asked me to pray with him. When Hicks touched my head, my sinuses, congested by all this hemorrhaging, suddenly cleared, and I could smell all of the roses in the room! Nancy, that man has something—some quality of tremendous spirituality. I'm delighted he came to this room."

Did Luis secretly sense his great danger? Happiness and hope flooded my being—maybe a miracle had happened.

"So cheer up my love, before you know it I'll be as good as new. That transfusion really did the trick." He ruffled my hair—his eyes were full of light again.

But, by afternoon, while I watched in panic, the hemorrhaging turned into a deluge. Luis complained of a dreadful headache. Narcotics and oxygen were administered, but eventually even they could not control the pain. Luis's last words to me before he went into a coma were, *"Qué dolor, mi pobre cabeza—mi querida, mi querida."* I held his hands, and the doctor and I watched as his respiration stopped. His strong heart kept beating, and then gradually, without oxygen, his pulse disappeared and my Luis was gone from me.

The doctor left the room. I sat there with Luis's quiet hand in mine. . . . I became aware of the fragrance of roses in the room.

Later, when I was taken home, Miss Julia, the nurse, said that María Luisa started to cry inconsolably at the exact moment of her father's death.

Early next morning I went into the garden and cut all the beautiful blossoms off of Luis's favorite tree. They would cover his casket. Then I gathered my three sons and gently broke the news that our Luis had left us. Rikki, the eldest at ten, asked, "Will we have lots of problems, Mom?" My answer was, "Yes." He volunteered to get a job to help the family.

The months that followed brought an agony I cannot describe. Slowly through my overwhelming sorrow came the realization of our predicament. It arose like a slow sunrise, its rays lighting up the valleys of my dilemma. It would have been easier to lie down and die of a broken heart the way dogs often do after losing a master. Until then grief had been a foreign sensation for me; now I was overwhelmed by its unrelenting persistence. It enveloped me during sleepless nights, it made my throat refuse food—and yet I had to pull myself together—I was in a faraway land with four dependent children and almost no money.

Our protector, benefactor, and interpreter was gone, and the wolves were forming a ring outside our door. Amongst them were some of Luis's immediate family who had never met or accepted me. As we were never legally married in Argentina, now I was not recognized as the legal wife, and all payments from the office ceased. Four months before, we'd bought our wonderful old house out of a German estate. I paid the first payment of $35,000 cash, the money I'd brought to support the boys; Luis was to pay me back when his money from Uruguay arrived, but this never happened.

It wasn't only a financial dilemma. I had brought my children to Argentina without the permission of their father. Now, from bitterness he wrote, "You made your own bed, so lie in it." He refused us any help and let me know he would take me to court on my return to the United States. So bridges had been burned behind us.

But maybe in the long run it was a blessing to have all these problems. It made me stay busy. I had to discipline my thoughts—if I cried all night, I was useless the next day. It was as though I couldn't even afford the luxury of my own terrible grief. Too much depended on my staying strong.

As much as Mother feared flying, she came from California. She will never know what this meant to me—meeting her at the airport brought the first ray of sunshine into my heart since Luis's death. After appraising our situation, she got us moving. We had a sale such as diplomats often do when leaving an assignment. We sold the house and many of our valuable belongings. The boys set up a table and sold their blue jeans and boxes of bubble gum.

Mother left after two months, but it took more than a year to unscramble our affairs—between legal matters and the revolution which ousted Perón, it was a tumultuous time. The only time I felt any serenity was when I sat by Luis's grave. I accepted the fact that there was a reason why he had to die; I never questioned God's will, but thanked that force for allowing me the three years of happiness we'd had.

I couldn't bear the word eternity and had engraved on Luis's headstone, "SLEEP PEACEFULLY BELOVED UNTIL WE MEET AGAIN." If there were justice in the universe, and there had to be, I figured it involved continuity of lifetimes. (I wasn't familiar with the term reincarnation then.) I continued to dwell on Mr. Hicks and his remarkable conviction and longed to believe myself.

I had so many questions to be answered. I envied him his unquestioning faith. Shortly after Luis's death he sent me a note saying, "Do not worry about your husband's soul. His talk with me had the quality of a full confession. He died with God's grace."

I believed him, and it was then that my thirst began, a thirst for answers, a thirst for a trust to be used as a faith, a support, should such a terrible grief engulf me again. And I knew that when I found a belief that worked for me, like Mr. Hicks, I would tell the world about it.

The warm Indian sun was shining in my room. It took a minute to realize where I was . . . in the hotel in Dharamsala. I had fallen asleep in a sitting position. Had it all been a dream? Sometimes on awakening I prayed my worlds were reversed, that Luis's death had been just a nightmare. But this was reality. However, I knew one question had been answered—my search was not ended, it was just beginning. It was time to take some real steps into a new dimension, the world of going within, the world of spirit, of justice and self-knowledge. I hastily dressed. I had many questions to ask Kazi—this was an opportunity not to be lost.

---

## 4

---

# Island Romance

IT TOOK TEN MORE DAYS for Tom and me to wrap up India. Leaving the
mountains, we headed back to Delhi airport. From there we flew to
Bombay to visit Tom's friends, Piloo and Vina Mody. After the
primitive travel conditions we'd endured, I will never forget the luxury
of the Mody home on Carmichael Road, the city's most prestigious
street. My suite of rooms was beautifully decorated, clean and welcoming—to wash my hair under a shower and to sleep on a real bed! The
contrasts of India certainly sharpen one's appreciation.

The Modys are a highly respected, powerful, and moneyed Parsee
family. Sir Homi Mody started the conservative party of India, the
Swatantra. His son, Piloo, was a popular Member of Parliament whose
hobby was cooking. Our great friendship started when I asked for a third
helping of his Goa curry. He and Vina had met at architectural school
at the University of California. She left her home in Oakland and
completely adopted her husband's culture—more than that, she improved it by working with all sorts of Indian artisans, bringing to them
her Western know-how.

Tom still had people lined up to interview, so between social events
we called on more swamis, healers, and fakes; then it was time for me to
be homeward bound. It had been an amazing six weeks! Tom had more

*Vina and Piloo Mody with Nancy in Bombay*

than delivered the adventure he promised. I left feeling rested, in balance, and full of joy in spite of the hardships of our travel. The little black cloud of apprehension which used to visit me frequently seemed to be gone. I had come to a momentous crossroad, and now I knew which direction to take. So it was with sadness that I said goodbye to Tom, to India, and to my new friends, but I knew I'd be back.

Now, heading homeward, I was aware that my image as an explorer would certainly be enhanced by this trip with Tom. The San Francisco papers had followed my career, the local girl, from the time I'd gone off on a troop carrier during the war to marry Dick Cooke. Next came my move to Argentina and then Luis's death just before the revolution which ousted Perón. In the winter of 1958, I went Brown Bear hunting in the Arctic Circle with Finnish Laplanders, as the first American

*Nancy's wedding day to Tony Jackson, May 5, 1962.*
*Left to right: Brett, Tony, Rik, Nancy, minister and Starr.*
*María Luisa in front.*

woman to do so; later several of the hunters and I went to Russia. It all made good copy, both for the papers and my lecture series.

Soon the rumors connecting me with Tom started. They particularly loved the Yeti hunt. However, the columnist did not know that for several months before going to India, I had been seeing Tony Jackson, a divorced American who had recently returned to the U.S. after living in Bangkok and Geneva for many years. He had joined a law firm in Los Angeles. His amusing letters had followed me around the world, and now he would meet me in Honolulu. A Harvard graduate, he was one year older than I. He was quick, bright, outgoing, energetic, and extremely good company. Fluent in several languages, he was not a typical American male. I was very curious to see him again. My sisters had met him and thought he was terrific.

Luckily, I felt no qualms about returning to the Islands. All my problems with the Cooke family were over; Dick and I had settled our legal battles and we were friends again. The boys spent their summers with him and occasionally I took short vacations there.

Tony arrived several days after I did—complete with tennis racquet and surfboard. I laughed. "A surfboard for Hawaii! Isn't that like coals for Newcastle?" His smile revealed sensational white teeth. "Guess that's the lawyer in me—I don't leave anything to trust."

We spent a joyous week sunning, surfing, eating, and drinking with my many local friends. They all approved of Tony. He was witty, played excellent tennis, and fit into any group. Also, important to me was his enthusiasm for my new spiritual interest. We spent hours on the beach reading out loud to each other from the books I'd brought back from India. Besides sharing this, he was increasingly attractive to me both mentally and physically . . . would he also be my spiritual partner?

Charlie the Palmist, a widely known character who sat outside the Taj Mahal Hotel in Bombay had told me, "You will be married within three months to someone you hardly know, and it will be successful." Was this he? I had to be careful. I didn't want to be lured into marriage again by the magic of the Islands.

Then, on the other side of the coin, it would be nice to have a companion with whom I could share love and also opinions, daily worries and all the fears that accompany our lives. It would be a luxury to share responsibilities, after being mother, father and breadwinner all rolled into one for seven years.

Tony had discussed marriage with me. He'd been a bachelor for nine years and was ready for a real home again. Although not yet a partner in his firm, his future seemed bright. As a team we would be O.K. financially. It would mean having to sell my home, leave my partnership, and establish a new foundation for the family in Los Angeles. I had a lot to mentally weigh back and forth.

After I arrived home and got caught up with the children and Mother, Tony flew to San Francisco. He was very complimentary about my family and my Mediterranean-style house. Naturally, the family members were curious about him. The boys, Rikki, now seventeen, Starr, fifteen, Brett, fourteen, seemed to like him. They admired his interest in sports and the way he played basketball with them. He reminded Mother of her favorite actor, Rex Harrison. Only María Luisa, now eight, seemed a bit aloof, but asked questions about his two daughters aged ten and twelve. Of course, we knew he was looking us over as much as we were appraising him.

He was most diplomatic: "I congratulate you on your children; they adore you and behave so well." It was true; we had a wonderful, happy relationship. I had been a strict mother and it had paid off—we could go anywhere, and I could trust them to behave. Having come through hard times together had made us a strong unit. The boys were excellent students, athletes, and had never been involved with liquor or drugs. María Luisa was a constant source of joy for me; she was very like her father.

Several weeks later, with the urging of my two sisters, who pointed out, "Tony is great; everyone likes him. It's time you get married again . . . María Luisa needs a father. The boys are all for it. Why don't you just set the date and get it done," we did it.

On May 5, 1962, before I knew it, I was standing in front of a minister in the living room of my younger sister's home. As we said our vows, I heard my slightly senile grandmother ask, "Who is that stranger standing up there with Nancy?"

Nobody was happier at our wedding than my old friend, Cobina Wright. Now we would be neighbors in southern California. We'd been close friends since our meeting in Honolulu in 1948. A mutual friend had written requesting that Dick and I entertain her, and we loved each other on sight. She referred to herself as my second mother; we had traveled all over the world together. She had been against my marrying Luis—it was too far away—and now she was elated. I'd once said to her, "You wouldn't care if I married a gorilla, as long as he lived in Los Angeles." She'd agreed.

Louella Parsons, Hedda Hopper, and Cobina were the three Hollywood gossip columnists who could often make or break a movie star's career. Having been a top socialite herself before becoming a columnist, she was far less "bitchy" than the other two.

How much I owed this lively woman. It was her scheming that had resulted in my becoming the U.S. Ambassadress of Fashion in 1957. A nationwide contest had been sponsored by a number of magazines including Town and Country, Vogue, and Harper's Bazaar, along with Twentieth Century Fox Movie Tone News. The winner was to accompany Cobina on a world tour promoting U.S. fashions, all to be reported in her column.

Saying nothing to me, she convinced the executives of the hosiery firm, which had put up the money for the contest, that they couldn't take a chance on some inexperienced housewife to represent the U.S. on such a diplomatic mission. The contest winner would present fashion gifts from highly-respected American designers to an outstanding woman in each country visited. This woman, selected by her own countrymen, would in turn give the Ambassadress a costume reflecting the fashions of her country.

Among these women were Madame Jacques Heim, wife of France's famous couturier, Princess Marcella Borghese of Italy, and Queen Soroya of Iran. Some countries planned large charitable functions for the exchange of the gifts. The format of the tour exploited glamorous people and exotic places. The international wardrobe collected on the trip would be modelled at an Embassy Ball to be given in New York for the benefit of UNICEF.

Cobina had warned them about their choice. "She could make terrible blunders and embarrass us all. I have a young woman you should meet. She would be a perfect candidate."

It was a year after my return from Argentina, and I was in New York being interviewed by Elizabeth Arden for a job when Cobina called. "How about joining me and a group for lunch tomorrow at *21*." I was delighted. How well I remembered that day.

As I stepped through the entrance door, Charlie Berns, one of the owners of *21*, greeted me, "How's my old Hawaiian pal? You're looking great. Cobina's around the corner."

Two arms caught me in a bear hug as I pushed through the crowd. "Hi, Baby. Watcha doin' in little ole New York without first checkin' in with your drinking chums?" It was Robert Ruark with his wife, Ginny. They had been my houseguests in Honolulu the night I had hosted a party to meet Cobina. It was quite an evening. After dinner, we sat on the lanai listening to the music of Bob's favorite Hawaiian singer, Mickey Fo. The musicians encouraged each of us to do a hula. Cobina performed an impressive "round the island" with her hips, then collapsed laughing to smoke a cigar.

Bob's rough face was filled with warmth and mischief; his tweed jacket exuded tobacco as he lit one cigarette from another. "Guess who's in town? Little ole Mickey Fo. I got her an engagement at the Blue Angel. When can we get you for an outing?" I promised to get back to him and headed for Cobina, who was waving from her table.

"Nancy, you know Earl Blackwell." We kissed; we'd had dinner the night before. He had suggested Cobina for the fashion trip. The other three men appeared to be typical New York businessmen. "Mr. Sandy Brass is the president of the hosiery company that is sponsoring my upcoming tour."

I smiled and nodded. "Well, you certainly picked the perfect Ambassadress of Goodwill. Cobina is a diplomat and knows everyone in the world."

Over luncheon I described my days at Arden's, being put into shape from ten to four, and then staying out late every night ruining the good work they had done. Cobina asked if I were going to take the job that had been offered at Main Chance, Arden's swank health farm in Scottsdale, Arizona. I told her that I didn't think I wanted to spend my life drinking carrot juice cocktails with fat ladies, while my children waited at home.

It was a lively lunch with people dropping by to say hello to Cobina, and we were soon finishing our demitasses and ready to leave. Suddenly Mr. Brass turned to me and asked, "Nancy, how would you like to win a contest?"

Cobina bubbled. "I knew you'd like her. She'll make an excellent Ambassadress, and with a name like Nancy Cooke, she already sounds like the typical American housewife."

Only then did I realize that the luncheon had been arranged as an audition. Not a man to waste time, Mr. Brass went on. "There are technicalities we will have to adhere to, but we can guide you right up to the final judging." He asked if I could write the obligatory twenty-five words on why hosiery was important to a woman's wardrobe.

Before I could respond, Earl offered, "Burt Bacharach can handle that one for you." (The slogan he did write was later adopted by the company: "Hosiery is the best cosmetic for the legs.")

By the time I left 21 my head was whirling. It was so tempting. Should I take a chance? Daddy would continue to help me out temporarily, and I could pay him back later. Mother and Miss Julia could run the house—the kids would think it was great. As it turned out, it was a lucky day for both Cobina and me. I won the contest, and a few months later Cobina, a publicity man named Gino, and I took off.

After two hectic weeks covering Europe, Cobina fell ill and had to return to Los Angeles. We agreed no one need know about her absence. Gino and I would carry on with my writing the news and sending it back to Cobina. This worked well until just after we finished Turkey, Iran, Thailand, and Australia, when Gino also got sick and returned home. I still had to visit Chile, Argentina, Brazil, and Venezuela—at least I would have a wonderful homecoming in Buenos Aires—before I could collapse.

Seventy-two days after the trip had begun, Gino and Cobina sneaked into Idlewild Airport so that we could pretend we had all arrived together. Later, while we were being interviewed, I heard one reporter remark, "Look at that fabulous Cobina. She looks so fresh, and Nancy, who's much younger, looks worn out." It had been a back-breaking trip, but it propelled me into a new fashion career for which I would always owe Cobina a debt of gratitude.

The United States Information Service became interested in my role as a goodwill personality—governments from all parts of the world invited me to see their fashions and advise them. Then, on my return to the United States, I would report on what I'd found. This started my "Around the World With Nancy Cooke" shows, which helped me support my family.

During the past few years, I had visited Cobina's home in Beverly Hills often and made many friends through her. I couldn't have a better sponsor to help introduce me to my new life with Tony.

## 5

# *Adventure In Meditation*

EVERYONE SEEMED HAPPY WITH THE FACT that an eight-year widow and a nine-year bachelor had found each other. Even Tom shared this sentiment. Several times before the wedding he'd called and I'd been honest with him about Tony. His reaction had been, "Frankly, I have mixed emotions; I'm happy for you, but I'm feeling sad inside for what might have been;" to which I assured him, "No one will ever take your place with me, dearest one—we have a special friendship. Maybe you are meant to stay single—a wife might hold you back, and the planet needs you." He sent a lovely wedding gift and promised to visit us in the near future.

Up until the final moment, I had vacillated about remarriage. Enjoying my independence, I was accustomed to coming and going at will. Tony had assured me, "Nothing has to change. We each have our own careers. If there were not so many children involved I'd say let's just live together and forget the legal part." He had a full schedule with his law practice, his T.V. program, *A Political News Analysis*, and his passion for classical music.

"In fact, I'll probably encourage you to go off on your travels and lecture tours, so I can have time to myself."

This sounded great and we did have fun together. We had the same energy level and laughed a lot. Sexually we were enthusiastic partners, but there was not the overwhelming intensity of attraction and bonding which had existed between Luis and me. That seems to come only once in a lifetime—and maybe just as well, the loss of such a love is so traumatic. I continued to dream of Luis and sometimes called Tony "Luis," but it seemed so natural to be married again. The first month was hectic with house-hunting, moving, and all the million details involved in setting up a new life. Finally, by July, we'd settled into our new California ranch-style house in Beverly Hills. The boys had gone off to Hawaii for summer vacation. We would have a honeymoon around our own swimming pool, which pleased Tony.

The only negative part of July and August occurred when Tony's two daughters, Lisa and Maggie, arrived for two months. They were disrespectful to their father, expected to be entertained constantly and mean to María Luisa. Always a loving child, anxious to please and help out, María Luisa, who had looked forward to having sisters, was now being accused by her step-sisters of being "Miss Goody Goody Two Shoes" for being obedient. How many times I had to bite my tongue and hold my temper!

Eventually I got it across to the girls, "We can have a lot of fun if we work together, but when you are in my home, you will obey the rules as my children do. If you don't grow to love me, you will grow to respect me." That set the tone for their yearly visits and Tony did support me in this matter.

One day Cobina's secretary called me, "We used all the social parts of your letters from Iran and India, but the *Herald* was not interested in the religious personalities, so Cobina let me send those particular letters to a friend of mine who is interested in spiritual matters. Her name is Helena Olsen, and she's dying to meet you."

We arranged a date and Helena came immediately. After a torrent of questions, the pleasant, middle-aged woman gently asked me if I'd found a guru, and then next, "Are you practicing some form of meditation?"

"Well, yes and no."

"What do you mean?"

"I had a technique, but I don't practice it anymore. I visited a swami in Bombay by the name of Sharma. Sharma taught a technique which didn't require renunciation, so I decided to try it."

"Good, what did it involve?"

"I had to kneel on the floor for half an hour with my eyes closed, visualizing a cross. When it stood still, I was to dive through the apex and thereby transcend normal consciousness. Only after I had dived for three months would he send me a *mantra* and further instructions."

"Did the technique work?"

"No. It was maddening. I would close my eyes and try to see a cross, only to see everything but a cross. All I got out of that meditation were headaches, sore knees, and a lot of frustration. After three weeks I stopped."

"How lucky you did. You were trying to drive the boat, and in meditation the boat should direct you."

"But I'm interested in spiritual advancement—not that I want to be a monk."

"That's not necessary," Helena insisted. "Nancy, I follow a guru who says there are two roads of spiritual evolution—the way of the monk and the way of the householder—and they're equally fast."

Now I began to question her. "What do you mean by 'householder'? Do you mean to say your guru doesn't ask you to give up anything?"

"A householder lives in the world. A monk retreats from the world." Helena peered at me. "Didn't you hear of Maharishi Mahesh Yogi while you were in Rishikesh? He doesn't ask you to give up—he wants to add to your life, not take away from it. You should enjoy an integrated life—spiritual and secular."

Then I realized he was the man Chidananda had suggested. The one who had left for the U.S. Was it only a coincidence?

"He's coming to Los Angeles in October. His organization is called the Spiritual Regeneration Movement, or the S.R.M. He always stays with us. He calls me Mother Olsen. Why don't you try TM and then meet him?"

"What is TM?"

"It's Transcendental Meditation. It works on the natural tendency of the mind to seek the source of bliss. You sit back, relax, repeat your *mantra* a few times and the rest is enjoyment," she chattered on.

"My husband and I have been meditating for two years—it's greatly improved our lives. We're more relaxed, happy, creative—we get more accomplished with less effort. Things just seem to go better for us now. I could go on and on."

Well, Helena did go on and on—bubbling about the delights of TM, describing her master in loving detail, and finally explaining the simple process by which we could become meditators.

Jerry Jarvis, the teacher, was just about to start a new course. Tony and I decided to take it. "For fifty dollars, what can we lose?"

We took an immediate liking to Jerry, who had joined Maharishi two years before. In his thirties, he was a serene, sandy-haired man, full of devotion and mirth. Even more, we liked what he taught. He told us about Maharishi's master, Guru Dev (Sri Bramanandam Saraswatim), who followed and taught the wisdom of Shankara.

The Hindu religion is based on knowledge from the Vedas, the oldest known scriptures in the world, found by the side of the Indus River thousands of years ago. Different individuals have passed down their interpretations of these scriptures, creating various sects. Gautama the Buddha's explanation became the basis for Buddhism. Shankara created the swami tradition of India. The pontiffs are titled Shankaracharya (*charya* means "place"). There are four Shankaracharyas, one each for the north, south, east, and west.

Guru Dev (*guru* means teacher, *dev* means beloved) was designated Shankaracharya of the North, the most revered of the four, as the region encompasses the origin of the Ganges and the Valley of the Saints. Maharishi was totally devoted to him, wearing the robes of a *bramachari*, or disciple, and invoking his name as a salutation, "Jai Guru Dev." Apparently, from stories we heard, he had been a stern master to Maharishi, breaking his disciple's pride through countless tests, but at the same time earning his devotion.

There were times when the lectures were almost sleep-inducing. Modest and quiet-spoken, Jerry had devoted his life to spirituality and meditation—reading these lectures was a profound responsibility. Accordingly, he treasured every word. No doubt it would have been more interesting to hear these lectures from Maharishi himself, but after a slow beginning Jerry's lecture would accelerate as he began to penetrate the profound visions of Maharishi's teachings.

He described a simple technique. "This will enable you to experience enjoyment of the reality—the inner bliss, the consciousness of 'Being.' This you will learn when you receive your *mantras* at your initiations." He explained, "The *mantra*, a sound vibration specially determined for each individual, attracts the mind naturally back to the source of thought, where it is most powerful." This reminded me of my conversation with Lama Govinda, where I first heard the word *mantra*.

On a portable blackboard Jerry drew a column of six circles, each larger than the one below it. He went on, "A thought begins in the transcendental sphere as a small notion. Like a bubble in water, it expands and takes shape as it rises. It is larger as it passes through the subtle states of the mind and keeps expanding until it reaches the gross state and bursts as a thought on the conscious level."

He had indicated each strata by pointing to the corresponding bubble. "What we want to do in meditation is to reach the transcendental level of consciousness. This we do by reversing the process of thought and following it back to its original source. To do this, Maharishi uses the vehicle of sound, the *mantra*, to take the mind to the source of thought, which is also the source of everything, including joy. Once it has been to its source, the mind will always want to return."

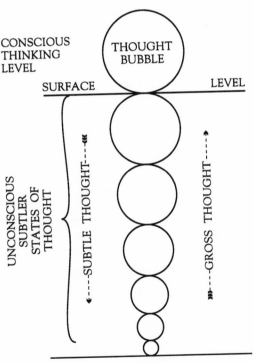

CONSCIOUS THINKING LEVEL

THOUGHT BUBBLE

SURFACE       LEVEL

UNCONSCIOUS SUBTLER STATES OF THOUGHT

SUBTLE THOUGHT

GROSS THOUGHT

STATE OF PURE CONSCIOUSNESS
OR SOURCE OF CREATIVE INTELLIGENCE

*From The T.M. Primer by Patricia Drake Hemingway*

On occasion I was skeptical. Would this really work? My other meditation hadn't. Will I be down on my knees again, only to close my eyes—and nothing?

Finally, after two months of meetings, we finished the course, and the day of our initiation arrived.

July 30, 1962 started as a bright, sunny day. Later on, the news promised, it would turn hot and smoggy. A trace of fog still lingered from the crisp night air, which the sun would soon chase back to the ocean— typical of Los Angeles in summer.

Anticipation had awakened me even before the alarm rang. Not waiting for Tony to get out of bed, I slipped into the garden to linger a bit. Today was an important day.

Walking on the cold stone path, I was surrounded by swirls of color and fragrance from the flowers planted around the swimming pool. Camellias, roses, marigolds, daisies—all blooming in intense hues. Was the fresh atmosphere quickening my senses? Or was there something more behind my feeling—in fact, my certain knowledge—that something momentous was about to happen?

It seemed as if the pieces of my jigsaw puzzle were finally falling into place, and today still another jagged edge would connect.

A finch twittered from the ivy-covered eave above me, awaiting its turn to approach the bird feeder on top of the garden wall. Standing barefooted in my nightgown, I felt close to nature as the morning rolled out before me; but there was a lot to do. With another quick glance at the sun, already bringing the cool stone to life, I went to the kitchen.

Jerry had requested that we bring flowers, fruit, and white handkerchiefs to our initiation. I was not surprised; Tom and I had followed the Indian custom of paying homage to religious teachers with such offerings. Today we were honoring not Maharishi, but Guru Dev.

As I gathered our gifts into a bag, my heart brimmed with gratitude. I picked white daisies and saffron roses thinking of Maharishi, who had chosen to remain in white robes, while Guru Dev wore the traditional orange robes of the swami order.

After dressing and before going to the Olsen's, I wanted a quiet moment to myself. I knelt and silently prayed, "Please dear God, let this be what I have been searching for. Please bring me closer to you, and make me a better instrument to carry out your will."

Tony's honking reminded me that we had to leave. I grabbed the offerings and my purse and ran out into the hall. Standing by the front door was my son, Brett. As I kissed him goodbye, I reminded him that, should anyone call, no one was to know where we were or what we were doing. Tony was concerned about the effect of our initiation on his growing law practice and reputation. He didn't want any mystical labels attached to himself.

A short time later we were sitting at Helena's house waiting our turn. I looked around me. How ironic it was. Not long ago I was in the Himalayas visiting renowned swamis and lamas. Everything had been so strange and colorful—I thought back on the "ice yogi" and his reaction to the word "science." Now, after all those exotic meetings, I was back in California, sitting in a typical middle-class American living room, about to adopt as my guru a little-known yogi, whom I had never met. I filled out the mimeographed form I'd been given.

I thought to myself, once I learn the technique, I don't necessarily have to be part of the organization. I can just meditate on my own. The last question, "What do you hope to gain through meditation?" was followed by several suggested answers: "Self-Realization," "Relaxation," "Spiritual Advancement," "Mental Tranquility," and so on. I checked most of them, but how could I explain my reasons, my longings, my needs—the form was too short, and I left the answer incomplete.

"Nancy, come with me now." Helena leaned over and whispered. "Here's your tray." My questionnaire lay on it with my offerings. We went through the kitchen into the broad backyard. Tall hedges provided privacy; spreading trees, shade. Birds called raucously. Was I really in the middle of Los Angeles?

Helena led me to a small frame house nestled under a huge maple tree. The door was open. A middle-aged woman looked out. It was Beulah Smith, the only initiator in America. She looked like someone who might be seen on television demonstrating how to make meatloaf. I trusted her immediately. As an initiator, Beulah would introduce me to the Shankara tradition through a *puja*, an offering, to the masters of the line. She would select my *mantra*—how she did this was not explained.

"Jai Guru Dev." She placed her hands together in *namaste*. "What a happy day for us all. I welcome you in the name of Maharishi." Incense filled the small, panelled room. There were no windows and, with the door closed, one flickering candle provided the only light. A portrait of Guru Dev was on an altar-like table, surrounded by flowers, fruit, and white handkerchiefs from earlier initiations. Brass dishes held rice, water, a cube of camphor, and sandalwood powder.

She took the tray from me and invited me to come in and take a seat. She sat next to me. "What beautiful roses; did you know they were Guru Dev's favorite color?" She glanced at the questionnaire as I settled back into the chair. "Your handwriting is so clear. Fine, we shall proceed." Her voice was soft, warm.

After placing my tray on the table, Beulah asked me to stand next to her. "The ceremony I am about to perform is to express my gratitude to the tradition of the Masters in appreciation for giving me this wisdom of integrated life. After I have finished, I will give you your *mantra* and teach you how to use it. However, I must ask you to keep your *mantra* to yourself—not tell anybody—in order to derive maximum benefit. Maharishi says, 'When we plant a seed, we don't dig it up to see if it's growing.'"

I nodded, very anxious to do everything correctly.

She selected a rose for me to hold. Then, picking up one of the daisies, she dipped the blossom in the water and shook it about the room, as if purifying the air. She began to chant the Sanskrit, "*apavitah pavitro wa, sarwa wastan gatopi wa . . .*"

I did not try to follow her invocation, but I recognized the names of Brahma and Vishnu. She intoned the chant carefully, speaking intimately to the portrait, as if conversing with Guru Dev himself.

I suppose any ritual looks strange. Jerry had spoken of a Sanskrit ceremony, but I was unprepared for this. However, it was absorbing—nothing seemed to exist outside the little room. I gazed at the yellow reflection on the portrait. The incense was intoxicating.

Beulah picked up grains of rice and placed them on a plate in front of the portrait. Then she added a pinch of sandalwood powder, all the time carrying on her litany.

The daisy was touched to the water, then laid by the offering plate. My handkerchief received the same treatment, followed by the fruit and remaining flowers.

Beulah lighted the cube of camphor, producing a pure, white flame but no odor. Picking it up, she slowly swung it from side to side. She ignited more incense and broke into a low song. Soon she came to the end of her chant, and told me to sit again. Shifting her chair, she sat close in front of me. Looking at me intently, she leaned forward, and in a hushed voice whispered my Sanskrit mantra. She repeated it, then asked me to do so.

Satisfied with my oral grasp of the sound, she said, "Now repeat this word quietly."

I did so.

"Now, close your eyes, and repeat the word without using your lips or your mouth—without making any sound."

I did so.

"Now repeat the word in your mind."

I repeated the word. It rippled above my eyes. I repeated the word again . . . and again . . . and again . . . and again . . .

Then the word . . .

REPEATED ITSELF! . . .

And repeated itself . . . and repeated itself . . . and reped iself . . . n repeth isef . . .

A warm physical humming enveloped and permeated my body. I gazed blankly into a blue expanse. A humming welled up out of that blueness. I lost feeling in my arms and legs. The chair dropped. I was descending into that pleasant humming and blueness.

I had transcended.

The following weeks were full of excitement. My *mantra* became a beloved friend, and each meditation something special. In the beginning, Tony and I tried to meditate together, but it didn't work—especially our sessions before dinner. The children were home from school and even though they tried to maintain quiet, something always seemed to happen, and the noise disturbed Tony. He would come out of his study like a raging bear and roar for silence.

Jerry had taught us, "Noise should not disturb you. Meditation is part of the thinking process; you think during the day with all sorts of distractions around you. Eventually you will be able to meditate in the middle of Grand Central Station."

However, it worked better for me to meditate before the children came home or Tony returned from the office. This way I enjoyed the luxury of quiet time and then could be on duty to provide the same for Tony.

Eager to learn more about TM, we often visited Jerry and listened while he read lectures written by Maharishi, who was at that time lecturing and opening new centers in Europe. Nowhere in the lectures was there a trace of the religious fanaticism characteristic of the devotees of so many of the notorious mystical and occult sects founded in Los Angeles.

I sensed none of this in either Jerry or in the students he attracted. Before TM, he had worked as a landscape architect. Now among his students were engineers, housewives, school teachers—many professionals. They were drawn to the practical dimension that meditation offered.

Many questions came to mind, but the big question was, "Jerry, how long will it be before we notice any effects?"

"It is difficult to see the process of meditation's influence, just as it's hard to see a flower grow. After a month, however, you should notice changes in yourselves."

To further encourage us, he added, "It's very subtle." Maharishi likens it to the dying of cloth. First one soaks the fabric to reach a particular hue; then the cloth is exposed to the sun which fades the color. Back into the dye goes the material and again exposure to the sun. This process is repeated many times until the color is fast. So it is with meditation. Drop by drop we bring the benefits into our life and one day we realize that bliss is there to stay—we have become completely integrated, the inner and outer lived simultaneously."

During those first few weeks, Helena kept reminding me, "Don't look for anything in your meditation. If you sit and wait for something to happen or spend your time analyzing and dissecting your experiences, your mind will be held on the gross level of thought. You will defeat the very purpose of the *mantra.*"

"But how am I supposed to tell if it's doing me any good?"

"Look, Nancy, when you brush your teeth, you don't count the germs you've killed. You do it with faith that it is helping. In six months when the dentist finds you have no cavities, you understand the benefits. Approach meditation in the same way. Don't think so much about it."

"But Helena, when I brush, I can at least tell whether or not my teeth are clean."

"You will not see results within your meditation. In fact, you are the worst judge of your own meditation. If you feel some sort of discomfort, then perhaps I should check you again to make sure you're doing it correctly. Otherwise, look at your outside life. Ask yourself if you are sleeping better, if you feel lighter, younger, more energetic, if you are more serene. Does your mind feel clearer? Do you worry less? If the answers are yes, then you probably are feeling the results already."

"Well, the answer to more energy is negative. I have been sleeping soundly, but I can hardly put one foot in front of the other. All I want to do is sleep."

She laughed. "Nancy, your *mantra* will cause you to realize the true state of your nervous system. You've probably been running on nervous energy during all the changes in your life, moving to Los Angeles, marriage. Your *mantra* is very likely forcing you to get the rest you need."

In the following weeks, my energy did pick up—but that could have been the extra rest. I felt more serene. The children's pranks and minor accidents around the house didn't bother me as much. But with moving and other adjustments over, my life was settling down again. How could I be sure? Where should I look for proof? I did feel better and attributed that to my meditation, but maybe I was auto-suggesting benefits.

Early in September I received some outside encouragement. Ruth Dillingham, María Luisa's godmother, came to Beverly Hills for a visit. We had lots of news to catch up on as we hadn't seen each other since my wedding in May.

While she unpacked, I chattered about Tony's new office, our home, and all we had accomplished in so short a time. I could feel her eyes on me and wondered if I should describe my meditation or not. Before I could make up my mind, she plunked herself down on the couch opposite me, looking conservative and elegant in her designer suit. She eyed me silently, lighted a cigarette, and leaned back as she exhaled. "Nancy, I don't know what it is, but you are definitely doing something different to yourself. At first I thought it was your make-up or your hair, but it's something else." She shifted to a more comfortable position and tucked a leg under herself.

"What do you mean?"

"I can't put my finger on it. It's not just being a happy newlywed. You look younger. Your face is more relaxed. You seem calmer . . . radiant."

Had Ruth noticed the effects of my meditation? Was it really working? I could have hugged her for joy. Now, without hesitation, I told her all about TM. But she seemed perplexed.

"Meditation? I thought you had given that up after your unpleasant experience with what's-his-name . . . Sharma?"

I tried to explain the difference between the techniques, but the perplexity remained on her face as she smiled and said, "It sounds sensational, if it really does all that you say. I'll be interested to see what happens. But you've got to admit, you do get into some of the strangest things!"

---

6

---

# Twenty-Six Miles Across the Sea

A MONTH AFTER OUR INITIATION, Helena called about Maharishi's Catalina Island course to be held in mid-October. "Even though the course is to train new lecturers for the movement and the prerequisite is one year's TM experience, they will admit you," she said. She was thrilled and we were delighted. We made plans.

Finally the weeks passed and the morning of our departure for Catalina arrived. Although not yet eleven hours old, the day had already climbed into the eighties. It became cooler as we left Beverly Hills behind and approached the coastline of Santa Monica.

Although we were alone in the car, Tony said in a strangely hushed voice, "You know we needn't go through with this. Are you still sure? We could just . . . turn back."

"I have never been so sure of anything." I peered ahead. It was necessary to be quite firm. "As we agreed, you can go back after the first week."

"Provided we look over the group first. If only old ladies in shawls or beatniks show up—you can count me out. Thanks, but no thanks."

"Yes, of course." I stretched and yawned. Who would be there? I wished that I could be sure. Tony turned into the pier parking and circled the lot, looking for a shady, protected spot for his Jaguar. An empty slot by a young palm tree was the best available.

"I don't like to just leave a car like this around," Tony grumbled.

"I doubt there will be any danger with all the action around the pier." Actually, there was little activity for a Saturday morning. Only a couple of T-shirted sailors could be seen lounging on the rear deck of the ferry. "Why don't you wait here with the bags? I'll go check if that's our boat."

"Oh no you don't. The deal is that we look the people over; then we decide whether or not to go."

"Okay, but let's get up closer where we can at least get a look. The bus should be here any minute."

Just then a yellow bus roared up to us. Above the green-tinted windshield, the sign read "Santa Catalina."

"Talk about good timing." I nudged Tony with my elbow, "want to hide in a bush?" But there was neither foliage nor tall trucks in this part of the parking lot.

I was excited. "Helena should be one of the first out." Tony smiled but retreated a step.

As the bus pulled to a stop, a uniformed driver hopped out, holding the heavy door with one hand and offering the other to his passengers. A balding, pudgy fellow in bermuda shorts and a baseball cap promptly stumbled on the first step. He then started toward us as if he recognized us, but a woman in a straw hat and butterfly sunglasses hooked him by the arm and wheeled him around toward the boat.

A teenage boy in a striped T-shirt with an airline bag slung over his shoulder bounced by the couple and up the plank onto the ferry, pausing briefly to spit. More gold-wedgies, clam-diggers, and dark-blue tennis shoes followed.

Tony blanched and steamed. We had blundered too close. At any moment Helena would skip out and we would be stuck, unable to back out. I expected him to explode, "To hell with this! Let's get out of here."

But the metallic voice of the public address system interrupted. "Will the Kiwanis Group please board now for Avalon."

"God, I thought that was our group. Just hold on until we see the S.R.M. bus."

"You don't know how close you came to losing me," Tony said.

He had a point. After all, we were still new to the whole thing—not only to the S.R.M. organization. We didn't even know if our meditations were working. Some meditations had been pleasant and the time passed swiftly; but I had also shifted and squirmed through half-hour sessions that seemed to last five hours. These times were frustrating, and I felt like a fool sitting in a corner mumbling my little word. Actually, we had had few measurable results so far. Being newlyweds, life was already exciting and full, so meditation couldn't take credit for that.

Tony tapped my shoulder and pointed in the direction from which the first bus had come. This time what looked like an old gray World War II naval bus chugged around the corner and pulled up alongside the first.

The door had jammed and we heard pounding on the inside. But soon a tall, grinning black man squeezed through the door and wedged it open with his foot. Dapper in a blue blazer and gray slacks, he continued to laugh and banter with the driver inside as the other passengers, dressed in tweed suits, sportcoats with sweaters, cravats, and handkerchiefs tucked neatly into their breast pockets, got off the bus.

Tony looked relieved. "Say, they don't look too bad."

Stroking his back I said with relief, "Well, I'm game—how about you?" Tony nodded and headed back to the car to get the luggage. My excitement surged back up again.

Helena bounced off the steps at the rear of the group, spotting me immediately. "Nancy, Jai Guru Dev! Come on over and meet our Canadian friends." Helena had mentioned the majority of students would be from Canada, where the S.R.M. was strong and well organized. Maharishi had firm bases in Montreal and Vancouver.

A tall, blonde woman dressed in a tweed suit and low heels was escorted over by Helena. This was Ailene Leroyd, editor of the Canadian S.R.M. monthly news.

Ailene shook my hand firmly and said, "I am delighted to meet you. Helena tells me that you just returned from India, where you tracked down all sorts of famous saints and lamas . . . perhaps we could sit next to one another on the ferry and I can ask a few questions for the benefit of my readers. They love to hear about new meditators."

"Gladly." How delightful to have such an audience.

Helena then led me to the smiling man who had opened the bus door. "I want you to meet Joe Lindsey."

Joe had a rich, resonant voice. "Is this your first meditation outing?" When I nodded, he replied, "Oh, you are going to enjoy it. I attended last year's course on Catalina, and I have been looking forward to this day ever since."

"You mean to say that you came all this way just to hear the same course again?" asked Tony.

"No course of Maharishi's is ever the same. There is always something new to learn from that man. He has so much bliss to share. You'll see."

Another bus had drawn up and I watched Helena mingle with the new crowd, flitting all over, kissing and greeting everyone. Catching her eye, I asked, "Isn't Jerry coming?"

"Not with us. He and the Lutes have gone to the airport to meet Maharishi's flight. They will fly over to the island later this afternoon and be at the lecture this evening." We had met Charlie Lutes, who was the head of the S.R.M., but we did not know his wife.

The public address system beckoned us on board. It was time to start across the twenty-six miles separating Catalina from the mainland. Soon the boat glided out into the clear, calm water; we would have a smooth crossing. Leaning on the railing, I could see the scrubby, bare mountains of the island ahead. Gulls soared alongside.

Behind me, Helena talked with other meditators about the previous course.

"The food certainly was lousy. I'll never forget those soggy vegetables."

"But look at it optimistically," Helena countered. "It was easy to go on a fast as a result."

"Yes, whether you liked it or not," grumbled a husky voice.

"Maharishi doesn't want us to fast. He wants us to feel our best for meditation." I recognized Joe's bass.

"But I 'm not used to living on vegetables."

Helena said that a new cook, a chef from the Aware Inn, a well-known Los Angeles health food restaurant, would be preparing meals this time.

A quiet, high-pitched voice with a light Spanish accent said,

"Food isn't that important in any case. There's no time to exercise, so it's better to eat little."

I turned around and asked the group, "Who cooks for Maharishi?"

*Walking with Maharishi on Catalina Island, 1962.*
*Charlie Lutes on the left*

The same tall, thin woman with a baby's demeanor and milk chocolate complexion explained, "Last year Maharishi had an Indian along to take care of his meals and laundry."

"But he didn't bring him again, Sheila. Maharishi has someone new this year. Haven't you heard about Devendhra? He was a lawyer in London and left his practice to become a disciple to Maharishi. He's young, handsome, very dear, and quite serious."

I didn't know that Maharishi had disciples. "Will he be cooking and doing the laundry for Maharishi?" I asked.

"Yes, it is part of his devotion to his master. He will use a little kitchen which has been set up near Maharishi's suite."

Ailene tugged at my sleeve. "How about that interview?"

Tony was deep in conversation with Joe, so I agreed.

She pointed to some chairs in the shade of the awning on the port side of the ferry. Sitting close, with pen and notebook in hand, she launched into her questions. "Nancy, did you hear about Maharishi while you were in India? Oh, really, you were in Rishikesh? Very interesting. Tell me about it. . . ."

Before I had answered half of her questions, we arrived at Catalina.

Noisy gulls welcomed us to the sleepy town of Avalon. Launching themselves from the weathered pylons as the ferry glided in, they looped and swirled with the gulls that had soared just off our stern.

Two bellboys from the St. Catherine Hotel busied themselves loading our bags into the jeeps standing by the pier. They indicated the direction of the hotel. Since it was only a short distance, Tony and I decided to walk and look at the town on the way. An uneasy mixture of Spanish adobe with rose tile roofs and modern stucco with garish signs, Avalon took comfort in its many swaying palms and clean air. Beige, weathered mountains served as a backdrop. Being mid-October, the tourists had migrated for the winter. According to Sheila, the well-informed Panamanian, we would have the hotel to ourselves. The room-cleaning service had also left after peak season, so we would have to be on our own. No wonder the rates were so low.

It was a huge hotel, dominating its own cove and beach, surrounded by towering palm trees. With wood-panelled walls painted a faded light green, bay windows with ornate, gray frames, and a massive shingled roof weighing it down, the hotel so possessed the air of another age that I half expected to see a parade of bloomers, knickers and lacy white parasols step out of the high, wide entrance.

Room 323 was at the end of a long, rambling hall. With a high ceiling and tall windows, it was situated at a corner, providing a panoramic view of the spacious, manicured lawn below. I looked out at the parallel paths leading to the bright yellow beach, then to the mountains, then the blue and white surf beside the swaying palms—could Helena have arranged for us to have this nice room? She seemed to have her fingers into everything.

Gentle winds ruffled the curtains. What a lovely place for two weeks of lectures and meditation. Tony eyed the armchair. While he tested it for comfort, I opened the bags on the double bed and unpacked into the high, mirrored chiffonnier. Our bottle of Scotch and the transistor radio were plainly in view—our link with the outside world.

At dinner, Helena brought Helen Lutes, Charlie's wife, over to our table and asked if they could join us. Helen's thick auburn hair made her seem younger than the middle-age I knew her to be. The seriousness of her face was broken by a folksy smile when she was introduced, and she seemed completely in her element.

As she put down her plate and pulled up a chair, Helen wryly commented, "I hope you like garlic."

"Does the cook own a garlic farm?"

"No, he's Jim Baker, who runs the Aware Inn. Probably thinks that garlic is good for your intestines or something." Her high-pitched, gravely voice indicated warmth and humor. I took an instant liking to her.

"Is garlic necessary?"

"Don't ask me, 'cause I don't know." One eyebrow lifted in skepticism as she pursed her lips. "But it does nothing for your meditation." She repeated that expression when I asked about the vegetarian diet we would subsist on during the course. Wasting neither words nor gestures, her statements were sharply honed with natural authority.

"Look, when you get tired of the food, sneak into Avalon. Charlie and I know a good restaurant on the right side of the street down near the pier. There you can get something substantial, like a good steak."

"Won't Maharishi mind?"

"No!" She threw her head back and laughed. "Why should he? After all, he said that you don't have to give up anything for meditation, didn't he?"

I had forgotten that she had just flown over with Maharishi an hour ago. Her husband was still upstairs with him and wouldn't appear until the lecture. Finishing my plate, I looked around and saw that the dining room was emptying quickly as the students, excited to hear of Maharishi's arrival, were hurrying through their dinners and leaving for the lecture hall. Helena had already left to find Roland, her husband, and get settled in their reserved seats. As I made a move to get my things together, Helen restrained me. "Oh, don't rush. Maharishi has never been known to be on time for anything. Just finish your meal, then look for me in the front row. I can save some seats behind Charlie and me. There you'll be able to see Maharishi perfectly." I was going to like this woman.

The lecture pavilion was a high-ceilinged ballroom set up with folding chairs in theater rows. Three of the four walls were composed of glass-panelled French doors. The sun was fading and darkness was rapidly descending. Potted palms were arranged along the walls and the view was directly out to the sea. This elegant sun-room must be spectacular during the day, I thought. During the season, a band probably played on the low wooden platform set against the single solid wall.

There would be no dancing tonight, I mused, looking at the sheet-draped chair where Maharishi would sit. A coffee table holding a microphone, a portable blackboard and a picture of Guru Dev completed the props. The whole platform was ringed by tall vases of cut flowers.

Helen winked at me from the front row and gestured to the seats behind her. Helena and Roland sat at the far end of this same row. Evidently, these were positions of pride or rank, coveted by everyone in the organization.

There was a low murmur throughout the audience. Nobody laughed, though nearly all wore expectant smiles. The flowers were fragrant, and the air in the hall was unusually fresh. Looking around the pale green room, I noticed that all the windows were closed. Nobody was smoking. The air was perfectly clear.

Helen explained, "Out of respect for Maharishi, no one smokes around him as it drains his energy. He believes tobacco has a negative influence on our vibrations."

Although we were staying at a seaside resort, we as students dressed carefully, out of respect for Maharishi. Most of the women wore knit suits, sweaters, and skirts. One woman had a high beehive hairdo. Tony wondered what the salt air and two weeks would do to that. A few stood or walked around; the majority sat patiently, glancing at the door expectantly.

Finally, the hall was silent. Everybody focused on the door. A tall, athletic looking man in a dark blue suit strolled in carrying a small deerskin. He moved with the control and discipline of a former Army officer. This was Charlie Lutes. With a grace belying his carriage, he stepped onto the platform and carefully spread the skin on the seat of the chair. Charlie had no need of a microphone. Stepping off the platform and turning to the audience, he announced with authority, "Will you please stand. The Maharishi is here."

The room hushed. Standing as one, we clasped our hands in *namaste*. Maharishi glided into the room soundlessly. The tall portal dwarfed his small image, but riding above immaculate white robes, his knowing smile seemed a vision. Cradling a bouquet of roses in his robed arms, walking with a leonine gaite, revealing a sandaled toe at the apex of each step, he welcomed the audience with an exultant smile, nodding slightly in recognition of familiar faces in the gathering and then looking for more. His head held high, there was confidence, warmth and grandeur in his demeanor. A mane of long, casually-groomed sable hair crowned his visage and blended into a full beard. His dark, liquid eyes were luminescent with love and joy; his look held a sense of profound responsibility.

Stopping in front of the platform, he put his large, powerful hands together in *namaste* and slowly, sweetly enunciated, "Jaaaai Guru Dev."

With our answer of "Jai Guru Dev" we took our seats.

Maharishi climbed onto the platform, putting the roses down on the coffee table. Slipping off his thonged sandals, he sat on the draped couch and tucked his feet under his white robes. He pulled at a shoulder to arrange his vestment and pushed a wayward lock over his shoulder. He adjusted the microphone so that he could speak comfortably and then leaned forward to place the flowers on his lap. From the bunch, he selected one stem to hold. Then he sat back and calmly, sweetly asked, "How do you feel? Are you all happy?" His English was very clear.

No one answered. We beamed in anticipation. Maharishi then instructed, "We will meditate for five minutes." The room was again silent except for a few squeaking chairs.

With a gentle "Jai Guru Dev," he started the evening. "You make me very happy when I see your bright, intelligent faces. You will be the ones to help save the world. You will help men to live in harmony with each other and to solve their problems brought on by over industrialization. You will spread the word that suffering is not necessary in life. Man is meant to enjoy. Discontentment is the result of poor achievement. Through meditation, man earns the goodwill and support of nature. When he earns the support of nature, he will accomplish all that he may desire."

My reaction was, "He certainly thinks big. He's not afraid to shoot for the stars."

In a carefully enunciated, high-pitched, melodic voice Maharishi asked each student to stand and state his name and occupation. I admired his manner. Like a benevolent grandfather, he took a lively interest in each response, often nodding approval, "Very good." After some introductions he made further comments. To a physicist he said, "You will show the world that transcendental meditation is the answer to physics; it gives us an understanding of matter." Helena had told me that Maharishi had a degree in physics from his university. To a doctor he said, "You will learn to cure your patients with meditation. It will be your new wonder drug."

While watching us, his large, smooth hands played with the flowers, plucking petals and dropping them back into his lap.

"What will he say to me?" I wondered.

Finally, his eyes reached mine.

"I'm Nancy Cooke." I still used my professional name. "I am a housewife and a lecturer."

"Good, very good. You will carry my message to all parts of the world. You will tell your audiences that you have very special news for them!" He threw his head back and went off into gales of laughter, high, light, rippling laughter. He looked like a jolly Indian Santa Claus.

After the introductions, Maharishi looked at Charles Lutes, who had been standing off to one side and said, "Let's have Charlie tell you your schedule."

Mixing a corporate board manner with a midwestern accent, Charlie stepped forward and began to outline the program in clear, unmistakable terms.

Maharishi sipped a glass of water while Charlie spoke.

"Within a few days, Maharishi will expect you to be up to four or five hours of meditation at one time."

Impossible! As if a half hour weren't long enough. I was flabbergasted. Helena hadn't warned me of this. How could I ever sit still for that long? I looked around to see how everyone else was reacting to this news, but their expressions had not changed. They still beamed in anticipation.

I looked at Maharishi. He too was beaming, not the slightest trace of sternness in his face. His eyes glowed with happiness. He didn't look as if he had just assigned a difficult task. He was beaming in anticipation of joy, our joy. So this is what it meant to have a guru; he will push you, impelling you on your way to spiritual evolution, anticipating your future, perfect bliss. Tears started in my eyes. Had I found him at last? If so, I hoped I would prove worthy.

As the days passed, our anticipation of each lecture increased. They were on a variety of subjects such as living without tension, evolution and death, reincarnation, the Shankara tradition, God con-

sciousness, to name a few. Then we'd return to our rooms for practice
. . . our periods were gradually getting longer.

Actually our room was cozy and friendly with our personal articles
scattered around. We referred to it as our cave.

Tony took the chair and I, wearing a loose caftan, settled on the
rather lumpy bed, pillows stacked high for a backrest.

Jerry had said, "Take any position you find comfortable, except
lying down, which will encourage you to fall asleep. If you want to sit
on the floor, on your bed, with your legs up or down, fine. You don't want
your mind going to aching joints. If you need to get up to stretch your
muscles, do so, and then continue your meditation."

Sometimes there were small annoyances. The valves in the shower
were hard to shut off completely.

Jerry had also warned us, "If there is noise, don't try not to hear it.
Meditation is a mental process; you think all day with all sorts of noise
around you, and unless it is overwhelming, it doesn't bother you. As for
thoughts, that is the same; we do not push them away or follow them
out. We simply return to our *mantra.*"

The dripping shower was no longer heard. I had not pushed the
sound away, it was simply accepted. My *mantra* took command, and I
slowly descended into the more subtle stages of creation.

I had hovered in the blackness for some time. Slowly, I began to
glide down, feeling cooler air around me. Now, at first only perceptible
as a new color, a dark shade of midnight blue began to blend away from
the black and lighten. Keeping my eyes closed I saw azure project below
and in front of me, and finally an amorphous, mingling mass of aquamarine shades under me. The borderline between the indigo and the azure
became distinct. Suddenly my vision became all-encompassing. I could
see in back of me and at the same time view the azure in front! I gazed
at the turquoise below, and at the same time, could see the cobalt
above.

Slowly turning my closed eyes, but not my head, I found that I
could see in all directions, as if I could see the entire universe.

Then I felt cool air on my chest and I began to glide forward. The
coolness increased; I felt a firm pressure on my forehead. The turquoise
was gradually slipping behind me, and I was heading toward the midnight blue; now sinking into blackness. I felt myself falling and falling;

there was nothing I could do to break my fall into the darkness, nothing to hold on to.

My body was shivering. I opened my eyes and rubbed myself with my hands. I was still sitting on my bed in the darkened room. There was no draft, yet I felt cold. I continued to shiver, my heart pounding. I was alarmed, frightened by my fall through the blackness.

To whom could I go? I didn't want to disturb Tony. Who would calm me? I rose off the bed, toed around in the murk for my slippers and crept out of the room.

Once outside, I shuffled down the dark, long, gray hallway. No doors were open. The only light came from the distant stairwell. There were no pictures on the walls, the doors began to flicker by, but the only sound was the friction of my slippers on the coarse mat. Of course everyone will be meditating, I thought. I could still feel traces of the cool on my arm, the sensation of falling, losing control, my heart in my mouth—but they were only traces.

Should I go to Maharishi? But I hadn't met him up close yet—how could I barge in on him now? He had stated, "Nothing that comes to you in meditation can harm you." I paced up and down the hall. Warmth returned to my limbs; I returned to my room, but I would have to get reassurance before I could return to meditation.

The next morning, before class, I didn't want to meditate, fearing an encounter with the great black pit again. I had no desire to fight my way free of that enveloping blackness.

My mind rumbled with the problem. Should I admit that I had experienced panic in meditation? Had I confused a source of pleasure to be a cause of terror? Was I using my *mantra* incorrectly? There had been problems with it before but they only caused physical discomforts such as headaches, or extreme restlessness. This was different.

Maharishi skipped the grand entrance in the morning, taking his seat relatively quickly, greeting us with "Jai Guru Dev," and then slowly looking around the audience. He took a deep breath and asked, "Are you feeling happy? Good, very good." Still looking us over, he announced quietly, "We meditate for fifteen minutes."

"Jai Guru Dev."

We opened our eyes to Maharishi's smile. I had deliberately not used my *mantra*. A few meditators waited a moment before opening their eyes and Maharishi sat quietly, smiling until all faces were turned up. He asked if we had any questions, then sat back on the couch after recognizing a pudgy, bald man near the back of the hall.

"Maharishi, I get such a terrible pain in my heart when I meditate. I'm afraid that I might hurt myself."

"No, no!" Maharishi leaned forward so quickly that he seemed to hop on his deerskin. "You cannot hurt yourself in meditation. You must continue. The pain indicates that something is breaking down in that area. This is due to a lack of coordination between mind and body." He went on to explain this important point.

Maharishi picked up a piece of chalk and pointed to his illustration of rising bubbles on the blackboard standing next to the couch. "When the mind transcends to these subtle levels of the mind, you will perceive sensations in the body you could not feel before. If you feel pain, it shows that damage has already been done on that level." He slowly circled one section of the diagram saying, "By putting your attention on the area of pain, you can send your vital resources to help reestablish the balance necessary for health."

The heads in the first row nodded in agreement. Somewhere, sometime, they had heard this before; I had seen this power demonstrated by the yogi in Delhi who could direct a supply of blood to any part of his body, causing that area to become red and warm.

A blonde woman with a Nordic profile raised her hand and stood up. "Maharishi, would that explain why my hands used to ache during meditation?" Maharishi nodded; She turned to the rest of the audience and explained, "It is very curious. For years my hands would ache whenever I swam in cold water. I figured I had some sort of arterial weakness there, or that I would have arthritis in my hands one day. However, I went to Lake Tahoe last month and when I dove into the water, I noticed that my hands didn't bother me at all, and they don't ache when I meditate."

"Very good!" said Maharishi, plainly delighted to hear her testimonial. "Your imbalance is now gone. For all of you who experience pains in the back, in the heart, or anywhere, continue your meditation and one day they will stop and you will have avoided a developing illness. Meditators will enjoy better physical health for this reason." He smiled and looked around for more questions. Should I ask? The words were still caught in my throat. I wasn't sure how they would come out. But Maharishi's gaze rested on me, as if waiting.

"Maharishi, I was afraid to continue with my meditation yesterday. I felt as if a great black hole would swallow me up. My body started to sort of—fall away."

Maharishi looked out and asked, "Ah, how many of you have felt this?" Hands shot up all around the hall. So I wasn't alone. I sat down as Maharishi addressed his answer not just to me but to the whole group. "This is when you must continue to meditate. Always, always, take it as it comes. Nothing can harm you. You feel this when large chunks of tension are coming to the surface. Afterward, your nervous system will feel freer. This is how we prepare ourselves for spiritual experience."

Maharishi paused and gazed out over the audience. A hand waved for his attention in the back, but he ignored it and, picking a pencil from the table, said, "Let us imagine this is the nervous system. During the day, your senses are constantly experiencing—every kind of experience, whether it is of joy, sadness, or pleasure." He turned the pencil in his brown hand. "Each experience will leave a deposit on the nervous system, like that and that." He patted the pencil on all sides, then rubbed his fingers along it.

"Soon it is covered by a film of tension from the many experiences and we feel fatigue. What do we do? We go to sleep. Nature cleans away this coating through dreams; the tension flakes off and floats out through the mind without disturbing the conscious level of thinking. If we have slept properly, we feel fresh when we awaken; we feel optimistic. Our nervous system is clean and flexible."

His brow darkened. We sat silent, anticipating. "But what happens if we do not sleep enough, if we do not get rid of all the tension built up during our waking hours? This builds up over days, months, years, and yes, even lifetimes."

"Even lifetimes?" I reacted mentally.

Maharishi wore a sad frown. "Then we have a nervous system encrusted with tension. Life becomes dark. We are tired upon arising. We are full of complexes and pessimism. What to do?"

"Could the black pit be the dark cloud I have often felt hanging over me?" I silently asked myself. I didn't know the answer.

He threw an arm out and smiled, "We meditate." We smiled and began to chuckle. The answer was simple, but we sensed its potency. Maharishi began to briskly rub his fingers along the pencil, as if trying to wipe it clean.

"The thoughts which arise during transcendental meditation are similar to the dreams we experience in sleep. It is a natural method to cleanse the nervous system. When it is healthy and clear, it is ready for spiritual experience."

I sat back and looked around. Other students also expressed relief at Maharishi's words. So I had been upset over the black pit for nothing. It would pass like all problems; I just had to persevere.

Maharishi sat looking over our faces for questions, scratching his head with the end of the pencil.

A freckle-faced woman stood up, crossing her arms as she asked, "Maharishi, isn't that what a psychiatrist does on his couch?"

"No, no, no!" Maharishi waved the pencil at her. "By bringing old experiences up to the conscious level of the mind, the psychiatrist disturbs his patient all over again. He stirs up the mud from the past. If the sun shines on a glass of muddy water, nothing will be reflected, but when the mud settles, the clear water will reflect the glory of the sun."

I remembered this example from India. "In order to reflect the glory of God, we do not stir up the mud, we cleanse the water through meditation. Meditation, one day, will be the ultimate technique used by psychiatrists to cure their patients."

He shook his head in wonderment. "I do not understand how the American people, who are so advanced, can place their trust in psychiatry. Such a new science, not a hundred years old. No, looking back over a crooked road will never make it straight."

That afternoon, alone in my room since Tony had returned to Beverly Hills to "put out the fires on his desk," as I piled up the pillows on the bed to meditate, I heard a light tapping on the door. Helen Lutes stood at the threshold and peeking in whispered, "Sorry to disturb you; I want you to come with me. Maharishi would like to meet you personally."

"What? Now?" I couldn't believe it. Although Tom Slick and I boldly approached holy men in India, usually without invitation, somehow it didn't occur to me that I could simply do the same with Maharishi. It was like a royal summons.

Helen swung her hand out as she said, "Sure. Why not? You've got to meet him sometime."

"Why not?" I scrambled about the room to get myself ready. As we stepped out the door, I turned to grab some flowers.

Helen stopped me, "That won't be necessary; we're going to see him on business. I got to talking to him about you and told him that you ran a public relations office in San Francisco once."

"Up to this year." I struggled to keep up with her fast pace.

"Well, whatever. He asked me to bring you to a meeting we're about to have on promoting the movement." Her voice lowered—we were passing some closed doors where students would be beginning their long meditations. "Nancy, he really needs people with experience in communications and promotion. Maybe you can help him."

Although we had to walk through a small anteroom to reach Maharishi's bedroom, we could see him as soon as Helen opened the door to his suite. His bed was pushed against a wall and draped with a sheet and his deerskin. On it sat Maharishi, surrounded by papers, open books, and correspondence. Cut flowers stood in a vase on his bedside table. He looked up as we approached and greeted us with a gay "Jai Guru Dev," then turned to ask Arthur Granville, an old time meditator, to pull up a chair for me. Several others were there, including Charlie and Helena.

Maharishi looked at Charlie, who sensed the cue to begin. Charlie turned to me, "Nancy, we have been discussing the various alternatives we have for spreading TM and making Maharishi and the S.R.M. better known. Maharishi wanted you to sit in; with your background you might have some suggestions to make. We aren't getting anywhere at present.

"At this moment we have initiated roughly 200 people in Southern California, most of whom are still meditating, and the number seems to grow by about fifty each year. But that's all."

He turned to the rest of us. "Remember that Maharishi left India with the goal of teaching one percent of the world to meditate.

"This is necessary for maintenance of world peace," Maharishi said. "If one percent of the world meditates, they will give off such vibrations that war will not be possible." His eyes glowed with his vision. "Then mankind will embark on an age of peace."

As conversation opened up, I got the dreary picture. Except for Charlie, these followers were loyal, beautiful souls, but didn't have a clue as to how to go about making their guru well-known in order to attract seed money; without it, they could not expand the movement. As things stood, one initiator, Beulah Smith, and a couple of hard-working volunteer lecturers like Jerry Jarvis constituted the entire activity of the U.S. movement. It wasn't enough.

Though reticent, I decided to put my oar in. "Maharishi, given the right connections, a lot of things can be obtained for nothing."

"What do you mean?" Now all eyes were on me.

"Well, if we let the papers know that you are a person of interest, they will want to interview you. Radio, television spots can be arranged. Programs use up so much material, producers are constantly looking for new faces. Also, my husband has a program on T.V.—it's a political news analysis. He'd be glad to interview you."

Then, I took another jump. "Actually, I have some good friends, Maharishi, whom I think can help you. One is Cobina Wright; she is nationally syndicated and has a column in one of the L.A. papers. If we could arrange something interesting, she would write about it. However, because she writes a social column, we would have to provide names, VIP's that are newsworthy. Let's arrange an event involving community leaders, business executives, actors.

Helena was aghast. "But shouldn't Maharishi be the center of attention?"

"Well, yes, but for the press, no; at least not until they realize how newsworthy he is." I turned to Maharishi and explained. "Other Indian holy men and teachers have come to Los Angeles in the past, setting up centers like Vedanta and the Self-Realization Fellowship, so that's not big news. What we need to do is get successful, creative people interested in you, and have columns written telling how these people came to hear you speak. The public will read this and associate you with these active, successful people and become curious about your teachings."

"What type of interesting event do you envision?" asked Maharishi.

"Well, in order to attract them, we will have to make the event social. Most of these people have already committed their time and energy to worthy causes, but they'll come if they think it will be fun and enjoyable."

"And that rules out the S.R.M. center," said Charlie.

"Certainly. But couldn't we have Maharishi give a lecture at my house? It's very central for my friends." Was I being presumptuous? "Cobina would cover it for the papers."

Maharishi leaned toward Charlie expectantly. "What do you think Charlie? Good?"

Charlie nodded.

Maharishi turned to me and said, "It would be better to give several lectures and make sure that your friends hear enough to become enthusiastic about what there is to gain through meditation. We will tell them it is not necessary to live with tension. We will teach them how to enjoy the fruits of their labor."

When the meeting was over, we stood and waited to receive a flower from Maharishi as he departed. Charlie came over to me, smiling warmly. "Let's set up a date soon." He liked to get down to details. Maharishi was lucky to have a businessman in his inner circle.

When my turn came, Maharishi pronounced "Jai Guru Dev" with special warmth. Smiling, he picked out a ruby red rose and presented it to me in triumph. How I treasured that blossom! I cupped it in my hands and left the suite. "Wait until Tony hears all that has happened!"

## 7

# Good News . . . Bad News

ONCE AGAIN BACK IN MY ROOM, my inner being purred in comfort and happiness over the meeting. The rose I'd received still held warmth from Maharishi's hand. Yes, we could help him. My mind started to review a prospective guest list, but no, now it was time for my *mantra*.

With my body glowing all over from the effects of the meeting, I decided not to take a shower, lest I wash away Maharishi's *darshan*. Rather, I plopped on the bed, not even changing into a robe, still cupping the fragrant blossom. I was in such a mood to get cozy amongst the pillows and meditate.

My *mantra* . . . his smile . . . my *mantra*, I could hear it in the back of my mind, while faces and names rotated in front of my eyes . . . the delicate scent of the rose touched my nose. My attention shifted from one to the other, one to the other. . . .

I had hovered in the blackness for some time. Again my body felt cool. I began to glide down, lightly. The blackness in front of me began to blend away and lighten, blending into a band of azure below and in front of me. I surveyed the expanse. Large, swallowing spaces floated on all sides of me. I concentrated on the aquamarine, hanging on to it. I could see everything; I had been here before. What would happen now?

"Take it as it comes. Take it easy." I was gliding forward. The turquoise slipped behind, and now I again faced the black, the yawning pit. "Take it as it comes. Take it as it comes," as I let go and I fell and there was blackness all around me.

But the black was thin. A ray of gold broke through and suddenly there was only gold. Gold and warmth flooded through me. I was filled with joy and excitement.

Had the sun sought me out? I opened my eyes. The shutters were drawn. The room was dark, but the darkness was suffused with gold, the gold was within me. I closed my eyes again, and the gold was there and everywhere. I swam in the gold of my ecstasy, in the glory of the gold, of the sun, of God?

Slowly, so slowly, but too quickly, the gold paled and faded from my eyes. Closing my eyelids tightly wouldn't preserve the gold. Other colors, other patterns returned. The room, the drawn shutters, the empty armchair, the rose in my hand. I sat quietly on the bed, stunned by my experience.

Later I practically tackled Helen Lutes when I saw her in the hall, I was so eager to talk. "Let me tell you what just happened to me."

She calmly examined me with her laughing eyes and slowly tipped her head with a smile, "Oh, how lovely, Nancy, you have experienced the 'golden glow.'"

"What do you mean? Does everyone have it?"

"Well, it is one of the guidelines we look for; it indicates that you have really transcended. The golden glow, the ecstatic feelings, you experience them in the Field of Pure Bliss Consciousness. It is a sign of your progress in meditation." Helen was happy for me, but not overly so.

"Two months of meditation have brought me this far?"

"Let's not forget that you've been doing long meditation while here with Maharishi. That makes a big difference. Still . . ." Helen looked up at the gray ceiling. She put her hands on her hips and slowly shook her head, pensively. "Maybe, just maybe Maharishi threw you a little whammy."

"A whammy! You mean that he caused my experience?"

"Why not? After all, in the Shankara tradition, gurus can give instant spiritual enlightenment to their chosen successors. Guru Dev did this for Maharishi after years of testing him. Masters have all sorts of powers. Maybe Maharishi had this happen to convince you of the joys that are awaiting in meditation." With that, Helen turned and walked off to the lecture hall.

Convinced? I certainly was convinced. Nobody, nothing could take this experience from me. I could doubt the earlier sensations of meditation, the cozy warmth, the indistinct lights, vague scenes, the lightness of my body, most of which I forgot upon arising afterward. But this I did know. My experience was so solid, so powerful that it seemed more real than life itself. I was still in a state of euphoria.

Who is this Maharishi? Does he truly have such powers? And, if so, what other powers does he have? I stood on the sharp edge of the fence and I was steadily pushing myself over. If he has these powers, then *who, what* is he? Is he a prophet, a saint? Why should he hide such capabilities; why doesn't he just use them and convince everybody beyond any doubt that they should follow him?

Later, while everyone went to their seats, I stood by the door outside the lecture hall waiting to present Maharishi with a flower when he arrived. But when he approached, he held a hand up indicating that I should keep the flower. He looked at me intently with his glowing eyes and smiled, asking, "Ah, Nancy, are you happy?" We shared a secret.

The suspicion lingered in my mind. Maybe Helen was right. Maybe Maharishi arranged a special bit of grace for me. An experience of such ecstasy certainly would help a person to believe.

But my ecstasy was short-lived; from the heights I was to be plunged into despair.

Late one evening, after the lecture was over, I flipped on the portable radio to check the eleven o'clock news. My heart almost stopped when they gave the headlines for the news to come following the commercial. "Tragic death of Tom Slick, prominent Texas millionaire, businessman and scientist."

Tom had gone to Vancouver. Because of Maharishi's course, Tony and I had declined the invitation to join him. I had said, "I'm going off on a search of my own," and filled him in on TM. He had been curious to know more and we had made a date for when he came back.

"Slick left in a storm; his chartered plane was struck by lightning over Montana. He and his pilot fell thousands of feet after the plane exploded in midair." Tom's body had already been recovered; there was no hope. Several times in the past he had been reported dead but had survived. The last time was after a crash near the Amazon in thick jungle-infested country. After many days, the searchers had given up hope. Then Tom walked out on his own and announced to the world, "It takes more than a few thousand Chivanti Indians (cannibals), piranas, and the Brazilian jungle to kill a Texan." He felt he lived a charmed life and would fly in anything, under the worst conditions.

I wouldn't believe it . . . it was a mistake, but after checking with the radio station, there was no hope; his body was undeniably identified. It was that of my beloved friend. What would I do?

"Why don't I go to Maharishi?" was my first thought. "Helen says he sleeps only three or four hours a night, and he's always up 'til early in the morning." I felt timid about intruding on his privacy, but I pushed myself into it.

"Come in, come in." On opening the door I saw Maharishi reclining on his bed with papers spread around him. Devendra was also in the room. At least I hadn't awakened him.

My words of shock and sorrow poured out in a torrent. "You did the right thing in coming to me, Nancy. I'm here to help you, and in order to understand life, we must understand death." His voice was soothing.

"Death is just a resting place on the path of evolution. If one understood correctly, one would cry at a birth and celebrate at a death." Lama Govinda had said the same words to Tom and me!

"It was his time to go. He has passed the tests he had come here for. He will go on to more important matters now, if he is the kind of man you say he is. Do not think of death as a tragedy. Where he is at present, he knows it is a release, and would want you to understand. You can help him now by remembering the happy times you spent together."

During the next days I tried to follow his instructions. Whenever grief would return I'd try to concentrate on a happy time Tom and I had shared. I thought back on that day with the Dalai Lama. I must notify His Holiness. I doubted that Tom's family and foundation would stand behind their agreement. The foundation was Tom's special project, financed out of his own pocket.

Even with Maharishi's help, Tom's death haunted me and brought back my grief of Luis's death—but thank goodness I was with someone who understood what life and death were all about. I realized the support I was seeking in Maharishi's philosophy *was* helping me. Maybe TM would be the emotional insurance policy I had longed for, ever since I had loved so completely and been so vulnerable.

Tony returned and the days passed rapidly, highlighted by our daily group meetings. During lectures Maharishi would pick up the microphone from the table and lean back on his couch, revealing a smooth, powerful forearm. With his left hand, he often stroked the dark wooden beads of one of his two necklaces as he discussed the principle of the *mantra.*

"In order to bring our attention to the subtle fields of thought, we have to start with the experience of a thought from the conscious level; then reduce that state of thought to a subtler and subtler state until the origin of thought is reached."

He paused and looked out into space, his deep eyes tracing the pale green auditorium walls. Nobody took advantage of this break in his monologue to interrupt his train of thought with a question. We had learned that when Maharishi pauses, he seems to be leafing through some spiritual book, some divine source of knowledge, for it was after such quiet moments that pearls of inspiration would flow from his lips. We sat and waited, not stirring. Maharishi opened his mouth, paused, and then spoke.

"We know that the power of the *mantra* increases as it is reduced during meditation. We enter into the subtle states of creation."

He picked a rose from his lap and held it up for our attention and lightly shook it.

"If we throw this flower at someone, it might hurt him," Maharishi shrugged his shoulders, "but it is not likely." A high, joyful laugh welled up within him but he did not lose his train of thought. "But if we could enter into the subtlety of the rose and excite the atom, the flower would bombard the whole atmosphere. As power is greater in subtle states of creation, so is thinking. When we reduce a thought to great subtlety, it is found to be much more powerful than it was on the gross plain of thinking."

As he reflected on the rose in his hand, turning it, observing its parts, he said, "If we choose for a *mantra* a word like 'rose,' we do not think about the rose as a rose, but as a sound, 'rose.' If we were to contemplate the rose as a rose, we could not reduce our thoughts to subtle states of consciousness. We may think of the parts of a rose, the petals . . . the thorns . . . the stem . . . but our consciousness will remain on the gross level of thought. We must not think about or visualize our *mantra,* we must use it only as sound. In this way it leads us to subtle

states of consciousness." His voice gradually lowered and warmed—
"Rose . . . rose . . . rooz . . . roouozz . . . erroouaaoozzz . . ."

It was such a seductive sound, I felt like closing my eyes and transcending right there on the spot instead of waiting until we got back to our room.

Later, sitting on my bed, I reflected on my good luck in having found Maharishi, or was it luck? I remembered the saying, "When the chela is ready, the master appears." Evidently I was ready. Already I was looking at life from a different perspective. Everything was a test to get through, and my choice would be to strengthen myself so that no test would overwhelm me—Maharishi would teach me this.

As for Tony, the spiritual dimension didn't attract him as much as the practical goals. He looked forward to needing less sleep, having more energy, and becoming more prosperous as a lawyer.

On the final day of the course, we were all called out onto the front lawn of the hotel to take a group photograph before our departure for the ferry. As Maharishi told each person which chair to take, Helen whispered, "This is when you literally find out where you sit with him." Slowly each took his place. Instinctively, I felt I would always sit in his esteem as I was seated that day.

I was getting nervous when, nearing the end of the placement, Maharishi noticed me. He pointed to an empty seat in the stand and said, "Nancy, go sit next to Charlie." I couldn't believe it. Out of a hundred, I would be in the middle, only a couple of feet away from my guru. Tony was seated on the other side of me.

Maharishi climbed past the first row, settled on his deerskin, took a final look at the palm trees and told the photographer to take the picture.

## 8

# The Selling of a Guru

WHILE IT HAD BEEN EASY TO PROMISE Maharishi press coverage, actually coming up with it proved to be a different matter. Filled with enthusiasm after Catalina, I expected the local papers to pounce on my news about this wondrous teacher bringing the source of happiness to America. Once people heard about this cure for virtually every ailment, they would demand to know more.

Then came the stark truth. I couldn't interest a single editor. They dismissed Maharishi as just another of the stream of swamis who had sought their fortune in California, and saw no reason to investigate further. Having succeeded in getting press coverage for horseraces, fashions and parties that I had promoted in the past, this was a challenge. I would not be easily discouraged—I would try others.

Even the best of contacts were cool. After soliciting help from Roy Larsen, the publisher of *Time, Life* and *Fortune,* he suggested that I see Mac, the head of their L.A. office. Responding to Larsen's name, Mac invited me into his cluttered office, pushed a pile of clippings aside so that I could sit down, and patiently listened to what I had to say. He asked no questions, resting his grizzled chin in his small, dry hands as I talked. His lined brow and steady eyes betrayed no reaction. When my presentation ground to a halt, I asked him if he would do an article on Maharishi.

Mac swiveled his chair to look out the window. "So what's so newsworthy about this guy, this—Maharishi?"

I took a deep breath and chose my words with care. "I believe that Maharishi will have a great influence on bringing about world peace."

Mac spun around in his chair. "Listen, lady, he'll have to do better than that. Peace doesn't sell magazines."

"On the contrary," I bristled, "one day peace is going to sell a lot of magazines, and maybe Maharishi will be one of the leaders of that mind shift. You could be in on the ground floor, one of the first to interview him." All that was missing was his yawn. It was pointless to try to persuade him, or probably any other reporter, even though the U.S. was involved in the agony of the Vietnam war. It was frustrating.

As I walked out into the bright sunlight, I comforted myself. "They're the losers. No use getting upset. We'll get someone interested and then the fireworks will begin." But who? I'd stuck my neck out—now I had to produce. I needed a friend. I'd go back to my original idea— Cobina. She'd have some ideas. Maybe it was a bit frivolous, as Tony had said, but nobody else in the press would listen.

Not bothering to call, I headed for her house. It was early and I knew Cobina would not leave before noon. Moreover, it was difficult to get past the constant busy signals—even with three phone lines. One of the social arbiters of Los Angeles and the Hollywood film crowd, Cobina's occupation was parties—either giving them in the grand fashion befitting the movie world, or attending them—often two and three a night.

Coming in late most nights, she slept well into the morning. Her first waking hours were then spent answering the phone, gathering news, and responding to numerous invitations. Sometime in the afternoon she would draw on all this activity and write her daily column for the Herald Examiner. As I drove in her direction, my optimism returned. Cobina considered me a daughter, second only to Cobina, Jr.

She had followed my involvement with Maharishi, asking to meet him, and offering him coverage if he should need it. This was no small favor, as she was syndicated throughout the country.

We would have to figure out a dignified gimmick—it wouldn't do to have a holy man seen at some smoke-filled cocktail party. We'd have to bring the celebrities and notables to him under proper conditions.

*Cobina Wright*

*Visiting King Hussein in Aman, Jordan in 1962.*
*Left to right: Charlie Adams (the cartoonist), Nancy, Joe Devers,*
*Joan Fontaine and Hugh O'Brien.*
*Nancy was sending news about this trip back to Cobina for her column.*

Here I was stuck. But I felt that wily old Cobina would find a way. I needed not only her interest, but her active participation.

I honked the horn as I wound up the steep, winding road to her house, which was built on a cliff overlooking Beverly Hills. One had to be part billy goat to live there, but the view was magnificent. The large windows and patio of her Spanish-style house surveyed the Los Angeles basin from Palos Verdes to Malibu. At night, the city lay below as a luminescent carpet. From here, one could keep an eye on everything. I huffed a bit going up the steep stone steps; they must be the secret of Cobina's agility. Going up and down them each day would keep anybody in shape.

I opened the door without knocking, but paused in the front hall to catch my breath before taking the next leg to the second floor bedroom where Cobina held court. Photographs of the celebrities she had feted covered the walls of the front hall and stairwell.

"Yoo hoo, Cobina. Are you receiving yet?"

"Come on up, Nancy dear. I'm on the phone." Her strong voice, the heritage of a singing career, resonated down the hall.

Bright sun from windows on three sides lighted the raspberry-pink walls and thick, wine-red carpet of Cobina's office and kingdom. She sat in the middle of her satin-covered bed, surrounded by photographs of ministers of state, movie idols, presidents, and other luminaries. Notebooks, newspapers, address books, and three telephones were in a fan around her. She motioned me to a chair while she talked. "Thank you, Duke, I knew we could count on you. I'll look forward to seeing you and Pilar next Tuesday. Give her my love."

Though still in her robe, Cobina had donned her blond wig and false eyelashes. As she put down the phone, she flashed her eyes at me. "Hello, darling. I want you to know these damn phones haven't stopped ringing all morning." I could believe it.

Always a good sport, with a lively curiosity, Cobina was interested in meeting new faces with colorful personalities. This she invested with an energy belying her age, roughly estimated by her daughter to be about seventy-five. Even Cobina wasn't sure—or so she would have you believe—waving off inquiries with a jewelled hand, "I've lied about my age for so long, I don't remember it myself." It didn't make any difference; she seemed more like thirty with all the enthusiasm she had displayed on our many trips and adventures together.

"Well, what are you up to this early in the day?"

After a bit of small talk I told her what was on my mind. Then I persuaded her to drop her plans for the afternoon and come with me to the Olsen's to meet Maharishi. Uttering only a few words of surprise, she canceled a dentist appointment, leaned back on one of her pillows and announced that she was at my disposal.

Later, as she headed toward her dressing room, she pointed to the balcony and asked, "Be a dear, Nancy, pick a couple of roses from the vine. I'm supposed to bring flowers to your holy man, aren't I?"

Her three miniature poodles dogged her feet as she dressed. Their names, Scherzo, Allegro, and Tarantella, recalled her years as a singer. She also owed her own name to that career; "Esther Cobb from a ranch in Oregon just didn't sound like an opera singer in Italy, so I changed my name to Cobina."

I called the Olsen house to alert them of our arrival, then looked around the room as I waited for her to dress. On every table celebrities peered out of silver frames. A portrait of the British Royal family had the inscription "Dearest Madre, you have a special place in our hearts." It was written by Prince Philip, who at one time had been engaged to Cobina, Jr. The war intervened and she married someone else, but Philip never lost his affection for Cobina, Sr. When he married Princess Elizabeth, Cobina and the Trumans were the only U.S. citizens invited to attend the festivities and stay at Buckingham Palace.

It was during this episode that William Randolph Hearst suggested that she write a column for his paper. She reputedly told him, "There is no such thing as real society in Los Angeles. I shall call my column, 'Society As I Find It.'"

Before the financial crash of 1929, Cobina had been married to a wealthy socialite stockbroker, William Wright. With his flock of houses, yachts and unlimited funds, she had been one of New York's foremost hostesses. After the crash and the loss of her millions, Cobina became an entertainer at the Waldorf Astoria, earning the admiration of her many friends. Cobina, Jr., became a much-talked-about young debutante, and she and Brenda Frazer were the darlings of the social columns. "Mama Cobina" was a natural for such a column.

Next to the royal family was a portrait of the Eisenhowers, then Kay and Clark Gable, Queen Frederika of Greece, the Nixons, and the Roosevelts—all graced with warm dedications. Above her bed, in antique frames, hung Italian saints. These must have seen plenty of action during their days on those walls. Cobina was frank about her lusty appetites.

Once, while talking with my mother and me, she had referred to "an active night in the feathers with an old friend." Mother laughed, "Oh, Cobina, you are such a devil. You didn't really?" Cobina answered, "Marie, of course I did. Just never forget, the petunias have to be watered from time to time."

Around the room in glass cases were displayed costumed dolls of all nations. Tiny poodle figurines frolicked about the bedside tables and dressers, along with miniature dog beds and houses. Many mirrors reflected the friendly confusion of the room.

Cobina's voice rang out from the dressing room, "Nancy, do you think your Maharishi can help me with my teeth? I had Katherine Kuhlman up here yesterday, but no healing took place."

Cobina lived in constant hope of finding help with her problem of painful gum tissue. But it was hard to be optimistic. By now, she must have been on her twenty-eighth set of false teeth, and there was no counting the number of dentists she had consulted.

When I had used the metaphor of approaching meditation in the same way she brushed her teeth, Cobina had cut me off with, "I put my teeth in a glass and have no faith at all."

I wondered how she would react to Maharishi. Was she just tagging along to please me, or would her curiosity become real interest? Although she spent most of her time occupied with a frivolous world, she nurtured her spiritual concern with the *Daily Word*, Rev. Emmett Fox's sermons, and other Unity readings. So it was not as though I was leading an old lamb to slaughter.

"Okay, I'm ready. How do I look?"

Cobina was a spectacle. Her smart, silk print dress, carefully tailored for her strong, full figure, couldn't hide the impression of a lusty, exuberant old girl. She had propped a Mr. Rex hat atop her wig and artfully made up her face to emphasize her eyes. As she posed in front of a mirror, touching perfume to the backs of her ears, her heavy gold bracelets jangled. She flirted with her reflection. "You know, I wouldn't want to appear too seductive and tempt your holy man to break his vows."

When Cobina and I arrived at the Olsen house, shoes were on the porch, and flowers were everywhere, but no one seemed to be waiting in the living room. Usually, everyone flocked to the Olsen's for the few days Maharishi spent there every couple of months. While he received individual meditators and helped them with their personal problems—

often for twenty hours a day—the place bustled with people wanting to help with preparing meals or other little jobs. Some simply enjoyed meditating near the good vibrations of their master. They knew that all too soon he would continue his mission elsewhere—in Canada or Europe, where the movement was growing more rapidly—and they would go back to their jobs and normal life.

Helena greeted us, then excused herself and went into the small library where Maharishi received people, to announce our arrival. Taking my arm, Cobina whispered, "I hope we don't have to kneel or sit on the floor. In this God-awful corset, I'll have a terrible time." But on entering, she knelt gracefully.

Maharishi sat, as usual, on a sheet-covered divan with flowers surrounding him and on his lap. He picked one and offered it to Cobina with a smile. "Jai Guru Dev. Come in, come in. Nancy tells me you are a good friend of hers."

"It is a great honor for me, Your Holiness. I could hardly wait for this meeting after all the raves I've heard about you and your meditation." Not only correct about titles, she was a diplomat. "I may have been the catalyst which brought you and Nancy together." Maharishi looked surprised.

She continued, "Last winter, Nancy took my place on a Celebrity Service cruise to inaugurate a new Italian liner. As a favor to me, she filed pieces for my column as they cruised around the Mediterranean; later she sent on news from Iran and India."

I wondered if Maharishi was following any of this, though he appeared to be fascinated by Cobina. She went on. "Her reports were excellent, but my editor wouldn't let me use the spiritual material. My secretary asked if she could send the letters on to a friend named Helena Olsen when I finished with them."

"Ah, so that is how Helena and Nancy met. How fortunate."

He nodded his head slowly and turned to smile at me.

"Fortunate for both of you, Your Holiness. You have brought something special into her life, and for that I will do everything in my power to help you." She was at ease and in control of the situation. With a chuckle she added, "I was already on your side when I heard you don't require a person to give up anything. I confess to being very fond of my vices!"

I could feel a current flowing between them. Cobina's heavy French perfume soon overpowered the mild incense in the small room.

As they bantered on, I sat back in the cozy atmosphere and let my thoughts wander, until a familiar plea brought me back to the present.

"Maharishi, you must help me with my teeth!" Cobina implored. "It's such a bore for me. I appear a lot on television, and they interfere with my speech. You must work a miracle for me!" This was the problem closest to her heart.

He replied, "Anything that will help your general health will strengthen your gum tissue as well." Cobina's cheeks glowed. Here was the opening. I knew she would give meditation a try.

Later, as I drove her home, she said, "What a shame more priests and ministers can't be like him. So charming. So full of humor." She folded her hands in her lap and sat erect. "Nancy, you must tell me how I can help this man."

"First, become a meditator. Then decide for yourself." I answered.

During the days that followed, rather than lose her enthusiasm to Jerry's seven week course, I read her the lectures in a couple of sessions—skipping over much of the material. Then Maharishi honored her by performing the initiation himself. He was grateful for the news coverage she had already printed, and when I brought her to him, he instructed, "She is not to be asked for a donation. She is showing her devotion to me in other ways."

Cobina was elegantly dressed for her initiation. Her tray of offerings was filled with orchids and exotic fruits. Enjoying the festivity, she laughed and tilted her chin coyly, "Now, Maharishi, you don't expect me to really tell you my age, do you?"

This had turned out so well, I was encouraged to introduce another friend to TM, Robin Ray, a syndicated beauty columnist. She grilled celebrities and movie stars about their formulas for health, vitality and youth. She had taken their lessons to heart, for although past a mentionable age, she looked wonderful and her lithe, agile frame was charged with remarkable energy.

Robin had been one of my few friends to take an interest in my Indian odyssey, besieging me with questions throughout a four-hour tea. When I mentioned that TM was a good beauty treatment, providing for relaxation of the facial muscles, better sleeping habits, and, in general, good health, she insisted on meeting Maharishi. I arranged it quickly, already envisioning another enthusiastic column.

However, as we walked up to the Olsen's on the appointed day, she seemed nervous. Her lips were set. When she saw the shoes on the porch, she huffed, "Why does your Maharishi insist on an Eastern custom when he expects to be successful in the West?"

"Robin, he doesn't insist. It's just a simple courtesy by which we honor him." She didn't look satisfied, so I added, "Besides, it's always more comfortable without shoes."

"Maybe for an old Hawaiian like you, but not for me." But in spite of her annoyance, she bent over and slipped hers off.

Upon being introduced to Maharishi, she bowed formally as she presented flowers to him. Then she sat on the sofa in an upright position. When I began to chat with Maharishi, she interrupted me with a loud hush, "How can you talk in the presence of such powerful vibrations?"

Robin closed her eyes and began to inhale deeply, still holding herself erect. I looked at Maharishi. Had he winked at me?

Having filled her lungs with good vibrations, Robin lifted her chin abruptly and addressed Maharishi, "I understand from Nancy that you say anyone can meditate. I thought Jesus said, 'Cast thee not thy pearls before swine.'"

My smile vanished; I held my breath.

Maharishi replied in a gentle voice, "We do not consider people as swine. Everyone's level of consciousness will be raised by meditation, no matter what level he starts from."

Robin turned and nodded to me, "Very good!"

Her next question was, "Do you claim to be a healer?"

"No man heals another. However, a man can be helped to heal himself."

Once again, she exclaimed in approval.

"Do you believe Jesus was the only Avatar?"

"God has never left man without a guide. Whenever the quality of life starts to deteriorate, a prophet appears."

I didn't like this; I had no intention of introducing Maharishi to the Grand Inquisitor. He looked nonplussed as he awaited her next question.

"Nancy says that you say Transcendental Meditation is a beauty treatment. Would you please explain that?"

"The state of your nervous system reflects on your face. Tension restricts the blood flow. It causes wrinkles and ruins the complexion."

Robin's arched eyebrows registered respect. "Very true. By getting blood into the face, you are able to rejuvenate the muscle tone." She turned to me and whispered, "Oh, Nancy, be sure to remind me to show you a new facial exercise I found the other day. It's absolutely marvelous!" Then she continued to interrogate Maharishi.

When we parted later, she said, "It's lucky that I came to meet him today. That man is going to use you."

"Great! I hope he does."

She stared at me. Turning her eyes away, she huffed, "You noticed he was not interested in me. He knows that my lamps are already lighted."

I decided not to ask her "How?" And she was gone.

Embarrassed to have brought someone who quizzed him like a schoolboy, I hurried back into the Olsen's to apologize to Maharishi. Also, I was sure that it had been a total loss as far as having any publicity potential. But Maharishi was amused. He smiled and calmed me, saying, "Do not be worried. She is an interesting woman. Obviously she has been concerned with spiritual matters. However, you must remember, there are various roads to enlightenment and many people will not wish to accompany us on ours."

"But I thought she could help you. She has a very large following."

"Someday, when she sees people becoming more youthful, more beautiful, more happy as a result of meditation, she will realize that it is the best beauty treatment." He broke into a pealing laugh that broke the tension clutching at my heart. I realized that I needn't be so protective, he could handle whatever was dished out.

Robin never wrote about him in her column, but on many occasions she defended him as an "intelligent, sensitive man of God." Maybe I was the one at fault; I had tried to use her.

Maharishi's lack of notoriety wasn't Cobina's fault. She seized on every permissible opportunity to slip a good word about him into her column. If Tony and I attended a party, she would mention us the next day, always identifying us as practitioners of meditation—which naturally demanded a passing clarification of whose technique we used or what meditation was about.

Cobina's own meditative experience, however, was not persuasive. After initiation, her blood circulation improved; the flow of blood to her extremities increased; her hands and feet felt warm and comfortable. Nevertheless, her meditation was irregular, despite my pleas for consistency.

One day I dropped by to check her meditation and found her sitting on the floor of her bedroom. She was leaning back against her bed with her eyes closed, holding a telephone in her lap, while a record player gave out some sort of soft chant.

"Hi, Cobina. What're you doing?"

She opened her eyes with a start. "What do you mean? What am I doing? I'm meditating, that's what I'm doing."

"With a record going and a telephone in your lap?"

"Nancy, dear, I am a newspaper woman. I cannot be away from my phone."

"And the record player?"

"Well, let's just say that it's . . . it's very soothing."

She was never going to get proof of what her *mantra* could do for her. I tried to explain the importance of keeping the technique pure, but after awhile I decided to forget my frustration and let her do as she pleased. It is impossible to teach an old columnist new tricks. She felt that meditation was doing her good, so what could I say? Besides, something had to be better than nothing.

In spite of all the good will in her heart, there was a limit to what Cobina's column could do for Maharishi. Tony and I were fairly low-grade as celebrities and the fact that we meditated did not justify much comment on a social page. We needed to persuade people of notoriety to meditate. It seemed her notices were like dropping stones in the ocean trying to cause a tidal wave, when it came to making the public aware of Maharishi and his teachings.

However, the phone did begin to ring. A few friends had noticed our names in the paper and wanted to know more. We knew the potential was out there. Everyone who has a problem lives in hope of finding help. But to send my friends down to the center, or to enroll them in Jerry's course, was as good as losing them. We had to devise more exciting activities to win their attention.

Also, Maharishi's concern about the tense, politically-dangerous state of the world, made it imperative we get the movement rolling. The Cuban missile confrontation had taken place during our Catalina course.

So as a first step we followed Cobina's advice. "We will invite some newsworthy friends to an occasion that sounds attractive and socially exclusive as well as intellectual. It must be worth their time; they must hear about TM directly from Maharishi. He is a well-known Saint from the Valley of the Saints. They will all benefit from being exposed to his wisdom; everyone is interested in getting more energy, staying younger, developing more potential—you must bait the hook. And, stay away from the religious aspects." This we already knew.

We agreed on a two-evening coffee and dessert format, to be held at our home, featuring an "Introduction to Maharishi Mahesh Yogi." No cocktails would be served until after Maharishi left. We made up a list totaling about a hundred, from which we expected thirty or forty would accept.

We had gone through Cobina's telephone books and she had offered to call many of her contacts directly. "If you call their agents, they will never return your call. But no star will fail to call me back. They all love to see their names in the paper."

Finally with Cobina's and my cajoling, we corralled thirty. It was an interesting, mixed group: several businessmen; a couple of prominent lawyers; George McLean, the architect; Adela Rogers St. John, the writer; some people from Moral Rearmament, including Bonnie Green and her husband, John Green, the award-winning music composer; Glenn Ford, the actor. Most of the men were roped in by their curious wives.

One morning I answered the kitchen phone to hear a warm, compassionate voice, and found myself talking to Efram Zimbalist, Jr., who was at the time just finishing his stint on "77 Sunset Strip."

"Nancy, I told Cobina I could not come. The first lecture falls on my birthday and my daughter has made plans. Then, thinking about Cobina's enthusiasm, I have changed things around with my daughter so that I can come, if that will still be all right?" It sure was.

The night of the party arrived. Following Helen Lutes's suggestions, I had place a draped chair on a small platform in our living room. I surrounded it with flowers, Guru Dev's portrait, and a portable blackboard. We had Maharishi wait in the spare bedroom until all the guests had gathered in the semi-circle of chairs in front of the platform. We didn't want late arrivals to disrupt his quiet entrance.

They were good sports, putting off their cocktails until later, and rising respectfully as Maharishi entered the room. Cobina settled herself to one side and began to make mental notes.

I had told Charlie about the responses to our invitations, and, properly coached, Maharishi lost no time getting to the topic of most interest to his audience—tension.

"I had a big surprise when I came to the United States, the most progressive country in the world. Their progress is killing them. The statistics on divorce, nervous breakdowns, alcoholism and suicide are terrible—all a result from living with too much tension. With Transcendental Meditation, one strengthens his nervous system and avoids unnecessary tension." He went on to describe the process.

After his talk, Maharishi accepted questions.

Dr. Anna Maria Benstrom, who ran the famous Golden Door Health Spa in Escondido, California, raised her hand to ask, "Maharishi, do you practice yoga *asanas?*"

While Maharishi described the exercises that kept him fit, improving circulation for meditation, I surveyed the room for other eager eyes. Miss St. John then asked Maharishi if TM were nothing more than self-hypnosis.

"No! No! It is not self-hypnosis. In hypnosis a man can pretend he is a king. He can say to himself, 'I am a king. I am a king.' But when he opens his eyes, he will still be a pauper. Transcendental Meditation leads a man to the realization of what he is, not what he is not."

She was not able to pursue her question, as actor Glenn Ford quickly raised his hand. His face still flushed from an earlier cocktail hour, he asked, "Maharishi, can you levitate?"

I held my breath.

Without a blink, Maharishi said, "Oh, it is not necessary. There are so many airplanes to take one anywhere." As his voice again pealed with laughter, I wondered why he evaded the question. He didn't say no. That was significant.

Evidently, Glenn was seriously interested in physical phenomena, for he rephrased his question. "Do you develop unusual powers through meditation?"

"It is not the object of meditation to develop powers. The purpose of meditation is first, to develop your full potential, and second, to attain spiritual enlightenment."

But that is not what Glenn wanted from meditation. He did not return for the second lecture. Neither did some of the other guests. However, their places were filled with new faces. Some of the first nighters brought friends the following evening. When half the group asked to be initiated, we knew the series was a resounding success.

As they stood for Maharishi's exit, I studied the faces of those who wanted to learn. Cobina was looking at them also. She had her celebrities, and that guaranteed her extra space in the paper. It looked like we finally had a format we could use in other cities to introduce Maharishi to our friends and the press.

---
9
---

# An In-house Miracle

URING THE WINTER OF '64, Charlie looked for a quiet place in the
mountains near Lake Arrowhead for Maharishi. There Maharishi could get away from the heat and smog of Los Angeles and
enjoy a cool, clean environment more like that of his native Himalayas.
Although the lake is but two hours drive from Los Angeles, it would also
provide him an escape from the constant intrusion of visitors at the
Olsen's house, where there seemed to be a steady stream of people
morning, noon and night. He wasn't able to work on the book he was
writing until two or three in the morning.

I asked Helen and Charlie, "When does he sleep?"

She replied, "Sleep? He hardly sleeps at all. At the most, two or
three hours a night."

"I don't see how he keeps from being exhausted."

"That's the problem. Do you have any idea of the schedule he
keeps?" I did not. Who ever thinks of a guru being busy? Or of his having
time to himself.

Helen accounted, "First, he bathes early each morning before his
private *puja* (ceremony) for Guru Dev. Then he has a glass of yogurt
mixed with hot water. That's all he takes until his one main meal in the
afternoon; the rest of the time it is a constant crush of appointments."

She then added, "He has a different source of energy than we have, but periodically, when his batteries run down, he goes into total seclusion—he calls it 'going into silence.'"

"How does that work? "

"He is not seen at all. He takes only water during the 'silence.' It's usually for two weeks at a time—what he does is like meditation, only it is deeper, more profound. We would have problems if we attempted this; our nervous systems are too unrefined. But Maharishi's is purified from all those years he spent with Guru Dev, so he goes directly to the source of energy. You ought to see him when he comes out. He's as bright as a shining light bulb."

Charlie added, "The silence also serves to cleanse Maharishi of other people's vibrations. You don't know it, but your vibrations affect everyone around you, especially someone as sensitive as a holy man. That's what happens to him; he picks up vibrations from all those people who crowd in to see him and they deplete his energy. His body temperature begins to rise and he gets tired. That's why he has to get away to restore his balance."

"Is that why he seldom touches anybody?"

"Exactly."

"But I thought the deer or goat skin he sits on wards off vibrations."

"Just from the furniture," Helen said. "There are vibrations all around him in the air."

"I bet the smog is no help. How often does he go into silence?"

"If possible, he likes to go every six months. He gives so much of himself, it's a terrific strain. You can tell when he's run down." Helen paused. "He moves slowly; his complexion gets darker. That's when it's time for him to go."

"It's also a time when he gets to talk with the Hierarchy."

"Charlie!" But Helen's reproach was too late; the cat was out of the bag. I asked who the Hierarchy was.

Charlie leaned back and began to describe in layman's terms just what the Hierarchy was. I had never heard the term before. "It is the government of the cosmic force which controls the universe. Maharishi consults it in his silences when he needs guidance for his world mission. He obeys Mother Divine and honors this force, although the name is not mentioned in public."

There was so much we longed to know. Many of us in the S.R.M. wondered about Maharishi's powers. Was he divine in some way? This was especially true of the members in the inner circle, the meditators who had known him the longest. In complete awe, they elevated every small coincidence involving his presence into a first-class miracle. We commonly spoke of him as an Indian saint, while some meditators thought he might even be an avatar, another Christ. All were quick to share any new evidence of his divinity, without his knowledge or consent. Maharishi did not discuss himself; his concentration was completely on his goal of spreading TM as rapidly as possible. Talk of miracles was a distraction, but he could not stem the flood.

Charlie Lutes was the best source of new stories. Often accompanying Maharishi on trips through Canada, he never failed to return with entrancing tidbits. He and Helen came to the house often, and this was a time for catching up. Relaxed after a full dinner, and some of Tony's aged wine, Charlie would make himself comfortable on the living room couch, place his hand across his stomach, and begin to relate. "This one day, we were running late to catch the ferry. We had to catch the six o'clock boat or we would miss the lecture date in Victoria. I was really pushing it—breaking every speed limit. Maharishi just sat in the back seat and said, 'Don't worry, Charlie, we will get there in time.'"

"What do you mean, 'Don't worry.' It's six right now, and we've got fifteen miles to go.

"But he just sat there smiling and, holy cow, when we reached the landing, the ferry was still there. The gate was stuck. It had never happened before. We drove on board, the gate became unstuck, and the ferry left." Charlie flung his arms up in wonderment. "I looked at Maharishi and asked him if he had anything to do with the gate, but he just smiled."

It was hard to believe and we, new to the movement, didn't believe. But it was entertaining nonetheless.

Helen would glower at Charlie and try to restrain him, saying, "Now Charlie..." But there was no stopping him. He would ignore Helen and continue.

"Flying into Calgary, we got into a terrible fog. We thought we wouldn't be able to land. Maharishi had a big lecture all set up, but it looked like we'd have to miss it. Just after our pilot turned to tell me he'd have to fly on to another town, this tunnel of clear air suddenly appeared through the clouds. It led straight into the landing strip, so we landed. The pilot couldn't believe it. He'd never seen anything like it."

Once again we would show our amazement and laugh and Helen would reproach her husband, even though Charlie was only relaying what he personally observed.

Yet we were to become believers, too.

One bright Sunday morning, Tony felt a severe pain in his side while playing tennis. He thought it was a pulled muscle and continued playing. However, the next morning the pain was worse, so he went to see his family doctor. Dr. Pendelton announced it was a fairly large hernia and scheduled an operation for that same evening. Tony, with an important business meeting in Cincinnati at the end of the week, wanted to delay the operation until he got back, but Dr. Pendelton was not to be put off. The hernia was dangerous. Furthermore, he advised Tony not to think of leaving the hospital until the wound was closed and the bandage removed: "You will have to forget that meeting; you're not going anywhere for a couple of weeks." With the doctor's scheduling of an operation so rapidly, I worried about his suspecting something more serious than a hernia.

On the way to Good Samaritan Hospital, we dropped by the Olsen's to see Maharishi and get his blessings. After seeing him for a few minutes alone, Tony came out to the car treasuring a rose in his hands. He seemed more calm and reassured. "I received special instructions from Maharishi," he murmured, but would say no more.

The operation went well. At 11:00 p.m., Dr. Pendelton came out of the operating room to assure me that everything was fine, Tony was still under anesthesia, and he would check on him the next day. I had been meditating during the operation, asking nature to support the surgeon's hands—also it helped me.

Returning the next morning, I found Tony sitting up in bed, bursting with excitement. He hushed my greeting with a wave and said, "Wait until you hear what happened. Yesterday, Maharishi gave me some special words to say mentally the minute I came out of the anesthetic."

"Why didn't you tell me this?"

"I didn't think it would work! But as soon as my head started to clear, I remembered Maharishi's instructions. I did as he said, repeating the words 'body and mind are one' while concentrating on my wound. Soon an amazing current of energy began to flow through me. I felt as if I were swinging in an electric hammock, suspended in a net of currents. I swung slowly, back and forth, back and forth. It must have lasted for a half hour. All the soreness left my wound and now I feel great!" A flush of goose bumps spread over my body; I knew I was hearing the truth.

When Dr. Pendelton came to check on Tony, he slowly went through the preliminaries, asking the usual questions, "How do you feel? . . . Have you been resting fairly comfortably? . . . Does it hurt when I press here?" Then he removed the bandage.

"How strange." Dr. Pendelton's ruddy face looked perplexed. "I did operate on you last night, didn't I?"

"Yes, at nine thirty."

"I don't believe it. I have never seen such rapid healing. Your wound is completely closed." At sixty, Dr. Pendelton was an experienced surgeon, yet he did not trust his own judgment. He called in some of his colleagues. They marvelled. The wound was healed. There was no reason to put a bandage back on, and Tony left the hospital the next day.

I did not know what to think of what I had witnessed. My heart filled with awe of Maharishi.

As he carried the bag out to the car, Tony chuckled softly. "Maybe we had better start listening more closely to what Charlie has to say."

He made his meeting in Cincinnati.

Another story worth repeating came about when Helen Lutes called me one day with sad news, "Millie's cancer has returned."

"Millie Hoops had cancer?" It was a surprise to me.

"Oh my, yes, she didn't like to talk about it, but it was cancer of the breast. She thought she was cured, but then it returned. That was why she had to maintain silence at Catalina; she was only to talk to her husband."

"I thought Maharishi made her do that for spiritual reasons. She could attend lectures but not speak."

"No, he did that to preserve her energy. He warned her to retreat from the world and concentrate her strength on healing herself. At first it worked. She was very good, but you know Millie; as soon as she started feeling better, she couldn't stand the silence, the inactivity, and she was back on the phone. Eventually she got real busy again and weakened her defenses. It's such a shame; her case is now terminal."

Millie, a pert, outgoing blonde woman, had been so good to me during my first month of meditation. She would call often to check my progress. It seemed strange to me that as a consistent meditator she should get cancer. Helen answered my question with, "It must be her karma, nothing will change that."

One day when I visited Millie at the hospital, on opening her door I heard Maharishi softly saying, "Put your thoughts on God and on love." Is he here? How could he be? He had gone to Canada. The voice came from a tape recorder on Millie's bedside table, and as soon as she saw me, she reached over to turn off the machine.

"How nice to have that tape, Millie. What is he talking about?"

"About God, but I can't describe it to you. Maharishi made it especially for me; no one else is supposed to hear it."

*Efram Zimbalist, Helen and Charlie Lutes, Nancy, and Tony Jackson
at TM Conference*

Millie looked so pretty propped up on her pillows. Her blonde hair freshly washed, she appeared thin, but healthy and happy. It was impossible to believe she was dying.

Looking up at the ceiling with a beatific smile, Millie confided, "This has been an incredible experience for me, Nancy. Between meditating and listening to the tape, my day is full. All the rest, the shots, the doctors, the pills—all that seems so unreal."

However, when her eyes focused on me, I discerned a note of concern, of pleading.

"Have you heard from Maharishi, Nancy? Do you know when he will return? He promised to be with me when I die."

"But Millie, you're not going to die," I insisted.

She shook her head, but her smile was warm. "Yes, I am, and I'm not worried about it. There is no fear. We all have to die someday, and Maharishi promised that he would be here to guide me across to the other side, where Guru Dev would be waiting." Sadness engulfed me; I wished I could share her faith.

On my way out, I asked the nurses how much more time they thought she had. They indicated amazement that she had survived this long, and with an apparent lack of pain. She refused pain killers, despite the malignancy and the cobalt treatments.

A month passed; Millie hung onto life by a thread, praying for the day of Maharishi's return. Finally it came.

Helena alerted the inner circle of the plane's arrival at midnight and we met Maharishi at the gate. After greeting him we raced back to the Olsen's, while Efram Zimbalist, who had become an ardent follower, drove Maharishi there in his Rolls Royce. We always wanted the best for our Master.

It was 1:00 a.m. when they reached the Olsen's. We were settled comfortably on the floor, anticipating the intimate moments we enjoyed when "the family" came together. It had been a long, busy trip and Maharishi looked tired when he entered. However, our questions and enthusiasm soon roused him and he announced his success energetically.

"The Canadian Foundation is growing fast. They have centers springing up here and there and very good people are coming forward." His fingers plucked the petals of a rose. "Their plan is to buy a small airplane for me to use. With it I can fly from there to there to there," waving his hand over an imaginary map in front of him. He went into more detail about future plans.

Suddenly he grew quiet. We waited. Then in a hush, he said, "I will leave you for a moment." He uncurled his legs, picked his way through us and left the room. He looked somber and intent on something. Standing by the door, I saw him hike up his robes and run up the stairs. I had never seen him hurry before.

I mentioned this to Helena, but she thought nothing of it. "With Maharishi, you never know whether it's in response to some spirit or merely a call of nature."

"But to hurry like that?"

I looked at my watch, 1:50 a.m. For a moment I considered leaving, but a few minutes later Maharishi came down the stairs. Smiling and looking over the gathering of his favorites, he returned to his seat.

"Tell us, Maharishi, when will you start on your book?"

Maharishi was planning to collate his lectures and course materials into a comprehensive introductory book on TM. Assured it would be soon, we decided to call it a night. It was close to 3:00 a.m. by the time we got to bed, tired but happy.

The next day, Helen called and told us of Millie's death. She had died early that morning, quietly and without pain.

There was a note of excitement in Helen's agitated voice, but I was sunk in my thoughts.

"How sad she never got to see Maharishi again. That hope kept her alive for weeks."

"But that's just it! She did!" Helen's voice exploded through the phone.

"What do you mean? How could Maharishi have seen her?"

"Nancy, this is what is extraordinary. Charlie was just down at the hospital to help Dick Hoops with Millie's things. The nurses told him that just before Millie died, they saw a person in a long white gown come down the corridor out of the darkness. As the figure got closer, they saw that it was a bearded man in white robes. He was carrying a bunch of red roses. He smiled as he passed the nurses and walked right into Millie's room as if he knew where she was. One of the nurses left the station and looked through the open door. She saw him make some kind of gesture over Millie's head. After a few moments, he turned and left the room. Shortly afterward, she died."

Her words really struck me, "Maharishi had promised her that he would be there to guide her across the river of death. That is why she had no fear."

"I know. We were all praying that he would arrive in time, that he wouldn't let her down."

Slowly Helen said, "Do you realize what happened, Nancy?" I waited.

"Millie died at 2:00 a.m. At that time, we were all sitting in the living room of the Olsen's. Do you remember when he left us to go upstairs?"

"Yes, but St. John's Hospital is at least a half-hour away."

"Exactly." I felt a chill as Helen continued. "Now do you believe in teleportation, the ability to be in two places at the same time? It is on the nurses' register that he was there!"

## 10

# *Enter Doris Duke*

THE NEXT WEEK, I RECEIVED A CALL from Debbie Jarvis, Jerry's wife, who was taking care of Maharishi up at Arrowhead. "He has come out of silence and is again working on his book, *The Science of Being and The Art of Living*. He wants you to come for a visit. However," warned Debbie, "no one outside of your family is to know. Not even Helena."

After hanging up, I consulted with Tony. His reaction was, "That is an invitation you can't refuse." I began to pack.

Maharishi's mountain house enjoyed all the seclusion, quiet and darkness of a cave in the Himalayas—or so I thought as I carefully picked my way down the narrow path from the road, trying to balance my food and flower packages without slipping on the pine needles. Though the sun was still high, only a little light filtered through the tall pine trees onto the low, dark shingled roof of the house.

Further down was a nearby cabin; the windows were shuttered fast, the pine needles were deep and evenly strewn, undisturbed. December was the off-season, everybody had migrated into town for the winter.

As I approached Maharishi's house, I saw that the far end rose to two stories with large picture windows. The trees thinned out, unveiling a beautiful vista of the bright, blue lake below. The sun brought out the red still living in the wood panels and smoke hovered over the chimney.

Seeing Debbie through the kitchen window, apparently leaning over a sink, I headed for the back door.

"Jai Guru Dev! What are you cooking? It smells delicious."

Debbie pushed her hair with the back of her flour-covered hand. Even her freckled face bore traces of flour as she smiled and greeted me, "Jai Guru Dev, Nancy. I am making *puris;* they're like an Indian tortilla."

Setting down my load, I made myself at home. The air was warm and full of flavors. The cedar of the cabinets and sideboards mingled with the scents from the stove.

"What's that aroma?"

"Clarified butter. What the Indians call *ghee.* You need it to deep-fry *puris.*" Debbie shaped a handful of wet dough in her palms, then flattened it and placed it in the hot pan.

I could not keep count of the variety of little jobs I had seen Debbie do for the S.R.M., whether it was arranging flowers at the center, checking initiates, typing for Maharishi, cooking at the Olsen's when he was in town, or handling his laundry at Catalina after Devendhra had gone back to India.

The patty turned golden brown and puffed up. She removed it with a spatula and laid it on a paper towel to drain away the ghee. By that time, another patty was ready for the pan.

"What do you feed Maharishi?" Despite all the time I had spent with him, I had never seen him eat.

Debbie shrugged her shoulders, but kept her eyes on the *puri.* "Oh, he's very easy. He eats only one large meal a day. Today, I'm giving him these *puris*. He'd like them every day, but with typing out his daily dictations, sometimes I simply don't have the time to make them. Ma was here helping, but now only Guri Mehellis is here to take over the housework and shopping. She's the head of the movement in Norway. So, if we can't do *puris*, we do something else that's special." She motioned to the sideboard. "Tonight I have a ripe avocado."

"I bet he doesn't get that in India."

"Never. In Rishikesh, the *sadhus* often subsist on little more than *dahl.* It's ground lentils and is very bland."

"So it must be a treat for Maharishi to stay in California and enjoy all the marvelous variety."

"No," replied Debbie shaking her head, "Maharishi does not expect variety. He is happy with whatever I give him. Today I'll serve him a dish of cut tomatoes, some sauteed almonds, and a combination of different kinds of squash. Also, there will be a lot of rice with curry and other spices, and finally, some fresh papaya."

"That seems like a lot." After all, Maharishi was a small man. I didn't think he could eat so much.

Debbie continued to shape *puris*, her brow wrinkled in judgment. "Not really. He likes to have small portions of many things, except the rice, he likes a large portion of that—very Eastern. Then, later on, maybe he'll have a glass of milk or a little yogurt—nothing else."

"Does he ever eat meat?"

She shook her head. "Never. He says that when one eats flesh, one takes on a trace of the animal's karma, as well as some of its death trauma. You are affected by these vibrations. That's why he says if you are going to have meat, it is best to eat small animals which are killed quickly. A large animal often experiences pain and fear, traumatizing its meat. Of course, the worst is the meat of a trapped wild animal."

"That sounds like a vote for kosher slaughter. But wouldn't a butcher bear a terrible karmic weight from all the meat he handles?"

"Absolutely." The *puris* done, Debbie washed her hands as she said, "However, this doesn't mean you have to be a vegetarian to meditate; according to Maharishi, it is a mistake for Westerners to try to become vegetarians overnight. Our bodies have been built up over the years by a meat diet, and, if we want to change this, we must adjust slowly, naturally. Otherwise, all the toxins in our system will be released into the bloodstream too quickly."

"That would be a shock."

"Yes, and he knows with time, TM will weaken one's desire for meat. You will naturally begin to eat in a manner which purifies your vibrations and makes you feel lighter. You will also lose your desire for negative influences such as tobacco and alcohol." She spoke with conviction. "Take Maharishi; he doesn't even like to eat vegetables grown in the ground. Root foods pick up heavy vibrations."

"You mean garlic, onions, potatoes—he doesn't eat them?"

"Sometimes he makes an exception with carrots, if they are mixed in with something else. Actually, he's not finicky, he's very appreciative of whatever we bring him. It was Devendhra who learned and then taught us his likes and dislikes. Maharishi would never complain."

Through the window, I could see Guri Mehellis walking down the path, carrying four grocery bags. I ran out to see if I could help. With her powerful arms and shoulders, she had no trouble with her load. All she would let me take was the smallest bag. Tall, blonde, with cheeks ruddy from the brisk air, she steamed along the path, oblivious to the slippery pine needles, like an indomitable Nordic Brunhilde. Guri had come all the way to California for the honor of performing menial labor for Maharishi. She felt privileged and so did I.

Only after Guri set her packages on the sideboard next to mine did Debbie notice the bouquet of flowers I had brought. Both women were delighted, they had scrounged the neighboring mountain towns in vain for flowers, which they needed for Maharishi's morning *puja*.

There being so little that Maharishi needed in terms of physical comfort, his followers were always striving to express their devotion by getting him the best. They knew he loved fresh flowers and filled his room with them. They also bought silk sheets for him to sleep on, and damask napkins for dinner. All this without his request.

Guri said to me, "Maharishi was asking about you this morning; he wondered when you were coming. I am sure that as soon as he's finished his dictation, he'll be asking to see you. Why don't I show you to your room and you can unpack?" Her English was almost free of an accent.

Without waiting for a reply, she picked up my bags and led me out of the kitchen and through the living room. Though the house was large and a trifle short on furniture, the redwood walls and stone fireplace made it inviting. There were four bedrooms. Debbie and Guri stayed upstairs, while I was given a little room next to Maharishi's on the ground floor.

As soon as I had unpacked and washed up, I walked over to the wall that separated my room from Maharishi's. Could I hear him dictating? There was no sound. I pushed the narrow bed up against the wall and propped up some pillows so I could meditate. The room was small and cozy. The one window looked into the forest. I could feel my tiredness and tension slip away.

"Maharishi is probably leaning against the other side of the wall. Maybe some of his *darshan* will come through."

Later, Debbie tapped on my door and asked if I would like to join Maharishi for a walk. I pulled on a sweater and hurried outside where Maharishi was waiting, his robes inflamed by the setting sun.

Helen's "shining light bulb" popped into my mind as I walked up to greet Maharishi. He was radiant. His skin glowed, his smile was broad and his eyes swam with lights. As we traversed the hillside, he walked with a graceful stride, his hands gesturing widely as he spoke. His movements were joyful, easy, generous. He was in tune with himself. While I had bundled into a heavy sweater to fortify myself against the cold, sharp air, he positively revelled in the briskness, strolling along in nothing more than his thin robes, a light shawl thrown over his shoulders and his weathered feet bare.

"Aren't you ever cold, Maharishi?"

He shook his head and replied with a light, high pitch, "No, no, the air is nice. It is very refreshing; it reminds me of Rishikesh in the winter."

"Does it ever snow there?"

"No, but snowcapped mountains can be seen in the distance. We are in the low foothills of the Himalayas." I noticed the enthusiasm in his voice as he spoke of Jyotir Math, a holy village situated on the sacred Ganges and his spiritual home, where he had studied at the feet of Guru Dev for twelve years. "In the month of April, it gets very warm. Then we go to Kashmir. Those who stay behind meditate in caves to escape the heat of the day."

"Do you ever get homesick?"

"Homesick? The world is my home."

"But you do seem happier near water."

"Yes, water is life." He paused to look out over the lake. He studied the vacant houses, sleeping below us on the hill. "It would be nice, Nancy, if you could take a house nearby and come for a longer time. It is a good place to meditate."

I couldn't believe my ears, a chance I should jump at. However, I thought of my family, newly settled in Los Angeles. I gushed, "Oh, Maharishi, how I wish that I could, but I have my family to look after."

His eyes softened. "Yes, but you should try, even if only for two weeks. It would be good for you." He had no idea how I wanted to accept.

We walked on. My thoughts troubled me.

"Maharishi, there is something I would like to ask you."

"Yes, what is it?"

"Let's say that I, as a householder, simply gave up all of my responsibilities in order to follow a spiritual path. I am thinking of Jesus's words. I can't quote him exactly, but he said something like, 'Give up all and only then thou shall know me.' Wouldn't I be selfish if I were to do that?"

Maharishi turned his face to the last rays of the sun. "I think you misunderstand what he meant. What is the most important thing to you?"

Without hesitation, "My family."

"No, you just think that, for without thought you do not even know you have family, so thought of family is more important."

Aroused by the question, he walked faster. It was getting dark and we had turned back.

I was disappointed to hear him split hairs. "Maharishi, I don't see the difference."

"There is an important difference. What is the last thing you give up in meditation?"

"I'm not sure what you mean."

"Thought is the last thing you give up before transcending. Jesus meant for you to come into his realm: 'Give up your thoughts, transcend, and come to where I am; then you shall know me.' He was speaking of a momentary withdrawal. He did not mean for you to give away your worldly goods and family in order to worship or serve him. He wanted you to give up your thoughts so that you could know him."

"I like that." I pondered it before proceeding. "He did say, however, that it was as hard for a man of wealth to enter the Kingdom of Heaven as for a camel to pass through the eye of a needle."

"Yes, for as a man gets attached to his material possessions, soon they possess him. Then he has little time to think of God."

"Is that why Eastern religions stress the value of non-attachment?"

"Yes. When a man lives with no attachments, only then is he truly free."

I thought I heard a note of wistfulness in his voice. Was he thinking of his former attachments? Did he leave his family? Did his heart ever yearn for their company? But, respecting his privacy, I did not ask. He never betrayed such feelings to us, and we never had the courage to inquire.

One day in class he did describe his first meeting with his master. It seems it was announced that the Shankaracharya of the North would be carried through the streets of his home town. As a young college student, Mahesh and several of his friends decided to view the procession. After seeing Guru Dev, Mahesh then told his family what he wanted to do with his life. He would renounce the world and become a disciple of the Shankaracharya. However, when he went to present

With Maharishi on Lake Arrowhead with Charlie and Helen Lutes and María Luisa, 1962

Arrowhead

himself to the holy man, he was told to finish the University first. Then he would be of more worth. This Maharishi did. His family was honored to have their son accepted by such a famous saint.

We were thrilled when Maharishi spoke about his past and his family, but it didn't happen very often.

That evening in Arrowhead, after eating, Maharishi put down his dinner plate, leaned over and dipped his fingers into a silver bowl of water on the coffee table. Sitting on the floor, we watched, each of us in bliss to be there, gathered around the coffee table with our plates in our laps.

Maharishi then leaned back, indicating his satisfaction with the meal and thanked us. Setting the towel aside, he asked me if I had any news from Cobina. I was well prepared, carrying a fistful of her columns in my purse, though most were but passing comments on various meditators. He nodded his approval, but said nothing more than, "Good, good."

However, I did have one major piece of news to spring on him. With Efram's help, Charlie had obtained an invitation for Maharishi to appear on the Steve Allen Show. Considering the superficial content of much of the show, it was a bit of a risk. However, the program was popular, and Steve Allen did have serious guests, though no one like an Indian holy man. We would have to depend on Maharishi's ability to handle the situation. It would give him instant recognition if all went well. He had never been on television before, so it would be a major break.

Again, all Maharishi would say was, "Good, good." I suspected an extra twinkle in his eye, but that was all. However, what did get his attention was the fact that Richard Bock's company, World Pacific Records, had just released the first of two long-playing records on the subject of deep meditation and love. Things were beginning to happen—Maharishi was pleased—he then turned to Debbie and asked her if she had typed out his dictation from the day before. She got up and brought it.

"Very good." He drew his words out slowly, "If you are finished eating, will you read it back to us?"

Debbie held her transcript up to the light and said, "This is as far as I got yesterday. You started in the middle of the chapter, 'How to Use One's Full Potential.'"

I glanced at Guri. She had placed her elbow on the table, resting her head on her hand. Her eyes were alert and steady on Debbie. I wondered how much dictation Debbie had read and she had listened to. There was an atmosphere of serious intent to Debbie's reading, and an expression of fulfillment on Guri's face. At last there would be a textbook. For years the S.R.M. had bemoaned the lack of any authoritative body of knowledge on meditation. There was no canonical literature which could make for agreement on central points.

Answers to various issues on meditation all too often depended on the person you asked. A few of Maharishi's lectures had been typed up and distributed, but we often had to grope around by word of mouth. Now, at last, we would have our own 'bible,' written by the prophet himself. The Age of Enlightenment was about to dawn. How lucky I was to be here at the birth. Each moment was treasured. Debbie read on,

"The art of using one's full potential is the same as the art of shooting an arrow ahead; one begins by pulling the arrow back on the bow. As the arrow is drawn back, it gains maximum strength for going forward. A useless shot will result if the arrow is not first pulled back.

"The art of using one's full potential demands bringing the mind back to the Field of Absolute Being before it is brought out to face the gross aspect of the relative fields of life."

Maharishi nodded and looked over to me, "This is from the third part of my book, which is devoted to the Art of Living."

Maharishi sat back on the couch, his hands running along his beads. Often he smiled and nodded agreement to what Debbie read, almost as if he had not dictated it. Quietly he approved, "Very good, it came through so nicely yesterday."

What was he referring to? Did he consider himself but a channel for some sort of Divine knowledge? Did he receive it from Guru Dev, from the Holy Tradition of India's saints?

Now I began to understand the nature, the purpose of Maharishi's silence. He did not withdraw into the mountains merely to replenish his energy; the silence was preparation and spiritual nourishment. Arrowhead was for withdrawal deep within, in order to explode into the world with maximum force.

For me, time seemed to stand in its tracks that weekend. The days were prolonged but filled with quiet joys as we talked with Maharishi, cared for Maharishi, ate with Maharishi and meditated under the supervision of Maharishi. All my senses seemed more acute. Everything was enjoyed more. I began to understand Helena Olsen's desire to possess him. However, time accelerated considerably when I returned to my family and sped through the necessary household chores so that I could return to the mountains the following weekend. Then the clock would slow down and the bustling world of Los Angeles would recede again into the distance.

One evening as Guri and I were setting the table for dinner, the phone rang, startling our quiet. It was a woman who asked for me as if she knew me. However, I didn't recognize her voice. We were isolated here in the mountains, and none of my friends would know how to reach me, only my family.

"Nancy, I ran into Lloydie here the other day in New York. He told me you've been to India and that you are now remarried—"

Lloydie? Who would know Lloyd Pantages? Of course, Doris Duke! He's a director of her Foundation.

". . . So, you've been on my mind lately."

"Doris! How are you? I haven't seen you in ages."

It had been a very long time. I hadn't seen her since one of Cobina's parties back in the mid-fifties. That was the night Joe Castro improvised some Hawaiian music on the piano while she and I performed our versions of the hula. She stole the show. We had a great time together and then lost touch. Typical. When I met Doris in Honolulu during the early forties, she was having a flirt with Errol Flynn. From that time on we'd bump into each other, be close pals for awhile, then she'd drop out of sight, taking one of her trips. Years could pass before we'd see each other again.

"Just terrible."

Her answer caught me by surprise. Now I noticed the nervous timbre in her voice.

I wondered what had happened. Doris usually was the picture of health. She kept herself fit with daily ballet lessons and was interested in all kinds of folk remedies and natural food diets.

"What's the matter?"

"Oh, Nancy, I think I am just coming out of a nervous breakdown. Either that or I am still in it. It has been a bad period for me. I have broken off with Joe for good; it was quite a mess."

She began to describe their final tiff. They had had a real brawl; no wonder her nerves were shot. Now she needed moral support; how could I help her?

Joe Castro was a young Cuban piano player. She had gone with him for over ten years, to my amazement. Doris enjoyed anything to do with music, so she kept Joe as a playmate.

"I thought I'd come out to California, if you're going to be there."

And when she did, Maharishi could take care of her nerves. I burst out joyfully, "Not only am I going to be here, but I have just the man for you to meet!"

"Oh, really?" Her voice sounded distant, shy. "Is he attractive?"

"No, no, he's a holy man. He teaches Transcendental Meditation."

"Is it interesting, this meditation?"

"Oh, it's terrific. It sounds like you could use his technique, which is a form of *Mantra Yoga*. His meditation incorporates the eight steps in yoga. It is very good for strengthening the nervous system."

"God knows I need it."

Doris liked the idea. It gave her something to look forward to. We arranged to meet at her house in Beverly Hills the following week.

Doris lived in a large, Moorish-style villa known as 'Falcons's Lair,' built by Rudolph Valentino for Pola Negri in the twenties.

One of the classic houses of Hollywood's Golden Age, it provided the privacy necessary for its famous owners.

A tiny, twisting road served Doris's and one other house on a steep hillside. High white-washed walls surrounded the hideaway. Six vicious dogs roamed at will in the courtyard behind the large, wrought-iron gate, guarding one of the world's wealthiest women. One had to ring the gateway bell and identify oneself so the maid, Tabala, would round up the dogs before letting the person in.

Doris had also heard the bell; she stepped out the front door as I entered the courtyard and greeted me in Kanaka-style Hawaiian slang, "Hey, you, how you doing?"

The press had been unfair with their description of her "large forehead and jutting jaw." Doris has a handsome face. Her mouth is wide; her eyes are almond-shaped and widely set apart. They seem to tilt as she talks. Doris has a pleasant, musical laugh and displays it often when she feels at ease.

As we met, one of the police dogs, a black female, escaped Tabala's control, and circled around me as if to decide which would be the most delectable part of my leg to bite. However, Doris came to my rescue, shooing the dog with a stern, "Don't be a silly goose." She went on talking in her enthusiastic, girlish voice, brushing back her silky, blonde hair from time to time. She seemed genuinely happy to see me.

I noticed vestiges of bruises around her eyes and mouth, but only when Doris turned to lead me into the house did I notice the faded blue spots on her shoulders and arms. Her skin looked so translucent—she didn't look at all well. My face must have registered my thoughts. Doris quickly explained, "I locked myself into the courtyard and, when attempting to get out, I tripped over some scaffolding." I wondered.

Inside, her furniture was a mixture of new old and old old. She had collected art pieces and antiques from all parts of the world. Looking around as we walked, I noticed oil paintings by old masters, oriental tapestries, Russian enamel cups from the collection of Catherine the Great, malachite tables, and priceless Persian carpets, threadbare from years of use. The heavy drapes framing the barred windows looked as if they had been installed by Valentino himself.

It had been a half-dozen years since I'd been to Falcon's Lair, so Doris pointed out the new additions to her collection, commenting with the authority of a museum curator. The living room was dominated by a huge chandelier, made from pieces of rock crystal larger than a man's fist. While I arched my neck and expressed my amazement, Doris complained, saying, "What a headache it was to get that fixture anchored securely. We had to keep reinforcing the ceiling."

Next to the living room was an ornate door, inlaid with human bone. The sight of that door always sent shivers down my spine. I wondered what kind of vibrations it gave off.

Doris was well-experienced with India and Indian philosophy. She had been a friend of Paramahansa Yogananda, the revered swami who had founded the Self-Realization Fellowship in Los Angeles back in the thirties. Doris had practiced Kriya Yoga for ten years. With this background and her quick mind, I knew I had to come prepared and not bore her with preliminaries. She was never hesitant to challenge, and was quick to get to the point.

Soon I was reading and commenting on the introductory lectures I had stuffed into my purse, skipping redundant sections as Doris's interest waxed brighter. Skeptical by nature, Doris checked out what I had to say, questioning from all angles, but, finally, I won her interest.

"O.K. I'll try TM, but I want to be initiated by Maharishi himself." Accustomed to her status as a famous, mysterious heiress, she was not to be handled by a lieutenant; she wanted the general.

On contacting Maharishi, I got the go-ahead, and the following weekend we drove up to Arrowhead in her old, bubble-topped, run-down Oldsmobile, about which she remarked, "I don't know why I keep this old thing, but I love to look out through the top."

Although pathologically wary of strangers, Doris is outspoken and assured once she feels at ease. The transition was rapid with Maharishi. After being introduced to him, she curled up on a pillow at his feet and began to badger him with all kinds of questions. While most of us were over-obliging in his presence, almost to the point of being yes-men, she felt no such inhibitions.

One of her abstract questions was, "What is the most important quality to have in life?"

"Discrimination," Maharishi said quietly.

Doris had no qualms about challenging him. "Now, Maharishi, I cannot believe that. Wouldn't you select compassion or non-attachment?"

I was shocked by her audacity, but Maharishi showed no surprise at her manner. Rather, he said with assurance, "When you learn discrimination, only then can you distinguish between what is important and what is not important. With this quality, you begin to understand the truth of life."

"But what about personal magnetism? Isn't that a sign of an evolved soul, one who has good karma?"

"Yes, magnetism is one of the best qualities to possess."

"But didn't Hitler have terrific magnetism?" She smiled slyly, as if she had won a debating point. "Did *he* have good karma? I would not have thought so."

Doris studied his face, but Maharishi did not flinch.

"Yes, Hitler had very good karma; however, he misused his gifts. He had special qualities, and instead of using them to help mankind, he employed them to gain power and ravage mankind." His face darkened as he slowly shook his head. "It will take his soul hundreds of lifetimes to get back to where he was. We can feel compassion for the terrible suffering his soul must experience."

I jumped in, "The Dalai Lama said the same thing about the soul of Mao, referring to the genocide of the Tibetan people."

Maharishi said, "As the soul evolves, the tests will be harder until it is made pure."

There were other matters I was curious about. I seized this opportunity—

"Maharishi, Charlie says mankind is 'doomed;' is this true?"

He roared with laughter and exclaimed, "If all were truly lost, we would stay home and enjoy life and not work so hard. No, we do not dig a well where we know there is no water. Charlie sometimes likes to shock people."

After more laughter, I asked him what he thought about a medium purportedly in touch with a spiritual force known as the White Brotherhood. Maharishi confirmed this, saying, "We are satisfied that these spirits who call themselves the White Brotherhood are good spirits and they aim to help mankind; there are many individuals who are trance-channels for disembodied entities—some are good, some wish to trick you. We don't pay much attention to any of them. The best way to help mankind is through TM."

"Will a savior be born in the near future, as the Brotherhood predicts?"

Maharishi replied, "We do not worry about who is a savior or when he or she will be born. We just prepare the ground for him." He went on, "What we are teaching will influence mankind for the next five thousand years, and though these exact teachings may be diluted, their influence will remain—this is the wonder of having tapes to record all."

Again, it was Doris's turn. She tilted her eyes up to the wooden beams for a moment before asking, "So as one evolves, the tests get harder?"

"Yes, yes," Maharishi nodded, "but then you have a better instrument with which to work."

This fascinated me. I had many friends similar to Doris, born into great wealth and with potential talent. Yet few did anything worthwhile with their gifts, finding little fulfillment in their lives. Was that part of the test? The greater one's advantages in life, the higher and more elusive the threshold for happiness? Take Doris, heiress to the American Tobacco Company fortune—money had warped her life.

Maharishi continued, tapping his arm with a rose to accent his statements, "Leisure time is one of God's great gifts. With leisure time you can come to know yourself, and, after self-realization, the next step is God-realization."

"It is hard for the man with a family to support, who has his nose to the grindstone all day. He has no time to think of lofty things." With his rose, he pointed out, "If you are born into wealth, you have been given a good opportunity, but you also have the danger of being ruined by it."

"Don't you think that being born with too much money is one of the most difficult tests?" asked the heiress.

"Yes, that is why you must do something important with your money. Otherwise, it will control and ruin your life."

How true, I thought to myself. Although I had briefed Maharishi on Doris, he knew nothing of her upbringing. At birth, the newspapers labelled her the richest girl in the world. Fearing she would be a prime target for kidnapping, her parents kept her so sheltered that she was denied a normal childhood.

As a result, she was shy of the public, the media, and was suspicious of strangers, fearing that people were only interested in her wealth. She grew into a lonely woman, craving to be beautiful and loved for herself. Unfortunately, most decent men shied away from her, fearful of being called fortune-hunters. Both of her marriages to two well-known personalities, Jimmy Cromwell and Porfirio Rubirosa, lasted only a short time and ended in handsome settlements for each.

Maharishi studied Doris. "Nancy tells me much of your wealth comes from tobacco."

I held my breath. Maharishi was treading on dangerous ground.

"That and other things." Doris's face closed up.

Maharishi waved his flower. "Tobacco is a life-destructive plant; it brings bad karma to those who sell it to others. You must perform life-constructive acts with your money to offset this karma."

I did not like what was developing, so I broke in. "Doris does a great deal of good with her money, Maharishi. She has a foundation that gives to hospitals, to colleges, to research and other worthy causes."

But he ignored my words and continued to speak directly to her. "It is difficult to speak of this; you will feel that a person is seeking something for himself. I am asking nothing. I only speak of universal law. That is why I warn you."

He glanced at me and then back to her, speaking in a warm and intimate tone, "As for an offering gift to Guru Dev when you come for your initiation, give me some of your time. That is more valuable to me than your money, for then you will be giving of yourself."

I could have hugged him!

Doris was initiated, and she meditated enthusiastically, with wonderful results. Her complexion bloomed, the music returned to her voice, and she felt relief from her recent trauma. She soon stated that the little TM she had done was already more beneficial than her ten years of Yogananda's Kriya Yoga.

However, Maharishi was alarmed at the state of her nervous system (could he sense it in her vibrations?). Every time she came to see him, he told her to go back to her room and rest and meditate, rest and meditate. Finally, she asked him for permission to rent a house nearby. She would give him a month of her time. His reaction was, "Very good, very good. Nancy will stay with you." We went house-hunting, using my name, of course, and soon settled into a cozy cabin five minutes' walk away. My family supported my absence, knowing how important it was to Maharishi.

Doris eagerly shared in the cooking and soon learned to make *puris*. The atmosphere in the house was lovely. With more hands to share the work, there was plenty of time left over for walks, yoga *asanas*, long meditations, and simply being around Maharishi.

We became a harmonious unit.

From time to time Maharishi invited us into his little room to meditate with him. It was a special treat. Although he always offered us chairs, we preferred to sit on the floor, leaning against the wall. I wish that I could say exceptional meditations took place in Maharishi's presence, but nothing of the kind happened. Rather, I would worry about making the slightest noise and disrupting the others. Simply worrying about coughing or my stomach growling was enough to keep me from transcending. Maharishi advised me, "You are the worst critic of your own meditation. Just do it, don't think about it." However, I thought about it.

One day I handed Maharishi some Christian medallions and asked him to hold them while we meditated. After they were thus blessed by his touch, I planned to distribute them to my children.

At the end of the meditation, Maharishi brought us back to consciousness with a gentle, "Jai Guru Dev. How do you feel, happy?" Slowly we opened our eyes, still leaning against the wall.

Maharishi looked at the medallions in his palm and commented, "It is good, Nancy, that you worship Jesus as your prophet. As a Westerner, it is proper that you follow him. If you were born in the East, it would be different."

Doris, still blinking her eyes, asked, "Do you believe that Jesus was an avatar, Maharishi?"

"Yes, as was Krishna, Buddha and others."

"But how many avatars have there been?" Now her eyes were wide open.

"Hundreds. Every species has its avatar, its most perfect specimen, for a leader. Even the turtles had their own avatar to lead them out of the sea. Evolution is a slow process. For a species to change, it takes thousands of years and lifetimes; God would never leave a species without a guide."

I was especially interested in what he said about Jesus. From my days in catechism class at a convent I attended one year, I had expressed doubts about certain tenets of Christianity and drove the nuns crazy with questions such as, "How does man know the world was created in seven days? " "Who watched? " "Why did Jesus's birth have to be an immaculate conception?" "If the creator designed the reproductive system for man, why wasn't it good enough for Mary?"

"Maharishi, I don't understand why Jesus said that if a person does you harm, you should turn the other cheek. That seems cowardly to me. After all, the Jews taught 'an eye for an eye, a tooth for a tooth'; if someone did you harm, aren't you justified in doing harm back to him?" This had always puzzled me.

"Nancy, it is necessary to see things in the proper perspective." Maharishi arched his hand back and ran his forefinger along his open palm as he explained, "Imagine that when you are born there is a large scroll. On the scroll will be inscribed all of your past deeds from your earlier lives. These will indicate the tests you must have in your present life to pay back your past debts."

We followed his words carefully. "If you can look at the person who does you harm simply as a messenger delivering an old debt to you, you will not waste time on him in feeling hatred or resentment.

"You will get on with the test which has been presented to you. Whether it is an injury, an illness, or bad luck, the important thing is to face what has come to you and get through it, learning a lesson from it.

"If you know this misfortune to be some past action coming back to you, how can you feel bitterness toward the messenger? You will never be able to feel envy or hate if you really understand this law of life.

"If someone does you harm, don't try to get even. There is a higher authority which will enforce justice. Everything is recorded."

Explained this way, it certainly made sense. So there it all was—the justice in the universe I'd been seeking. This would explain the malformed child, the crippled beggar—they were paying off debts from another lifetime. Whatever we had, whatever we were, we'd earned it, good and bad. It made me happy to intuitively know this as truth. I wasn't worried about the exact particulars; what was important was to know that many lifetimes were required to work out this justice. I liked knowing that for every action there is a reaction; as you sow, so shall you reap. It meant that no one got away with anything.

How little I knew during that quiet, happy time at Arrowhead how severely tested I would be in the future on this exact belief.

Soon our enchanted time at Arrowhead was over, and all of us returned to Los Angeles. One afternoon Doris invited Maharishi for tea. Afterwards, his reaction to the visit amused me.

"Nancy, that house has very sad vibrations. You should tell Doris to get rid of all that old furniture which carries tragedy with it. Have her buy new antiques." It must have been that door of inlaid human bone that got to him.

Then, to our tremendous joy and surprise, Doris gave $100,000 to the S.R.M., asking that it be kept secret. Charlie and Maharishi were overwhelmed. It was such a generous gift. With it, the S.R.M. was able to complete the International Academy of Meditation in Rishikesh. There was even enough money left over to build a house for Maharishi at the ashram, with a special altar to Guru Dev in his *puja* room downstairs.

Unfortunately, word of the gift passed from mouth to mouth, all the way to India. When Doris next visited Bombay, she called on Sharma, my first teacher. He asked her about a gift for him such as she had given Maharishi. Angry that her wishes had not been adhered to, she ended all association with the S.R.M. and with transcendental meditation.

It was such a shame; she never knew how much her wonderful gift had accomplished.

---
### 11
---

# Triumphant Return to San Francisco

MAHARISHI'S APPEARANCE ON THE STEVE ALLEN SHOW almost back-fired. After Maharishi was introduced and had taken a seat, Steve Allen looked at the floor under his chair and asked, "Where are your feet?" Maharishi had tucked them under his robe. The audience roared. However, Maharishi handled Steve Allen very nicely, and left the show with everybody's respect, including the crew. But a variety show was hardly the proper introduction to a profound holy man and teacher. My friends and family, who had not met him, came away with the impression of a man with a strange, high giggle, and what seemed to be long, dirty, stringy hair . . . he definitely needed grooming for future T.V. exposure.

A friend, U.S. (Uell) Andersen, who was well known for his spiritual books such as *Three Magic Words*, commented, "I like your holy man. He's a clever little guy, but he still looks like a cardboard cutout from central casting."

Maharishi himself had once said, "My image will be a big hurdle for you to get over. That is why it is so important that we have people representing us who look like Charlie Lutes, the conservative business-man."

As time passed and Maharishi traveled nonstop, the movement seemed to do better in other parts of the world. Pamphlets and newsletters began to trickle in, describing triumphant receptions in foreign countries, summarizing speeches given to various international bodies, and announcing grandiose plans for the world.

Maharishi declared his teaching would achieve world peace within a few years. How was it possible? We were still having trouble paying for the secretary at the center.

But to Maharishi, all things were possible. From the very beginning of his mission into the world, he never lacked the vision, the courage to dream.

It was in Madras in 1958, while addressing a throng of over twenty thousand, that the inspiration came to inaugurate a movement aimed at no less a target than the spiritual regeneration of the whole world. From there he was invited to visit Honolulu. He accepted. He knew no one, but knew that when people heard his message, help would be forthcoming.

Flying on to the U.S. mainland, he went first to San Francisco, then on to L.A. On the plane a fellow passenger asked who he was, what he was doing in the U.S. and all the customary questions. Then the lady asking the questions volunteered, "My husband owns a fairly large hall, would you like to speak there?"

And so it was that the Lutes and the Olsens went to the Masquers Club in Hollywood to hear an Indian holy man speak, thinking at the time, "What an odd place for such a person to appear." When the question was presented, "Does anyone know of a place where Maharishi can stay?" Helena said she found her hand in the air, and that is how the Los Angeles center started.

It seemed a good place to start in the United States, but the results were disappointing.

Between home, family, and my lecture series, the next two years passed quickly. Tony had become a partner in his law firm, María Luisa was happy with her private girls school, Westlake, Rik was at UCLA, Starr was at Stanford, and Brett was at Yale. All three boys were meditating. It proved a buffer between them and the students experimenting with drugs. If a friend suggested, "Hey, Cooke, how about smoking a joint or trying a little LSD?" Their reply of, "No thanks, I have my own mind-expansion trip," seemed to satisfy their peers. It was at the height of the Vietnam war, a troubled time for students.

I felt such gratitude to Maharishi and wished I could help him more. Then I started thinking about introducing him to San Francisco, my native city. While I had a PR office there, the press had been very supportive when I needed them. Herb Caen, San Francisco's favorite newspaper personality, had always been interested in my activities. In one of his columns he had commented, "If you see Nancy Cooke de Herrera at a cocktail party, escorted by a strange-looking, ape-like man, you'll know she met with success on her Yeti hunt with Texas millionaire, Tom Slick."

After my engagement to Tony was announced, Herb again wrote, "Tom Slick has found the Yeti. His name is Tony—and he's just run off with Tom's ladylove, Nancy Cooke de Herrera." So San Francisco would certainly be curious if I now appeared with someone like Maharishi.

Charlie's response to my suggestion was, "Sounds good to me. We're not getting anywhere fast around here. But, you'll have to sell the idea to Maharishi; he's beginning to get busy with speaking engagements, especially in England, Canada and Germany." Tony thought it was a great idea, also.

Charlie found three days open in November, so the next time Maharishi came to Los Angeles, we agreed to a course in San Francisco similar to the one we hosted in Beverly Hills. There would be no trouble getting a newsworthy group to hear him, and the press would need no prodding.

The main concern was to arrange for a house and a host.

Fortunately, this was easily arranged. No sooner did I put out feelers to find a willing hostess, than two friends immediately responded. The first was Phyllis Fraser, familiar to the social pages as "the glamorous, blonde jet-setter." She was zany and fun-loving. She certainly added glamour, humor, and life to every party she attended—and there were many.

"Oh, Nancy, I would adore to have Maharishi stay at my apartment." Her husky voice curved in a gentle drawl. "I could use some of his vibrations. You can have the place completely to yourself if it is more convenient for you. Or if you prefer, I can stay and help you take care of him."

It was nice to have the offer. We were planning on having about fifty people, and I would need assistance. Since Phyllis and I shared many mutual friends, she took on the chore of telephoning invitations while I contacted civic leaders and the press. I could imagine the content of Phyllis's call. "Darling, I'm calling to invite you to meet Nancy's holy man, Nancy's guru . . . isn't that exciting! He will teach all sorts of profound, exhilarating things. You simply can't miss it." Phyllis would stir up a lot of curiosity. And as it turned out, we had sixty acceptances.

Then I received a call from Friedl Klussman, offering help. Friedl was a one-woman crusade, or so the city government found out when the mayor tried to replace the outdated cable cars with modern buses. She took the mayor on single-handed. "The cable cars are not only a great tourist attraction, they are practical as well. They are a part of the history and color of San Francisco itself." She made such an obstacle of herself that the city government had to give in, and the quaint little cars continue to clank up and down the steep hills.

Friedl also volunteered her house.

"Are you sure it wouldn't be too much trouble, Friedl? Phyllis also has offered her apartment."

I knew the two were friends. We had toured Russia together. But Friedl cautioned, "I do not think her place would be appropriate for a holy man. You don't want Maharishi too heavily associated with the party people of San Francisco. You bring him here, and Phyllis can help you with whatever you need."

This made sense. She had held many civic meetings at her house; it was large, with many rooms. Maharishi would be able to initiate in one room while the earlier students were meditating in others. Also, being at the top of a dead-end street, it was quiet. It was ideal.

I had a lot of planning to do. At night details floated through my mind—it was difficult to sleep. I would not only be responsible for getting the people to attend, but I would be doing the cooking, cleaning, shopping, answering the phone, making the appointments, and be general cruise director of the whole show! Yes, I would need lots of help. Friedl and Phyllis would be my team.

The day arrived—Phyllis met me at the airport full of enthusiasm. Every time I saw her anew, I marvelled at what a sensational-looking young woman she was. She had a voluptuous, tall body which moved with feline grace. Her long, swinging hair framed a face with a pointed, full mouth and large, open green eyes. Everything about her was seductive, and she played her role well.

Phyllis had exploded on the San Francisco scene after modeling for a nude statue sculpted by a well-known artist. Her name started to appear in Herb Caen's column.

After winning a large financial settlement from her wealthy contractor husband, Bob Fraser, she had ensconced herself in a spacious, chic apartment in Pacific Heights and wore fabulous, designer clothes whenever she did appear. She soon had the city's attention. People were in two camps. Some thought she was outrageous for having modeled in the nude. Others adored her, especially the men.

Phyllis and I became friends in the spring of 1960 when I led a Woman's Delegation from San Francisco to Russia, after receiving a high-level invitation from Mikoyan. It was in response to the gracious treatment Kruschev and Kosloff had enjoyed in San Francisco. They invited Cyril Magnin, director of the Port of San Francisco and well-known personality in the City, to bring a group of men to the Soviet Union, later to be followed by a women's group.

When word got out about the trip, Phyllis had asked if she could join the group. I thought, why not—a little glamour always helps. I already had a structural engineer, a pediatrician, a mathematician, Friedl Klussman, and several others—a bit heavy on brains. Phyllis turned out to be a great asset, especially when we put on a fashion show in Moscow at Gorky Palace and modeled our own clothes. She took the audience by storm, as she did later in a nightclub in Leningrad—doing the twist in a clinging, black beaded gown.

Phyllis and I formed a binding friendship. She modeled for my charitable shows and could be counted on to help me in any promotion—a great asset and beloved friend. Now she was here to help me present Maharishi to San Francisco.

"I have the car full of plants to take to Freidl's. They are all white and yellow, as you suggested. I'm so excited. Do you suppose Maharishi could teach me to be calm and disciplined like you, Nancy?" I laughed. Being calm was not always my nature.

Later, Friedl watched as we moved her furniture around. Fiftyish, her figure was square and dumpy. She boasted that she never wore a bra, washed her naturally curly hair in the shower, and wore sensible walking shoes. She was the antithesis of Phyllis.

Her house reflected her spirit. The mellow, aged wood of the walls and polished floor lent warmth to the rather spartan interior. Although she had lived alone ever since her husband ran off with the young German cook, she kept the house full and active with all her meetings.

She was a bit puzzled when we draped a small sofa with a sheet, surrounded the portrait of Guru Dev with plants, and set up the usual easel-type blackboard, but she said nothing.

It was late afternoon by the time we got back to Phyllis's apartment for a bit of fresh-up time before going on to dinner.

It was a beautiful, large apartment with high ceilings, thick white carpets, and a well-stocked bar. Modern oils covered the walls, striking *objets d'art* rested on book shelves, but what immediately caught the eye was the nude statue on her coffee table. It was a miniature of the original she had posed for. This undoubtedly started many conversations.

Later, coming out from a refreshing meditation, my footsteps muffled by the carpet, I found a dejected-looking Phyllis staring out the window. Her whole being expressed sadness. When I spoke, she jumped and immediately put a smile on her face.

"Phyllis, what is it that's bothering you? I saw that expression cross your face several times today."

"Oh Nancy, I just don't know what I am going to do. Bob, that bastard, is holding up my alimony. Just because he sends me money, he thinks he should still be able to sleep with me."

She picked up the statue from the table, turning it this way and that, without really looking at it. Then she set it on its side.

"I have so many bills. I don't dare walk into a store."

Looking around her apartment, her fashionable way of life, one could imagine the large budget she was used to.

"But surely you could cut back on expenses. Stop giving parties. Look at your wardrobe, you certainly don't need any more clothes."

"Yes, but when the opera comes around, what am I to show up in? Everyone expects to see me in something special."

"Phyllis, any designer would lend you a model. Couturiers are always looking for publicity. They know that anything you wear will be admired and written about. Why, for years, as the Ambassadress of Fashion, I had my clothes either given to me or loaned for special parties."

To think that she was not aware of this. What huge sums she had paid out unnecessarily for spectacular one-time gowns. As we talked, her mood changed. She began to brighten.

"Oh Nancy, do you think that meditation would give me strength, more balance?"

In response, I described some of the immediate benefits. All this appealed to Phyllis; she sensed a solution to her problems. She asked to be initiated as soon as Maharishi arrived. Our conversation became animated as I summarized the introductory course for her so that she would be ready.

When I went to sleep that night, I felt happy. Maybe I could do a good deed for a dear friend in a difficult time.

The next day was the day when I would introduce Maharishi to my hometown. The sun was shining. San Francisco had put on her loveliest gown to welcome him. Phyllis looked beautiful in a clinging knit dress.

"If anyone could get a holy man to forget his vows, that's you."

"I am as covered up as any nun."

"I grant you that, but there is a difference!"

Several members of the press met us at the airport, including some photographers. One of them focused his camera on Phyllis, commenting, "Well, your Indian friend is going to get a glamorous reception. Are you a meditator, Phyllis?"

"Not yet, but I intend to be very soon." She stopped and posed for the photographer, arching her eyebrows and batting her beautiful eyelashes. "Didn't I hear somewhere that Jesus loved the sinners? Perhaps I will be Maharishi's favorite conversion."

When the plane arrived, the photographers asked that I detain Maharishi on the plane until the other passengers had disembarked. They wanted him standing alone at the top of the stairway.

Maharishi was delighted when I slipped through the plane door, picked up his deer skin, and told him of the photographers. His eyes glowed as he said to me, "You have done a good job, Nancy. One more step on our way to winning the world."

The reception was delightful. A crowd gathered by the luggage counter as we awaited Maharishi's small bag. Few had ever seen an Indian holy man before.

As we drove into town we outlined the plans for the evening lecture. There were a few free hours before guests would arrive, so I asked Maharishi if he would initiate Phyllis during that time. He nodded his head and beamed with joy.

Phyllis leaned forward from the back seat and asked, "Have you ever been in San Francisco before, Maharishi?"

"Oh yes, I opened the first meditation center in the United States here. It was when I came in 1959." This was news to me. Obviously, his visit had been unheralded.

The car came to a halt. "Welcome to San Francisco, Maharishi," Friedl called from the top of the steep path. Her freshly-scrubbed face radiated hospitality. Once on the porch we looked out over the Bay.

It was a breath-taking panorama. Sailboats, taking advantage of the sunny day, glided past Alcatraz Island, dwarfed by a heavy oil tanker crawling through the waters toward the Golden Gate and the open sea.

Maharishi was delighted. He walked about the house admiring the view from various outlooks. He complimented Friedl on her home, her garden. She was beaming with pride. He also thanked us for the way we had arranged the flowers around Guru Dev.

Friedl led him upstairs to a bright, airy room. Maharishi was pleased with his lodgings; we had made the right choice. He had little unpacking to do. His suitcase carried his extra robes, his *Bhagavad Gita*, a small photo of Guru Dev, a silk sheet to cover his bed, and a few toiletries. Soon I was able to usher Phyllis in for her initiation.

The phone began to ring continuously. The doorbell rang. An unannounced group of four elderly ladies appeared on the doorstep with flowers in their hands. They had come to pay their respects to their master. They filled me in. "We are from the S.R.M. which originally brought Maharishi here in 1959." One lady stepped forward. "Maybe you do not remember me, Mrs. Cooke. I am Mrs. Mills. We only met once, when we arranged to pay that second mortgage on your house on Jackson Street."

I was stunned. "My house on Jackson Street? You were the ones who bought it?" I had lived in San Francisco when I first opened my office there, but had sold the house when I decided it was better for Mother and the family to live in Piedmont.

"Oh yes, we used it as the first center for Maharishi in the U.S."

I couldn't believe it—my house! An amazing coincidence, or was it? It seemed that I had been destined to meet Maharishi. I remembered the realtor saying the house had been bought for a swami, but I never asked for any details and promptly forgot it. How amazing; wait until Maharishi heard this news.

We chatted over a cup of tea until Phyllis's initiation was over. Then I took them in to Maharishi.

The rest of the afternoon disappeared in a whirlwind of preparations, answering calls from the press and somehow finding time to cook Maharishi's dinner. After her meditation, Phyllis left, saying, "I have an engagement I can't break. I'm sorry, but I'll try to be back in time to catch some of the lecture." I was disappointed, as she had not warned me.

I was pressing Maharishi's robes for the night's lecture when my mother and sisters arrived. They had come early, sensing that I might need help. Also, I had arranged for them to meet Maharishi privately.

"Now I've seen everything!" exclaimed my mother. "Do you even have to do his laundry?"

"Yes, darling, and I consider it an honor."

They were highly amused by my role. After the "Steve Allen Show," my mother had commented, "Sweetheart, if this teacher of yours brings happiness and spiritual inspiration, I don't care if he looks like Rasputin. Sorry about the comparison, but he does look unusual to me with that hair and beard, and his laugh *is* different. He doesn't come across very well on television."

Mother looked young and pretty that afternoon. Neither I nor my two sisters had inherited her dark, auburn hair, but we did have her blue eyes. Age had hardly dimmed her youthful beauty; in her sixties, she looked forty.

As children we used to love going to Grandma's, where we would look at old photoplays and see Mother when she was an aspiring actress. However, Mother never talked about this; she was more proud of having put on dance exhibitions with a fellow Nebraskan, Fred Astaire.

Mother was everything to us three sisters. She raised us with love, confidence and admiration. We could and did go to her with all problems, knowing she was there to guide and support us. Now she was here to meet my holy man. I was so anxious she would like him.

The meeting with Maharishi was a happy one. He complimented Mother, "Mrs. Veitch, what a gift you have given the world with your beautiful daughters. You are the Divine Mother—the hub of the wheel of creation. Because of your love, training, and inheritance, they will go on to sound accomplishment; this they will also pass on to their families." Mother was won over.

"Why, Nancy, he is a fine-looking man—such expressive eyes, so full of joy."

My sisters agreed, "We even like his funny laugh."

Mother added, "How different he looks in person. His hair is quite acceptable." Her reaction encouraged me for the meeting which lay ahead.

The phone was still ringing when guests began to arrive. One of the first was my father, who hugged me and said, "Well, honey, quite a night for you, isn't it? Your friends will soon decide if your holy man is for real or not."

Ever the skeptic, my father had always challenged me to defend my beliefs. If I had trouble expressing them, he was an exacting judge.

"If you can't put wisdom into words, then wisdom does not exist in your head."

Although he termed himself an atheist, Daddy was an agnostic. No atheist would know as much about religion or have so many books on the subject. He had insisted I take all the history of religion courses that Stanford offered. Actually, they only managed to shatter my informed beliefs and increase my confusion.

"Where is that pretty Phyllis?" Typical for my father to ask, with his love for beautiful women.

And the women loved him, with his handsome Scottish looks—thick, gray hair framed a high-cheekboned face with a perfect, straight nose, strong even teeth and a ruddy complexion. His passion also included boats and airplanes. A chemical engineer by schooling, he invented the bobby pin. This practical little gadget proved to be a real money maker, and Daddy retired from business at an early age. He was in the army in France in World War I, and in the Navy as a Commander in World War II. He was a brilliant, undisciplined man—a terrible husband, and an absentee father. Luckily, his father lived with us until I was seventeen—he was more like our real father, and we three girls adored him.

Mother finally got a divorce and we were all better friends because of it. Daddy became more interested in his daughters after they grew into attractive young women.

I answered his questions about Phyllis. "I don't know, Daddy. She was supposed to be here, but she said she had a date."

"Well, that is our loss, but then maybe it will be easier for us to concentrate on the wisdom of the Far East." He settled himself in a chair next to some of the other guests, while I returned to the door to meet new arrivals. He nodded pleasantly to Mother; they were still friends. My sisters came over to greet him with a kiss.

The excitement grew in the room as the seats filled. The afternoon papers had carried photographs and stories about Maharishi's visit. No one had to be dragged to meet Maharishi that day. They politely rose for his entrance.

His chair surrounded with plants, Maharishi looked like a white blossom as he tucked his feet under his robes. He began to speak in a slow rhythm. "Are you happy? Would you like to learn to be even happier? There is no reason to suffer in life. Suffering is the result of misunderstanding. It is the mind's nature to be happy."

He looked over the smartly-dressed audience before continuing. Success was no stranger to this gathering. But what about happiness?

"In meditation we take the mind to the source of happiness, and, once it has visited there, it will always want to return.

"How do we do it? Very easily. We use the natural tendency of the mind to go to that which is most pleasant. If there is an ugly woman on this side of the room," he extended his right hand, "and a beautiful one on the other side, it is no effort for the mind to decide, without thinking, to gaze upon the beautiful woman."

My father shook his head in silent laughter. Maharishi had caught his attention.

The evening lasted longer than we expected, as there were many questions. Among those who raised their hands was my father. "Maharishi, we have been taught that tension brings forth creative achievement. Now, you tell us that we should learn to live without tension. What about the great artists who lived under the stress of poverty, in garrets and the like, yet were still able to produce their greatest works? How do you explain this?"

Maharishi responded with his gleeful, high-pitched laugh. His whole body shook. This seemed to be a popular question.

"Because nobody knows how to cure it, they teach that it is necessary." Maharishi continued to laugh. "How do we know what would have happened to their productivity if their lives had been less stressful? Maybe they would have been doubly creative." He then went into a complete explanation of the dangers of stress. I watched the audience . . . they were hanging on his every word.

After the lecture, due to the late hour, my father decided to just say hello to Maharishi and save a longer visit for another day. On his way out the door he commented, "I like this holy man of yours, honey. He has a brilliant mind; he doesn't try to impress his audience with big words. He keeps his knowledge simple, and that is the most difficult way to present truth."

My father was a very critical man. That Maharishi could impress him was a good indication of the evening's success. Maharishi felt the same way. He was happy with the audience. "The movement needs leaders of this caliber."

I was especially pleased that certain people had shown up and I explained who some of them were. "Senator William Knowland is a powerful friend to have, Maharishi. When I traveled as the Ambassadress of Fashion, he gave me a letter to the Ambassador of each country I visited, requesting any support I might need. This put me in a special category diplomatically."

"He would be able to reach the U.S. President, would he not?" asked Maharishi.

I could see the wheels turning. "Yes, but let's not waste our ammunition yet. An interview such as that will be a one-time opportunity. . . ."

So, with that thought in his head, our optimistic little holy man retired for the night.

## 12

# The Haunted House by the Bay

ITH THE SATISFACTION OF A JOB WELL DONE, I slept soundly that night. I had moved into Friedl's in order to care for Maharishi. The next morning I virtually jumped out of bed when the alarm went off. Many guests had expressed the wish to talk to Maharishi privately. The press had asked for interviews. The phone would start to ring and visitors would be knocking on the door before long. I had to race through a lot of chores if the house were going to be presentable in time.

While straightening up the living room, I heard Maharishi start his daily shower. Running upstairs, I gathered up his laundry. As he had only two sets of linen sheets with him to use as robes, I needed to wash and iron every day. He wrapped one around his waist and threw the other over his shoulders.

His years in the Himalayas certainly acclimatized him; I noticed all the windows in his room were open, permitting the damp crisp air off the Bay to mingle with wisps of incense. Storm clouds seemed to be gathering.

Later, Friedl came to tell me to answer the phone. She found me kneeling on the floor of Maharishi's bathroom, cleaning. "My lord, look at all that black hair in the tub. Did he just wash his hair?"

"Yes, he does every morning; that's why I get cross with people who talk about his dirty hair."

"Then why is it so stringy-looking?"

Laying down the sponge, I got to my feet. "Maharishi has absolutely no personal vanity. He rarely uses a comb; he just towels it and kind of pats it into place." I was getting tired of this question.

I asked her if she knew who was on the phone.

"No, I didn't recognize the voice. I thought it might be Phyllis. Wasn't she supposed to be here to help you this morning?"

"Yes, and Maharishi has to check her meditation. But she probably had a late date. I'm sure she'll be calling soon."

It was Frances Moffat of the *San Francisco Examiner*. She wanted to know when she might get an interview with Maharishi, both for the newspaper and for some personal questions of her own. Before I was able to tell her a good hour to come, the doorbell rang. There were people with flowers in their hands. The next few hours simply disappeared in a whirl of phone calls, visitors, and arrangements for the second evening.

It was mid-afternoon before there was a lull in the activity and I wondered about Phyllis. It wasn't like her to simply drop out of sight, not even to call. Of course, the line had been busy and she might not have been able to get through. I tried to call her but there was no answer.

From the kitchen, I dialed Phyllis's number several more times. Still there was no answer. I became worried. This wasn't like Phyllis. Finally, with dinner needing only to be warmed up and taken to Maharishi, I told Friedl of my apprehension. She said she'd hold down the fort while I drove over to Phyllis's. "Perhaps she left a note or something." As I left the house she called, "Don't forget we have a big group of people coming in three hours and you should have a brief nap; you've been on your feet all day."

"I'll be all right. I won't be long."

It was now raining steadily.

With the end of the business day, traffic congested the wet streets. Lights were already flickering on the girlie-show marquees that cluttered the building facade of North Point. After the Broadway Tunnel I began to make better time. Soon I was parked in front of Phyllis's gray stucco, Locust Street apartment.

I carefully mounted the painted steps to the top floor and rang the bell. Although I had a key, I thought it better to wait a few minutes before using it, lest I walk into some sort of delicate situation. One never knows.

"Yoo hoo, Phyllis, are you there?" I let myself in and called again. There was no answer. The rooms answered with silence—a silence which seemed ominous.

The door to her bedroom at the back of the flat was shut. I knocked and called out again before turning the knob and opening it slowly. With the day dismal and the hour late, the room was dark, but I could make out Phyllis's form on her bed.

I turned on the overhead light and said, "Phyllis, wake up. It's Nancy. I've been wondering where you were."

Phyllis didn't stir. She looked beautiful in her sleep, but her skin had an unusually yellowish hue. I nudged her, but still she didn't stir, so I shook her roughly. Panic leapt into my throat when she refused to awaken. Her skin was warm. Her pulse was regular but faint. I tried to lift her into a sitting position to wake her up, but she stiffened her body, keeping her eyes shut tight as though she didn't want to awaken.

I began to yell at her and shake her. What had happened to her?

Finally she began to moan, turning her head from side to side. Slurred words slowly flowed out of her mouth, gradually taking shape, "Please let me sleep. Please. I don't ever want to wake up."

How could she? Had she tried to kill herself?

How long had she lain like this? Why? How do I save her? The questions roared through my head as I raced into the kitchen to put some water on to boil. I noticed an empty pill bottle on the drainboard. Then I ran back and pulled her up into a sitting position.

"What were those pills you took? Tell me!" I demanded. "I am going to call an ambulance."

That brought her to. "No, please. I beg you not to do that." Phyllis looked so pathetic; her blonde hair dishevelled, hanging over her face." They were just pain pills from the dentist."

"Then just sit here for a minute while I fix you some coffee."

I made the coffee so strong it was almost solid. She gagged on it, but swallowed obediently.

"Phyllis, what is the name of your doctor?" She stared at me dumbly, so I threatened to call my family doctor. She coughed up the name and I immediately reached him, urging him to hurry over.

While we waited for the doctor to arrive, Phyllis visibly revived with the help of the coffee. She began to talk, unloading her problems in a long torrent. Her personal affairs were in much worse shape than she had admitted to me. She felt as if the whole roof were about to cave in on her. She had taken the pills to fight off her depression when she returned late the night before. The dark, the loneliness, the lack of hope overwhelmed her. Sobbing, she insisted that she just wanted to sleep, sleep. She had no intention of killing herself.

The doorbell rang, cutting off her words.

"That'll be the doctor. I'll go let him in."

It was Dr. Deems, still agitated from his hurry to get there. He brushed aside my breathless description of what had happened and marched up the stairs. Evidently he knew the way to her bedroom, for he stomped right in and confronted her.

"I thought you promised me you would never try this again. You cannot continue to do this and not ruin your health for good—or you'll kill yourself." He reached out and roughly grabbed her wrist to take her pulse, still seething as he looked at his watch.

Phyllis looked at him dolefully and mumbled, "I just couldn't help myself."

"That is what you said the last time. Don't you remember when we had to pump your stomach?"

I was shocked—the newspaper stories came back to me. There was a report that Phyllis had had to go to the hospital from taking too many aspirins. Some people suspected an attempted suicide, but I pooh-poohed the rumors.

The doctor stood over her. "Well, it's back to the hospital. What are you going to tell everyone this time?"

"Please, don't make me go. I can't afford it. I have so many unpaid bills already." She was on the point of tears again. "Please, I promise you it was a mistake—I won't take another pill, ever!"

He was obviously fond of her. This explained his gruff treatment. "Yes, but where will you go? You cannot stay here alone."

I butted in, "She can go back to the house where I'm staying."

"Well, that might be the solution." He picked up his bag and motioned me out into the hall. "I hate to subject her to the hospital when she is so adamant against it. She seems all right now, with the exception of being a bit drugged by the pills, but she'll sleep that off tonight." He looked at his watch and said, "I'll wait a bit longer to make sure she's okay. Against my advice, she flew to New York last month with walking pneumonia, and has never fully recovered. She refuses to take care of herself."

After the doctor left, I asked Phyllis about the cigarette burns on the furniture and the empty bottles I'd noticed in the living room.

She seemed to be leveling with me. "I can't describe it to you. It is like a terrible wave of blackness that comes over me. I drank everything I could get my hands on, trying to shake it off. But I had almost no liquor here. That is why I took the pills—anything to get rid of that ghastly darkness." I could still see the panic in her eyes. She had no control over this depression. She said that the party she had been to was not the cause; she had enjoyed it. It was the dark curtain of despair that descended on her afterward.

"If it is your financial worries that are doing this to you, Phyllis, all that can be made good so easily. You have many friends who will help you. I can; once you feel better, we'll figure out a way for you to live more sensibly. You're so attractive; there's a world of opportunity open to you."

She took my hand. "I'm sorry you had to see me like this; I never wanted you to know how weak I am. You make me realize how fake my values have been and I do want to change. Please help me."

What was I to say to that? No wonder she hadn't confided in me. Her words were very dear, but they shook me. Why had I not been more sensitive to her despair?

While Phyllis got dressed, I called Friedl, who was about to send out a search party for me as eight o'clock drew near. I told her not to worry, we were on our way. We arranged that Phyllis would sleep there that night.

Poor Phyllis. She continued to apologize for all the trouble she had caused. "I promise I will never try such a thing again. I promise I will call one of you if that awful chasm opens up again."

On the drive back to Friedl's I told her what Maharishi said about suicide. "It is the worst sin against life. It is the most terrible thing you can do to your soul. If a person takes his own life, his bodiless soul is doomed to wander in a state of nothingness until the day when the body would have died naturally. And it is such a waste—the soul will be reborn to the same tests. It will have to relive them, only they will be harder."

It was strong medicine, but I thought it necessary. After all, Phyllis had broken her earlier promise to the doctor.

She bowed her head and whispered, "I guess I was lucky."

A thought struck me, a surprising, troubling thought. I turned to Phyllis, "You looked so well, so happy after Maharishi initiated you yesterday. I just don't understand. When you felt bad, did you think of meditating?"

"No, I just couldn't . . . I don't even remember my *mantra.*" She sobbed quietly and said nothing the rest of the way. Only a few minutes remained before the guests were scheduled to arrive when we reached the house, so we entered through the back door to avoid being seen. Once Phyllis was settled in my bed, I went down to greet the first arrivals.

Not wanting to alarm Maharishi, we had explained that Phyllis had food poisoning and needed rest. Concerned, he had stepped into her room for a moment to give her a flower, which she still held in her hand as she drifted off to sleep.

Word had spread about Maharishi's first lecture and many guests brought friends along, hoping to squeeze them in. And squeeze we did. My former partner, Dorothy Mackenzie, congratulated me. "You've done a wonderful job of presenting the Maharishi. I went to a luncheon today and everyone was talking about him."

Tired and troubled as I was, I rejoiced to the praise in the gravelly voice of an old pro. We had our public relations office together for only a few years before my marriage to Tony, but Dorothy had been in the business for ages.

It was midnight before I had pushed the last guest out the door and Maharishi had retired to his room. Friedl said that Phyllis had asked for water and then went right back to sleep. "I'm sure she's fine, Nancy. Now you should look after yourself and get some sleep."

A little after one o'clock, with my cleaning chores behind me, I slipped into Phyllis's room to take a peek at "Sleeping Beauty" and grab my cosmetic case. She seemed to be breathing very heavily. I leaned over her to listen, but at that moment she rolled onto her side and resumed a normal state of respiration.

"She is still under the influence of the drug; the doctor said she would be. A good night's sleep will probably restore her completely. Then we'll sit down and make some plans to straighten out her life. Maybe Maharishi can talk to her."

Though exhausted when I settled onto the downstairs cot, I felt our trip was a triumph. The whole series had gone like a dream. So many people had expressed their interest in being initiated that we would have to send up another initiator to handle the numbers. The papers were full of stories on Maharishi. He was thrilled.

Getting carried away with our success, I had proposed that I take Maharishi through South America. He said that if I could attract the quality of people that I had in San Francisco, he would go anywhere with me. We were euphoric. We could not have asked for a better reception.

Five hours of sleep seemed very short when the alarm rang out the next morning. Expecting early visitors, I got up and sleepily went through the motions of setting up breakfast and giving a final touch to the living room. I felt an obligation to Friedl that her house look its best when people came to call on Maharishi.

At about 7:00, I tiptoed upstairs to see if anybody was stirring. Not a sound came from either Maharishi's or Friedl's rooms. I cautiously opened the door to see how Phyllis was doing. My heart stopped. Phyllis, in her red nightgown, lay half out of her bed, her limbs frozen in place. Her head was thrown back, her eyes opened wide in a tortured, horrified stare. A translucent bubble had formed across her gaping mouth. I shook her arm—it was cold and unmovable.

I screamed, "Friedl! Call an ambulance, call a doctor! Something has happened to Phyllis!"

Friedl appeared at her door, still adjusting her robe. "What has happened?"

"I think Phyllis is dead." I again touched her still form. She had no pulse. There were no signs of life. "Call an ambulance, Friedl, maybe something can still be done."

I will never forget her answer. Friedl's jaw quivered as she turned away. "I don't want her found here. If she is dead, you must figure out some way of getting her out of here." I looked at her in horror. "But Friedl, Phyllis is dead. Don't you understand? We must get help. Call Dr. Spencer." I gave her the number. I was not thinking straight. Phyllis was dead, I knew, and yet I was still desperate to get someone to help her.

I rushed to Maharishi's room. He was just coming out of the shower. "What has happened?"

"Oh, Maharishi, something dreadful has happened. I think Phyllis is dead; maybe you can help her."

He walked into her room and stood silently by her side. Death is not terrible to a holy man, yet this one seemed so drastic that Maharishi looked shaken. She had met him at the airport just two days before. She had been so brilliant with life. Death didn't seem to belong to her.

Maharishi shook his head mournfully. "Nothing can be done for her now, Nancy. Such a shame. She was so young, so full of life. What happened?" He looked at me with sympathy.

I told Maharishi the truth about her taking the pills, my finding her and reviving her, and her promise to straighten out her life.

"Maharishi, even though she did try to commit suicide, she did not actually succeed, at least not when she intended. Although the attempt must have weakened her and brought this awful thing on, do you think her death will go down in the cosmic record as a suicide? Will she have to suffer it all over again?"

Maharishi gazed down on her. "No, you say she promised never to try such a thing again; she repented her actions. That she was never tested again in life is not her fault. It was her karma that she should die."

His words soothed me. Maharishi put his arm on my shoulder and led me into his room where he had me sit, as he continued.

"Try to remember the happiness you shared as a friend. Do not worry for her. Before I came down for the lecture last night, she called me to her room and asked forgiveness for all the trouble she had caused. She has a good soul—her journey will not be a painful one."

Friedl continued to fret about the publicity which would ensue. She knew she had made a mistake and tried to explain, saying to me as I sat hunched over on Maharishi's bed, "Nancy, you know I am very fond of Phyllis. I am very upset about her dying, too, but you know how I hate publicity."

I looked at her in disbelief. No one loved the press more than she. Friedl was always able to show a few clippings she "just happened to have in her purse." There was nothing for me to say; she had let a curtain down and I had seen what was behind it.

The doctor arrived the same time as the ambulance. His face was stricken with grief as he watched Phyllis's body, now covered with a sheet, carried down the steep driveway.

"I can't understand it," he said, mostly to himself. "She was perfectly all right when I left her yesterday. A bit dopey, but nothing else. I would have insisted she go to the hospital if it had been otherwise."

Only after the doctor had left with Phyllis's body did I realize we had to protect Maharishi from damaging publicity. "My God, what do I do now?" I called Frances Moffat at home. She would tell us how to handle the press. Thank God she was there! I knew her to be that rare breed of reporter whose humanity superseded her professional interests. She loved Phyllis and often had tried to protect her. I knew I could turn to Frances as a friend.

Frances was shocked and grieved to hear the news. Then she cautioned me, "Don't speak to anyone until I get there. Take the phone off the hook."

It was but a few minutes before she drove up. Her short, brown hair waving with her movement, she immediately took charge, gathering us in the living room to plot strategy.

"The newspapers must be informed immediately; otherwise they will hear about it through the morgue and suspect that something strange has happened."

I was anxious that Phyllis's death not be reported as a suicide. The doctor had told me to say she had a bad bout with the flu before taking a trip to New York against his advice. This so weakened her system that her heart simply gave out. Whether or not it was true, no one would know until after the autopsy. At least in death we could shield her from the press which had hounded her in life. Frances agreed with this.

Then, looking about the room at the flowers, Guru Dev's portrait, and other signs of last night's happiness, Frances said, "As for your Maharishi, you must get him back to Los Angeles immediately. You had announced that he would be here three or four days. Well, this is the third day, so he will be returning on schedule. This has all the ingredients of a real juicy story—the society blonde, the mysterious Eastern holy man, the big mansion on the hill, owned by one of the city's leaders." I began to understand Friedl's reaction.

She turned her eyes on me with a sad smile. "You yourself are pretty good copy also, Nancy. The papers are not always interested in the facts. They can make a Rasputin out of Maharishi. They can insinuate wild parties, strange rites. Phyllis's death will be twisted to look like a mysterious suicide."

I understood what she was saying; I had to protect Maharishi. When we called Charlie Lutes to ask advice, he yelled across the line, "Get him on the first plane you can and I'll be there to pick him up. This is like sitting on a time bomb!" Five minutes later Tony called with the same warning and also to express his sorrow and shock over Phyllis's death.

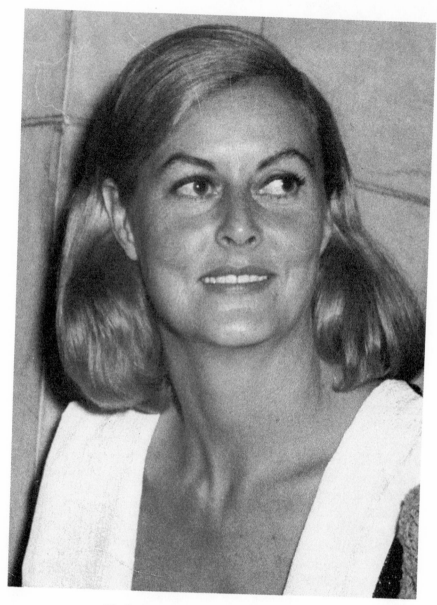

*Phyllis Frazer, 1965, just before she died*

Maharishi needed no explanation. He got the picture; every minute he stayed on in that house increased the likelihood that the newspapers would undo all the progress he had made in San Francisco. And they wouldn't stop there; if a scandal boiled up, meditation would be slandered across the U.S.A. As I put Maharishi's bag in order, he went to the living room to thank Friedl for her wonderful hospitality.

Shortly after we left, the first reporters arrived. At the airport I was allowed to drive directly out on the field and put Maharishi on board. I heaved a huge sigh of relief as the plane taxied out on the runway and Maharishi was safely away.

On returning to Friedl's house, much activity was evident. Cars jammed the driveway. Thank God my sisters arrived to help me. Ardagh Marie took one look at me and said, "You look dreadful; lie down and put up your feet while I get you some brandy—or you'll be the next to go."

She took over just in time; I never thought I was the fainting type, but now the initial shock of Phyllis's death took effect. While I lay on the couch, my other sister, Doryce, went upstairs and packed up Phyllis's things and also mine.

Knowing I would be needing a change of scenery, my sisters insisted on driving me across the Bay to Mother's house. I thanked Friedl as best as I could. I doubted I would ever forget her initial reaction to Phyllis's death. She expressed relief that Frances Moffat had handled the press so well, smoothing over suspicious clues. We left her standing on the porch. She was busy looking at a newspaper.

Crossing the Bay Bridge, I looked back—there stood the Klussman house as it always had, hanging out over the Bay. Nothing in its appearance had changed, yet it looked haunted to me after the nightmare which had occurred there.

Nestled in a little flowery dip in the Piedmont Hills, my mother's house provided sanctuary. In almost every way it was different from Friedl's. No corner lay bare. Everywhere I turned I saw the carved Victorian furniture I had known since childhood. On every tabletop and dresser sat little potted plants, surrounded by family portraits and knick-knacks, especially Mother's collection of porcelain pigs.

Daisy, a miniature gray Schnauzer, scampered about my heels, yapping for attention.

What comfort to have Mother's arms around me. Seeing the strain on my face, Mother invited me to join her in the kitchen while she fixed dinner. I had no appetite, but the bright room and the familiar little white table, cluttered with leftovers and fresh fruit, gave me comfort. Between mouthfuls and comments on new recipes, Mother threw in little questions, drawing the sorrow out of me bit by bit, and I talked and described the sad events.

When I finished, she again expressed her sympathy. Then she made a comment that disturbed me.

"I still don't see why Maharishi couldn't have helped her. Especially if he is supposed to be some kind of saint. Why didn't he get a warning of what was going to happen? After all, she was in the room next to him. She couldn't have been more than twenty feet away."

I didn't know what to say to that.

Later I tried to meditate, but it was no use. As soon as I closed my eyes, doubts and questions besieged me. "If saints bring people back to life in India, why couldn't he resuscitate Phyllis? She had only been dead a short while."

Then I remembered what Maharishi had said about healers while up at Lake Arrowhead. He believed in their feats, but did not choose to emulate them, saying it was not his way. To be a healer, he would have to concentrate all of his energies on healing; he had another mission. This provided me with ammunition.

I was able to beat off the first wave, but more doubts rushed up. Why couldn't he tell what was going to happen? If he had, we could have warned doctors and they might have saved her.

Indian tradition is full of stories of how great masters are able to announce the date and hour of their coming death. Didn't Maharishi tell us that six months before a person dies, a certain sound, a vibration, leaves his body? Holy men could hear this sound, and, when it fell silent, they knew how to make their plans to leave the earth. Guru Dev did this. So did Yogananda; a personal account could be found in his *Autobiography of a Yogi*. He called his followers together one day and said, "Take careful notes of my talk tonight." When he finished his speech, he sat down and his soul left his body.

Did the Cosmic scroll, which holds all knowledge, say that she was to die that night? Couldn't Maharishi have warned us? I thought of the many times we had seen Maharishi pause before answering a probing question. He would look off into space—we used to imagine that he was searching through some cosmic archives. Then he would turn and look directly at the questioner and give him a concise, profound answer. So what would be his answer?

Again I thought of Maharishi, sitting by the fire at Lake Arrowhead, as he explained, "The difference between a God and the most advanced soul is that even if the man can do everything, only God can do all things at once." I thought of his reply that in order to watch the health of his friends, he could do nothing else: "It would be like taking a cannon to shoot an ant." Again I turned back my doubts. Maharishi had never said a word about having any special powers.

But there was another doubt, one hard to admit to myself. It attacked me from within, threatening my belief in Maharishi and in TM. Phyllis had been initiated by Maharishi himself, the day before she lost all hope and wanted to sleep forever. How could it be? Maharishi often talked about how TM affects the nervous system immediately, starting from the first day to lessen tension, to help the meditator cope with the world. And now a new meditator, fresh after her initiation, had gone the other way. What could Maharishi say to that?

As I tried to blot out the picture of Phyllis in death, another face took form. I recognized the peaked burgundy hat and the wispy white beard of Lama Anagarika Govinda. I remembered our visit to Almora. I remembered asking him how one finds his guru. His answer had been, "He will be full of peace, harmony and understanding."

Yes, that was Maharishi.

"He will carry a mantle of purity, and possess limitless love and patience."

"A teacher gives knowledge, but a guru is more than that. A guru gives himself. As he goes beyond words, beyond the power of human speech, much of his real teaching will remain unspoken. He will act as an inspirer; he will infuse you with his own living spirit. Yet, with all this, a guru is still a human being. Whatever part of him is divine, look to that only, and do not be distracted by his weaknesses."

Once again Govinda had led me to Maharishi. Now I could see his luminous, laughing face. Maharishi never talked about himself, claiming that it was unimportant. It was only necessary to believe in him enough to try TM, and even if one did not completely understand it and had doubts, if one continued to do it consistently, it *would* prove itself. He often said, "You will have doubts about TM until the final stroke eliminating tension, the final step to Cosmic Consciousness, has taken place."

Love filled my sad heart. Yes, dear Maharishi, I will have my doubts about meditation, but I will try not to have them about you. I realized many painful tests still lay ahead.

Several weeks later the autopsy showed that Phyllis had died of an "overwhelming lung infection." Her lack of self-care had caused her destruction.

## 13

# Invading Catholic Territory

THE PHONE RANG. It was Charlie Lutes. "You still game to take on South America? Maharishi has just said he'd like to go."

The acceptance scared me. What a responsibility. "What do you think, Charlie, is a Catholic continent ready for an Indian holy man?"

"Probably be wise to present him as a famous philosopher; no sense in taking on the Church if it's not necessary," was his advice. "He would like to plan for the month of October; think that's a good time?"

"Perfect! It'll be spring; the weather should be lovely."

"What places should we include?"

"I suggest we visit Caracas, Rio, maybe Montevideo, Buenos Aires, Santiago, Lima, and Bogotá."

"Boy, that's a big trip. How long will it take?"

I counted, "About six weeks."

He gave me the go-ahead, and I started setting up a schedule. Luckily, my PR background and lecture series had trained me to direct this kind of promotion. Out went letters to friends for suggestions on how to best handle each city. Luckily, I had good connections with newspapers because of my previous good will trip. It took several months to select the proper hotels and lecture halls, arrange fees, and set up newspaper interviews—all the fine tuning that makes or breaks such a venture. I often wondered why I had opened my big mouth! It was like pulling teeth to get the information I needed. But by October, 1966, all was set.

Maharishi and Charlie were to go to Trinidad, while I went on ahead to Caracas to get everything ready for their arrival. I was to be the advance man—a new role for me.

Soon I was on the first leg of my trip. I settled into the plane seat as we taxied down the runway, destination, Caracas, Venezuela—a city made wealthy overnight by American oil companies. A city full of *nouveau riche*, not my favorite place, in spite of having many friends there. How would they welcome Maharishi? This would be our first big test.

The pretty, young flight attendant handed me a newspaper. The bold-faced headline jumped out at me, "Heiress Doris Duke Kills Friend." Oh my God, what now?—Did she shoot Joe? The article went on to say that Doris and her decorator, Eduardo Tirella, had driven to her home in Newport, Rhode Island. While he got out of the car to unlock the gate, she sat inside waiting. The car started to slip backwards, and Doris, in an attempt to stop it, reached her foot over to the brake and hit the gas pedal instead. The car lunged forward, crushing him against the gate. How horrible for Doris, to say nothing of her poor friend who was killed instantly.

As soon as we landed I would wire her and see if she could join us. Maharishi would and could help her. I wondered if she continued to meditate. I doubted it. Nature didn't seem to be giving her much support.

To calm my thoughts, I closed the paper to meditate, but thoughts of the trip ahead invaded my meditation. What were the best points to stress in South America? Would I be able to translate for Maharishi? My Spanish wasn't too good. Thank God, I could call on the Indian Embassies for translators.

As a personal favor, Ambassador B.K. (Biju, as I called him) Nehru, the Indian Ambassador to the United States, had notified the Embassies to help Maharishi and me in any way they could. B.K. had been a friend from my Hawaiian days, when he had passed through on his way as a delegate to the U.N. So, only because of a long-time friendship did he do this. He laughed, "Nancy, last time it was Goldwater you were stumping for, now a Swami. What next?" But it was important—it gave Maharishi needed credentials.

On arrival in Caracas, after sending a cable to Doris, to which we had no reply, one of the first persons I called was a distant cousin of my late husband, Renaldo Herrera, a handsome man, popular with the New York society press. He and his stunning wife, Mimi, were a constant source of news; they spent half the year in Caracas, and the other half in Manhattan. When I called him, he was bemused. "Nancy, why in the world would I ever be interested in meeting your Maharishi? What could he do for me?"

I threw out the bait. "Meditation is supposed to make a man more virile, my dear Renaldo."

"Well, by Jove, I guess I'll have to come meet this man after all."

In my next call, I mentioned the fact that Renaldo would be there, and the occasion began to assume a more attractive profile. With a few more strategic calls, we were assured of an audience the following night. A newspaper ad would also pull in a number of people.

Several curious members of the press were at the airport to meet Maharishi and Charlie the next morning. The photographers loved him. Pictures in the afternoon papers would help the lecture hall.

The journalists asked, "How do we address your friend? Does he have a title?" This startled me; we hadn't discussed it. "Oh, use his Indian title. 'Maha' means 'high,' and 'rishi' means 'sage,' so 'Maharishi' is what you should call him. If that proves too difficult, call him 'padre.'" It was best to stay away from His Holiness, His Reverence, or His Eminence— these were saved for the Pope.

Maharishi seemed so happy when he arrived. It made all the effort worthwhile. Charlie remarked, "He is radiant because he has left behind the heat, humidity, and low vibrations of Trinidad. He didn't like that place at all."

When Charlie asked me how things were going, I could only answer, "How can we know? It is open to the public; we won't know until they arrive."

"Well, let's hope we attract enough to help pay for expenses." At least they didn't have to worry about mine. My air fare, expenses, and expertise, such as it was, were my donation to Maharishi.

Nothing spectacular happened in Caracas. The lecture went well; there was a fairly good turn-out, and twenty-three people asked to be initiated. It was enough to cover expenses and leave the beginnings of a small center behind. But the experience helped us refine our presentation. Now we'd be better prepared for the big one, Rio de Janeiro.

As the Corcovado came into sight through my plane window, I felt a thrill as the immense statue of Christ sprang from the mountain top, dominating the entire city below. The sea was azure blue and green velvet peaks jutted up from the Bay of Rio de Janeiro—the most beautiful port city in the world. I could see the wide sweeping curve of Copacabana Beach where we would soon be staying.

I looked forward to this stop; again as the advance man, I had gone ahead. Pushing my way through the crowds of people at the airport, I heard my name called. "Nancy, over here. I'll wait for you outside the customs door." A tall, vibrant-looking man was waving his hands energetically to attract my attention. It was Teddy Badin, who had been looking forward to our visit with enthusiasm. He had answered my letters almost before they were written.

Soon we were in a boiling sea of Brazilian traffic. "You look terrific, as usual." Teddy was always good for one's ego. "How has the trip gone so far?" He didn't pause for my answer. "Everything is ready here; there is a big press reception planned at the hotel tomorrow morning, and some of them will also meet Maharishi at the plane. Your friend, George Guinley, is out of town, but he asked his manager, Señor Vasconsuelo, to assist you with anything you need at the hotel." That was good news. The world-famous Copacabana Hotel would be our headquarters for the next week.

"How do you think it is going to go over here, Teddy? Does there seem to be much interest?"

"Interest! Wow!" His American English burst through; of Lebanese descent, raised in Brazil, he was educated in the United States. "You have no idea what is going to happen." His excitement started to get to me. "As you know, I'm giving a cocktail party for you and Maharishi, and everyone has accepted and wants to bring a friend."

"But Teddy, Maharishi won't come to a cocktail party. When you mentioned the party in your letter, I thought you meant it was for me, as you have done in the past."

"Oh, my God," he reacted, "I have senators, generals, the heads of Rio's industries, and all sorts of prominent people coming; they are looking forward to meeting the Maharishi in person. Several columnists have already written about the party. I thought the more excitement, the better." Teddy was a complete Aries, the leaping flame. How could I resist him.

"Let's not worry about it. When we see Maharishi in the morning, ask him. If he says no, we can explain to everyone and ask them to meet him at the hotel." That seemed to pacify him at the moment.

"Fine. When he gets the picture, he'll agree to come. Here's the hotel. While you register, I'll park the car."

The hotel had Maharishi registered as Mr. Yogi, I liked it and let it stand. The staff was very obliging; they asked me to select the room for the lecture. "It's difficult to know how many seats we will need," I began, just as Teddy walked in and offered an optimistic suggestion.

"Take a room that can be opened up into another in case you get a pleasant surprise."

For ourselves, we were given large, old fashioned, high-ceilinged rooms overlooking the beach. Maharishi would be enchanted. From the window came the beat of a carnival tune, a perpetual sound in Rio. "I bet he'll like the vibes here," I thought. "The Brazilian people are friendly and warm; unsophisticated, they are not self-conscious about enjoying themselves."

The telephone was ringing as I walked into my room. "Mrs. Cooke, this is Ibrahim Sued from *Do Brazil;* I met you when you were here as the good will ambassador in 1958. Would it be possible to have an interview with you before the Maharishi arrives?"

How nice to be remembered. Also, the timing would be propitious.

His article would appear in the morning press, as Ibrahim was Rio's top columnist and would begin to generate immediate interest. I agreed to meet him a short time later. I had a good feeling about Brazil. Everything was going to go well here.

Early the next morning Teddy was there on the dot, not a characteristic of most Latins. The November sun washed over the beach, while natives slept on the sand rather than in their stuffy apartments. Young children ran along black-and-white mosaic sidewalks, pulling their large kites fashioned like huge birds. Persian blinds were still drawn on most of the hotel windows, housing fun-seekers from all parts of the world. As Rio is a city of nightclubs and entertainment, theirs was a world of late nights and later mornings.

At the airport, Teddy really poured it on; Maharishi had never been better received. He took to this energetic man immediately, and shook his head in agreement to everything Teddy suggested. The cocktail party, a voodoo ceremony, a television appearance with a yoga group. Charlie and I just sat back and grinned. Teddy's face beamed with joy.

Maharishi did make one request in regard to the cocktail party. "I will come later. Maybe you could open the windows and ask that there is no smoking or drinking while I am there. They can have their drinks before I come and after I go. Will that be all right?"

Teddy was ecstatic; Charlie couldn't believe that Maharishi was going to a cocktail party. "Now I've heard everything." I knew Maharishi was being obliging because he had taken such an immediate liking to Teddy.

"How do you think the government will react to this visit?" asked Charlie.

"Very well. They feel the church has too much power. They like it when people have something else to consider. There is a lot of spiritualism in Brazil, but many just pretend it doesn't exist. Our basic roots are from Voodoo and Macumba brought here from Africa. This is why I felt it would be interesting for you to be exposed to a Macumba ceremony."

Maharishi nodded, "We shall go." Things were happening fast.

The hotel received Maharishi as though he were a visiting king. That night we were off to a terrific start. The second room was opened and there was standing room only. The fun-loving Brazilians were happy to hear it was not necessary to give up their sensual pleasures in order to evolve spiritually.

Seated in front of the entrance door, I attempted to give people individual appointments for the next day. I was inundated by pushing people speaking Portuguese, a language only vaguely similar to Spanish. I finally called to Charlie for help. "This is impossible. How can we keep it straight?"

Charlie responded, "Forget it. Just tell them to come tomorrow when they wish and we will take care of them as fast as we can."

The next morning my phone rang insistently. What time was it? I answered with a sleepy voice.

"Señora, we need your help. There are over one hundred people here already to see Maharishi. We don't know what to do with them!" I glanced at my travel clock; it was just before 6:00 a.m.

Señor Vasconsuelo was in the lobby to meet me, surrounded by Brazilians of all ages, sizes, and dress, carrying fruit and flowers to present to Maharishi. He assessed the situation. "The hotel wishes to please you in every way, but with these crowds of people streaming in, the regular guests will complain." As he spoke, the crowd was growing. "If you will agree, we will gladly open the main ballroom and have them enter through the back entrance. If that is not enough, we will open the two adjoining ballrooms." By late afternoon all three ballrooms were in service.

No wonder there was such a rush; the papers were filled with the smiling face of the bearded guru. He was quoted on how to enjoy life two hundred percent, how one did not have to withdraw or give up desires. He had invited the Cariocas to come and learn how to live without suffering, and they did come, in droves.

It was a chaotic day we couldn't have handled without the help of the interpreter sent by the Indian Embassy. When personal friends of mine appeared, they were pressed into service. It was a rat race.

By the time the party took place that night at Teddy's, all of Rio was excited by the presence of the Hindu Philosopher.

It was a party that really took off.

The steady hum of almost two hundred talking people was heightened by the combo that played from a side alcove. Overlooking one of the numerous bays that make up the landscape of Rio, the Badin's eleventh floor apartment reflected the tastes of well-traveled people. Elegant and spacious, it was perfect for the party now in progress.

"Nancy." It was Vania, Teddy's beautiful, blonde wife. She twisted her lithe figure between the wall-to-wall guests to get near me. "Mirna just called. She said Maharishi will be here in twenty minutes. Teddy will make his announcement."

He did, as planned. "We are honored to have His Holiness Maharishi Mahesh Yogi with us tonight," he said, not afraid of offending his Catholic friends in the room by using the proper title. "It is a rare exception for him to attend such an occasion; so out of respect, we ask you to put out your cigarettes and to refrain from drinking while he's here. I guarantee the bar will open again for business after his departure." The guests chuckled, amused by the whole affair.

"For those of you who would like to meet the Maharishi personally, Vania has provided a vase with yellow roses in it. Please take one, as it is customary to honor an Indian holy man with a flower."

As the windows were opened, people took deep inhalations of smoke before extinguishing their cigarettes and gulped the remains of their drinks. Soon all was ready. There was an air of anticipation as we waited for Maharishi to arrive.

When he entered, the guests watched quietly as he was led to a blue satin couch. Charlie spread out his deerskin, and Maharishi sat down, neatly tucking his legs under him. He patted his large bouquet of red carnations into place on his lap.

For the next hour, one by one, the guests came forward to be presented by Vania. Some immediately retreated; others stayed to ask questions. The tinkling bell of Maharishi's laughter could be heard from time to time; he was obviously enjoying himself. A senator asked me about the lecture scheduled for the next night. He promised to be there. My close friend, Carlos Leal, South America's largest ship builder, was impressed by the holy man's logic. "He has a degree in physics," I explained.

"Ah, now it makes more sense," he responded.

The hour passed quickly, and then Maharishi was gone. The bar reopened, cigarettes were lighted, and everyone talked about the man they had just met, each holding in his hand the red carnation Maharishi had given. The Badin's guest of honor had captivated the party—he had told these affluent guests that man was expected to enjoy the fruits of his labor. He had offered them a way of maintaining their energies and success.

The next five days were like a joyous nightmare. As soon as one ballroom filled up, we would send a signal of distress to the front office. A bellboy would appear on the run with keys in hand and open the doors into an adjoining room. They were huge rooms mainly used during Carnival or for presidential occasions. The walls were decorated with ornate relief moldings and silk coverings, the floors were of inlaid parquet. I didn't dare think what these rooms rented for. We would just have to work out something when we went to settle the bill. Now there was no time to worry.

One morning I attended a meeting of the hotel executive staff. "We have already added six extra phone operators, and we still can't free the switchboard for our own guests."

"So far they are taking it with good humor and seem curious. Several of them were at the meeting last night," said the public relations man.

In five days, Maharishi initiated eight hundred people. He had no time to eat, practically living on water, honey and lemon juice, which we provided every four hours. His day started at sunup and ended after midnight, but he looked radiant, while the rest of us had deep circles of fatigue under our eyes. "Where does he get that energy, Charlie? It's as though he gets it from all the people."

"He has a different source than we do, Nancy. You can be sure of that." I was. I knew how I looked and felt.

One facet of Maharishi which I marvelled at was his patience. He went over the same material again and again. Each person felt the grace of his undivided attention during the brief moment they shared together.

I didn't feel that patient. Sometimes the pushing and shoving got to me. One night after the crowds had left, I asked, "Maharishi, are we really supposed to love everyone as Jesus said?"

He laughed, "No, no, feel compassion for them, but love is a spontaneous emotion; even Jesus had his favorites—remember John, the Beloved."

Actually, people were in good humor, waiting for hours without complaint. The atmosphere was full of happiness and gaiety. Maharishi was giving his all to Brazil.

One afternoon we had an appointment at a T.V. station, but couldn't extricate Maharishi from the crowd.

"Besides the television producer, it will be an insult to Teddy and the Indian Ambassador if we are much later." I decided to try to liberate our leader. It seemed I had no choice; I took hold of the deerskin, apologized to him and the crowd, announcing, "Sorry, but we have to go," and tipped Maharishi gently out of his chair.

Charlie almost died at my effrontery, but Maharishi agreed laughingly. "Nancy was right; it was the only way to get me out of there."

After the T.V. interview was over, we picked up the Indian Ambassador and headed for the mountains above Rio for the voodoo party. While in the car, Maharishi was approached with a request from His Excellency, the Ambassador; he wished to be initiated! I was delighted and looked forward to telling Biju Nehru. It would be a feather in our cap.

Teddy drove the big, black Mercedes fast but well; he was hurrying to make it on time. We had been climbing rapidly, and now the lights of Rio were coming on far below us. "This will be a very high class ceremony, Maharishi. I helped these people buy the property. This is not the low-down macumba-voodoo where they kill the chickens and throw the blood all around." I thought I felt Maharishi wince; I wondered if he knew what voodoo was.

Darkness was closing in; there were no more houses. At the top of a hill, Teddy turned down a road and pulled up to a white-washed wooden gate. A middle-aged woman wearing a long cape over a white robe-like dress stepped forward.

"It is an honor to welcome the Maharishi," she said, and knelt down. Soon a man dressed identically came forward and asked, "Would you accept this fresh nectar and then follow me."

While we enjoyed the guava juice, we observed an unusual sight. Inside the compound was a small village of white-domed houses, neatly laid out. One large temple with an onion-shaped cupola dominated the entire area. Soon two tiny girls, I guessed them to be about four, came forward to guide us to this temple, which was enclosed within a high, white plaster wall. They were dressed like nuns, complete with head-dresses, and covered from head to toe. Each carried a basket of rose petals, which they dropped on the ground in front of Maharishi's feet as he walked.

Stepping through the gate into the temple courtyard, we found ourselves in a setting that would have been perfect for Star Trek. The sand-covered ground was combed into a wave pattern; lined up on both sides of the path were a hundred people, all dressed in the same costumes as those who had first greeted us. They certainly looked affluent. Standing with arms crossed over their chests, no one uttered a sound as we passed into the temple.

Once inside, we saw the white-washed cupola was covered with esoteric symbols. Our guide pointed to them. "These illustrate the many paths to spiritual attainment, but then, you will know them, Venerable Swami." Maharishi smiled in silence. He was led around the circular room to a seat on a small platform, while we sat on benches that hugged the side walls. The rest of the floor was covered with gold cloth pillows which were soon used by the people quietly filing in from the courtyard.

Teddy whispered to us, "To keep the spirits from getting to you, don't cross anything." We sat like awkward dolls propped up against a wall.

"What about Maharishi?" I asked Charlie.

"Oh, don't worry about him. This is child's play to him." It was true, Maharishi looked serene and comfortable.

At one side of the temple was what appeared to be an altar with mannequins on both sides dressed in elaborate gowns. Soft music was piped in, and everyone sat at silent attention.

"We are waiting for the High Priestess to arrive," whispered our host.

Every head turned as she made her entrance. She was straight from a Buck Rogers comic strip of the thirties. Her middle-aged figure was a bit too full for the purple velvet gown, train and all. Her gold cape was covered with brilliant stones, as was the heavy metal crown she wore on her head. She was definitely of European extraction with her light complexion.

I nudged Teddy, "How come there are no dark-skinned people here?" Approximately ninety percent of Brazilians have some negro blood.

"This is a very exclusive community," he replied. So, they too have some prejudice, I thought to myself.

Standing behind the altar, the Priestess raised her arms and spoke. "She is welcoming Maharishi and asking the program to start," interpreted our guide.

The first part of the program involved incredible calisthenics, the Candomble. Several men danced, twirling long sticks so heavy that one tap would easily break a leg or arm. Another man called out the rhythm, and the pace became faster and faster. The twisting, turning bodies leaped and somersaulted, catapulting themselves under and over the dangerous poles. It reminded me of the whirling dervishes I had once seen dance in Egypt; they were inexhaustible. Only by being in a trance could the human body take such punishment.

With a blast of a whistle, the Priestess brought the dance to an abrupt end. Low, somber chanting started; the sound was impressive. The rhythm evoked an African atmosphere; and I thought of the heritage of Brazil with its thousands of black slaves brought by the Portuguese settlers. The singers swayed to the beat of their chanting. Now the Priestess began an incantation, raising her arms to the ceiling.

One at a time, the disciples filed in front of her. As each in turn faced her, she dipped her fingers into a bowl of water on her altar and with a zapping gesture flung her hands out, sprinkling the person, who then started whirling with the music.

"Now is when she will cast the evil spirits out," said Teddy. Soon the entire congregation was whirling, faster and faster.

"I will go and get exorcised," Teddy volunteered. "It will please her. You all remain here." I was feeling stiff. Oh, to just cross an arm or a leg.

We watched with curiosity as Teddy presented himself. Soon he was reeling with the rest. "Do you think he is pretending, or did she actually get to him?" asked Charlie.

The beat increased; the hall became warm with calories generated by the moving bodies. Soon, one by one, people began to sink to the floor from exhaustion, Teddy among them. When all was quiet again, the Priestess smiled with satisfaction and indicated that the ceremony was over.

Maharishi had remained very quiet; not a change of expression had come over his face to betray his inner thoughts. Now, the gathering turned to look at him. At the Priestess's request, he rose and congratulated her on the ability to bring joy to her followers by releasing them from the grip of negative spirits that had invaded them. This seemed to satisfy everyone. When asked to sign their book, he suggested, "Better I send you a small gift from India for your temple." With that he rang a little bell, and everyone laughed. I had the feeling it was his way of getting out of putting his name in their book.

In the car going back to Rio I asked, "Were there really spirits there?"

Maharishi answered, "Definitely, there were spirits, but what a hard way to get rid of them." He told Teddy it was an interesting experience; he gave the impression that once was enough. I felt the same way. It was too weird, and my back ached.

Our outing was over. Now it was time to get back to business. Maharishi and Charlie returned to the hotel. Teddy and I would join them at the meeting after a dinner we had planned with Vania, who was beginning to feel like a forgotten wife.

It was after 10:00 p.m. when we returned to the big lecture for all those who had been initiated during the past days. Including spouses, there appeared to be about a thousand people. We sat on the side of the platform where Maharishi was speaking.

"What a joy to look out over all your happy faces," he began. It had been a productive time for the Spiritual Regeneration Movement: all those new meditators and a central committee had been established to head up the new foundation. He had reason to feel pleased; my thoughts wandered during the closing speech.

Suddenly I was brought back to the present; a man came running from the back of the hall, "Don't listen to him! He is a fake! He is telling you nothing but lies!" It was the French yoga instructor who had been on the T.V. program with Maharishi that afternoon. He jumped up on the platform, grabbing the microphone stand from in front of Maharishi. Charlie and Teddy moved forward to stop him, but Maharishi signalled to let him continue. As the Frenchman raved on, he sat calmly running his hand down his coral beads.

After a few minutes the Frenchman ran out of steam and the crowd started to boo him. Maharishi stepped in and took over. He addressed the back of the man as he walked up the aisle away from the platform, "You should call yourself a professor of exercise. Yoga means 'union.' You will never achieve union with God just by twisting the body."

The audience applauded; then he defended the professor for speaking out his thoughts. Charlie, Teddy, Vania and I held our breath, praying; a crowd can be so easily swayed. At the end of the lecture, the crowd gave Maharishi a standing ovation. Charlie heaved a sigh of relief, "It was kind of touch-and-go there for a minute." Thanking our lucky stars, I bid everyone goodnight—I had had it.

Unlocking the door to my room, I could hear the telephone ringing. I was tempted not to answer it. Relenting, I picked up the receiver to hear an agitated voice. "Hello, hello, Señora Nancy, ah, I'm relieved to reach you. This is Vasconsuelo, the manager."

As if I didn't know. "May I speak to you candidly?"

"Of course, what is it?" My heart went into my stomach. He must have heard about the commotion in the lecture hall, and that was the final straw. We were about to be tossed out in the street. I listened, waiting for the axe to fall.

"I have watched very carefully what has been going on here; I admit that I was skeptical about the whole thing." I knew we were in trouble. He continued, "Now I am convinced there is something to this. Do you think there is a chance that Maharishi could initiate me before he leaves tomorrow?"

I couldn't believe my ears. He wasn't going to throw us out. He liked us. My words came out in a torrent. "Oh, yes, bring a handkerchief, some flowers, and some fruit. Come to my room right away, and it will be done before the hour is out!"

We had been saved.

The following day, before leaving, the hotel informed us there would be no charge for the use of the three ballrooms. Thank God for my friend George Guinley, the hotel owner! So, we were in good financial shape; we had a "kitty" in case things did not go well in Argentina.

Now my thoughts turned to our next destination—my former home, Buenos Aires. Each time I returned to Argentina, I played a different role. My first arrival in 1952 had been memorable. My mind went back in time. Luis and I, the bride to be, thousands of miles away from everybody and everything I knew, were held up by immigration authorities at the modern new airport Perón had built.

By the time we were released, there were no more taxis, so we took an airport bus. Cursing, Luis growled, "This is not exactly how I planned your first impression of Buenos Aires." Instead of being impressed by the beauty of the Paris of South America, I saw a gloomy, browned-out city. Luis explained, "Because of a power shortage, there is a curfew on unnecessary light. This is what happens when a fool like Perón decides to industrialize an agricultural country." He shook his head sadly. He agonized at the way a naturally wealthy country was being economically ruined. "After World War II, Argentina had enormous gold credits. At the request of the British, we stayed out of the war in order to get our neutral ships through the German U-boat nets to feed the British Army and Navy."

This had surprised me. "Why does the press make Argentina out to be pro-German?"

"Lack of knowledge. Thousands of Jews were also given sanctuary here. But because we were neutral, the Germans also sought refuge for themselves and their money. It works both ways, doesn't it? Now this magnificent country is being robbed by a band of thugs, who know nothing about economic law."

Then in 1959, four years after Luis's death, I returned alone, but this time as the Ambassadress of Fashion. It was a good way to return. I had been apprehensive that the frightening grief would return when I was once again in the city where my husband and I had shared such happiness. But the days were so active that I had little time to wrestle with the past, except during my visits to Luis's grave.

Now, in 1967, I was returning with an Indian holy man, my guru. What a lot of curiosity that would excite. There would also be a natural sympathy toward him from my friends, for having brought me spiritual peace. They remembered the terrible moments my children and I lived through after Luis's death. Also, they would meet my husband Tony, who had decided to spend a week there with us.

I prayed all would go well—Argentines can be very critical. I was putting my own credibility on the line. The meetings were well attended—Máximo Gainza, an old friend and the publisher of La Prensa, the world's largest Spanish newspaper, had made sure we got good coverage. Many priests and nuns came. I queried a Catholic friend about this. His bright, black-Irish face showed amusement. "What could be more natural? Don't they show by their vocation that they are interested in philosophy and religion?" Many of my friends came forward to be initiated, besides a good number of others. So, Argentina was considered a success.

The same was true for Santiago de Chile; Lima, Peru; and Bogotá, Colombia. Everywhere, friends came forward to help. Centers were started and we promised to send initiators and checkers as soon as possible.

One day, as we were preparing to do a bit of sightseeing in Bogotá, Maharishi turned to me. "Nancy, I think you should return to India with me and become an initiator."

I was thrilled. In those days, only a selected few were invited to take the teacher's course in India at the ashram. I was dying to become a teacher; Maharishi said that initiating new meditators is a rapid form of spiritual evolution and also of raising the initiator's level of consciousness. But I had to be realistic. "Oh, Maharishi, you have made me so happy. What an honor. But I have been gone a long time from my family. Could I come next year and take the course then?" He understood and it was agreed upon.

I was walking on air as we stepped out into the sunlit plaza. "It is the big religious holiday, El Día de Los Muertos (The Day of the Dead). It might be interesting to visit the Cathedral. Have you ever been in a Catholic church, Maharishi?"

He had not; Charlie agreed it would be a new experience for him.

It was a beautiful old church, built by natives under the supervision of the Spanish conquistadors, full of gold, silver and religious artifacts.

Mass was being held as we quietly entered the church, so we tried not to attract attention. This was a bit difficult, with our friend in his white robes, beard, and carrying flowers.

*With Charlie Lutes and Maharishi in Bogotá, Colombia, 1967*

"What are the little houses for?" Maharishi asked, pointing at the confessionals.

After my explanation he expressed surprise. "They are then forgiven for their actions? What about the reaction? Didn't Jesus say, 'reap as you sow'?" I agreed; it didn't make sense to me.

He surveyed the high, vaulted ceilings and richly ornamented walls. Proceeding further into the main part of the building, he saw the life-size statues over the altar; they had been hidden until then by tall columns. The statues depicted the crucifixion of Christ with all its gore. Blood gushed from His head where the thorns sank in, also from where the nails had pierced His hands and feet.

"How terrible. What a thing to put in a church!" was Maharishi's reaction. "Do they allow small children to see such things?" By now, every head in the church was turned in our direction, even the priest's.

"I think we'd better leave," I suggested. Taking his arm, I led him towards the entrance while he filled his eyes with the strange sights.

As we passed a group of black-veiled women on their knees, lighting candles, saying their novenas, and wiping away tears, Maharishi took a long look. We stepped out the door. "Oh, Charlie, we must help these poor people." This was his reaction to what he had witnessed in the Catholic church.

"Why do they instill people with fear by having sights such as those? Don't they know that God is full of love? Do they feel that as the Son of God, Jesus could have felt pain? If the Son of God can suffer, what chance does ordinary man have? There is a big misunderstanding there." He was very perplexed.

Our six-week tour finally came to an end. We returned to Los Angeles without a stop-over in Mexico City, as Maharishi's visa did not come through. He greeted the approximately five hundred people who had come to L.A. airport to welcome him. "Our trip was a great success. We have gained a whole continent!"

The world was beginning to hear about Maharishi. A month following our return, Charlie sent over an article for me to read. "Let me know what you think of the description of our trip to Brazil."

Written by the French yoga instructor, the article was filled with distortions. "A tall, blonde American woman, traveling in the entourage of the Maharishi, badgered the people about their donations; forcing weeping women to part with their last few cruzeiros. They were strictly interested in those who had the most money to give," read the paper. I thought of the donations—some were under the equivalent of 25 cents in American money.

It continued, "When their baskets were full, they left for Argentina, richer by thousands of dollars at the expense of the Brazilian people." It was a long article, taking each of us apart in turn.

"What are you going to do about all those lies, Charlie?"

"I will write an answer to the paper and ask them to publish it—other than that, what can we do? Maharishi says to forget it."

# PART TWO

*Reaching For The Stars*

## 14

# The Bumpy Road To Cosmic Consciousness

THINGS WERE BEGINNING TO SNOWBALL for Maharishi. Speaking engagements and articles on him appeared in national magazines. In the late summer of 1967, about six months after we returned from South America, the news broke that the Beatles were with Maharishi in Bangor, Wales. Their manager, Brian Epstein, had died suddenly and the group was devastated. George Harrison's wife, Patty, had attended several of Maharishi's lectures in London and convinced the young men to hear him. The papers reported that they were all on a retreat together. I called Helen, "Have you heard the news about Maharishi and the Beatles?"

"Oh yes, Charlie talked to Maharishi yesterday. He said they are such nice young men. He thinks they should come to Rishikesh when he returns to India. I think they're considering it."

I thought of my plans to take off right after the Christmas holidays to participate in the three-month course. "Maybe they will be there when we are."

"I don't think he wants anyone to know their plans, in order to insure them privacy; they'll probably have come and gone before you arrive."

Oh well, it was an exciting thought; and it still could happen.

A week later, *Life* magazine featured a centerfold, in color, of Maharishi sitting in the middle of the Beatles and their wives. I called Helen back. "I'd like to take that article and personally shove it down that *Time* magazine manager's throat."

In the weeks that followed, stories mushroomed in the press about "the Beatles' Guru." The Beachboys, the Rolling Stones, The Doors, and other artists started to take an interest in TM. My phone rang constantly—friends demanding to know more about the subject we had tried so hard to tell them about previously. Now it was "in." Would I become their teacher when I returned from the course.

Before I knew it, fall was over and the time arrived for my return trip to India. I got butterflies every time I thought about it. Even though Tony approved, Mother, who had always supported me in my desires, was dead set against it.

"You have no right to leave your family and go off to such a remote place for so long. What if you get sick, which is likely considering the primitive conditions you'll be living in?" She was primarily worried about my well-being. On the other hand, the rest of my family were encouraging me to go. The boys were away at school, and María Luisa would stay with my sister, Doryce, in Piedmont. Mercedes, our house-keeper, would take care of Tony and run the house.

Helen, who had taken the course the year before, gave me advice. "It gets cold! Take thermal underwear, a long, padded robe in which to meditate, and heavy walking shoes. Hot water bottles will be available in New Delhi." One would have thought I was going to Antarctica.

My doctor gave me a list of medications to take care of emergencies. At night I lay awake and wondered, "Am I doing the right thing? Can I stand up under the living conditions such as I had seen in Rishikesh?" Several times I came close to canceling out, but I knew I'd be disappointed in myself if I did. I remembered the crude living quarters for the students at Sivananda's Vedanta Forest Academy.

There was no concept of physical sanitation. Toilets were holes in the ground with a foot pedal on either side. It would take a strong nose as well as spiritual desire to live in most ashrams, and one would have to take extreme precautions to avoid dysentery. There were no medical facilities closer than Dehra Dun, an hour and a half away. Not to mention the cold and dampness.

But then I would weigh my doubts against the opportunity of having all that time with Maharishi. Our conscious levels, the only thing we take with us at the time of death, would certainly be elevated by three months of long meditations. The spiritual tug was there, and Tony understood. Most of his energy went to his law practice anyway.

One day, shortly before departure, Charlie dropped some news, "That actress, Mia Farrow, and her sister, Prudence, will also be at the ashram."

I was aghast. "How is it possible for non-meditators to join us? Won't that affect the level of the whole group?"

Charlie assured me, "They are going only as guests, not as potential initiators. Maharishi feels they will attract good publicity." In addition, the rumor persisted that the Beatles were coming to the ashram. Maharishi, however, would not comment. It seemed we were going to have a mixed cast.

Several times I got down on my knees and prayed that I was doing the right thing in going. I worried about my daughter. She had no father and had never felt close to Tony. She was still young enough to very much need a mother. My sister assured me she would be fine at her home, the boys were all away at college, but I still hesitated. Then Genie McLean asked if she could also attend the course. I was able to get special permission from Charlie. She would not become a teacher, but would take the course, as a guest, like Mia and her sister. The fact that I had a friend going with me made Mother happier.

Then it was take-off day—as I kissed the family goodbye, María Luisa and the boys repeated, "Remember, Mother, if the Beatles are there, you must write everyday and give us every detail!" I had the famous group to thank for making my departure easier.

It was January 20, 1968, when the Pan American plane circled New Delhi before landing. The sky was black, but below us the capital of modern India was a blaze of lights. The city was ready for a week's celebration of Independence Day on January 26. What a sensational welcome back to India! Excitement engulfed me as we prepared to land.

In the poorly-lighted night, as the plane came to a stop, I could see raggedly-clad figures carrying trays of earth on their heads to a nearby runway, which was under construction. It was like being projected a thousand years back in time. As we waited for our luggage to appear, the pungent smell of India assailed my nostrils. Everything seemed familiar as six years fell away and India welcomed my return.

"*Memsahib*, are you Nancy Cooke?" a frail, dark-complexioned young man asked. "Mr. Khanna has sent me to take you to your hotel."

This was comforting. Tom Slick's old friend, Gautam Khanna, the managing director of the Oberoi Hotels (and that means most of the best ones in India) also owned the travel company, Mercury Travel, which sent the car to meet us.

Relaxing in the back seat, I said to Genie, "Well, we've made the first part of the trip." Our luggage, which seemed especially dear to us with all its carefully selected items, was intact, and now a room awaited us in a brand new hotel—not the Imperial this time.

Soon we were driving down Embassy Road. It was encouraging to identify to Genie such old friends as Germany, Italy, and Sweden. There was the widely-publicized architecture of the U.S. Embassy, designed by Edgar Stone shimmering white under flood lights. Across the road stood the USSR's, looking severe and unwelcoming. A bit further down we passed the British Embassy; how different from the days of the British Raj when Calcutta was the proud capital of the subcontinent.

"We are here, *Memsahibs*. This is Oberoi Intercontinental."

A huge, modern hotel, partially designed by my friend Piloo Mody, stood there. Its well-lighted porte-cochère was full of cars and smartly dressed bellboys in wine-colored jackets, carrying luggage. There were tall, Sikh doormen dressed in Mogul costumes with high, four-pleated headdresses, and ladies in bright-colored saris. All seemed familiar and lively. Through a wall of swinging glass doors, I could see the marble floors of the huge lobby with a fountain playing in the middle.

"This way, *Memsahibs*, to Mercury Travel. Mr. Kohli is waiting for you." Mr. Avi Kohli turned out to be a young man with beautiful, humorous dark eyes. In a soft voice he inquired about our trip and welcomed us on behalf of Mr. Khanna, who had to be out of the city. Soon we were on a first name basis. "Anything you need, you are only to ask," Avi pointed out in perfect Oxford English.

"What I really need after a good night's rest is to find Maharishi Mahesh Yogi. Do you know him?" Did I detect a hint of a smile? Most Indians laughed at us foreigners who came to their country to study under a guru.

"No, but I will certainly look forward to meeting him," he replied politely. "Tomorrow we will find out if he is in the city."

Our carpeted bedroom was comfortable and inviting. It looked out over the Delhi golf course. Later, while relaxing in a warm bath, I thought to myself how comforted Mother would feel if she could see me now.

Tomorrow came quickly, and so did the next day and the next, but no word from or about Maharishi. While Genie rested, I spent the time seeing Indian friends and making new ones. It was nice having a few days on my own. A visit to Connaught Circle, at the suggestion of Avi, produced many of the necessary items for Rishikesh—a flashlight, wire hangers, soap, canned butter and cheese, peanut butter, cookies, jam, powdered milk, instant coffee and tea. Memories of my previous trip to the Himalayas helped me prepare for whatever conditions lay ahead. Daily I felt more confident that all would be well.

Then one day Avi informed me that Maharishi had arrived. "Mia Farrow and her sister, Prudence, have come with him and are here in the hotel. Is Mia some sort of movie actress?"

"Yes," I said, and nothing more. "Did you find out where Maharishi is staying, as well as the others in the group?"

Avi answered, "Let's go to the YMCA. That seems to be headquarters for the moment."

The YMCA was stark in contrast to the Intercontinental. It was cold, clean and functional. The price was right, but most members of the group were traveling on little money and were already worried about the extra days' expenses. Young and old, they consisted of an assortment of eager students from twenty different countries. Many had arrived on a Syrian-chartered flight from Germany and already some of the younger men and women seemed to have paired off. Tom, an unknown Hollywood actor, had found a pretty, frail-looking blonde with big blue eyes. Larry, dark and unshaven, was an aggressive PR man from New York. Hilda and Ingrid were straight from Norway with their sensible walking shoes. Sudad was a Christian from Lebanon, while Annalei was a Hindu from Sweden. The largest delegation came from Germany. It was a friendly group.

"Have you any news of Maharishi?" we were asked from all sides. "When do we go to the ashram? Who is going to pay for all these days in the city? We were told we would only be in New Delhi one night."

Taking responsibility for our words, we assured them that Maharishi had arrived from Europe and would probably make an appearance at any moment. Positive input was needed.

Morale was running low, especially amongst the older members. Maharishi had better appear soon, or his group of fifty-odd would start to dissipate. The younger ones didn't seem too concerned. They were in India and had already discovered the delights of the bazaars, evidenced by their clothes.

So it was for me; each day was a delight. I spent hours perusing the Tibetan stalls, shacks barely substantial enough to be called shops, which lined Jan Path, Delhi's main shopping road. One shop owner remembered me from six years before.

"You're the lady who had the audience with His Holiness, the Dalai Lama." Her cheeks were bright red from berry juice; her long hair hung down in a broad pigtail. Around her neck were necklaces of coral and turquoise, the sacred stones of Tibet. Over her long, black robe was tied a colorful brocade apron. "You bought a Tibetan dress, hat, and boots from me in Dharamsala."

"You are right—how amazing. That costume has been shown to thousands of Americans. Do you live in Delhi now?" I asked.

"Only during the tourist months, then I go back to the hills."

As a people born to the mountains, Tibetans hate the heat of the plains, but they are great merchants.

Her store exhibited all sorts of bright, stone necklaces, bronze figurines, oil lamps, religious artifacts, wall hangings, thangkas—such a feast for the eyes. There were thirteen such stalls, each more tempting than the last. Further down Jan Path is the government-run Cottage Industry Shop, which assembles artisans' work from all parts of India. Every price is marked, so one can be assured of not being cheated; but the excitement and fun of bargaining is lost.

While wandering down the street, pleas came from merchants. "Please, Madam, come into my shop. You don't have to buy, just look." A turbanned old Sikh with a flowing white beard coaxed, "Mother, you have very good luck, the stars have big surprises for you. I will tell your fortune." Small beggars tugged at one's skirt, their grimy hands out, "Memsahib, baksheesh, baksheesh." Traders, with their wares spread out on the earth, vied for attention. My eye was caught in every direction by shimmering silks and intricate, hand-decorated fashions of all descriptions. Bronze locks and peacock feathers were thrust in front of my face. All was noise and smell—pungent odors of incense and dung prevailed. Cars, bicycles, and three-wheeled taxi scooters whizzed by.

I was so happy to be back in India. What was it about this land that made me feel this way? I was so at home. Maybe I had been an Indian in my past lifetime.

On January 26, I decided to see the Independence Day parade.

B.K. Nehru had said, "If you never see another parade, see that one." It meant getting up at 5:00 a.m. to meet Avi, but it was worth it.

What a spectacle! Camels, elephants, grenadiers, warriors from Nagaland and tribal peoples from all parts of India appeared in their distinctive costumes. The elite Bengal Lancers astride their black horses, mounted on tiger skin saddles, a tradition from the past, contrasted sharply with the modern men and women marching by in colorful, uniformed regiments, followed by column after column of heavy artillery and war machines. It seemed a paradox that they passed in front of Mrs. Indira Ghandi, the Prime Minister and daughter of Jawaralal Nehru, the devotee of neutrality and passivism.

The famous fighting men of Nepal, the Gurkhas, got a special hand from the cheering half million people as they marched in front of the honored guests, Marshall Tito of Yugoslavia and Mr. Kosygen of the USSR. Then came the planes. British and French jets led the way, but the big display was put on by Russian MIGS aircraft. Wave after wave flew past, dipping their wings. The U.S. was not represented in any way. "We could have at least sent a smiling Hubert Humphrey," I thought to myself.

The next day Maharishi finally appeared. By that time many of my Indian friends had expressed a desire to meet him. However, as time was scarce, only a few had the opportunity. One was S.K. Roy, Director General of Tourism. His comment, "But Maharishi, what India needs is more food, more production, not more religion," brought Maharishi's answer.

"No, no. You will never get production out of unproductive people. Only when they have energy will they become productive. Correct meditation will give people energy and then they will no longer put up with the mess India is in."

Another was V.C. Shuckla, then the Home Minister of Internal Defense. He had several other MP's come with him, and all left impressed by the wisdom of their countryman. Shuckla was to help Maharishi often in the months to come.

Finally, on the morning of the 29th, we prepared to leave for the ashram. All the gripes and complaints disappeared. On Avi's advice, I had rented a station wagon to take Genie and our precious belongings. Having traveled with Maharishi's groups before, I had little faith in their organizational ability.

At 9:00 a.m. the buses were assembled and ready to go. Then we waited. We waited for six hours because Mia and her sister were not ready to go. It was three o'clock when we took off. The two girls were put in a special car to themselves, and Maharishi followed in the last. Later I found out that all their expenses—hotel, plane tickets, and special cars—were picked up by the organization. Why did he find them so special?

So much extra luggage had been piled on, our station wagon could hardly move. We looked like a broken-down bunch of Oakies with our entourage of two old buses, covered with painted flowers, and our assortment of trucks and cars. But at last we took off. We were on our way to save our souls and those of the world.

One gets a true glimpse of Indian life by the roadside, if you are brave enough to take your eyes off the road as your driver pushes through bullock carts, bicycles, *tongas* (which are passenger carts usually drawn by emaciated horses), cows, and the mass of humanity. We passed village after village consisting of open-air markets, barber shops, dung factories (Indians make fuel from animal droppings), restaurants, repair shops, and businesses of all descriptions in small three-sided shacks.

Everything was in motion or else in a state of complete chaos. Constantly occupied with their little jobs, using any method of making the few rupees a day it takes to stay alive, Indians are an active people.

One large town was closed and under martial law. Bricks lay in the streets patrolled by soldiers, evidence of a two-day battle between Moslems and Hindus. Our driver observed that the communists incite each side against the other.

Often when we stopped at a railroad crossing, Maharishi would check to see if everyone was comfortable. He had his assistants buy oranges and bananas to pass out. He was working on housing charts on the way. As I spoke to him through the car window, he said, "We will put Nancy in the celestial blue room which Mother Olsen had." That was encouraging.

Also, he suggested I introduce myself to the Farrow sisters. Mia's first remark to me was, "Oh, you make me feel very secure and at home, seeing you in your nice suit and earrings and all." I really felt like a square.

About 125 miles northeast of Delhi, in the state of Uttar Pradesh, one passes miles of sugar cane and fertile green land. Antiquated means of farming were the rule. Water was taken from the wells in buckets as oxen slowly plodded around, supplying power. Women then carried their share on their heads in glistening brass containers. I admired their erect posture. Bullocks passed with loads three times their size. Everything was overloaded to the breaking point, whether it was a *tonga* with double the allowance for passengers, or a truck or bus. We were right in style.

Darkness fell by the time we reached Hardwar, the holy city thirteen miles below Rishikesh, where Tom and I had interviewed the "Ice Yogi." I felt his loss as we had our first glimpse of the Ganges. Lining the river were temples and bathing platforms, or *ghats*, giving a ghostly appearance in the faded light. The narrow streets are lined with dingy open shops selling *puja* artifacts, holy beads, candles, sari materials and foods.

Open sewerage ran alongside the broken sidewalks. Maybe it was just as well that it was nighttime and we couldn't see too well.

The forests started and the river disappeared.

Our driver pointed, "Ahead are the hills of the Valley of the Saints." I felt a thrill, half of happiness, half of fear, as they loomed in the distance. We were almost there.

Maharishi's ashram, the International Academy of Meditation, and Sivananda's Academy are only two of the many religious schools situated in the Valley. Dozens of India's most revered holy men attract disciples to come here to learn the ancient Vedic traditions. These sages keep the modern world out, preserving the primitive character of the area. Meat and eggs are banned, women dress in traditional fashion, and the only arrivals are pilgrims or spiritual disciples.

But it is primarily the water that renders the valley spiritual. Rishikesh is the last civilized outpost, closest to the headwaters of Mother Ganga, and there India's sacred river runs pure and clear.

That winter of '68, the ferry boats ceased at 6:00 p.m., so our entourage, instead of going into Rishikesh, went a mile further north to Laxman Jhula, where a British-built suspension bridge spanned the Ganges. As we emerged from our vehicles in the darkness at 10:00 p.m., the wind and cold of the mountains greeted us. Everyone quickly put on the sweaters and coats that were available. A ragged bunch of porters disappeared into the dark with our luggage. One had to have faith— there was no way to keep track of anything. In order to get to the bridge, we had to go down a steep stairway of over fifty steps. It was then that we discovered we had only two flashlights for 56 people! It was a miracle that we all made it without a tumble.

The bridge swung back and forth in the wind as we crossed over; I was glad I couldn't see the river far below. Maharishi was the last to cross. He was clad only in his thin silk robes. It was like entering a dark void, but, walking cautiously, we trailed behind the porters—negotiating a twisting, rock-covered path through a forest—the last two miles to the ashram.

After the dismal buildings we had seen on the other side of the river, our destination point looked inviting. The ashram manager had decorated the gates with flowers, flags, and a welcoming banner that proclaimed, "Jai Guru Dev." There were trees everywhere, a few decorated with strings of colored lights, adding considerable cheer to the stone bungalows.

Although it was almost eleven o'clock, a crowd of people from Swargashram, the small village adjacent to the ashram, waited to bow, greet, and present Maharishi with flowers. Uttar Pradesh is one of India's poorest states and the people reflected it. They were dressed in pitifully meager clothing for the cold night; nevertheless, they rejoiced in seeing Maharishi, who greeted them like a father returning to his family. Although some of the holy men in the valley resented Maharishi's flaunting of tradition in his secularization of meditation, the townsfolk loved him. They benefitted from the jobs and money he brought into the area.

Led to the kitchen compound to have something hot to eat and drink, we were introduced to Mr. Suresh, the manager. He welcomed us in a soft, friendly voice. "Please bear with a few inconveniences, as things were not quite ready for you." He then read out the room assignments which Maharishi had prepared on the way, after which I went off to find my luggage amid the confusion, eventually dragging it down to the bungalow myself.

As I looked at the two cement rooms that were to be my home, my spirits sank. One really had to be dedicated to come here. The pale "celestial blue" paint which had covered the rooms was cracked and peeling. The windows were spattered with putty and strung with cobwebs. "And we're expected to sit in these rooms and meditate?" My bathroom was particularly damp and loathsome: the toilet, a platform with a handcarved toilet seat covering a hole below, was reached by first walking through the shower. The meager furnishings included a small table and a board bed, on which lay a towel and blanket. At least I didn't have to sleep on nails. I lighted three candles to supplement the weak bulb. The scanty electricity rendered the old heater ineffective.

Putting on my thermal underwear, I took a medicinal drink of Scotch, and thanking God for inspiring me to bring a cozy down sleeping bag, went to bed. Like Scarlett O'Hara, I would think about it tomorrow. I had left my comfortable home in Beverly Hills to come here. I was where I wanted to be. My spiritual fervor would now get a good testing.

---
## 15
---

# The Valley and Its Saints

THE FOLLOWING MORNING WE GATHERED FOR BREAKFAST. The dining area consisted of tables and chairs arranged under trees near the primitive kitchen building. We were a sorry-looking group of future advocates of meditation, wrapped up to our chins in blankets. We looked more like escapees from a chain gang. Snow had fallen just north of us the night before, and it was damp and foggy. We were still shivering from the clamminess of our blocks.

As we sipped hot drinks and ate oatmeal porridge, we exchanged descriptions of our quarters. One girl had several inches of water across her entire floor and had to bed in with another friend. Dripping pipes, broken windows, and dirty rooms seemed to be the common complaints. I remembered Helen Lutes's comment, "Nothing really gets done until Maharishi arrives there."

But soon the fog lifted and the view was spectacular. The dining area looked out over the river and the entire Valley of the Saints. Mountains surrounding the area on three sides emerged. The location was dramatic. High on the hill, the ashram was down-river from the little town of Rishikesh; we would see the city lights by night.

Inside the ashram compound, six blocks of rooms nestled together on one side, with the big lecture hall, the dining room, and the caves

*Rishikesh across the river*

*Nancy on main street in Rishikesh*

*Maharishi and Nancy*

*Maharishi teaching with Divendra in Rishikesh*

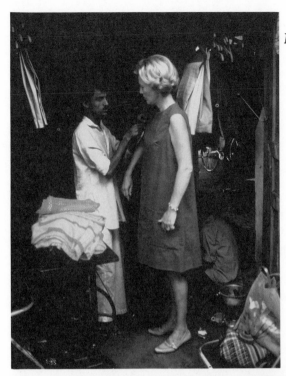

*Nancy having clothes made in Rishikesh*

*Nancy leaving her "block" at the ashram after doing her laundry in a bucket, 1968*

completing the half circle. (The caves are inhabited during the hot, Indian summer. Classes meet on top of them during the other seasons.) Between the buildings was a park with trails marked out by stone borders.

Surrounding the compound were beautiful forests filled with lacy, delicate teak trees that harbored an abundance of wild life—peacocks, crows, vultures, parakeets, monkeys, chipmunks and occasional cows. In addition, pythons, cobras, and wild elephants frequented the vicinity. Maharishi had little trouble discouraging us from wandering outside. We would be content with the fourteen acres the ashram afforded us for stretching our legs.

Maharishi was distressed to hear that his orders concerning our comforts had been ignored. He had asked that all rooms have plenty of blankets, candles, buckets, and heaters; but I gathered this was always the case at the beginning of a course. He set out to correct the situation, inviting merchants to come over from Rishikesh. They spread out their wares on the ground for us to select rugs, mirrors, saris, and other useful goods. The choice was limited, but we all found things to make our rooms a bit more cozy.

Many course participants contented themselves with pulling their beds into the middle of the room and leaving things as they were. On the other extreme, I was the nester. Without asking permission, I slipped away, crossed the river, and shopped in the little shacks lined up along Rishikesh's dusty main street, buying a variety of colorful, cheap cotton bedspreads, grotesque carpets, pillows, posters, religious calendars, and pots to put plants in. Also among my treasures were hooks, nails, and cleansing powder.

The ashram carpenter first hung my mirror at an angle for me. Three attempts later it was straight. The electrician brought another electric heater, saying "As soon as we string a second line across the river, we'll have enough current to use these." Everyone seemed anxious to please, but their world was so primitive. They had no idea of Western comforts.

Working non-stop, I brought about a complete transformation by the second evening. The peeling walls were now covered with the figured cloth. While working on this I almost had an accident. As I was pushing tacks into the moldy wall, a big spider popped out from a crevice and I almost fell off the table. I hate spiders! Then I had a decision to make—in this holy setting was it proper to take life? With my shoe I decided—there was no way I was going to meditate with that creature.

I sent him on to his next life. Hooks held my coats and robes, which added a touch of splendor. Tablecloths covered the desk and bed. The swan carpet was hung as a back to the bed, another carpet, which had been purchased from the merchants Maharishi invited to the ashram, covered the floor, and several more chairs scrounged from the ashram, completed the furnishings. Family pictures graced the walls and the three shelves were filled with my food stocks from Delhi. My rooms looked like a gypsy tent, junky, but cozy. Later on some of the students referred to my little suite as the "Park Avenue apartment." On several occasions when we had guests stay at the ashram, Maharishi asked me if they could use my rooms, and I would move out.

During this period of knockdown, Maharishi was on a constant tour of inspection. Within a week, the ashram had a different look to it, and so did the students. A miserable looking group on arrival, we were now colorfully dressed in our new Indian garb. Men grew beards rather than shave with cold water. We carried blankets, pillows, and hot water bottles to morning and evening classes to fend off the cold. We marvelled at the Bramacharis, celibate disciples who wore little more than thin robes, and the laborers, who wore only a thin layer of dirty rags. Warmer afternoons saw most of the classes held outside under the trees.

Gradually, the cool mountain air of the Valley refreshed us and provided the quiet that promotes good meditation. It was necessary to purify our nervous systems in order to become teachers of meditation. Maharishi had brought us to this exotic yet pristine environment to facilitate that process.

After getting our physical needs attended to, Maharishi gathered us together in the lecture hall to outline the structure and purpose of the course. The drafty lecture hall easily held two hundred chairs. Its dung floor was covered by a mat, and its whitewashed walls were plain except for a few posters. Birds had built nests in the high ceiling and flew from one open window to another. On the raised stage was a gold-covered sofa for Maharishi in front of a large portrait of Guru Dev. A few potted plants had been placed alongside. Warmly covered by blankets, we sat in the hall and listened as our teacher unfolded his plans for us.

According to Maharishi, "Ignorance of the mechanics of life, in the cosmic sense, is the cause of all suffering. Because man has failed to develop his potential, he suffers." Our guru was going to disclose his immense span of knowledge in daily lectures which would meet two or three times a day for the first month. At the same time, we would gradually increase our hours of meditation. Later, in order to slowly bring our conscious level of comprehension higher, so that we could absorb Maharishi's knowledge, we would have six intense weeks of almost total meditation.

I thought of Maharishi's illustration of this point, "Water in a lake will not try to get out, but if a pipe is put alongside at water level, the water will naturally flow out. This is what a master does with his pupils. They cannot take knowledge from him, he must raise their conscious level so that his knowledge will flow to them."

Only when we understood the mechanics of creation could we become teachers of meditation. We would try to create a society based on the support of life by nature. A big task.

After the meeting I went to Maharishi's house, as we had not yet talked in private. His house was set off from the other buildings, situated on a cliff overlooking the Ganges. His gardens were well tended and fenced to ward off stray cows. Unlike the rest of the ashram, Maharishi's house had had the benefit of an architect. One story, Indian style, with a veranda running around it, the building was cared for. It was screened, painted, varnished, and had polished stone floors. Maharishi had built it with the funds donated by Doris Duke. Stories had frequently appeared in the press about huge fortunes gleaned away from misled followers and hidden in secret Swiss bank accounts, but the little house at the ashram was the first luxury in which I saw Maharishi indulge himself.

While others waited to see him in the outside reception room, he had me brought into his small, private quarters. After presenting flowers, I sat on a pillow on the floor, but Maharishi ordered one of the Bramacharis attending him, "Please bring a chair for Nancy." When I protested that I was fine, he insisted, "You have come all this way to help me, you must be made comfortable at all times. Our primitive conditions are not good enough for Westerners; however, when they get into the bliss of good meditation, all else will be unimportant."

He asked me what I thought of his house. "Where is Doris now?" he asked. "I would like her to see what her money has done." When I mentioned that she might be coming to India soon, he confided, "I'm not saying anything yet, but the Beatles will be coming the middle of next month. Maybe Doris would come then. Other young people with creative talents are also expected."

That was exciting information, but I reminded him that Doris had been angry when the news got out about her gift to him. He shrugged that aside. "Tell her I feel great love for her; I expect nothing more from her but for her to accept my devotion and hospitality." I told him I would try to track her down. He suggested I send a cable from the office.

He asked me to be his liaison with the students, to come to him with suggestions for their comfort. (I was to come quite a few times before the course was over.) As he stated it, "You will be my eyes and ears. This way, at all times I will know what is in the hearts of the meditators as a group. At meals you will hear their praise and their complaints. Please come to me with this information."

I almost wept with joy when he exclaimed, "Oh, Nancy, I'm so happy you are here. I always feel good when you are around. You make me happy." He then gave me one of the first copies of his *Commentary on the Bhagavad Gita*, bound at the ashram with an inscription written inside:

"The song of life as sung by the Lord is to be sung here and now to echo down through the ages, dear blessed Nancy. Enjoy." (signed in his Sanskrit name)

I hugged the book and asked him, "Will I become a teacher?"

He just smiled, running his hands along his beads and said, "It will depend on the purity of your nervous system. All those attending the course will not be made initiators, but that does not mean that they will be of less importance to the movement." He paused and added, "You will be the group that the world will judge me by. This is the biggest group we have had, and there will be a lot of publicity about it. Think of the numbers it will attract."

This was an opportunity to voice some of my doubts about those attending the course, "Maharishi, most of the class participants I recognize as long-time meditators, and I don't doubt their qualifications or sincerity. But there are maybe ten persons I'm puzzled by. They don't appear to have the qualities of leadership necessary. From their conversations, they were heavily into the drug scene at one time. Are they going to have the strong nervous systems necessary?"

"Time will weed them out, Nancy. We took several people because the countries they come from have no one. The movement is growing fast, and we must take some chances. Don't forget, our goal is to get one percent of the world's population meditating. Then we will have world peace."

I could understand his rationale; his words calmed my doubts temporarily—however, my intuition kept saying, be alert—danger is ahead. I persisted slightly. "When will we know if we are to be an initiator or not? Will it take the entire three months before we find out?"

He laughed merrily, "Patience, Nancy. All in good time." I could tell I still had my tests ahead of me.

From Maharishi's house I went down the hill to the office to send the cable. I couldn't believe what a mess it was. No wonder nothing ever got done. The Suresh family ate and slept on the other side of a loose curtain that divided the room. Cooking utensils and clothes protruded from beneath it. Every corner of the office was stacked high with papers; the place was utter confusion. It was also the spot where dirty laundry was picked up and clean laundry was delivered. The path to the door was littered with paper and refuse. If anyone from outside came to call at the ashram, this was the spot to which he was first sent. What a terrible impression would be formed. This was the location from which leaders of the world would emerge! Impossible! I knew what my first suggestion would be. Get this place cleaned up!

A few days later, my second suggestion was to do something about the kitchen and the meals. The food at the ashram really depressed us. It was lousy. While many gurus and yoga traditions insist on abstinence from heavy animal foods, Maharishi has never made a vegetarian diet a prerequisite for meditation. He knew that meat-loving Westerners have difficulty in adjusting to such a diet, but unfortunately, within the Valley of the Saints, meat and eggs were banned by the whole spiritual community on the assumption that they excite the metabolism.

There was nothing to be done. We had to suffer, and we did. When people undergo such a sudden, severe change of diet as we experienced, the toxins in the body are dumped into the circulatory system, and a variety of problems ensue. We all felt achy and looked terrible. Some began to wonder, "If this is what intense meditation does for the body, who needs it?"

I looked at Genie one day and exclaimed, "Boy, you look as though one good sneeze would blow you away."

Urging her to eat more and gain a bit of weight, she reacted with, "Gain weight on the garbage we're served? You must be kidding." She was right. It had all the appeal of dining at the M.A.S.H. 4077th. Everything was green or gray-green. We all called it "glop" from the sound it made as ladles-full landed on our plates.

Maharishi erred greatly in not hiring Indian cooks who knew how to prepare an enticing vegetable menu. After all, India is a nation of vegetarians. Instead, two English youths worked their way through the course by supervising what was called the kitchen, a screened room approximately twelve-by-fifteen feet, with a dirt floor and a brick-wall-like counter out of which burned two open wood fires. Between English cooking and a Bramachari's diet, the menu was bland and uninteresting. They boiled everything in giant kettles over the fires. In addition, Maharishi eliminated spices from our diet. Evidently, they stimulate the senses which would have been counterproductive for meditation.

Breakfast consisted of soggy toast made from rough Indian bread, Quaker Oats (God bless the British for introducing that to India) and canned juice. Lunch featured a nameless concoction of various vegetables all boiled together. All raw food was off our list unless we peeled it ourselves (except in first class hotels and modern homes, toilet paper is not used in India—one has to watch out for dirty hands which prepare food, as this is the fastest way to transmit dysentery).

I soon decided to eat breakfast and lunch in my room, from the stocks I'd bought in Delhi. I especially blessed that psychological necessity for Westerners in India, peanut butter. This helped supply needed protein. Also there was a plentiful supply of cheap almonds and cashews. I had brought dehydrated onion soup and sometimes used it as a condiment for the bland food. Each night after the lecture I would fill my thermos with boiling water to make tea in the morning.

After I saw how the village boys, who assisted in the kitchen, washed up, I lost my appetite. Dogs licked the plates clean while they were stacked on the ground, and birds swooped down to peck at the sugar bowls. The kitchen boys, who always seemed to have colds, picked and blew their noses and continued peeling vegetables. No wonder so many students got sick! I took care of my own plate and utensils.

Knowing I could get to Maharishi, a group of German women came to my room one day. "Nancy, something has to be done about the kitchen and eating conditions. We came here to become spiritual teachers, but who can meditate with dysentery? Almost everyone has it!"

We went to Maharishi. He listened while they aired their complaints. "Very good, you take over supervision of the kitchen. The people here are poor and ignorant. You will teach them for this and future courses." He clapped his hands with delight.

In shifts, they took over supervision of the dining and cooking facilities. First they threw away all the dirty cloths, brought new ones, and screened off the dining area. The ashram carpenters were busy night and day.

Another convenience which helped raise morale was hot water, heated by members of the ragged ashram crew. When one needed hot water, they would bring in one or two buckets. This made it easier for us to perform our daily chores. We also knew that by staying cleaner we had less chance of getting sick. So, little by little, we settled into our exotic atmosphere and looked forward to receiving the wisdom we'd traveled so far to obtain.

## 16

# Mia, Mia, Quite Contrary

WITH IMMEDIATE PROBLEMS WORKED OUT, after a few weeks, necessity became the mother of invention. Practicality ruled the day. Indian pajama-type outfits became the favorite dress for the men. As for women, after a few experiences with the local laundry, which literally washed clothes in the river and beat them on a rock, we wore garments we could rinse out in our own buckets. There was not a pressed costume amongst us, nor a smart coiffure. Luckily, curly hair was back in style; shampooing in a bucket does not lead to smooth hairdos.

As Maharishi promised, a local dressmaker was set up in a tent, and quickly earned the title of the "ashram couturier." He sat crosslegged on the ground in his white dhoti made of handspun Khadi cloth, the fabric revered by Mahatma Ghandi. He worked on an old-fashioned hand-driven sewing machine. We made appointments for fittings; he carefully took our measurements, scrambled them up, and threw them away. Nothing ever fit. Luckily, most of the items were of loose design and could be traded around.

Many of the German women were wearing saris; but it's amazing how far wrong one can go in wrapping six yards of lovely silk or cotton on the wrong body. To be seen to their advantage, saris needed the supple, slim frame of a slender Indian.

For me, the most practical was the costume of the Punjab. It covered many sins. Consisting of a pajama-like top that comes to mid-thigh, which is worn over trousers, or *churidars*, gathered at the waist by a draw string and tapering down to slim, tight leggings, it has a good look for almost any figure.

The first one to adopt this Punjabi dress was Mia. She had bought an outfit in Delhi. Deciding she liked it, she selected fabric for more, and Maharishi gave instructions for her clothing to be worked on first.

"Why should she be first in everything?" the other students grumbled.

I put my oar in, "It's not her fault, Maharishi is impressed with the publicity that has resulted from her coming to the course. You all know how he is about that—the faster he can get the word out about TM, the happier he is." This seemed to appease them. Soon we'd get our clothes from the besieged tailor and all would be happy.

In class, Mia sat huddled with the rest, intent on wrapping her blanket to keep out drafts. With her youth and natural beauty, no make-up was necessary. Her short, cropped hair and bangs accented the largeness of her gray-blue eyes. She certainly was prettier than her sister, Prudence, who was plain in every way. Not only plain, but strange. Though Prudence looked like a scared mouse, not so much as a squeak came out. Poor thing, rumor reported that she had flipped out on drugs and had been in a hospital. Also she had been meditating on the *mantra* "aum," which we were taught was only to be used by monks, whose nervous systems could sustain its power. A monk's *mantra* helps a person give up life and become a recluse.

Within the first week, I had struck up a passing friendship with Mia and Prudence. Mia was usually with Maharishi when I saw him. He seemed almost star-struck by her and tried to think of her every need. She played him to the hilt with her little girl voice and wide-eyed expression. It seemed incongruous to me that she was Sinatra's wife. That was pretty rough company which surrounded him; not exactly the best ambiance for an innocent little flower—if that was what she was.

One morning while Maharishi, Mia and I were walking in the woods, a tiny black puppy adopted us. Mia picked him up, and looking at Maharishi, begged, "Oh, Maharishi, may I keep this puppy? He needs a mother and can stay in my room."

He smiled, "As long as it does not interfere with your meditation."

*Mia Farrow at
ashram, 1968*

"Oh, thank you, thank you, dear Maharishi. You have made me sooo happy. Now I must think up a name for it."

"Why not 'Arjuna,' the mighty warrior?" he suggested.

"He doesn't look very mighty to me. He looks like he needs a good meal," I commented.

"Oh, we'll fatten him up," she gushed in her little girl voice.

"On what?" Then I volunteered, "When my friends, the Cambatas, come, I'll ask them to bring some vitamins for him. He won't have any meat in his diet here." Mia went off hugging her new-found pet.

In the days that followed, I saw Mia frequently. She was very friendly; I liked her better and felt guilty about my first rather harsh impression. One day while sharing a cup of tea, she confided in me, "I don't know what to do. Maharishi is really bugging me. He calls me over to his house all the time. I know I should feel flattered by the special attention, but I did come here to meditate." I tried to explain that that was Maharishi's way of being hospitable, but promised to help her.

When I next saw Maharishi, I felt I had to speak, even though it was a delicate subject. "Maharishi, I think it's better not to pay too much attention to Mia. Movie people are spoiled, and you will get better results by treating her no differently than anyone else."

But he didn't see it that way. "Nancy, an international star like Mia can bring us such good publicity. We must treat her as a special person." When I tried to cite some examples of my experience with celebrities, I could see I was getting nowhere and left hoping he was right.

Each night during lecture time, Maharishi singled Mia out for special questions and opinions. I felt her replies were sometimes almost curt. Her mood was disturbing to me, but Maharishi seemed oblivious to it and continued to shower her with attention.

After lectures, she often walked back to my room for a hot drink. I sensed she was getting more tense with each day. I encouraged her to ignore the situation. "Soon other celebrities will arrive and his attention will be on them." As I had been told in confidence about the Beatles, I could say nothing more. I just prayed Maharishi would smarten up!

Life settled into a pleasant routine. As a group, we were looking more like a bunch of *chelas,* the students of an Indian master. What a mixture—doctors, architects, actors, agents, teachers, housewives, musicians, and businessmen, even a faith-healer from Germany and a card dealer from Las Vegas. Many of the younger students had been on drugs and in class described their experiences. Most of them felt they owed their lives to Maharishi for getting them off of drugs.

We also learned practical knowledge, such as how to press a sari —three women walked back and forth into the wind with it until it was dry. The only irons available were the kind filled with hot coals, and those were saved for scorching men's shirts. Every day we looked more like the natives.

But as Maharishi's wisdom started to flow to us, we all felt that no matter the inconvenience, discomfort, distance, or expense, it was well worth the trip. Surely this profound knowledge we were receiving would help Mia develop a more compassionate attitude and not be so easily annoyed.

Another week passed before Avi arrived with his good friends, Kersey and Phoebe Cambata. Kersey was easily one of India's most influential industrialists. It was a feather in our cap to get him to the ashram.

Kersey had a long meeting with Maharishi about the importance of having an accountant put his financial affairs in order. He warned Maharishi that he'd get in trouble with the Indian government otherwise. During this time, Avi was sitting in my room when Mia knocked on the door, saying she needed to see me. I answered, "Come in, our old friend Avi is here."

She seemed very agitated. "I've had it. I'm glad you are here, Avi. Will you take a cable to New Delhi for me, or could you send it from the office here?"

"Sure, glad to. First write it out, and I'll ask Suresh to get it off," he obliged. She wrote it out, handed it to him, and left. He looked at the paper.

"Holy Krishna, I can't send this! Every telephone operator in India will know about it. The papers will get hold of it in no time."

The message read, "FED UP WITH MEDITATION. AM LEAVING ASHRAM. WILL PHONE FROM DELHI." It was addressed to Frank Sinatra, who evidently was in Miami.

"Wow, what do we do now?" I asked. "It would really hurt Maharishi if the press blasted out that she's bolting the ashram. Can you imagine the headlines?"

Avi's handsome face reflected his concern. He also was starstruck by Maharishi—as we all were. Pondering the situation, he started to carefully express his thoughts. "Don't you think she's bored with the whole thing? I can't believe she's really that interested in meditation. She's already received a lot of publicity for being here. Why don't we suggest taking her on a side trip for a few days. Then when she's in a better mood, something can come up naturally which requires her presence in the U.S." It made sense.

It was decided upon. Avi spun a tale of where we were going that no one could have resisted. Mia agreed, then it was my job to sell it to Maharishi. He seemed very pensive when I approached him with our idea, but he could see the wisdom in it. He knew that the press would pounce on a story of disenchantment at the ashram, but woefully added, "I was planning a big celebration for Mia's birthday. Will you be back for that?" It was agreed that we would. I hated to miss even one day's lecture, but felt this was too important. Mia would not have gone without me.

Maharishi appeared sad as I took leave of him. His parting bit of advice, however, was amusing. "While you are in New Delhi, Nancy, go and eat a big steak." I didn't point out that buffalo steak, which is the only kind served in India, is not my favorite. My mind turned to eggs and chicken.

Even though I knew it was a detour on my road to spiritual advancement, it was a lark to take off. The first night we spent in New Delhi. After a scrumptious hot bath at the Oberoi, we went to the Chinois Room and ate ourselves straight through the delicious Chinese menu. Avi's cousin, Moni Kohli, joined us, and the music was great for dancing. Leaving only a few short hours for sleep, we took off at 5:00 a.m. the next morning. We were going to check on some American hunters at a camp which Avi's other company, Alwyn Mercury, ran for tiger *shikar* (hunts). It sounded most exciting to be part of a tiger shoot in India.

"But I don't approve of killing," protested Mia.

Avi reassured her, "You don't have to worry; the chance of this particular couple hitting anything is remote. They drink a bottle of Scotch every night, smoke like furnaces, and cough in the *machand* (a raft-like platform placed high in a tree, from which the hunters wait while beaters drive the forest animals in front of them). It is absolutely essential for the hunters to be quiet. It is not likely that a tiger will come near them."

By the time morning broke, we were halfway to our destination. The foothills were covered with sun-filled forests, reminiscent of the ashram. Before reaching camp, we saw several *samba* (deer), many peacocks and a herd of wild elephants. When Avi saw the latter, he ordered our driver to stop and for us to not make a sound. "When there are mothers and small baby elephants together, a herd is dangerous. If we annoy them, they could easily come this way, turn the car over and trample us with their feet." We didn't breathe.

Once at the camp, it was a delight. The guest bungalow built by the British was of stone walls and shingled roof. Smoke rose from an inside fireplace. The lawn terrace in front was watched over by tall mountains. "This place is a dream!" we exclaimed in a chorus.

Later at lunch, I couldn't help drawing a comparison between how this place was run and the ashram. Both had Indian staffs, but that was where the similarity ended. Our table was covered with a clean cloth; the food was largely vegetarian and delicious. Avi agreed,

"It is ridiculous not to have a first-class cook at the ashram. There are so many well-trained cooks for large *shikars*." What a difference it would have made for the course participants to have cleaner conditions and good food. This place was well painted, well lighted, the windows were clean, and the garden was manicured. I intended to take a Coleman lantern back to Rishikesh with me. Reading by the light of six candles was not conducive to good eyesight.

That afternoon, after a siesta, we traveled on elephants to where the spore of a tiger had been spotted. The pug mark indicated its owner was a large animal. A sense of anticipation went through the group. As we sat in a tree across from the hunters, Mia and I prayed the tiger would get away if he came within range of the guns. We knew Avi was a good shot; if the American hunters didn't get the tiger, Avi probably would.

The beat came closer. There was a flash of black and yellow, but the tiger suddenly doubled back and got away. Nobody could understand it; it was most unusual, as though the tiger had been warned at the last second. Mia and I secretly felt we had alerted the animal by repeating our *mantras* all during the time we were in the *machand*.

We thought it best to say nothing. We knew animals picked up the vibrations of meditation. Whenever we started our meditation time at the ashram, all the monkeys for miles around would descend upon us. We had men stationed on the block roofs to scare them away. Sitting in my open door one sunny morning, meditating, I felt a chipmunk nibble one of my toes. Other times, butterflies landed on me. Once, I got a real thrill when I opened my eyes to see three big, grey monkeys sitting directly in front of me. They looked like See No Evil, Hear No Evil, and Speak No Evil. They sat there showing no fear, just curiosity. Evidently they liked the vibes we gave out while meditating—we were in harmony with nature.

Anyway, we experienced the thrill of the hunt without the kill. That afternoon we climbed on our elephant again; this time to visit a thatched village we had passed that morning.

"*Namaste*," repeated Mia to the villagers, with her palms and long slim fingers placed in front of her. "Do you think, Nancy, that we could get down and go into their homes?" We decided to try, since the native women looked so welcoming.

Each villager tried to entice us into her particular thatched-roofed hut. Inside, the earthen floors were immaculate. Babies swung in little rope hammocks. The family slept in the raised lofts, and at night the animals were put in their stalls below. Mia cradled one of the babies while the mother looked on with approval. She had a darling way about her that was hard to resist. We were gradually becoming good friends.

She had a ribald sense of humor which took one by surprise. On the subject of her husband, I gathered she felt sorry for him. She disclosed that their likes and dislikes were at extremes. "He's given me all sorts of jewelry, but I don't like it; it's pretentious. We have a huge house in Bel Air, but that is not my bag. He really is a square." I wondered how Sinatra would have reacted to being called a square? He who always tried to be so independent and "with it."

Our hours went quickly. Soon four days had passed, and it was time to return to the ashram, as I had promised to get Mia back for her birthday.

Once back at the ashram, Genie, who had the room next to mine, helped catch me up on the news. "I have been biting my nails until you got back. Maharishi had me go to Dehra Dun with Raghvendra to buy little presents for each person to give Mia at the party tonight. It took us all day to select over fifty articles. Then we had a big feast of ice cream and chocolate sauce. My, did that taste good!" Her face radiated happiness.

That night at the lecture, Maharishi had Mia sit on stage with him. She was given a small silver paper crown to wear on her blonde head. She looked like a fairy princess receiving her gifts one by one. To each person, she flashed her even white teeth and murmured a thank you in a tiny voice, as though she were overwhelmed by it all. Her wide-spaced eyes expressed love and surprise. I wondered what was really going on in her head. Inwardly I moaned; instead of treating her like everyone else, Maharishi had put her on a pedestal.

Avi and his cousin, Moni, who had a summer house nearby at Misoorie, a well known hill station, had come to celebrate with us. We each took our turn to present a gift. Moni brought a coleman light; Mia's thanks for that had to be sincere. When I presented my small parcel, she muttered quietly, "Meet me in my room afterwards."

When gift time was over, the young cooks came in with large carrot cakes they had made—quite a feat over an open fire. All were served while Maharishi sat beaming on his couch, so pleased with the evening honoring his special friend.

What an honor he had bestowed on her, I mused. Let her accept it as such. But something negative nagged at me. It didn't take long for verification.

Back at the room it was a different Mia. "I'm so fucking mad! Have you ever seen anything like it! I felt like an idiot up there on that stage, with everyone bowing down to me. Avi, when you leave tomorrow, I'm going with you. That is final—this time you cannot change my mind!"

"That's fine, Maharishi asked me to send a cable to your brother, Johnny; he will go to Goa with you." She had heard about a colony of European hippies in Goa and had told Maharishi that she wanted to go there. Avi tried to pacify her. Moni had brought a cake and some champagne.

Mia raised her glass. "To the last night in this holy place. Hah, that is a laugh. Maharishi is no saint—he even made a pass at me when I was over at his house before dinner."

Moni raised his glass and joined in, "To more un-holy saints."

I interrupted, "Mia, wait a minute. How can you even think such a thing!"

I wasn't star-struck by her. I would not allow her to say such a thing about my beloved guru. Especially in front of Moni. I could imagine his story when he got back to the curious ears of Delhi society, "Wait till you hear my scoop about Maharishi . . ."

"Listen, I'm no fucking dumbbell; I know a pass when I see one."

"Then please explain how it happened."

"He asked me down into his private *puja* room, saying he would perform a *puja* for me on my birthday." Her laugh was derisive. "Big deal, but what could I say."

"Go on." I could feel my Irish temper begin to rise.

"He made me kneel on a small carpet in front of an altar-type table and a picture of Guru Dev. He went through some of the *puja* ceremony and then put a wreath of flowers around my neck. That is when he made the pass."

"But how so?"

"He started to stroke my hair. Listen, I know a pass from a *puja*."

"Oh, Mia, what Maharishi did for you was such an honor. When he ran his hand down your hair, it was all part of the ceremony. It is an honor for him to touch your hair. He did it for Helen Lutes, just like that. That is the way he presents you to his beloved master." I fought to stay in control.

She didn't want to hear any more and turned to the two men. "What time do we leave tomorrow?"

It was hard for me to speak; I was so angry and shocked. How dare she accept so much from Maharishi and then make such a rotten statement—especially in front of Indians who would be likely to repeat it. Avi wouldn't, but what did we know about Moni? It's a contaminated mind that would even think such a thing. My first impression of Mia was probably correct. She'd spent a lot of time around pigs, and some of the mud had rubbed off on her.

I remembered one day after I'd made a remark about Mia's sweetness, Genie had commented, "Don't be too taken in by that act. George (Genie's husband) knows that whole Sinatra group, and they're a tough bunch. Also, she was evidently quite a hellion while on the cast of Peyton Place. George has always been amazed at the way she got Sinatra to marry her—scores of women, really attractive women, had been after him, but she succeeded in getting him. She's no little mouse."

We arose early to have a group picture the day after Mia's birthday. I tried to dissuade Maharishi from this project, but nothing doing. He loved directing and told each person where to sit. Mia was asked to don the silver crown again and sit dead-center. She went along with the whole thing in a surprisingly good humor. Maybe it was because she was leaving the ashram that day. She promised Maharishi to come back after her trip to Goa. I hoped she would not.

He had instructed Avi, "You are to be Mia's protector until her brother, Johnny, arrives in Delhi. By no means is she to go off without him. We are responsible for her safety while she is in India."

When she said goodbye to Maharishi, leaving Prudence behind, butter wouldn't melt in that mouth which had been spewing four-letter words the night before. My admiration for her acting ability was growing.

Shortly before the threesome departed, V.C. Shuckla called the ashram. (He had defended Maharishi in Parliament the day before against an attack. Avi's friend was proving invaluable to Maharishi.) His message was, "Tell Maharishi that the Forest people have OK'd the temporary use of forest land behind the ashram for an airport." Maharishi was delighted. It helped to erase the sadness of Mia's leaving.

After walking to the upper gate to wave goodbye to Avi, Moni, and Mia, Maharishi suggested, "Nancy, let's drive over and measure out the land that we will need for the airport."

By the time we arrived at the Laxman Jhula bridge, it was midday, and the bridge was lined with begging lepers. I was again instructed to change money into little coins—a money changer sat close by—and drop some in each cup. As they raised their crippled hands imploringly, I dropped the coins and Maharishi blessed each one. What a pitiful sight; they were so small and deformed. "Oh, Maharishi, what terrible karma they must be living out! Do you think one of them could be Hitler?"

"Might be, might be," he smiled.

The bridge was barely wide enough for our small car to pass. Across the river, north of the ashram, was a large piece of open land.

It looked great for an airport. Maharishi directed the *bramacharyi* driver to start measuring. Evidently, Maharishi had found out how much space a plane needs to take off and land. "We will put stakes at four corners and tie them with strings. Then the world will know the location of the first TM airport." He was like a happy child with a new toy.

For me it was a joyful afternoon. What a pleasure to spend the time with Maharishi while he was in such a happy mood. "How are you liking the course?" he asked.

"Oh Maharishi, I love it. I hated the days away from the ashram."

"But it was best. Now Mia has gone away in a happy mood. When she hears the Beatles are here, she will come back in a happy mood."

"When do they arrive?"

The answer was, "Soon." And then, "Nancy, what are the lessons you seem to be learning?"

"I know one lesson that will be hard for me, Maharishi. That is the learning of humility. I get so impatient with the stupidity of the ashram workers; they are so dumb! Poor things, I know they have no training, but it seems sad you can't have more efficient people to help you. I'm afraid patience is not one of my strong points."

"With self-realization we come to know our faults. Then we bring them out into the light. They will gradually fade away as does color from cloth when exposed to the sunlight."

"I want so badly to become an initiator, Maharishi. My children will be very disappointed if I don't."

His laughter pealed out, "Don't worry about them. They have extremely good karma. Whenever I am with them I feel I am in the presence of pure being."

I hardly believed my ears. What a compliment from this holy man. I couldn't wait to get back to my room to write home and report his words.

The sun was shining, the crows were arguing in the trees. It was nice to be back in my cozy room with nothing to think about except meditation. Here was where the real jewel was to be found. It seemed weeks ago that Mia had come and gone. Now I understood the saying, "With the eye of a jeweler, one can see a diamond. With the eye of ignorance, one sees a rock."

---
17
---

# Beatles Invade the Ashram

OUR FIRST WEEKS WERE SPENT MEDITATING for increasing periods of time, reading Maharishi's books, *Commentary on the Bhagavad Gita* and *The Science of Being and Art of Living*, and attending classes three times daily. The afternoon lecture was an explanation of the discourse between Lord Krishna and the warrior, Arjuna, the central action of the Gita. We gathered around Maharishi under the trees, like children listening to a grandparent telling fairy tales. These were enchanted hours, the only sounds other than Maharishi's voice came from animals and birds in the forest—an occasional raucous call of a peacock, a bleating from the kitchen goat, the chattering of monkeys or the crashing sound of a large beast pushing through the underbrush—possibly a tiger or an elephant.

Maharishi believes Indians became a passive race through a misinterpretation of the *Gita*, the Hindu Bible. With great care and sensitivity, Maharishi unrolled his knowledge of the mechanics of life and the Shankara tradition as important points came up in the scripture.

No outsiders were allowed into the lectures as they would have interfered with the steady raising of our group consciousness. "I cannot give you knowledge," he said; "I must bring your conscious level up to the point where wisdom will flow out of me. This is what will happen in this course."

Each night he asked for a show of hands to illustrate how many hours of meditation we were accumulating. After a few days at the ashram, Maharishi had instructed us to meditate four or five hours a day, and he gradually lengthened these periods.

Whenever someone fell behind in his hours, he never criticized us for anything but complimented those who were accomplishing the most. If someone asked a stupid question, we would all laugh, but he was likely to encourage the asker with, "We must understand this point from all sides. We can easily be fooled by our senses, but we are never fooled by our intuition if we develop it and learn to trust it. This will come from long meditation."

The main social hour was held after the evening lecture. Most of us went to the kitchen to get our thermoses filled and have a cup of something hot to drink. The musicians in the group usually sat around the dining area composing and singing.

One day Maharishi called me to his house. He dropped the bombshell, "The Beatles and some of their companions will be here next week. I am counting on you, Nancy, to help me get Block Six fixed up for them." He had seen my room, and at the time commented, "Ah, with little you are learning to do more." No wonder he was in such a festive mood; it was an honor that he was sharing this with me.

What fun, was my immediate reaction, but the doing was something again. The first part of my job was to teach my raw, untrained work crew how to clean. They would pick up a filthy rag and make the bathroom fixtures dirtier. Starting from scratch, I made the best use of the two or three Hindi words I knew as I literally grabbed them by the collars to get them to do what I wanted. If I ordered the floors swept, I had to teach them how to sweep first; then, after they had swept all the dirt into the flower patch running around the porch, I made them take all the refuse out from around the flowers. If I asked them to spread and tack a blanket to a wall, I had to measure it for them, or it would certainly be out of place.

I needed patience to work with these workers. I remembered telling Maharishi I lacked patience; maybe that was the reason for giving me this job. There was a lesson in humility also.

One may think the caste system is dead in India. Not at all. For example, these workers would refuse to clean a toilet; that was a job for the untouchables, the Harijans, the lowest caste in India. And if none were available, they would stand by and watch me do it.

Although I was a strict task master to these poor, tattered-looking men, they all remember me to this day. Whenever I visit the ashram, like little children they rush to greet me with flowers saying, *"Jai Memsahib!"* ("Hail Boss!").

So, with patience and perseverance, slowly Block Six came together. Maharishi ordered a lot of special items brought from the village. Now the rooms had carpets completely covering the cement floors, mirrors and fabric hung on the walls, and there were thin foam mattresses and spreads on the beds. The bathrooms had tubs and showers, some of which actually worked in a primitive fashion. The closets had curtains with hangers inside. When the celebrities arrived, they would be comfortable and have no idea of what had been accomplished for them. It wasn't anything like the Rishikesh Hilton, the press later called it, but by the standard of the other blocks, it looked like a palace.

Maharishi was thrilled with Block Six, "You have done the impossible, Nancy; you have made something out of nothing!"

Then one morning, the third week in February, Maharishi made the announcement that the first group of Beatles and their friends were arriving that afternoon. "Please remember, I have offered these young people a quiet refuge from being celebrities. I promised them they would not be molested in any way by news seekers. Please do not have any cameras near them, do not ask for their autographs, and treat them no differently than anyone else here."

I wished he would take his own advice. He had even planned a private dining area for them. Actually, no one was that interested in the celebrities. We were more interested in the wisdom that Maharishi had to offer, and the announcement came as a surprise to no one. The minute we had started on the "beautification program," everyone knew it was for someone very special; who else could it be but the Beatles?

There were mixed emotions in the group as to the merits of the celebrities' impending arrival. Also, lacking information, we didn't know if it was going to be a quick visit or a longer stay. "Well, there goes our peace and quiet," was the general opinion, except for the younger members who were thrilled to be in the same place as the Beatles!

About 5:00 p.m. I heard cars drive down the road strictly prohibited from use during the course in order to protect the quiet for "Meditators Row." Genie and I watched as several young men in long black coats descended, followed by three young women. On top of the cars were sitars, guitars, and all sorts of psychedelic colored bags.

They had to be the Beatles! I wondered which ones, as I didn't know them by sight. We'd find out at evening lecture.

At dinner I was told it was John Lennon and George Harrison who had arrived with their wives. Naturally, there was a sense of excitement as we entered the lecture hall. I noticed the front row of seats roped off. I took a place in the second row and waited. Everyone was seated when John and George walked in with Maharishi. Both men wore long grey robes and hoods with tassels hanging down their backs.

They certainly were attention-getters. No one said a word or made a move. Once seated, Maharishi welcomed them from his platform sofa and then went on with his lecture as though nothing unusual had happened.

Sitting directly behind them, I looked straight at George Harrison's shiny hair, clean and beautifully cut in its long, shoulder-length fashion. The delicate girl next to him was his wife, Patty. She was the one who had originally led the group to Maharishi. Next to her was her look-alike sister, Jenny Boyd. The third girl was John Lennon's wife, Cynthia. Although wearing glasses, she was the prettiest of the three. Then came John, who looked like a stern school teacher with his granny glasses. His white skin had an unhealthy tinge of grey. During the lecture his hands never stopped moving; he seemed to be doodling. Later I learned he'd been a heavy drug user, especially LSD, but was now off drugs. He undoubtedly had a lot of tension on his nervous system.

My mind went back to the only other time I had seen these two boys and the rest of the Beatle foursome. It was at Dodger Stadium with my daughter and fifty-five thousand other howling young people. I never heard a note of their music over the din! They were brought in by armored truck and taken out by helicopter. I had asked María Luisa, "How do you know if you like their singing? You never heard it." Now, here I was, sitting not more than two feet away from two of them.

María Luisa would be so excited with my news. I tried to notice every detail possible so I'd have more to write. John's cockney accent certainly was hard on the ears. From their spoken words, the girls appeared to be more cultured than the boys.

A third man accompanied them. I found out later he was their road manager, Malcolm Evans. Maybe because he was heavy-set and had a businessman's haircut, he seemed older than the two famous young men, who were very slight.

George looked around at the other students with a pleasant smile on his face. John stared straight ahead as though he were alone in the hall. After the lecture was over, everyone left the course as always, going over to the kitchen to fill their hot water bottles and thermoses. I was very proud of the way we all behaved. It was as though nothing new had occurred. Maharishi must have been pleased.

The next morning a message came for me to come to Maharishi's house. That was exciting. I hoped I was going to meet the Beatles. When I arrived, the newcomers were there. "Come in, come in, and meet our new guests," he cordially called out to me. "Nancy is one of my liaisons with the students. If you have any problems, I want you to come directly to me, but if she can help with any of your needs, just ask her," and he went on to tell them which room I occupied. I was delighted with the turn of events. Of course I would help them!

They were very friendly. Immediately, the girls asked me about getting some clothes made. We made plans to do some shopping in Rishikesh.

Maharishi was so happy. He gave out such energy and joy. What a compliment that the Beatles actually came to his ashram. Paul McCartney was due in a few days. He was seeing a bit of India before reporting in to the course. Nothing was said about Ringo. I asked Patty later, and she said he didn't think he could make it. But, to have three of the world-famous quartet was incredible!

The celebs seemed happy with their rooms. They indicated that they didn't want to take their meals alone, that they would eat with the rest. Evidently the casual reception had reassured them that they would not be bothered by the other students.

That afternoon the Beatles, their women and I set off across the river with Raghvendhra, one of the head Brahmacharis, in tow as interpreter. George wore a shirt that spelled out in flowers, "All you need is love." John's pants were multi-colored stripes, accented by a wildly-printed shirt. Nothing quiet about the boys. They admired my Punjabe costume. "Take us where we can get some of those." It was quite thrilling to be complimented by the Beatles.

The three girls wore long, slim dresses under their overcoats. It was the last of February, still winter in India, and crossing the Ganges one felt the cold humidity creep through.

It didn't seem possible that the ramshackle city of Rishikesh would have much to offer the shoppers, but in an hour's time our arms were full of purchases—colorful fabrics, saris, long sleeveless vests, thin embroidered *kurtas* (Indian overblouses), swaths of plush, cheap velvet, and Kashmiri shawls. I'm sure the merchants unloaded a lot of merchandise they figured would never sell.

John and George were decisive shoppers; they knew what they wanted and paid the price asked. The girls were supportive, but the boys made the purchases. They refused to barter, even though Raghvendhra told them it was expected. They especially loved the Khadi shop and all its hand-spun fabrics. Even John dropped his cynical expression and became excited at the wealth of exotic fabrics. He picked the brightest. Pointing to the gold plush cloth covered with red dots he proclaimed, "I'll make me a coat out of this one."

What fun it was for them to leisurely shop around, no one molesting them in any way, no one suspecting that they were special. For the time being, they were completely offstage. As for me, I had to keep pinching myself. Was I really here shopping with two of the most famous personalities in the world?

Several days later, after our shopping trip, costumes began to emerge from the tailor's tent which were to influence fashion trends of the world for a decade. At first, the tailor, whose creations were to have more impact on the world than Dior or Balenciaga, was completely confused—George and John were using women's saris for their shirts, and John did use the red and orange velvet for a long coat. It was wild!

The girls used men's *dhotis* (white cloths wrapped around the waist and brought up through the legs) to fashion pajamas, while saris were turned into long, flowing dresses. Long shirts hung below sleeveless vests, accompanied by pajama-like, baggy pants. On the Beatles it looked good—and comfortable. Other course members started to copy their zany styles. Most of the men were sporting beards by now, and soon it was difficult to tell a Beatle from a *chela*.

Patty and her sister, Jenny, were very chatty and friendly; Cynthia Lennon seemed depressed and quiet. I wondered what it must be like to be the wife of a Beatle; obviously she wasn't handling it well, even though the other girls explained that she'd known the group the longest.

The most outgoing was Mal Evans, the road manager; he loved the whole show. One day he asked me if I'd like to drive into Delhi with him and Raghvendhra to pick up Paul McCartney. It was tempting, but I decided to save my next request for going in to pick up my son, Rik, who was arriving shortly. He had taken a sabbatical from studies before going on to architectural school. I could imagine María Luisa's, "Oh Mom, how could you refuse!" I was a bit concerned about myself. Everything seemed more tempting than staying in my rooms meditating. Maharishi was going to have a problem with me.

Soon the world press appeared at the locked upper gate. With small effort they broke the lock. At this same moment Maharishi arrived—he was quiet but firm when he requested, "Please, we will receive you after a little time with the course—then the interviews will be more meaningful; we will send for you and give you two full days to interview everyone." He finally dismissed them. I think the Beatles were very happy at the way it was done. That afternoon both George and John and their wives came to the afternoon lecture. George asked intelligent questions. The girls looked terrific in their colorful robes, a mad mosaic of color. Everyone complimented them and they seemed pleased. They appeared more relaxed around the other students.

When Paul McCartney arrived he brought a total surprise. It was Ringo Starr, who said he could only stay for ten days at the longest. Paul was also accompanied by a slim, willowy red-haired girl he introduced as Jane Asher, a British actress and his fiancee. He made it clear that they would share the same quarters. George warned me, "Prepare for rain—it rains wherever Ringo is."

Ringo was small and just as much of a Rumpelstiltskin as his pictures made him out to be. One's first impression was of a big nose pushed along by vitality. Paul was outgoing and friendly. He seemed delighted to catch up with his team. Maharishi was the happiest of them all—he had all four Beatles as his guests. What a catch! It rained that night. But it didn't dampen my spirits—every day got more terrific.

"Do you mean that Maharishi condones Paul and that actress sharing a room?" asked an indignant Genie, who was a supporter of Moral Rearmament, a Christian movement with strict moral values. "Do you feel that is a good example for the rest of the course members?"

"Maharishi's eyes are on far more important events than who is sleeping with whom," I countered, in spite of being a bit baffled myself. "He isn't going to treat us like children. We are responsible for our own behavior," I reminded her. "Don't forget Maharishi's definition of sin; it involves an action which is 'life destructive.' I don't think it's 'life destructive' for Paul and Jane to share a room. Neither are married, so who are they hurting?" But her Moral Rearmament training was too deeply imbedded; I didn't make an impression.

When the world press found out that all four Beatles were at the ashram, reporters from all parts of the globe flocked to Rishikesh. Now there was no holding them back with a polite little request. Security guards stood by the gates.

Several of us pleaded with Maharishi, "You must prepare some material to hand out to the press. After five hours in taxis, crossing the river by boat, and climbing the hill in the heat of the day, all this, and then to be turned away with nothing! You can't do it, Maharishi. They have to file something. After all the expense, they'll be in trouble if they get nothing."

He agreed; the printers would put something together. Later, thinking it over, he felt an explanation given at the gate would be enough to make them understand why they could not enter the ashram. He was looking at the situation from his level! The press looked at it from their own. No press material was prepared. I reminded Maharishi of my PR background, and offered to put together a press release, but he dismissed me.

"I promised the Beatles they would not be molested by the press or anyone else. They are enjoying being away from the world of activity— do you see how rested their faces appear?" He smiled as he added, "No, the world can get along for a few more weeks without their Beatles."

But Maharishi overestimated the goodwill of the press. There was a confrontation at the lower gate. One journalist insisted he was going through the gate, after being told by Raghvendhra that it was impossible. Raghvendhra bodily threw the man out in the clash that followed. The newspaper man threatened to sue Maharishi for being "assaulted by one of his monks."

Walter Koch, an old time meditator, was sent down to talk with the angry arrivals, but he could do little to pacify them. He was a scholarly, professional type who made no impression on them. Maybe they would have been more understanding if they could have left with pictures of the ashram, the Beatles attending class, and a little news of the daily routine. As it was, they took the absolute "no" as an affront, and made up all sorts of lies in their articles. Maharishi was to learn the importance of PR the hard way.

Often I was called to answer the phone and talk to different members of the press. I tried to point out how important a course like

*Nancy going into the Ganges (fully clothed) with Sadhu watching, Rishikesh*

*Nancy's funny room at the ashram with its swan carpet on the wall*

*John Lennon in a happy mood at the ashram singing "Prudence, Come Out and Play," which he wrote for Prudence Farrow*

*John Lennon photographing in front of Maharishi's house at ashram, 1968*

*John Lennon signing an autograph at ashram, 1968*

*Maharishi and George Harrison at the ashram*

*Mia Farrow, John Lennon, George Harrison and Patty,*
*going to class carrying blankets*

*Mike Love, Donovan and John Lennon with Maharishi at the ashram, 1968.*

*Donovan Leitch (famous singer) at the ashram, 1968*

*Rishikesh, 1968 Puja. Nancy, Cynthia and John Lennon, Patty and George Harrison attending class*

*Maharishi and Mike Love of the "Beach Boys" at the ashram*

*Avi Kohli and Mike Love in one of his colorful costumes at the ashram, 1968*

*Maharishi in Kersey Cambata's helicopter, Valley of the Saints.
This appeared in the world press.*

*Phebe Cambata, Maharishi, Avi Kohli and Kersey Cambata
They brought the helicopters to the Valley of the Saints to take Maharishi and
the Beatles for a ride.*

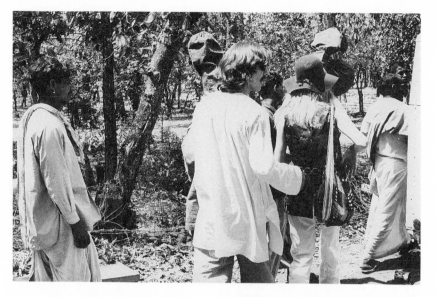

*George and Patty Harrison packing up to leave, 1968*

*Khumba Mela (gathering of the saints) at Maharishi's ashram. Charlie Lutes and Jerry Jarvis is front of Maharishi and Tatwala Baba on his left, Nancy behind.*

**LOOK**  50 CENTS · FEBRUARY 6, 1968

CALIFORNIA
CAMPUSES:
MEDITATION
REPLACES DRUGS

WHITE COP,
BLACK REBEL
A searching report on our crisis in
law and order, and a possible solution

WHY I'M BATTLING LBJ
Senator Eugene McCarthy's own story
of his decision to run

AND NOW—
MEDITATION
HITS THE CAMPUS
How Hindu monk Maharishi
turns the students on
without drugs

MEDITATORS
AT YALE

1968 Look Magazine *cover*
*Direct center is Nancy's son, Brett Cooke, who introduced T.M. to Yale*
*while he was a student there*

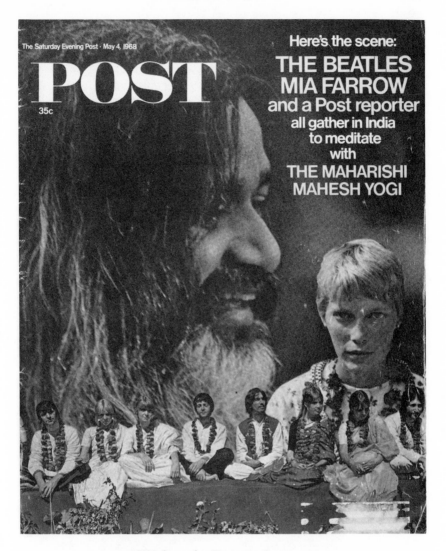

1968 Saturday Evening Post *cover*
*Left to right: Ringo Starr, Jenny Boyd, Jane Asher, Paul McCartney,*
*George Harrison, Patty Harrison, Cynthia Lennon and John Lennon*

*Portrait at the Ashram, 1986*

this was for the world, but they didn't hear me. My name got mentioned somewhere and each day I made more trips down the hill to the phone, only to find it was some agitated newspaper man. I did my best to explain why Maharishi had to be so strict, but it didn't make a dent.

When Maharishi sent me to Delhi with instructions regarding his airport, he suggested, "While you are talking to Mr. Shukla, would you tell him we are having a problem with the local police? They are harassing the meditators who walk into Swargashram, demanding to see their passports. Everyone has already been cleared by the police, so it is completely unnecessary. Also, tomorrow, another singer from England will arrive; bring him back in the car with you. His name is Donovan." Even I had heard of him—more news to write home!

V.C. Shukla again proved a good friend to Maharishi. His reaction to the news I carried was, "We will not allow such rudeness. I will send a Gurkha to stay at the ashram and protect the visitors. Maharishi can feed him, give him a room, and pay him ten rupees a day ($1.50). He will be told to report to *Memsahib* Nancy each day for instructions."

Avi and I picked up Donovan the next day. He would stay at Avi's for the night, in order to avoid any press hanging around the Oberoi. A thin, delicate-looking young man with the whitest skin, Donovan was gentle in every way. That evening he took out his guitar and sang some of his ballads. He absolutely captivated us with his sensitivity and beautiful voice. His pale face and gentle eyes were a picture of spirituality. We knew that Maharishi would love him. I liked his Scottish accent, which was far more appealing than the cockney accents of the Beatles. I didn't know what he meant when he asked me, "Luv, have you got a cough?" He was asking for a cigarette.

The Cambatas had joined us, and they shared our enthusiasm for Donovan. Kersey came up with a smashing suggestion. "Do you suppose Maharishi would like it if I flew two helicopters into the ashram and took him and the Beatles for a ride?"

"Do you have any idea what will happen to the Valley of the Saints if you fly in there?" asked Avi. "The place will go wild." I immediately thought of the publicity value—what a gimmick. We'd have to leak it to the press. A great bone for a hungry dog.

They started planning how it could be done. It was decided that Kersey would send a truck ahead with extra gasoline. Then he would fly the first one in and land on the side of the river below the ashram. Hours later, the second helicopter would follow. What news we were to take to Maharishi!

Before returning to the ashram, we went clothes shopping for Donovan. As we drove through Connaught Circle, we saw amazing news posters pasted to the columns of the buildings. They were headlines of the daily papers—"Wild Orgies at Ashram," "Beatles Wife Raped at the Ashram," were two that caught our eye. We bought copies of three or four papers, and Avi, Donovan and I read aloud to each other as we left Delhi.

"Listen to this one, 'Cartons of whiskey were seen delivered to Maharishi's guests at the ashram. Evidently the guru doesn't want his disciples deprived of their pleasures while learning about the spiritual world. Maharishi teaches that all desires must be satisfied.'"

"And this, it's unbelievable, 'Sources close to the Academy of Meditation located in the Himalayas above Rishikesh report that attempts are being made to suppress the fact that one of the Beatles' wives was raped two days ago. It has not been determined as yet which wife was the victim.'"

"This really is a silly one," I reacted. "Listen, 'Ringo Starr stated he will leave the ashram as he cannot tolerate the spicy food.' Boy, I wish that were the truth; we could use a little spice in our dull, daily fare."

It was tea time when we arrived. The Beatles came over to greet Donovan, whom they knew and respected. We showed them the newspapers. They were incredulous. Donovan asked, "Come on, who was the one who got done?" The girls, Patty and Cynthia as the only Beatles' wives, claimed they hadn't had the honor. In fact, Cynthia was in a very happy mood.

We asked Ringo to be a good sport and share some of that spicy food with us. His reply was, "After me, man, after me." The stories were complete lies—"Where there's smoke, there's fire," did not apply.

As far as the wild parties were concerned, we figured someone had seen whiskey cartons filled with vegetables and other food stuffs being unloaded and made the assumption that liquor was being brought in. There was no way Maharishi could protect the ashram from such blatant lies. The best thing was to laugh and forget it.

Maharishi was thrilled with the idea of the helicopters' arrival. That was right up his alley; his eyes shown with excitement!

Several days later the gasoline arrived by truck, with a message that the following day Kersey would fly in at 10:00 a.m. At 9:30 that next morning, Maharishi led us all down the hillside. We'd been given the morning off; what a big event for the meditators! We carefully stayed away from the river front, not knowing how much landing space Kersey would need. Soon, in the distance, we heard the sound of the aircraft, good old Kersey, a really prompt Parsee (original Persians who migrated to India). Before long we saw the faint appearance of what seemed to be a large mosquito. The sound grew louder and louder as the helicopter invaded the silence and tranquility of the Valley of the Saints.

Soon we were waving as the chopper passed us and started circling before making its descent. *Sanyasis*, holy men, were appearing from all directions. It was amusing to see these people, who usually move so slowly, now running to see what was happening. One can only imagine what went on in the minds of many who had never seen a movie or TV and were only now getting used to having a meager bit of electricity.

Around and down came the helicopter. I could see Kersey at the controls; alongside was his pilot, Captain Engineer.

"Stand back a bit, Maharishi, so that sand won't hit you as the helicopter settles," warned one of the Beatles. We turned away and shielded our faces as a blast of air hit us just as the aircraft landed. The propellers came to a stop and out stepped a smiling Kersey, saying, "Jai Guru Dev, Maharishi."

After being presented to the celebs, Kersey asked Maharishi if he'd like to go for a ride. Maharishi couldn't get into the plane fast enough. What a picture it made to see our little bearded guru waving from the window as the chopper took off. Cameras clicked like mad—many of the pictures were to appear in newspapers and prominent magazines around the world. Kersey didn't know it at the moment, but he'd just given Maharishi the greatest PR exposure possible.

They flew up and down the Ganges. Crowds standing along both river banks watched in wonderment. Maharishi's stock must have really gone up in the minds of his neighbors! Of course, there would also be criticism.

Landing once again, Kersey instructed Captain Engineer to take the Beatles up. The other helicopter was due in two hours.

The next one up was John Lennon. With his beard and white *dhoti* he looked like a *sadhu* himself.

What a day of excitement. Most people had no idea of the tremendous expense involved in bringing the two helicopters; of course, it helped that Kersey owned the company.

That night, Maharishi asked Kersey, who also owned a movie company in Bombay, an appropriate question. "I am concerned about something. I have given the Beatles and their Apple Corporation the right to make a movie about Guru Dev, the movement, and myself. It will be a glorious film, and all the world will want to see it," he announced dreamily. "But the Beatles insist on the distribution rights. I'm wondering if we cannot do that ourselves. I would like your advice."

"Maharishi, you couldn't do better than to have Apple Corp as your distributor; it is the most difficult part, and determines whether you have a big success or not."

After discussing the pros and cons, one could see that Maharishi was not completely convinced. Something else puzzled me. I thought Charlie Lutes had been told to make a deal with Four Star Productions to make a movie on Guru Dev's life—I'd better ask Tony to let me know. My mind came back to the conversation when Kersey asked me aside, "Do you suppose Maharishi has seen even a home movie?" I understood his skepticism. Once before Maharishi had sought his advice and then ignored it.

Within a week, the pictures and stories of the helicopter in the Valley of the Saints were front-page news around the world. Life and Look magazines devoted pages to the story. My stock went up with Maharishi. He told the Beatles, "It was Nancy's friend who brought the helicopters." I modestly pointed out that it was really Avi's credit. But when I'd have a guilty conscience about not meditating enough, I'd console myself with thoughts such as, "If I hadn't gone to Delhi to get Donovan, none of this would have happened." I was great at rationalizing.

---

## 18

---

# The Mechanics of Creation

A FTER THE EXCITEMENT OF THE HELICOPTERS, life at the ashram returned to normal; the long days became serene, the focus returned to extended, continuous meditation.

The course proceeded well and Maharishi was in a relaxed, happy mood. Every afternoon the Beatles and other stars would join him on top of his house, after the regular class, and be given an additional private course. Ringo left after his promised ten days, but John, George, and Paul were basking in the privacy and quiet of Maharishi's hideaway. They seemed unconscious of the uproar they were causing on the outside and the ill will of the world press they were bringing on Maharishi's head.

Every day Mr. Shukla's ghurka would come to me, "Memsahib, reporting for duty," and neatly salute. He was a tough little bowlegged man. He wore the famous hat of the ghurka, turned up on one side. England had long considered them the fiercest fighting men in the world. He tightened up security at the gates and flushed newsmen out of trees on the ashram's perimeter, trying with their telescopic lenses to get some sort of a scoop. No one wanted to tangle with this wiry warrior.

Quiet settled over the ashram. We looked forward with renewed enthusiasm to hearing Maharishi's wisdom flow. Each evening lecture dealt with different phases. He attacked many theories most Westerners

239

were raised with as basic truths. He used simple terminology and often explained things in several ways to make sure we understood his points. He suggested we not bother with notes, saying, "When you need knowledge, it will be there, or you will know where to seek it. Now it is better to comprehend the course as a whole, and let the knowledge flow from me into you." I disobeyed, thrilled with what we were learning. I could not resist putting some of it down, wanting to pass it along to my family. In that way it would also serve as a record for later on. Each day the course took on greater excitement for me.

Maharishi referred often to "The Tragedy of Knowledge." "Wisdom is handed down incorrectly. Look what has happened with Christianity. A suffering man saw Christ as suffering. Suffering is resistance to evolution; so how could the leader of man suffer? If he is the Son of God, how could He suffer? It is humiliating to teach that Jesus, the Son of God, could suffer in the world of man!" I thought back on the day in Bogotá and our visit to the Catholic Church—how dismayed he'd been.

Maharishi continued, "A bishop in Italy once said to me, 'If you took suffering out, Jesus' life would have been a comedy.' I answered, 'Better his life a divine comedy than a tragedy.'" We chuckled at Maharishi's practical approach.

"When Jesus was called into the Garden of Gesthemane, he started to review his work and didn't want to leave. He wanted to know why he was being called back, 'Why have You forsaken me?' But, 'Your will be done,' showed his complete devotion. If he went on to suffer, it means he was not a proper instrument for the Divine; either that, or, as Christ spoke from his level, suffering men heard him from their level and brought the whole incorrect story about."

Maharishi shook his head. "If a man in communion with God can suffer, then what is the use of self-realization and God-realization?

"No, the misunderstanding is the reason for the continuation of suffering." I found myself nodding in agreement; it all made such sense.

"It is taught that suffering is necessary to know God. What brought about this misunderstanding?" he asked, and went on, "When a mind in complete desperation calls out in total helplessness—everything else is gone. The mind can slip into transcending. This is the mechanics of it. This helplessness is termed 'surrender to God.' Surrender is complete when one loses the ability to think or act. 'Your Will be done.' This complete giving up of ourselves slows down the thinking of the mind. When there is no mental activity, one can easily slip into the transcendental. But then it cannot be repeated systematically. Maybe after being miserable and suffering for another six months, the mind will slip again. This is how the whole system of purity through suffering was established in order to gain the Grace of God." The profoundness of his words overwhelmed me—my admiration knew no bounds.

Maharishi advised us, "If you want to pray, meditate first. That is systematic communion, and then pray. When man has the sympathy of nature, creation will support his desires." Also he added, "A loving son eventually will not even have to desire; the father will know his needs and simultaneously fulfill them. This is the role nature will begin to play in your lives."

I was so impressed with what we were learning. Every day the course took on greater excitement for me. Maharishi discussed each phase of divine construction. Partly by lecturing, partly by answering our questions, Maharishi laid out the spectrum of life before us. One night he talked about death, advising us how to approach it and how to help others face it, even those already dead. This in particular gave me much to think about. Another time he dealt with the question of sin. Each class was a unique exploration into the familiar but poorly understood life around and within us.

As the weather improved, we held some classes down by the river and read from the scriptures. The atmosphere was rich and tranquil.

One day, Maharishi called me in to announce, "Mia wants to come back."

My reaction was curt. "Naturally. All the publicity about the celebrities here would certainly lure her back. Do you really feel she's sincere about her meditation?"

He ignored my question. "She called and will be in Delhi in two days. Why don't you meet her? It's the same day your son arrives." How dear of him to remember. I had been checking off the days, my excitement mounting—my meditations were full of anticipation to welcome Rik and get first-hand news from home. I was feeling a bit homesick.

Maharishi had another exciting piece of news. The following week, Mike Love of the Beach Boys was due with Paul Horn, the jazz flutist and longtime practitioner of TM. We certainly were becoming a center for musicians.

Maharishi suggested again that I try to find Doris Duke. "She'd enjoy the young people and their music. I would like her to see what her money built."

As soon as I got to Delhi, I sent another wire, but again heard nothing—I felt we should give up on her. Avi agreed with me. "Maharishi doesn't need to court anyone." We were on our way to the airport, "Yes, but I'm glad he doesn't forget old friends."

What a joy it was to welcome Rik. His first remark warmed me. "Mom, you look great . . . ten years younger."

Avi and Rik hit it off right away. Rik was carrying his rifle. "What do you plan on doing with that gun at the ashram?" Avi asked.

"I don't expect to spend my whole time there. I want to go on a hunt. Mom said you often had groups going out for samba, leopard and tiger."

"How would you like to tag along on a tiger *shikar?*"

"Boy, are you serious? Would you go, Mom?"

"I'd have to ask Maharishi, but I doubt it."

Avi cut in, "I have a tiger *shikar* coming up in a block fairly near the ashram. We'll pass very near and could pick you up. I'll let you know exactly when it is to be. But it's time for Mia's plane, so let's get over to the other gate."

Rik was filled with chatter. "Boy, what excitement has been coming out of the ashram. You lucked out to be there at the same time as the Beatles. For me though, Donovan is the top of the list." He went on to say how the whole family was enjoying my letters, copied and sent out by Tony's secretary, and that María Luisa was spreading Beatle news to all her friends at school.

Rik's first reaction to Mia was, "She looks like a spook with those funny round glasses." She didn't look at all well. She appeared thin and pale, but seemed happy to see us. In her hands she carried a little metal box. Later she told Avi there was nothing in it, but she wanted to arouse people's curiosity. She had spent a couple of weeks with young people from the U. S. and Europe on the beaches of Goa. I had heard descriptions of the filthy hippie life that had taken over there, but she raved about it. My Indian friends reported it was a source of hepatitis, and that VD was rampant. Evidently, when the kids ran out of drugs, they sold their girls as prostitutes to the locals for seven or eight rupees (about a dollar) to get money to buy hashish.

Mia was very chatty during the five-hour trip back to Rishikesh. Maharishi was full of joy to have her back. You would have thought from her words that she had counted the hours until she could return to the ashram.

Maharishi also gave Rik the warmest of welcomes. Rik had just finished a season's racing on the UCLA crew team and had the leftovers of a crew cut. "I sure feel like a square here with my short hair, button-down shirt, and khaki pants," he mumbled, after seeing what the rest of the group looked like.

But Maharishi was delighted with his appearance. "Rik looks so nice, so clean, so tall—he is a good example of a meditator." (Rik had been meditating six years, which was much longer than the majority taking the teachers' course.)

That first night at dinner, Mia paired off with Donovan and the Beatle group and no one ever saw her again. For the time she remained, she became Donovan's shadow. I couldn't blame her; he is such a beautiful soul. Maharishi had put him in one of the newly-constructed thatched huts. It was bright and full of colorful Indian cloths. Daily, a group would gather there to play music. Both George Harrison and Donovan were studying the sitar. An Indian sitarist stayed permanently during this time to give instruction.

One day a car drove in and a tall man with a large red beard stepped out. He looked like a cossack in his floor-length camel coat and high round hat. As he walked, glimpses of bright red silk lining showed. This was our introduction to Mike Love of the Beach Boys. He had a friendly, melodic voice and a contagious enthusiasm. "Man, am I in rapture to be here." He quickly became one of Maharishi's favorites.

In spite of the musical activity, Maharishi kept to a regular schedule of classes and quiet time for meditation. Only during meals and after evening lecture were there any signs of socializing. This was a pleasant schedule; the longer days of meditation would soon be approaching.

Late one afternoon, I answered a soft knock at my door. It was the Bramachari Satyanand. Also one of my favorites at the ashram, he'd been with Guru Dev at the same time as Maharishi. Then he married and went into the business world. After the death of his wife he rejoined Maharishi. At present, his head and beard were shaven—a sign of the recent death of his father. His eyes twinkled, his face always ready to break into a smile.

"The master would like you to come eat with him."

My first thought was, "Great, maybe I'll get some nice, spicy food." Later, as I scooped up delicious morsels of curried vegetables, I reported that morale was up and that the new regime at the dining area was working well. "Someday you should get a European couple to come and run the ashram for you," I advised. "Rajmohan Gandhi, the grandson of Mahatma Gandhi, has done that at the Moral Rearmament Center in Panchgani; everything is beautifully organized there."

I hoped I hadn't hurt his feelings, but the locals would never run the place well. Dunraj, Maharishi's cook, offered me a second helping. While I continued eating, Maharishi asked specific questions about several of the course participants.

It was an opportunity for direct talk. "Maharishi, I'm still worried about some of the people here. There are several who hardly meditate. Can they become initiators?"

He acknowledged my doubt but added, "We will need many to teach. The publicity we are receiving will create a big demand. We must be ready to strike!" He licked his fingers before dipping them in the silver bowl. "I will multiply myself through all of you. Now that things are running smoothly, we can better concentrate on our course. In a short while, we will bring up the conscious level of all." Always the optimist.

At the beginning of March, Maharishi asked us to meditate in our rooms as long as possible. It became a routine of sitting up and meditating, then lying down and sleeping. After a while, one action flowed into the other and we took no notice of night or day. Occasionally, we got up to receive the food and hot water which had been brought to our doors or visit the toilet. Otherwise, the long meditations resembled hibernation.

While meditating, I often had the sensation of sunlight bursting all over me. I would open my eyes to see if a ray had entered my room, only to find I was sitting in the dark. It was a feeling of ecstasy, similar to my experience at Catalina. I began to understand why holy men often say their experiences are beyond description. Our descriptive language is based on the senses and these feelings transcend the senses. I sometimes felt disembodied, as if I stood on the top of the universe, surveying the whole of Creation, and my life was spread out in front of me.

Sometimes I felt electric shocks and pains in different parts of my body. Maharishi explained that these sensations were due to an imbalance in the body which meditation would put right. He advised us, "Do not open your eyes if you experience panic or something unpleasant. Stop repeating the *mantra* and sit quietly until you are confident of proceeding again. These are deep icebergs beginning to surface." My mind went back to the terror I'd experienced at Catalina. Now I understood what the blackness was.

Back and forth between chair and bed; every couple of hours I lay on the floor, stretched and gently did some yoga *asanas*, exercises, perhaps drinking a cup of tea as well. Time held no importance, little distinguished night and day. With my metabolism low, I had no appetite and required scant food. Though I lost fifteen pounds, I looked and felt fit.

Yogis commonly perform *asanas* in order to keep in shape while meditating ten and twenty hours at a time, but Maharishi didn't want us to raise our metabolisms. He was experimenting with us. However, eventually he allowed some *asanas* so we could remain healthy. Nowadays he insists on meditators breaking for these exercises every twenty minutes—it is called "rounding." He found from our experience that it is too hard on the nervous system for householders to maintain such long hours of continuous meditation.

Except for a spider bite which became infected, I was one of the few students who stayed healthy the whole time. From the very start, I was religious about my exercises as well as taking the vitamins and food supplements I had brought with me. Thank God I had those extra goodies. Rik caught a terrible case of dysentery. Finally, he lived on almost nothing but cheese sandwiches; he couldn't face the food served by the kitchen staff.

When Tim, one of the English cooks, turned twenty-one, we decided to have a little celebration. We needed to blow off steam. With a bit of foresight, I had smuggled in a bottle of vodka from Delhi on my return to the ashram with Mia and Rik. After midnight, twelve of us secretly met in my room. By candlelight it looked like a place you might find if you made a wrong turn in the Casbah, with the heavily-bearded men in Indian shirts and the women in saris.

Raghvendhra joined us. Ascetic looking in his white robes and brown shawl, his black hair cut cowl fashion, he drank two bottles of cider with some alcohol and pronounced the drink to be quite good. We laughed. The mood was conspiratorial and happy. Sipping vodka mixed with tomato puree, the others began to talk about LSD and acid trips.

I said, "Maharishi has always said that if we knew the importance of our nervous system in regard to its being the vehicle for all our past and future incarnations, we would never do anything that might endanger it. He claims that LSD can blow out your nervous system."

"That is an exaggeration, man. Has he ever tried it?"

"One doesn't have to commit murder to know that it isn't for the best of society," volunteered a youth.

Then Sudad from Lebanon said, "I've taken acid at least sixty times." We all stared at him. "If you keep your cool, nothing bad can happen." A quick survey showed that only Raghvendhra and I had not experienced it.

When the Lebanese complained that Maharishi needed to revise his opinions on LSD, Raghvendhra volunteered a surprising remedy. "You get some," he said, "and I'll take it, then I can advise Maharishi better." He suggested I find him some in New Delhi, but I wasn't going to help satisfy his curiosity.

We celebrated until 3 a.m. Everyone left except Mal Evans. He no longer wore his business suit and now looked more like a meditator than a road manager. His life was easy, with the Beatles' attention taken up with Maharishi. He was in a playful mood. He complimented me on the warmth and comfort of my rooms and wondered if I'd like a roommate. I tickled him as I pushed him out the door, remarking that breaking one rule was enough for one day. Then, before going to bed, I put a sign on my door:

MEDITATING—DO NOT DISTURB

That would camouflage the incriminating evidence—empty bottles, cigarette butts and general disarray—"Householders will be householders."


With so many musicians in attendance, dinner time became a time of entertainment. Guitars and sitars were brought to the table, lyrics flowed, and Donovan composed a beautiful song about Jenny, "Jennifer Juniper."

At lunch one day, Raghvendhra made a special announcement which soon spread through the entire ashram. "With the full moon tonight, Maharishi feels it is auspicious to take a moonlight ride on the Ganges instead of the evening lecture." He went on to give directions as to where to meet.

The night was perfect, almost balmy. We had two large, flat barges waiting for us at Swargashram. Rik, an Australian named Terry, and I walked down the hillside and along the river front to the boat landing. Maharishi put us in the boat with the celebrities. He sat at the rear, on a bench slightly elevated above us. Alongside him were two pundits, wise men, to chant the Vedas. As we floated down the river, the two boats stayed alongside each other.

Soon the off-key chanting of the pundits was replaced by far lovelier music. The Beatles sang Donovan's songs; and in turn, Donovan and Mike Love sang the Beatles' songs. Paul Horn played his flute and began to teach Patty Harrison. Some songs became group efforts.

It was a magic night—the temples alongside the river looked ghostly in the moonlight. We tacked from one side of the river to another, not really going anywhere, just enjoying the glistening water, the moonlight, the mountains above us, and most of all the realization of where we were and with whom. It was enough of a thrill to be there with Maharishi, but what great material for my family letter—cruising on the Ganges with the Beatles!

Later, returning to the ashram, rather than wait for a car to come back for us, we walked along the river. While strolling along leisurely, Terry happened to remark, "Did you hear that a tiger or leopard ate the kitchen goat outside the compound last night?" My stroll became a race up the hill—I saw a tiger behind every rock. It was almost too much for the mind to absorb—tigers, Beatles, chanting Pundits, moonlight on the Ganges—we certainly were enjoying life two hundred percent!

---
19
---

# *Storm Warnings*

Most of March was devoted to more meditation and fewer classes; some people did not emerge from their rooms for more than two weeks. Blocks of tension were being freed from our nervous systems. When these fragments reached the conscious level, they often terrified the meditator, but with Maharishi in control, we knew nothing dangerous could occur. He circulated through our blocks, checking on us. In the afternoon, he sat in the park so that we would know where to reach him in an emergency. Although he was in complete control, I don't think he knew exactly what to expect.

Debbie Jarvis, who also hoped to become an initiator, told me that earlier classes had not undergone such long meditations. Jerry took the course in '67. It was an experiment Maharishi was putting us through, and we guinea pigs, unaware of this, simply did as told. It was a first for Maharishi as well as for us, and the results were sometimes frightening and traumatic.

It was unnerving to be around people after long periods of withdrawal. Our metabolisms were low, and activity and excitement were draining. Some people fainted from the slightest exertion. One day, Rik, who joined the long meditations, went to Rishikesh and could not make it back under his own power. Fortunately, no one was allowed to go alone, and the accompanying student half carried him back. I never understood why Rik was not permitted to take the final course; he'd meditated longer than most of the others.

One woman remained alone for three weeks. Twice, I meditated for five days, but could not continue any longer. Five days in itself was a miracle to me. If anyone had told me I could sit in my room for five days, not seeing anyone, not talking, and doing nothing but sleep and meditate, I would have said he was crazy. But with the metabolism gradually falling, there was little desire to come out of hibernation.

One "day" (I had completely lost track of time), deep in a trance-like state of "poised alertness," I felt a strange sensation and heard music in the distance. The music came closer and closer. It sounded like "Auld Lang Syne." Finally, with the music crashing all around me, I opened my eyes to look for it. It continued, but there was no apparent source; I was still in my room and nothing was moving. I shut my eyes. Although I was meditating, I was definitely awake.

I kept on meditating, for Maharishi had instructed, "No matter what happens in your meditation, take it as it comes." My face was wet with tears. Suddenly, I was sitting on Luis's grave in Argentina. My mind's eye must have returned me to the days just after his death. I sat on the raw earth which covered his casket before grass was planted; the headstone was still unfinished.

It was as though I had been teleported. I was there, yet I was also aware of watching myself at the grave. As if I were two people, I observed and felt myself reliving the painful experience.

During the course many of us had experiences such as watching ourselves while sleeping, as if one body had floated out of the other. But what was happening to me was more dramatic. I heard the music enveloping me and felt tears flowing down my face. It was a devastating sensation as I relived the heartbreak of that time—all the despair. I have no idea how long it lasted. Several times, I touched my eyes to make sure they were shut. The scene would not go away, even when I opened my eyes.

Repeating my *mantra*, the scene came and went. Gradually, the music faded away, and I became aware of sitting on my bed, tears still flowing. There was no question in my mind that the scene had happened, and that momentarily I had been there in the past.

I felt confused, but I enjoyed a sense of lightness. Making a cup of tea, I tried to sort out my feelings. The vivid recollection of that experience haunted me for days.

When I told Maharishi about it, he smiled and said, "Very good! That was something you had to get out of yourself."

According to him, if an experience makes a deep impression on the nervous system, it remains there as a big "iceberg" until it is chipped away through dreams, meditation, or even a psychiatrist's couch. Perhaps this "iceberg" had been the source of the ominous feelings I used to have, as if a cloud were hanging over my head. For this experience alone, it was worth going to India. My heart again felt full of love and gratitude for Maharishi.

A young German awakened us one night with terrifying screams. A number of us ran to his room, but he had bolted his door. Looking through the window, we could see him sitting on his bed with a large rock in his lap. He threatened to kill anyone who dared to enter. After a few minutes, Maharishi calmed him enough to come out. The German explained, "I was reliving a lifetime in which I was killed by my neighbors. It was terrible."

Maharishi nodded, "Yes, events from past lives can make up an iceberg, and these submerged experiences are relived as they are released."

One woman described her execution in France! I asked her when this might have happened, but all she would venture was, "Many lifetimes ago."

Some of the younger students, who had been on drugs before they started to meditate, had to endure the worst trauma. Various hallucinogens suppress the dreaming stage during sleep, causing the icebergs to accumulate, so instead of relaxing the user, drugs were adding to their tensions. Generally, the more experienced meditators had less tension to throw off, having chipped away at it for years.

When I met Jane, an Englishwoman from Fiji, everything about her seemed grey—her sari, her face, her hair, her expression. As her room was close to mine, Maharishi asked me to look in and check on her from time to time. On one occasion I knocked softly and inquired if she needed anything. When she came to the door, I could see her swollen eyes. I went to Maharishi and reported that Jane seemed very upset, and that evidently she had been crying for days.

Listening attentively, he asked me to describe her appearance. As he often does, Maharishi paused before replying, "Tell her to rest and to continue meditating. This is something she must get through. If she is tired, she can sleep, but she must return to meditating until this pain is gone."

When she finished that long period, Jane looked like a completely different person. The change was remarkable. It was as if a light had been turned on inside her. Her eyes sparkled and joy seemed to radiate from her innermost being; she appeared to have been reborn. It was hard to recall the former sadness of her face. Later, she confided she had mistakenly carried the burden of thinking she had caused her mother's death.

According to Maharishi, three months of this kind of meditation and cleansing of the nervous system can significantly change one's personality. For me, my experience brought conviction. I felt changed. I felt such joy. Embraced by a serenity I had never known, everything seemed to be at peace within me. Evidently it showed, and people commented on this change.

The long meditations also provided physical improvement. Years before, Genie had been in a severe accident and retained scar tissue and calcification in her neck and shoulders; this restricted free movement of these parts. After several days of continued meditation, her arms suddenly lifted without any conscious direction on her part. She then performed what she described as "a rhythmic-type of movement one would expect to see in a Balinese dance." She found herself bending and stretching in all directions for a long time. When the involuntary movement left her, she got up from her chair and discovered that her former stiffness was completely gone. Months later, x-rays showed that the calcification around her joints had disappeared.

Originally, Mia brought Prudence to the ashram in the hope that Maharishi could help her sister. The rumor we had heard was true; Prudence had flipped out on drugs, and finally landed in an institution where she had undergone shock treatment. After a month in Rishikesh (by this time Mia had left), she had let her appearance deteriorate, dressing sloppily, not combing her hair. By two months she became almost comatose; she could not feed herself. Now she screamed day and night, "Maharishi save me! Everyone go away! Help! Help!"

I begged Maharishi to send the girl to a hospital in New Delhi, worrying that the press might hear of her madness and claim that he had driven her crazy.

"But how could I send her away? She is in no condition to travel. This is the price I have to pay for wanting publicity from her sister, Mia," he said. "If I send her to a hospital, they will just put her back on drugs and give her shock treatment. That way she will never recover. This is what she is afraid of and pleads against." He sighed, "I will work with her."

And he did. Every day, Prudence was brought to his house, literally led by the hand. In her pajamas, with a vacant look on her face and saliva running down her chin, she looked like a mad Ophelia. I doubted that anything could be done for her. Nevertheless, it took Maharishi only three weeks to bring her back to normal, making her again a responsive, happy-looking young woman. (Today, Prudence is married and has two children. With her husband, she is active in the movement in New York.)

One by-product of Prudence's illness was a song by the Beatles. When her screaming fits started, Maharishi asked us to take turns sitting outside her room so she would not feel lonely. John Lennon took his guitar along when his turn came and sat cross-legged on the ground outside her door strumming. Trying to cheer her with his company, he picked out the tune that became famous as "Dear Prudence (Won't you come out and play?)"

I was thankful that the block where Prudence stayed was far from mine. Some of those near her asked to change places with individuals less sensitive to noise. It was an eerie sound to hear in the middle of the night. Luckily for everyone, one meditator came forward and asked to help—Irma, a slight, grey-haired, trained nurse. "Maharishi, give me the room next to Prudence. I have had training with this type of sickness." She had a calming influence, and soon the screams in the night ceased.

While keeping control and supervising the long meditations, Maharishi continued to give special attention to the celebrities.

Again I tried to warn him about feeding their egos, "Sometimes it boomerangs if you cater to them all the time. It might be better if they stayed a bit in awe."

It fell on deaf ears. The stars came and went at will, their will. It spoke well of those who were there to become teachers that their noses didn't get out of joint. Everyone could plainly see who were the Master's favorites.

As I was now in seclusion myself, I was less aware of the situation. However, on several occasions, I was requested to go on shopping trips for the celebrities. This was no hardship. On one occasion, Rik (who stayed on and had a small room nearby) and I went to Dehra Dun—an hour and a half by car—and headed straight for a restaurant, where we gorged ourselves on chicken and ice cream sundaes. Our first feast made us both ill. We were no longer used to rich food.

Since other students did not have an opportunity for such outings, I brought back several cartons of hard-boiled eggs and smuggled them into the ashram to distribute. They were like golden apples. Mia's little dog ate all the shells—it was probably his first source of calcium since mother's milk.

One day I was given a long list of Beatles' needs, so I called Avi for assistance. "We need a copy of Swami Yogananda's *Autobiography of a Yogi* for George, a fixture for Paul's tripod, sandals and hair tonic for John." The list went on.

Avi interrupted, "I finally got John's movie film out of customs. He will never know the trouble this has been; I had to pull every string imaginable—hope he appreciates it."

I reminded him to give me all the bills for Raghvendhra. Maharishi didn't want the Beatles to pay for anything.

Avi went on, "I'll drop the things off on my way to Sitabani. I've given that American couple a free fifth week. How about you and Rik going along? It would just be for two days and it would be nice for the Burkes, they especially like you." They were the hunters Mia and I had joined.

He made it sound as though he'd rather arrive at the camp with the two of us, not with just Rik alone. He added, "We won't say too much about Rik's shooting. The Burkes have paid seven thousand dollars for their original month. They have had several good opportunities to get a tiger, so they can't complain."

It sounded exciting. I requested permission to go when I next saw Maharishi. He had asked me to perform so many special duties, I guess he felt he had to say yes to my request, so Rik, Avi and I took off.

Before leaving the ashram, Avi gave John Lennon his precious film. He accepted it like a king does a small gift from a loyal subject, with hardly a thank you.

I spoke up, "John, Avi struggled with Indian customs for weeks to get that out." He looked at me with a "so what" glance. He was not an attractive personality, although he was looking healthier by the day with the regime of fresh air, meditation, and no drugs. I never doubted his creativeness. He was brilliant, but charismatic he was not.

We drove through the night and arrived in Sitabani before sunup. There was great excitement in the camp, as fresh spore had been sighted. So after hot coffee, toast and eggs we climbed into jeeps and drove to where the elephants were waiting.

Rik and I were put on the lead elephant with Navob, the gentle-man *shikari* (professional hunter) and a *mahout* (the elephant boy). There was no *haudah* (a riding platform), just a large straw-filled mattress roped onto the animal's back. The other seven elephants followed us, while Avi and the Burkes sat in the machands with their guns ready. The pug marks had indicated the whereabouts of the tiger; from a distance we were to form a half-circle and beat the area to drive the animal towards the hunters.

Rik sat facing backwards with his camera ready, "This way I can get great pictures of the beat, and what a way to see a forest!" Sunlight filtered down on us, as birds chattered away and monkeys swung through the trees, attracted by all the shouting and noise we were making. Our elephants moved along, plowing through everything in their way. A sambha (deer) panicked and ran into us—what an uproar that caused.

The air was full of excitement and anticipation. I had semi-straddled the mattress and hung onto a rope for balance. Suddenly, our elephant stopped in front of a large grove of lantana about ten feet high. He growled and trembled all over. The *mahout* jabbed him repeatedly behind the ear, urging him forward. Then came a heart-stopping roar. Our elephant raised his trunk, gave out a deafening trumpet, whirled and bolted as the tiger, a flash of black and yellow, hit the second elephant. It was mating season and evidently we'd interrupted a roman-tic interlude.

Pandemonium took over—all eight elephants crashed through the forest and crossed a river, hurtling stones and breaking trees and any-thing that stood in their path.

Rik, awkwardly hanging on from his backward position, shouted, "Hang on, Mom; if you fall off, the elephant will trample you out of fear." I had wrapped myself around Navob, who was commanding the helpless *mahout* to stop the elephant. My leg struck a small tree. Luckily the tree broke. Rik yelled to the other *mahouts*, "Go back, you chicken shits, let's get that tiger!"

Nothing seemed to stop the stampede until finally the elephant carrying us got caught in the crook of a large tree and stopped, which served to halt the rest. While the *mahout* chopped a branch from the obstructing tree there was time to round up and calm the rest of the pack. I didn't envy the elephant boy who was in that tall grass. My ears were still ringing from the ferocity of the tiger's roar. I now understood how they can paralyze an intended victim.

Navob suggested, "*Memsahib*, it's best you go back to the camp. The other elephants will begin the beat again."

I said, "Oh, no, I'm sticking with all of you." I felt secure on the elephant, as long as I had something to hold on to. It wasn't 'til later that I learned a tiger can run up the back of an elephant, chew on its neck, and sometimes kill the huge beast.

In the meantime, back at the machands, the hunters had heard the commotion caused by our flight, including the roars from the tiger. When we finally reassembled and got back to Avi's group, they were eager to take over our positions and go after the tiger again. "He'll return to his mate," Avi was sure.

Rik and I stepped from our elephant's back on to a small raft-like machand. Rik was given a light gun with a telescopic lens—a gun for deer or other small animals. Avi stayed in the machand across from us as the others returned to the beat.

As our machand was too small for both of us to sit, I stood behind Rik. He whispered, "I have a feeling we're going to see that tiger again, Mom."

I was confident. "Yes, and you will shoot it just as though it were a deer on Molokai." I sounded more calm than I felt.

The beat started—suddenly, I was aware of a movement in the underbrush. I saw Avi point. As I kicked Rik to look, we heard a furious roar—Rik said it startled him so much that he almost pulled the trigger right then. A second later, the tiger broke in front and like a streak of lightening leaped at us. Rik's gun went off instantaneously, hitting the animal's head and stopping its charge. At almost the same instant, Avi fired, hitting it also near the ear and killing it. For a second all was quiet and there was a tiger lying dead two feet from our ladder.

"Rik, I'm so proud of you!"

"Mom, I've never shot so fast in my life. That was real luck. I'm sure glad Avi had that big gun, or that animal could have recovered and been up in the machand with us!"

The elephants returned; everyone was shouting and congratulating Rik. After the initial excitement was over, Avi said to us, "Cool it, unless you want to pay $7,000. You don't want the Burkes to get uptight." Against the real tradition of the hunt, they claimed the skin, saying it was just a fluke they were not in the machand at the time. Rik didn't care, he had had the thrill of shooting the tiger.

As for me, once I got down the ladder and saw the tiger up close, I felt sick. There wasn't a blemish on his coat; he'd been shot down in the prime of his life—what a terrible thing to kill such a magnificent young animal. I would never go hunting again.

The next day, on returning to the ashram, we went directly to see Maharishi. John Lennon, Paul McCartney, Jane Asher and George Harrison were there with him. Rik was worried about his killing the tiger, "Is that bad karma for me, Maharishi?"

The answer was, "You had a desire, now you have satisfied it and will no longer have the desire." (Maharishi must have been right, for Rik hasn't been hunting since.)

"But wouldn't you call that slightly life-destructive?" sneered John.

"Well, it was the tiger or us, " I volunteered, getting into the act.

Paul, with Jane sitting alongside, her head on his shoulder, asked, "Tell us the details, man—what an experience." He always went out of his way to be friendly to everyone.

Later on, John wrote the song, "Bungalow Bill,"—its lyrics telling the story of the tiger hunt: "Hey, Bungalow Bill, what did you kill?" It described Rik as "an all-American, bullet-headed, Saxon mother's son (his crew cut) who always dragged his mom along . . ." Everything was grist for John's writing.*

Maharishi invited Rik to stay on for another month and become an initiator. But Rik had made arrangements to go trekking with a friend

---

*from *Beatlesongs* (1989), by William J. Dowling, "The Continuing Story of Bungalow Bill." Lennon: "That was written about a guy in Maharishi's meditation camp who took a short break to go shoot a few poor tigers, and then came back to commune with God. There used to be a character called Jungle Jim, and I combined him with Buffalo Bill. It's a sort of teenage social-comment song and a bit of a joke." September 1980, *Playboy Interviews*.

*Nancy and Rik Cooke in Sitabani Forest, northern India, 1968*
*with tiger Rik just shot (his last victim!). The tiger hunt inspired*
*"The Continuing Story of Bungalow Bill" by the Beatles*

in Nepal. He'd have to think about it; he would at least stay until the
course was over in Rishikesh.

One day George Harrison wandered over to our rooms. We sat with
him often at lunch and talked about life. This day he had a particular
request.

In his gentle way he asked a favor of me: "Nancy, this means a lot
to me; please convince Maharishi to let us go to the *Kumbha Mela* on
our own." (This is a special religious gathering of holy men in Rishikesh
and Hardwar that takes place every six years.) "He insists that we go on
elephants."

His brown eyes were earnest, "Being a Beatle is already seeing life
from the back of an elephant; we want to mix with the crowds. Maybe
I'll find Babaji (a famous Indian saint) sitting under a tree." He stayed
and talked for several hours. He told us about the two seances they went
to after Brian Epstein died. With his cockney accent, he is such an old
shoe. Being very spiritual—quite a mystic—he was loving every minute
of the course.

One night he and Donovan took their guitars and went to play for Maharishi. Donovan sang for hours, his voice an ethereal breeze floating over the ashram. (His real name is Donovan Leitch, so like my maiden name of Veitch.) He and the Beatles had all written special songs for Maharishi—"Happiness Runs" was Donovan's, and "Cosmic Consciousness" was by Paul.

Actually, George said they had written ten new songs in the five weeks they'd been there, and he was up to twelve hours of meditation at a time. They should have been happy with the treatment they were receiving. When most classes were suspended, they were still having daily sessions with Maharishi—and all of this for free. I hoped they appreciated it.

One day I asked Maharishi directly what they were being charged. "Nothing, Nancy. Just by being meditators they will bring the world to us. In their own way they will repay for all this happiness they are now experiencing." Love filled his face as he spoke of them. But I had my doubts.

What I didn't like were some of the deprecating remarks Tom, the American actor, had made one night at the dinner table—they were aimed directly at Maharishi. Then, when the Beatles' friend, Magic Alex, arrived, I saw him constantly with Tom and his girlfriend. I felt Alex resented Maharishi's influence on the Beatles. Without his noticing it, I watched his face while Maharishi and John talked one evening. The hostility was so evident I wrote home that night, suggesting that Charlie join us as soon as possible. I felt things were getting out of hand.

I'd begun to hear about all sorts of deals involving Maharishi. Mike Love, whom I liked tremendously, was planning a tour for him with the Beach Boys; two other PR men also had a plan—Charlie was needed.

People were getting antsy. Maybe the long periods of silence were being overdone. Course participants complained about never seeing Maharishi. Was he going overboard again? Were my doubts a sign of a weakening devotion? I thought not, but didn't he remember the near disaster with Mia?

As for Mia, she soon had to leave to make a film in England with Richard Burton, and was in the process of getting ready for her departure. The tailor was busy for days making a gown out of Kashmir shawls for her to wear on the trip to London.

Later, we laughed at *Time's* description of her arrival at Heathrow:

"Trying to escape the press, Mia jumped on a milk truck, but was later tracked to her hotel. She was wearing an exotic Indian costume and carrying a mysterious metal box. When asked what it contained, she refused to answer."

Before leaving, Mia went to Maharishi and cooed, "I hate to leave you and all this knowledge." She batted her beautiful wide eyes, "But I will be back to join you in Kashmir." She knew Donovan would return after his concert series; and she had also talked Maharishi into letting her brother, Johnny, be one of the directors for the Guru Dev movie.

I often wondered if she repeated the story of "Maharishi's pass" to Donovan or the Beatles. I now regarded her as a self-serving, selfish young woman. With all the money Mia carried for herself, she left Prudence with nothing. The S.R.M. had to lend her money and pay for her plane ticket home.

I agreed with Genie when she pointed out, "That is not fair. There are so many others who would be good teachers, but could not afford the trip to India." Maharishi's blind spots sometimes puzzled me.

Whenever asked if I think Mia is a good actress, my answer has been, "She's never off stage." Her whole life seemed predicated on an illusion of being what she really was not.

Jane Asher and Paul had to leave the last week in March, after six tranquil weeks; Jane had a theatrical commitment she could not break. It was a heart-warming scene when they said their goodbyes. Paul got on his knees and said, "Maharishi, you will never fathom what these days have meant to us. To have the unbroken peace and quiet and all your loving attention—only a Beatle could know the value of this. You kept your word to us, you protected us from the press and all outsiders. This has been the ultimate luxury. We will never forget you. When John and George get back, we'll work on the plans we've made here."

As Rik and I walked to the upper gate with them, Paul gave Rik his tripod. He said to me, "I'm going away a new man." Jane beamed with happiness. John stood by the gate and, strumming his guitar, bid them a fond farewell. John almost seemed like a different person from the white, pinched faced man who had arrived. He posed happily for me as I took a picture of him with his foot on a rock, playing his guitar.

One night, the first week in April, the two remaining Beatles and their wives met with Maharishi to discuss the Guru Dev movie. John held Cynthia's hand, the first sign of affection I'd seen him show her.

She looked almost happy. The movie was to be focused on Guru Dev, Maharishi, and the movement, and would be shot at the ashram and in Kashmir. George kept coming up with ideas, which John would then contradict or affirm. It was clear who the dominant personality was—clearly John had the highest I.Q., but it was George who was the spiritual leader.

John was in a rare mood that night, ideas for songs and scenes poured from him. "The only thing is, Maharishi, I miss me little son, Julian. Maybe Cyn and me could go back to England and bring him to Kashmir with us. What do you think?"

Maharishi thought it was fine, but I was bold enough to suggest, "It might not be wise, Cynthia, to bring such a young child to India. The food situation would be difficult for you, and dysentery is so dangerous in children. If you have him in good hands, leave him where he is." Cynthia seemed to agree.

"Well," stalled John, "We can make that decision later."

It was a cozy scene; Maharishi lay half-reclining on his bed, tapping his flower to emphasize various points. We all sat on cushions on the floor, our backs resting against the wall. John's guitar lay alongside him; he wore his now habitual white baggy Indian pants, an embroidered white *kurta*, and a sleeveless, long vest. His face was as relaxed as I'd seen it—meditation certainly was bringing good results. He had reached up to fourteen hours of continuous meditation. But I also sensed he was getting restless to get home. Paul's leaving probably brought that feeling out.

"Maharishi, what about our doing a big musical event in New Delhi?" asked George. "With all the artists here, we could put on quite a show. Ravi Shankar is keen to do it with us." Maharishi was all attention.

"Paul and Donovan both said they'd come back if we got something going. Also, Mike says the rest of the Beach Boys could be counted on," added George.

They started making plans. Maharishi was now sitting up, tapping his arm continually with the carnation. Soon he'd torn the flower to bits and it ended up a pile of petals on the couch and the floor.

"Yes, yes, we should have an all out effort and proclaim to the world in one big strike that everyone can enjoy life two hundred percent." Maharishi's enthusiasm was catching. "We will make enough money to start a TV station here as you suggested and broadcast our messages to the world."

"Right on, Maharishi," said John.

This was the first I had heard of the TV venture, but evidently it had been discussed before.

"What is this about a TV station, Maharishi?" I asked.

John answered, "We're going to build a transmitter powerful enough to broadcast Maharishi's wisdom to all parts of the globe—right here in Rishikesh."

They certainly didn't think small. I wondered where they were going to get the labor for such a feat, thinking of the chore it had been just to get their rooms in presentable shape, but I wasn't going to be a wet blanket by being practical. Let Maharishi dream of a big new toy. How wise he'd been to ask nothing from them. My respect grew.

"This will be done after the picture is finished. We don't have a lot of time to waste, man. We'd better start getting the crew and equipment out here if we're going to shoot the ashram before Kashmir." John was now getting down to business.

Maharishi agreed, "Right, it will be too hot here after we return from Kashmir. May is a very bad month—everyone must meditate in the caves."

"O.K., let's put down on paper what we need and get a cable off to Apple Corp tonight," decided John. "Can you send this for us, Nancy?"

Maharishi assured them I could. "Nancy, call Avi and have him send it straight from Delhi."

I suggested sending it in the morning, but got nowhere. Half an hour later, I was on the phone with a two-page message to send, full of technical details, addressed to Neil Aspinall, managing director of Apple Corp, who had visited the ashram previously.

While I was on the phone, George and Maharishi went into a side room to talk privately; John and the rest went off to their rooms. It was well past midnight. Finishing my call, I waited, hoping to get a word with Maharishi. By 1:00 a.m. he still hadn't reappeared, so I left a note saying I'd be over early in the morning as I had something important to discuss with him. I felt uneasy and wanted to remind him of some facts he seemed to be ignoring.

## 20

# Explosion By the Ganges

I T WAS A SHORT NIGHT OF TOSSING ABOUT. At 6:00 a.m., I made my way through the forest to Maharishi's house. Everything was quiet; it was the start of a beautiful sunny day. I knew I would miss this place when we left in a couple of weeks.

"Maharishi, I'm worried. I didn't want to say anything in front of John and George, but you gave Charlie the right to make a deal with Four Star Productions. Tony mentioned in one of his letters that Charlie was on the brink of an agreement with them, and was feeling very enthusiastic about it."

Maharishi listened intently and then threw his arms out as though to encompass the world, "If Charlie has a contract, then they can all work together for the glory of Guru Dev. There will be enough work for all."

"Maharishi, I don't think it works that way. Maybe you'd better phone Charlie? The Beatles have already asked their people and equipment to come without delay. That's what worried me about that cable."

"Yes, you're right; maybe it's better to hold up that message after all. Charlie will be here next week."

But by the time I reached Avi again, with all the difficulties of the Indian telephone system, it was too late; the wire had been sent. We sent another, requesting a delay until they heard from us again. All we could do was pray.

A week later, Donovan and Paul Horn drove to Delhi with me. The first discotheque in India was opening that night at the Oberoi Intercontinental Hotel. Paul was the featured musician, and I would present a fashion show of discotheque costumes. Our timing was coordinated with Donovan's leaving India and Charlie's arrival. I was so looking forward to seeing this level-headed businessman—then I could stop worrying and go back to meditating.

Charlie arrived with the Four Star lawyer and a signed contract. In the car, returning to the ashram, I heard Paul say to the lawyer, "Do you realize what you have? Wow, man, you're going to have the Beatles, Donovan, the Beach Boys, and even Mia promised to come back for the movie. You have just made yourself a million-dollar deal!"

Later, I asked Charlie about it, but he could say nothing until he got to Maharishi. However, he shared my misgivings. "This man has a signed legal document, and that's it. They're not going to share this with another company."

"The whole idea of the movie is sensational—it will be a shame if anything were to happen, " I said.

"Yes, but it will be made one way or another. It's a hot item and everyone wants a piece of the action," he assured me.

Back at the ashram, Maharishi greeted Charlie with love and enthusiasm. In their business suits, Charlie and the lawyer seemed like creatures from another planet.

I asked Charlie if he would stay for awhile.

"Yes, once this deal is set, I could use a little meditation myself. Man, that's a long trip!" His fresh appearance belied his fatigue. They'd been held up by a typhoon in Manila. "Matter of fact, I'll go to Kashmir with you."

During the next few days, there was a lot of activity at Maharishi's house, but I was not included. Taking advantage of this lull, I spent needed hours in meditation. The weather was heating up. Often we sneaked away to have a dip in the river. One morning, early, the day after the first members of the Four Star movie crew arrived, Rik and I crossed over to do some shopping in Rishikesh. We needed to get back before it became too hot, but misjudged our time.

"Oh, that water looks so inviting," I sighed, looking at the Ganges. Perspiration was running down my legs.

"Why don't you just go in—you can't hurt that dress." Rik's inflection indicated he didn't particularly like my denim A-line.

Not wanting to walk around barefoot on the public steps by the boat landing, I wore my shoes into the water also. It was pure heaven. As we sloshed our way up the hill to the ashram, Rik remarked with a laugh, "Our fellow students are in for a shock when they see you, Mom. They've been impressed, the way you're always so well-groomed in spite of the primitive conditions. Wait 'til they see you now."

He didn't look too great himself. Wet pants and shirt clung to his tall frame as we walked through the forest on the dirt road that led to the ashram gate. Now the trees lent welcome shade to a hot Indian afternoon. It was quiet and peaceful except for the constant "craw" of the black birds. It was the hour to stay inside and wait for the cool of the evening.

Coming around the last turn in the road, we met a puzzling sight. A taxi stood at the ashram entrance and George Harrison was loading suitcases. His shiny, long hair hung over his flushed face as a result of his efforts.

He paused to greet us, "Well, you're just in time to say a fast farewell."

"What do you mean? Where are you going?"

At that moment, a teary-eyed Patty Harrison joined her husband. Patty, delicate and pretty, was usually serene and friendly. At this moment she was obviously distressed. "We have to leave because of a misunderstanding."

"But only a few nights ago we were discussing all your plans for making the movie of Maharishi's life. You had definitely decided to go to Kashmir with the group and finish the course. Will you still meet us there?"

As I asked this, an angry John Lennon strode up to the car, "We're not going to join Maharishi there or anywhere—we've 'ad it. If you want to know why, ask your fuckin' precious guru!"

His thin face was tight. Behind his granny glasses, his sharp eyes were full of fury.

"Cyn, get your ass out here! I want to get out of this bloody place, now, for Christ sakes!"

Cynthia was also in tears. I asked the two girls, who had been so thrilled with Maharishi and his course, "What has happened? I have the things you asked me to buy for you." Taking packages out of my tote bag,

I handed them over. "You were all fine this morning. Does Maharishi know you're leaving?" I could not comprehend what was happening.

Before she could answer, John snorted, "Does he know we're leaving? That's the laugh of the day!"

Cynthia spoke with great distress as she was hustled into the taxi after Patty, "We are so unhappy. I can't explain what happened. It is all a big mistake, but the boys insist on leaving."

Rik helped George fasten down the last bag, and in a few moments the car took off, leaving a cloud of dust to settle over our wet clothes.

We stood there stunned—all had been so violent and now the quiet returned. "My God, what could have happened to cause such anger that they'd just leave?" asked Rik. "It's amazing! Let's find Maharishi and get the story."

"Agreed, but we have to get out of our wet things first."

While changing into dry clothes, my mind reviewed the past weeks. The Beatles and their entourage had seemed blissfully content. Several groups of personal friends from England had visited them at the ashram; Jenny Boyd, Patty's sister, had left with one of these groups. Also, Paul and Jane had been so happy when they said goodbye.

A few days before there had been a special *puja* out in the middle of the ashram; a space had been cleared for a flower-covered trellis, which shaded an intricate design of colored rice and combed sand. Patty and Cynthia had appeared in gowns made from saris, their feet decorated Indian fashion. Their soles were painted vermillion and scalloped around the edges. On each toe was a toe ring and they wore anklets with bells. Everyone admired them. John had been popping up everywhere snapping photos. He seemed open and happy with everyone.

Now something else had happened that disturbed me; Tom, the young American actor, and his girlfriend also left. Just as the Beatles disappeared, they had come up the path, dragging their bags, asking if their taxi had arrived yet. What was happening! I didn't like the idea of their being with the Beatles at this moment. They were not true Maharishi supporters and, with John in such an ugly mood, it was dangerous to have them around.

On our way to Maharishi's, I paused, "Wait a minute, Rik; I want to peek in and see how they left the place." We were in front of Block Six. There was nothing much to see, except in John's room. A large photo of Maharishi was torn in half and thrown on the floor.

Rik quickly picked it up in dismay, "What bad karma he's tempting!"

Maharishi was sitting on his bed in his private room when we arrived. He looked sad. We asked him what had happened and told him that we'd seen the group taking off as we returned. He said very little—something about celebrities having fragile nervous systems and icebergs coming to the surface. He suggested we not talk about negative things, that we put our attention on the course. He said the rest of the Four Star crew would be coming and there was much to be done. He obviously didn't want to discuss what had happened, so we left him to his thoughts.

"Mom, it's too big a coincidence. The Four Star lawyer comes and departs happily. Obviously he has a signed contract. Then Maharishi breaks the news to the Beatles—he still expects them to be in the movie, but now they won't be making it. Then some of the movie crew arrives, and a day later the Beatles leave. Wouldn't you say two and two adds up to four?"

In my mind, it couldn't have been anything else. But even then, how could John behave that way after almost two months of enjoying Maharishi's hospitality? And what would happen to the big musical program they had planned for Delhi? The other artists had already agreed to perform.

We felt deeply sorry for Maharishi. So many plans had been made, such beautiful dreams were about to be realized. Would the Beatles voice their anger publicly, or would they keep this disappointment to themselves. Time would tell.

Charlie's opinion was, "With a little time and distance, maybe John will calm down. The others may remind him of what they received—all for nothing. They were never asked to pay a cent; if nothing else, where could they have gone and had all that loving care and attention?"

His optimism was encouraging, but then his next words alarmed me. "The one I don't like is that Magic Alex. I feel he was very threatened by Maharishi. However, now that they're no longer here, maybe Alex has nothing to worry about."

Charlie's optimism did not prove correct. News came later that "the Beatles were critical of Maharishi's materialism." One of them was quoted as saying, "We thought Maharishi was a saint, but he turned out to just be a man." They certainly forgot quickly that it was a dispute over a business matter that got them to leave in such an unfriendly way.

Most of the course participants knew little of the stars' departure. Even when the rumor spread, it was given little importance; everyone was interested in his own rising consciousness as the end of the course in Rishikesh approached.

Summer arrived the last two weeks at the ashram. We were allowed to go on top of our blocks for meditation and sunbathing, so long as we were not observed by the natives. As the trees around us were evergreen, the forest looked about the same except for the hot sun filtering through. Our period of long meditations was over; we looked better with more color in our faces. During the preceding months, most of us looked terrible—pale, with circles under our eyes. Unstressing certainly wasn't a beauty treatment—no wonder Maharishi didn't want people from outside coming in.

Our last day at the ashram was my birthday, April 12, 1968, which I will always remember as special. It started out as a beautiful, clear day, with the promise of afternoon heat. Outside my door was a little copper pot, stuffed with a paper package. The note attached wished me many happy returns from Rik. Inside was a string of beautifully-carved wooden seeds, gold beads and little brass bells. I was delighted. By the time I'd opened my present, he had entered my room. "Here is another combination of beads, Mom; they're for you also."

"Rik, they are simply smashing. When the others see them, you'll have to go into the necklace business."

He handed me a fat envelope, "This is from the family." It was a little album of current pictures of each member of the family during different occasions, including the dogs. Our labrador, Poppy, had had puppies, and we were keeping two. I felt a real pang of homesickness when I looked at those photographs. I realized what a difference it made having Rik with me and told him so. It was María Luisa's birthday also.

She had written ecstatically, "Please thank George and Patty Harrison *especially* for the birthday letter. To think of having my own letter sent and signed by three of the Beatles! Everyone at school had to touch it. Imagine George asking all about me; I'm glad you told him he and Patty are my favorites." It had been George's idea to send the letter. Often I'd thought how María Luisa would have enjoyed being here.

At lunch we were informed, "Because it is the Kumbha Mela, a group of saints are coming today to visit Maharishi. You are invited to come to his house at 3:00 this afternoon. You may bring your cameras if you wish."

We'd all been anxious to see something of the Kumbha Mela, a festival which brought *sadhus, sanyasis,* and holy men of various descriptions from all over India to the Valley of the Saints. George Harrison had wanted to go, but now he was gone. He had missed his chance to view it, even if Maharishi insisted it was to be from a vantage point atop an elephant. I hadn't been able to change his mind about this.

As Rik and I walked into Maharishi's garden, many had already assembled around the small group of holy men sitting in a semicircle, holding hands. One old saint, Satchadananda, in saffron robes, looked a hundred years old with his long, white hair and beard. He seemed to be the most revered and sat holding Maharishi's hand. The other five saints also wore yellow robes except for one; clad in white, as was Maharishi, he had black hair and fierce dark brows. The last to arrive, the real attention-getter, was Tatwala Baba.

We had heard stories of this saint, who lived in a cave in the mountain above the ashram. Some said he'd been there for over eighty years. Maharishi once said he was older than one hundred. As he walked into the garden, he looked like a magnificent Hawaiian king; Kamehameha should have looked like him. He wore nothing but a small G-string and carried a staff. His heavy black hair, coiled in ropes, hung down to the ground. His shoulders and chest were powerful. His face was a mask of serenity. He strode slowly, head held high, over to the group of holy persons. I got some shots of him with my polaroid camera.

Later on, I asked Rik if he thought it was okay for me to give a photo to the saint. He said, "Why not, everyone is moving around snapping cameras." Tatwala Baba was sitting in the lotus position on a mat. I walked up, extending my hand to give him the picture; he raised his eyes. I've never seen eyes like that before or since, so full of purity and strength. Light literally flowed from his face. He took the picture quietly and smiled. I went back to Rik, still entranced by the power of his eyes.

Each saint spoke to us. One went on at great length. Satyanand interpreted, "He compliments Maharishi for what he is doing for the world. From your faces, he sees you are absorbing spiritual knowledge."

Tatwala Baba alone sat quietly, but it was his presence that dominated. When the time came to leave, he quietly arose, nodded his head to Maharishi, and left to go back to his cave—a place I was to visit frequently in the following years. As he passed me, I noticed the smoothness of his dark skin; only his knees showed signs of age. They were wrinkled, maybe from years of stretching in the lotus position. Except for that, he looked to be in his thirties, not one hundred. He made a quiet gesture with his hand—it was a large, beautifully-shaped hand with long, graceful fingers.

After the visitors left, we gathered on top of Maharishi's house. It was an enchanted hour—a warm summer twilight, all the trees in blossom. Maharishi told us of his life with Guru Dev. As he talked, it slowly became dark. We each lighted a candle; the Ganges moved quietly below.

Rik and I floated back to our rooms on a cloud of happiness. "What a birthday present, Mom; one you'll never forget!"

It wasn't over yet. We went to work on our rooms and finished packing. We had ordered a car to come to Laxman Jhula at midnight to pick up Rik, Genie, and me. We'd decided not to accompany the group on the bus. For weeks Maharishi had procrastinated with Avi's office about arrangements for our mode of transportation to Kashmir. In desperation, Avi had exclaimed from his travel office, "What is the matter with that organization! First they ask for one thing and then another." He was really exasperated. "Maharishi wanted a plane chartered, which we did; then he decided it was too expensive and had me cancel it. Two days ago, he instructed me to cancel out the commercial reservations and get the charter again. I finally told him it couldn't be done. As it is, we can't get the whole group on one regular flight. I've had to pull all sorts of strings to get seats on the next."

The phone had cut in and out, but his impatience was clear. "I'll do anything for Maharishi, but he's got to stop changing plans after each person tells him something different; now he's canceled the cars they'd ordered from Delhi, and the truck to carry all the luggage. He's been assured that cabs from Rishikesh, a bus, and an independent truck can do the whole thing from there. I'll go along with whatever he wants, but pray to God they get to those planes or my name isn't worth a rupee!" Then before hanging up he had reaffirmed that our car would still come for the three of us.

Just before going to dinner, Maharishi sent word for me to come to his house. With a greeting he asked, "Did you enjoy the afternoon of your birthday with the Saints?" He looked radiant himself. "It has been a very auspicious day, and now I would like to do a special *puja* for you in front of Guru Dev." It was a surprise; I was thrilled.

Unfolding his legs and gathering up his robes, he signalled me to follow. We went to the front veranda and descended the steps that led underground. The doors at the end of the stairs were usually kept locked, but were now open to us. It was the first time I had been in Maharishi's private *puja* room. It was a small room, draped with yellow cloth and softly lighted by candles. Small, high windows let in a bit of fresh air and light by day. A delicious, spicy aroma of incense permeated the room. Against one wall was a small altar and portrait of Guru Dev. A garland of fresh flowers lay on the table. Maharishi asked me to kneel on a small pillow as he lighted a candle and more incense. He then put the flowers over my head, on to my shoulders, and began chanting his devotions to his master.

During this time, I was in a state of rapture. It was such a privilege. Maharishi performing a special *puja* for me. Each moment was precious. Maharishi took the lei from my shoulders and placed it in front of Guru Dev. He then placed his hand on my head and ran it down the length of my hair. The warmth of his hand permeated my head. All the time he was chanting in Sanskrit—I felt I had just been personally presented to his lord and master. Tears of happiness ran down my cheeks. I knew I'd had an experience of bliss consciousness.

When the ceremony was over, Maharishi led me upstairs and said, "You will go forth, Nancy, and represent me in wisdom." He also mentioned we'd meet later in the lecture hall. There were no words with which to thank him. My heart was so full of love and devotion.

When I described my hour with Maharishi to Rik, he reacted, "Mom, in your entire life you will never again have such an important birthday." And to think that Mia had tarnished the same honor by looking at it through her own dirty glasses.

Then, from the divine to the mundane. As I disassembled my room, I felt nostalgic. I had spent such happy, serene hours in this little haven of pleasant vibrations. I decided to leave the swan carpet on the wall—someone else would enjoy it. Everything was packed and ready before the three of us went over to a late dinner—our last dinner in Rishikesh with the group.

Everyone felt as we did. There were no more complaints; everything was rosy-hued and covered with nostalgia. Even the boiled vegetables tasted good.

When we met at the lecture hall, it was dark as usual, but I felt Maharishi could see my shining face glowing above the others. My dearly beloved Guru.

We meditated for a few moments in silence; then, on hearing his quiet "Jai Guru Dev," we opened our eyes.

"Tonight we have Nancy's birthday to celebrate and also our departure for Kashmir. For the double celebration, the cooks have made us cakes, which we will now enjoy, and then afterward we will have a display of fireworks over the Ganges."

Huge trays with pudding-like carrot cakes were passed down the aisles. I sat on the stage next to Maharishi and ate my helping. It was delicious—again the cook had worked a miracle. With the primitive facilities they had, it was unbelievable.

Fireworks were set up on the gravel path in front of the hall entrance. Maharishi instructed a Brahmachari to light the first fuse. "To the glory of Guru Dev!" he exclaimed with delight, as the rocket went up into the air and out over the river. He clapped his hands together in joy—his face was wreathed in happiness like a young child.

His enthusiasm was so contagious that a rather insignificant display of fireworks became a feat of magic. I continued comparing my reaction to my birthday festivities with Mia's reaction to hers. "It is in the eye of the beholder."

It all ended too soon. It was after eleven when Rik and I walked back to Maharishi's house with him. Others followed. He knew we were leaving and would meet again with the group at Delhi airport. My words of thanks were inadequate, but he knew the emotions that existed deep in my heart.

Without Rik, I couldn't have done it. We half-carried Genie and half-dragged our suitcases along the rocky, dirt path to Swargashram. Thank goodness we'd sent things ahead with Avi. Finally, we encountered our waiting cab driver, who then helped us on to Laxman Jhula, where we crossed the swinging bridge over the swirling waters and climbed the steps to his waiting cab.

The buses and a truck for luggage for the group were parked alongside our taxi. They were scheduled for a 9:00 a.m. departure. Luggage was to be put outside each room to be picked up by the porters.

I was so happy in the knowledge that mine was going with me, even though it had almost broken my back to carry it out. We hardly spoke as we left the Valley of the Saints behind us—each deep in his own thoughts.

---
21
---

# The Vale of Kashmir

I T WAS A MIRACLE, but at the appointed time, two days later we were all
ready and waiting to board the plane in Delhi. There were tales of a
chaotic takeoff from the ashram, but all that mattered was we were
on our way to Kashmir.

Mike Love got the prize for travel costumes; his floor-length Raja
coat with lining and pants in matching blue were stunning. It had been
fun seeing his different outfits and wild collection of hats. One evening
he came to dinner in a full length, red velvet chemise. At other times,
he copied the Beatles, wearing the wide pants of the laborer and the
Indian *kurtas*—this also had been Donovan's favorite.

Our plane circled over Delhi and then headed north. Maharishi
was surrounded by members of the movie crew; he looked tired. No
wonder, while he had been giving our course, receiving outsiders,
handling individual problems, and teaching a group of Indians in the
lower part of the ashram during late afternoons, he was being pulled from
place to place by these movie men. Maybe he'd get some rest in Kashmir.

The engines hummed on monotonously, and within a short time,
we were looking down on snowcapped mountains. As far as the eye could
see, the huge, silent Himalayas lay below. Mountains untouched by
human exposure gleamed pristine white in the thin sunlight. Purple

shadows began to creep across the range, adding a dimension of forbidding cold.

Soon, with the snowy peaks behind us, we looked out over tree-lined lakes and lush, green fields. The cragged, white mountains looked down with envy on this bowl of spring beauty. The Vale of Kashmir seldom fails to thrill the first time seen. As we came closer to the ground, we saw trees in full blossom, golden acacia blazing across the hillsides, and willows silhouetted in still waters. This was the home of the fabled Shalimar gardens, and the colorful houseboats, a tradition left behind by the British Raj. Tom Slick and I had spent several days here.

A group of reporters surrounded us at the airport terminal in Srinagar, the capital city. Maharishi amused me when interviewed. "God has blessed this place with majestic mountains, an invigorating climate, and beautiful land; what a shame you are such miserable people." It could be taken two ways, but I knew he was referring to the political unrest. News of Sheik Abdullah's release from prison had been in all the Indian papers; street riots and uprisings against the Hindu government of Kashmir were the order of the day. Maharishi had almost canceled our coming because of the trouble.

My friend, S.K. Roy, had explained it to me briefly when I last saw him in Delhi, "It seems to be a situation without solution. Actually the Kashmir government outsmarted itself and is now stuck with a Hindu ruling body and a populace that is eighty percent Moslem."

He put it in simple terms, "As partition approached and the day of the British Raj came to an end, each large state was consulted as to which way they wished to go—to become part of Pakistan, or to stay within the subcontinent of India. Only Hyderabad, in south central India, was refused the choice. Its Naizim, or ruler, was a Moslem, but being surrounded by Hindu states, it wouldn't have been practical to become Pakistani for all its sentiments."

The old Naizim of Hyderabad was reported to be one of the world's richest men. When the Bank of India tried to ascertain approximately the value of his huge holdings, they sent a jeweler to appraise the valuables in his palace. After a month of listing cigar boxes filled with diamonds, rooms full of gold bars, an armory of jewels, weapons, and all sorts of *objets d'art*, the jeweler gave up, estimating he'd listed less than ten percent of what was there. It was impossible to stay on; the Naizim made a continual fuss about the amount of electricity the jeweler was using by turning lights on at night.

"However, Kashmir was different," my friend continued. "Geographically it could logically join either country. The Maharajah of Kashmir, a Hindu, began to play games with both sides, waiting to select the highest bidder. He waited too long; Pakistani troops moved across the border to grab the wealthy prize—the fruit and grain bowl of India. By the time they occupied one-fifth of Kashmir, the Maharajah appealed to the New Delhi government for help. The government's reply was, 'How can we send troops to help you; you are not even part of us.'"

"With that, the Maharajah threw his hat into the Indian ring." S.K.'s voice was sad as he concluded, "And since that time, Indian and Pakistani troops have faced each other across that unnatural border—a constant cause of irritation. The Kashmir government wants that one-fifth back, while the Moslem population demands the right to join their Punjabi brothers in Pakistan. Sheik Abdullah has become their leader. Nehru promised them a plebescite, but never kept his promise. There doesn't seem to be a practical solution; neither side will give an inch."

After the expected confusion of collecting luggage, we took taxis to Dal Lake. From a small landing we boarded *shikaras,* small gondola-like boats covered in gay printed fabrics, each sporting its own name. We were paddled to a tiny island of green lawn, on which sat the Greenview Hotel, which would be Maharishi's quarters. All around the large landing area were boats and wooden docks leading to other boats. One barge would serve for the dining area.

"Riki, this is where we really take care eating. Foreigners always get sick in Kashmir," I cautioned. After his bout with dysentery, he was having trouble gaining back the weight he'd lost.

The Garoo Brothers, Moslem owners of this particular group of boats, looked like an unkempt bunch of ruffians. I chuckled as they assumed the *namaste* salutation and greeted Maharishi with a pious and very Hindu greeting, "Jai Guru Dev." Kashmiris could be such con men.

The movie group suggested I stay on their boat—a lot of meditating I would have done. I was flattered, but, laughing, I declined. As directed by the rooming list, Rik and I took *The Flower of Kashmir,* docked next to the landing. All trimmed with filigreed wooden panels, this was one of the nicest boats.

The entrance was a small gangplank extending into the pantry area. Our large dining room was furnished with a high boy filled with glasses, an ornately-carved dining set for twelve persons and a crystal chandelier. The whole boat was covered from stem to stern with

Kashmiri-made, Persian carpets. The living room was cozy with over-stuffed chairs and sofas. With everything covered in a different print, the place was a riot of soft colors. The effect was "faded British," but with a sense of festivity. The floorboards creaked as one walked the length of the boat. Gathered curtains covered the doorways to the bedrooms. Rik and Terry, another student, took one room and I another. Genie, not taking the teacher's final instructions, was on another boat and would leave before the course was over.

The air was cold; the bed mattresses felt damp. I looked for the customary wooden stove used on these boats during the winter, "No, *Memsahib*, we never use stoves after March," answered Ramzoo, our number one house man.

"I don't believe it; I was here on the *California* in April years ago, and our boat was heated the whole time." I'd inquire tomorrow. A Kashmiri boatman would figure costs down to the last *pisa*.

Later, we all met for a hot bowl of soup. The truck with luggage was not to arrive until the next day. Some people hadn't realized how cold it would be and were insufficiently dressed. We passed out the extra warm things we had.

"Boy, am I glad we brought our luggage with us," exclaimed Rik. Years of traveling with groups had taught me that.

Within three days, because of damp beds and no extra clothing, half of our classmates had colds. Finally, with tenacious insistence, we got little wood stoves for each boat. They were quickly assembled; a panel came out of the side wall of each bedroom and the flue was attached. Every morning the houseboy, Ahmed, would come in with a hot coal and get a fire started. Soon the bedrooms were nice and toasty—a bit smoky, but warm.

Serious grumbling was disturbing an otherwise serene atmosphere, but finally, *four* days later, the luggage truck arrived. The driver said he had broken down; we figured he took a nice sightseeing trip and called on a few friends.

I complained to Rik, "If all these details were attended to in advance, it could have been a shorter course." Finally, housekeeping problems were solved and classes began. Much time was devoted now to learning the *puja*, written and spoken in Sanskrit and difficult for Westerners to learn.

One morning in exasperation, I exploded, "This damn Sanskrit! It seems to be following me! When I took the entrance test for Stanford, the thesis, which I was given to read only once before answering the questions concerning it, was all about Sanskrit. I remember everything seemed to look alike and start with an 'S'!" I think Rik learned it faster than I from checking me each day. Thank goodness he stayed on.

But pleasant days followed in rapid succession. In the afternoons, we went by *shikara* (small boats) past Nehru Park, an amusement playground on the lake, out into the large part of the lake where Maharishi had a big, two-storied barge set up as a classroom. On sunny days, Maharishi sat on top under an umbrella while we baked in the welcome rays.

We all looked rested and healthy, except for Maharishi. The movie crew was making terrible demands on him. Rik and I went to see Charlie, who after a short absence had recently returned.

"Charlie, each day Maharishi looks more tired. That crew had him up at dawn on top of Gulmarg (one of Kashmir's highest mountains), riding a toboggan in the snow; another time he was on a donkey. Yesterday they photographed him in the old Fortress in a little silk dhoti while they were all bundled up in woolens—they're going to kill him!"

Charlie, who had a terrible cold himself, soothed us, "Don't forget, Maharishi is not an ordinary man. He knows what he's doing. He'll be all right." I wish I could have believed him.

One afternoon, Rik and I went to call on Miss Helen Stravides, to whom we had a letter of introduction. She was a tiny English-Greek lady whose factory, Kashelen, turned out beautiful, hand-embroidered fashions. Not even five feet tall, she made up for it with her spunk and vitality.

"After working for thirty-five years with these thieving, irresponsible Kashmiris, I'm about ready to give up! What I'd give to have a young man like you, Rik. Stay here as my assistant." They had such fun putting their creative heads, one grey and one brown, together. Sitting on the floor they designed shirts for men, and *pherrans*—long, knee-length, baggy Moslem over-blouses—for me. From carved wooden blocks Rik stamped out various designs on paper. Then, after selecting wool or cotton fabric, they would pick the shades to be used for the embroidery from balls of colored yarn.

Afterward, sitting in Miss Helen's garden, sipping tea, it seemed like paradise. Willow trees hung over us, violet wisteria dripped from the roof of the house. Lilac bushes sent us their fragrance. The earthen beds

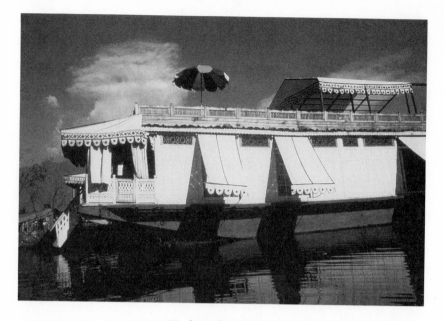

*Kashmiri houseboat*

*Class on Dal Lake, Kashmir*

*Maharishi on boat
in Kashmir*

*Maharishi's boat (shikara) in Kashmir*

*Jerry Jarvis with Maharishi in Kashmir, 1968,*
*just before Maharishi became ill*

were bursting with every spring flower California had ever seen—between the garden and a river was a field of brilliant acacia.

"Can you believe it, Rik? It's breathtaking!" He had a Pekinese dog in his lap—several others lay at his feet.

"And, Mom, did you see the *objets d'art* Miss Helen has in her house? What wonderful sculptures, and such carpets. What a place."

"This is the reason I'm still here, Rik," Miss Helen said. "Kashmir is a mixture of all that is good and evil. It is a difficult place to live and almost impossible to work. For five months each year we're snowed in. This is the time when the people do their intricate handwork, whether it's carving furniture, making *papier maché*, Persian-type carpets, intricate jewelry or embroidered woolens. But nothing is organized. The minute someone makes money, he brings in others to do the work and the quality drops. There is no consistency. We should have a big leather and fur business, but nothing is well done."

Her prematurely wrinkled face showed concern. "Some of the worst people in the world are merchants here." She went on to tell us stories about one called "Suffering Moses" and warned us not to shop at his business. "He beat up his American wife and I had to take her in. His brother, Abdullah, who has Asia Crafts and is very reliable, no longer speaks to him." I Am a Jew, Cheap John, and Sulhim the Wurst were other merchants' names we loved.

Walking down Srinagar's main street, Polo View, we passed little wooden stores that hugged the broken sidewalks. "The Butterfly," "Ali's Art Palace," and "G.M. Shah" were some of our favorites.

We did most of our shopping and ordering those first days before the course schedule started. Maharishi was busy with the movie makers.

Then sickness struck our boat; both Terry and Rik came down with the flu. When Rik's fever stayed high, Miss Helen arrived one day with her doctor, "You can't let this go; this is a tricky climate. You do what he says, Rik." We were touched by her concern. Later, she confided to me that she had lost her baby, born prematurely, after receiving news of her English husband's being killed by an avalanche in Norway during World War II. Her son would have been exactly Rik's age.

The doctor left, saying he would be back the next day.

As Maharishi had been off with the movie crew all that day, class was held late in the afternoon out on the barge. Maharishi looked terrible—his color was gray, and under his usually vibrant, luminous eyes were black circles.

His voice was hoarse as he lectured to us. Someone suggested he recline and rest a bit as he talked. In his weakened voice, he said, "I am now a bad example for you. Because of too busy a schedule, I have not tended to my own body's strength. You must let nothing in life interfere with your meditation; there will always be a force trying to keep you from it." Finally, we insisted we end the meeting in order for him to get some rest; we couldn't bear to have him sacrifice himself further for us.

Maharishi returned to the hotel in my *shikara*. "Nancy," he implored, "Please ask Charlie to give me one full day of rest. Twenty-four hours and I'll be all right."

His request almost broke my heart, after all he'd done for us. I remembered those first days in Rishikesh. All night Maharishi had wandered from place to place with workmen, getting broken pipes fixed, windows insulated against the cold, and tending to a hundred things. Now he was begging for our help.

"Maharishi, if I have to stand in front of your door all day and night, you will have that time. I'll talk to Jerry and Charlie immediately when we get back."

He smiled weakly, "I'm always happy when you are around, Nancy." Nothing could have spurred me on to faster action than that!

We arranged to take turns in front of his door. At the same time, I concentrated on learning the *puja*. The only person allowed in was the cook, Dunraj, who also gave Maharishi a rubdown. That evening, when the doctor came to see Rik, I convinced Maharishi to allow the M.D. to check him also.

The report was ominous, "He has double pneumonia and should be in a hospital. Do you have an antibiotic from the U.S.?" Yes, I did. He gave it to Maharishi, with instructions on how much to take and said he'd return the next day.

When we asked him how long Maharishi's sickness would take, he replied, "That man can't do anything for two weeks at least; it would kill him."

Charlie was in a real bind. The movie group was at his heels, badgering him about their schedule, about the money they would lose if they missed their dates in Benares, Chandigar and other chosen sites. Shortly after that they were scheduled to be in Turkey and Greece. All this with Maharishi.

"Well, you aren't going to have much of a picture with a dead man on your hands," Charlie pointed out, but he agreed to discuss it with Maharishi. However, Jerry, who had recently joined us, and I took a firm stand. We wouldn't even let beloved Charlie in to see Maharishi! We had guaranteed him those twenty-four hours.

As promised, the doctor arrived the next day. He pronounced Rik well enough to start getting up and around. Next he called on Maharishi. Twenty minutes later, it was an amazed doctor who returned. "I've never seen anything like it!" His face was a mask of incredulity. "He is completely cured—I could find nothing in his lungs. He has no fever, his eyes are bright, and he's feeling fine. It is not possible, but I've seen it myself!" He left talking to himself, shaking his head in disbelief.

We laughed, both from relief and amusement. He didn't know the power of a Maharishi. I later wondered if Maharishi took my acromycin as ordered. Probably not.

The course wound down to its last days. Some people left; some as initiators, some as lecturers and checkers for the movement. Thirty-two of us were selected to become teachers. I was so relieved to be one of them. Now Jerry gave us minute instructions regarding initiations; even

Rik could not be told these details. This was a confidence we shared only with Maharishi and other initiators. Sporadically, Maharishi called individuals to perform the *puja* for him; then gave the final instructions, which only he passed along.

As I kept waiting to be called, Charlie explained, "Nancy, his schedule is so hectic trying to make up for lost time, he may not make all of you initiators until he gets to the States in June."

I was *so* disappointed. I wanted to perform the *puja* and get it over with, while it was still fresh in my mind. Also, I wanted to arrive home as an initiator. But the time came to leave Kashmir, and I was not a teacher.

We were now a small group as we arrived in Delhi for an overnight stay at the Oberoi Intercontinental Hotel, before Maharishi's going on to Chandigar in the morning. As we entered the lobby, I asked Maharishi, "May I bring Mr. Gautam Khanna, the managing director of the Oberoi chain of hotels, to meet you?" He agreed.

Gautam Khanna, husband of the Oberoi daughter and a quiet, serious man, was highly respected in India for his business ability. On being introduced to Maharishi, he made an offer. "We feel it is an honor to have you here, Maharishi, and we would like to be the first hotel in India to offer a meditation room. We would make it part of our health club complex, where we also offer saunas, pools, exercise, and massage. We would put a card in every room telling our guests about it."

"Excellent, excellent. The atmosphere in your hotel will be irresistible," and Maharishi went off into peals of laughter. It was contagious and we all joined him.

"Maharishi, Mr. Khanna may run for the Maharani of Jaipur's seat in Parliament." (The Maharani had been initiated into TM by Maharishi several years before.)

Oh, very good, what party do you represent?" Maharishi asked. "The Swatantra Party, Maharishi, the conservative party in opposition to the Congress Party."

"Yes? But don't you think it would be better to run for the Congress Party? They always seem to get elected," offered our seemingly naive guru.

"But, Maharishi, I don't agree with their policies," countered Gautam.

"Fine, I understand. But it is better to first get elected, and then, secondly, start enforcing your policies. You can do little on the outside," said our Saint from the Himalayas to the astute businessman. We all laughed—even Gautam agreed that he might be right.

As we took leave, Maharishi said, "Nancy, would you remain behind. I think it is time for you to be made an initiator." I almost collapsed with surprise and joy. Maybe this was the best way for it to happen. I had no time to get nervous. Half an hour later, I walked out of Maharishi's room a teacher of Transcendental Meditation. What a joy, and what a relief! On joining the Khannas and Avi in the Chinois Room for dinner, my first request was to place a call to California to tell my family that I had made it!

Later, in bed, I examined the reasons for my delight. Of course, there was a sense of achievement, of fulfilling a hard-earned goal, but it was more—now I knew the power and value of meditation. It had been worth the sacrifice my family had made. I felt so honored to be entrusted with the wisdom I'd been given. Now I could share with others something I considered a great jewel in my life. It was all of these reasons, but also it was the relief of having performed well for my guru. He had complimented me on my *puja*. I had justified his faith in me.

---

## 22

---

# Dark Forces Attack

ONCE THE COURSE WAS OVER, the pull was to head directly home. I had been away for three months, a long time; but it was Rik's first trip to India, and he was anxious to see more. B.K. Nehru, now the governor of Assam, the easternmost state of India, had invited us for a visit. "Fori and I will be most interested in hearing firsthand about your course, and you will find Assam fascinating. It is the home of many colorful tribes, such as the Mizus and Nagas. Also, you should visit Kazarenga, the one-horned rhino sanctuary. Rik will have a field day there with his camera."

Rik had implored, "We can't turn down such an opportunity." However, I was worried about being gone even longer than originally planned, even though in his letters, Tony constantly referred to how busy he was and how lucky it was that we were all away at the time—he had no energy left over for anything but preparing for and moving into his new law offices.

I held up my decision until I reached Tony by phone. Then his strong commentator's voice assured me, "By all means don't miss seeing Biju and Fori. Actually it will give me an extra week to get ready for your return." That decided it and we accepted the Nehru's invitation.

Sometimes it occurred to me there might be other reasons for Tony's enjoying my absence. The year before a doctor had diagnosed Tony as having rheumatoid arthritis. He said not to worry, it could be controlled with increased dosages of cortisone. Until then I had not known that Tony had been taking a steroid for what he thought was gout. It was a very mild dosage, but a steroid is a steroid. I protested, but to no avail.

Slowly our physical relationship changed. Lovemaking became a sporadic event rather than a regular activity. Tony felt guilty about this in spite of my assurance that all was well and happy—maybe my not being there took the pressure off of him.

On the way to Assam, we stopped over in Calcutta. S.P. Jain, an Indian business tycoon and friend of Maharishi's, had invited us to be his guests there. Uneasy about the stories of abject poverty he'd heard, Rik rationalized, "If we're going to the 'Black Hole of Calcutta,' it sounds like the right way to do it."

Right he was. We were met at Dum Dum Airport by Mr. Jain's personal car and secretary and whisked to his white marble home. The guest cottage, which we occupied alone, could comfortably hold up to two hundred people. We were not crowded. "What a contrast to the ashram!" Rik exclaimed. However, with all its cavernous pretentiousness, it had neither taste nor charm. For all the marble, we still had to sleep under mosquito nets and provide our own toilet paper and soap. Nowhere was there a plant or a scroll to please the eye.

The first evening, as we sat in a small group on a huge, bed-sized divan, eating off of silver trays, or *talis,* with our fingers, Indu Jain, our host's pretty daughter-in-law, asked, "Nancy and Rik, my friends are so curious about Maharishi and TM. When you come back from visiting Governor Nehru, would you give us an evening? I'll get a group together." We agreed; they would have friends who were the kind of people Maharishi wanted to reach.

Leaving for Assam early the next morning, we sped by the race track, the country club, government house, and the Calcutta museum, a huge stone structure built by the British Raj. So far we had seen only the elegant side of Calcutta. On arrival we had been so deep in conversation we hardly noticed the pitiful, rag-covered bodies sleeping in the gutters and along the streets, their faces turned to the moist, crumbling walls. Millions of

Pakistani refugees had reached a nadir in human suffering, in what had once been the cultural pride and seat of the British Raj.

Now, alone in the car on our way to the airport, there was no diversion. "Oh my God, Mom, how can people exist like that?" Rik pointed to an entire family, one of many, living on a sidewalk. Several were still asleep, while a young girl cooked over an open fire and the mother washed things out in a battered pan by the gutter. Further down, a man was squatting using the same gutter as his toilet. "Even animals live better than these people. Where is the justice which forces man to descend to such depths? What terrible karma these people must be paying off!" Just wishing them well with their tests did little to assuage our shock.

The streets were total confusion; filthy, over-crowded buses pushed their way through traffic partially composed of wagons and flat beds, pulled not by oxen, but by men, as were the rickshaws. Horrified by the squalor and suffering, we were glad to leave Calcutta behind.

Flying low over rolling green hills, palm groves, rice paddies and tea plantations refreshed us. We felt we had entered another country, as it was necessary to get special military permission to visit Assam. Infiltrated by Chinese-trained guerrillas, various tribes, especially the warlike Nagas, had been plaguing the Indian army with uprisings, demanding independence from Mother India. A challenging position for B.K. Nehru, whose car and driver awaited us at the airport.

It was a beautiful drive to Shillong; tropical lushness enveloped us. As we passed through the town, it looked more like a small village than the capital city. Soon we arrived at the governor's residence. Guards in British-influenced regalia stood at attention as we passed through grilled iron gates. Ahead, on a small hill, stood Raj Bhavan, the governor's mansion. It was a marvel of Victorian gingerbread architecture, with leaded glass windows (impractical in the tropics), high peaked roofs, and dormers. Biju and Fori, his Hungarian wife, who appeared more Indian than the Indians, were at the door to greet us.

"Welcome to Raj Bhavan! You are our first guests since we arrived in Assam." Biju embraced me. I had not seen him since he had helped me with the Indian Ambassadors appointed to South America. There was more gray in his abundant dark hair. Tall and slim as always, he conveyed a regal dignity.

*Rik and Nancy in Kazarenga, the one-horned rhino sanctuary*
*in Assam, 1968*

*The swami in Shillong, Assam*
*who invited me*
*to speak to his congregation*

*Nancy in Assam with*
*Gov. B. K. Nehru*

When I complimented him on his trimness, he explained, "We have an indoor tennis court which is a joy. Very thoughtful of the British. They did know how to enjoy life."

I thought how the British must have hated to give up the fabulous life they had in India; middle-class people lording it over a whole continent—not that they hadn't left some good traditions behind. They were certainly better colonizers than the Portuguese, who raped Goa of its wealth, and did nothing for the people except to build Catholic churches during their years of occupation.

Fori embraced Rik, "I'm so thrilled to have an architecturally-trained person here to help me. This gigantic place is in need of so much work, I don't know where to begin."

They had arrived only three days before and had yet to see the city of Shillong. "We will be your pioneers and scout the land," we volunteered. As governor, Biju was tied down receiving one welcoming tribal delegation after another. He had just returned by helicopter from the Naga front that morning. This would be a far different assignment from being the Ambassador to the U.S. for ten years.

Shortly after we arrived, the governor's aide came to my room. "Mrs. Nancy, the Swami of the Ramakrishna mission sent this note. He asks permission to call on you." It was an honor, but we decided it would be more correct if Rik and I were to visit him. We sent a message back that we would call that afternoon.

When we did arrive at the mission, the swami greeted us warmly, his chubby, middle-aged face wreathed in a wide smile. No *namaste* for him; he took my hands in both of his and expressed his delight that my son and I had come.

Over a cup of tea, he explained, "My congregation is so interested in hearing about what Swami Mahesh is teaching. Our newspaper has carried all sorts of tales about the celebrities at the ashram," his eyes sparkled with humor, "We feel Swami Mahesh must have special wisdom to attract Westerners to leave their comfortable, full lives, and come to live in primitive conditions in India." Oh, if only there were more people like you in India, Swami, we thought.

"Would it be an imposition to ask you to come to our mission tomorrow and give a small talk?"

I protested that I wasn't qualified to speak to Indians about meditation.

"Yes, yes, that is fine, but you could give us your impressions and maybe answer a few questions. We are starved for news here in Shillong." There was no way out; I hoped that Biju wouldn't object and told the swami I'd clear it with the governor and get back to him.

Later, seated at a small table in a corner of the huge dining room, I brought up the subject of our invitation. Biju chuckled, "I have to hand it to you two. You haven't been here a half a day, and you're already out proselytizing the natives!"

Fori told him to behave himself, adding, "I think it would be a very nice gesture on your part, Nancy. I will attend the meeting with you. Also, we've decided to take time off tomorrow to have a picnic and do a little sightseeing."

To go on an outing with a governor was an experience. As our official car went through the gates, the soldiers came to attention and then did a doubletake—the governor was driving himself. Immediately following us was a car with his aide and a secretary. Following them was a troop carrier. It was the first time the Nehrus had seen anything of their local surroundings.

Rik and I were able to point out a few landmarks we'd discovered the day before. The land was productive, but one crop puzzled us. Finally, Biju stopped and asked his aide, who came running up, to find out what it was.

"Potatoes, sir," came back the answer. We laughed, expecting something more exotic. When we walked through the fresh produce market, the word went out and a crowd began to gather.

After an hour or so of sightseeing, Biju suggested, "How about finding a place for our picnic?" We finally saw the perfect spot and stopped. The crew of soldiers and aides spread out blankets and a large tablecloth, and we were served our picnic lunch on silver platters and bone china. After lunch, Biju picked out a comfortable spot for a nap. He slept blissfully while armed soldiers kept watch. Rik was amused, "How do you like this 'informal' picnic?"

Too soon it was evening and time to be at the mission. Inside, rows of benches were filled with eager faces. The air was pleasant, with windows open on three sides. At Fori's suggestion, I wore a sari.

The swami introduced me graciously as the governor's guest and I took it from there. Rik had suggested I give an outline of our course and a simple explanation of Maharishi's fundamental wisdom. To that, I added stories about the celebrities, such as our musical night on the

Ganges. It was a quiet but responsive audience. From every window faces looked in. After I finished, Rik and I answered questions. They seemed delighted with Rik's explanations, especially when he described coming back from the tiger hunt and being accused of a life-destructive act by the Beatles.

Fori complimented us in the car going home. We responded, "Can you imagine a Catholic priest inviting a Protestant minister to come to his church and speak to his congregation? What a marvelous man that swami is."

When we saw Biju, Fori announced, "Well, they did you proud. They not only had a full house, but each window was filled from the outside."

Then it was time to return to Calcutta. Fori and Rik had spent hours perusing the huge building and had come up with many plans. I think she hated to see him go.

Indu Jain met us at Dum Dum Airport with a confession, "The group has grown a bit, so we're going to hold the meeting tonight at the Park Hotel." We assured her that was fine and told her of our success at the mission.

Wearing my sari again, I decided to follow the same format as in Shillong, pitching my talk as, "A Westerner's Impression of Meditation." What a surprise we had when we arrived. Our audience consisted of over seven hundred people!

Later, after my talk was over and questions started, we realized we had a different audience on our hands. Respectful and attentive, but steeped in Vedic tradition, they were threatened by what Maharishi taught. We were very cautious; if a question became too technical or religious, we fielded it with, "We are not experts in the field of religion or traditional Indian philosophy. We can only pass along to you some of the wisdom we have received from Maharishi and explain how it will help in our Western lives." The whole thing went well, but we were happy when that evening was behind us. Indu was delighted and asked to be initiated. We agreed to send an initiator to Calcutta. (Years later, she became a teacher of TM and the head of the Calcutta organization.)

It was the middle of May when we returned to Los Angeles. It had been almost four months since I'd left; what a joy to get home to my family. It was the longest time I'd ever been away.

When Tony met us at the plane, I was shocked by his appearance. He had mentioned in his letters that his rheumatoid arthritis had been acting up, but I wasn't prepared for this dramatic change. He looked thin and haggard. I felt guilty—I had thought my course had come at the perfect moment. My absence had left him free to devote all of his time to this big move into an elegant suite in Century City. He finally had his own law firm and was the senior partner. "But," I thought to myself, "at what cost? I must call the doctor tomorrow and question him about Tony's health."

Mercedes had the house in apple-pie order. The dogs climbed all over us. Then Starr, Brett, and María Luisa, all home again, started to grill us on our news. "The most exciting thing is that Maharishi will give a month's course at Squaw Valley during August," we announced.

Tony and I agreed we would find a house nearby and attend the course while the boys went to Honolulu. María Luisa could bring a friend. Tony looked as if he needed a good rest; the timing would be perfect.

June and July were busy months, between business entertaining and initiating many friends into TM. At first I felt shy teaching personal friends and performing the *puja* for them, but gradually I became confident in my role as initiator. The house became a small center, with people in each bedroom meditating. The chimes on our grandfather clock were silenced and phones were taken off the hook.

One initiate stands out in my mind, C.V. Wood. A well-known character, Woody bought the London Bridge and brought it to Havasu City, Arizona, a city built by McCullough Oil, the company of which he was president. He was also a director of Tom Slick's Mind Science Foundation.

One day he cornered me. "I've been watching you. You've got something different from other folk. I've gone down the list and decided it has to be TM. I'd like to give it a go." He was a heavy smoker, and his silhouette showed he loved food and wine. But he was a sparkplug of energy, with the personality of a Texas circus-barker. He could sell anything. "Man, I want to keep all the good things in life. I like this little feller, Maharishi—he don't ask you to give up nuthin'. When he gets here, I'd like to have him over for a bowl of my special chili." From the day of his initiation, he was to tell hundreds of acquaintances, "When I feel a band of tension around my head, I just close the office door, put my feet up on the desk, turn on my *mantra*, and give it a whirl. It works every time."

When he did meet Maharishi at Squaw Valley, six-foot, two-hundred-pound Woody walked right up to the tiny guru, put his arm around his shoulder, and patted him on the back, exclaiming, "Maharishi, this is a great day for me; I'd like to tell you, Little Feller, what a wonderful thing TM is for me. I just give that mantra a whirl and it never lets me down."

We were aghast. No one ever touched Maharishi. Only occasionally would he shake someone's hand when it was offered unknowingly. But Woody's bearlike friendliness and enthusiasm were irresistible.

The course went well, and the merchants and hotel keepers of Tahoe City said Maharishi's group was the best behaved group they had ever had—all eight hundred of them.

In addition to the course participants, the Four Star movie crew accompanied Maharishi to Squaw Valley. Gradually, we heard rumblings of discontent. What the crew wanted and what Maharishi wanted were two different things. With the celebrities gone, bad press from the Beatles' departure, and the failure of the Beach Boy Hour featuring Maharishi to materialize, world interest seemed to lag. So did the movie makers'.

"We're going to have a picture with all the zap of Pablum!" groaned the director. Finally it came to a showdown in front of Maharishi and a small group of us sitting at his feet.

Arguing over a technical point, the director complained, "But Maharishi, I am the director of this film, and I have to do what I feel is right." He had been a man of great patience, taking endless reels of Maharishi "imparting wisdom."

"Wrong!" announced Maharishi in a loud, firm voice. "I am the director, and do not forget it." I was shocked. This was a new aspect of our little guru. It wasn't long before the movie crew disappeared, and as far as I know those reels are still moldering in cans at the studio.

One day, as we were walking to a lecture, Efram Zimbalist noticed bruises on Tony's arm and asked, "For heaven sakes, Tony, are you on cortisone?" When Tony affirmed that he had been on a mild dose for eight years, Efram went on, "You've got to get off of that. Those are hemorrhages; one could occur in your brain. It is worse than whatever you have. My sister is eaten up from heavy doses of cortisone, but now it's too late for her to get off it."

Thank goodness Efram said this. When I called it to Tony's attention he rebuffed me. "Nancy, I'm under a doctor's care; stop playing nurse." He dismissed the subject as nothing, but I couldn't help remembering the bruises that appeared on Luis's arms before his leukemia was diagnosed.

When we got home again, I decided to take matters into my own hands. Several years before, I'd tried to get Tony to the famous Dr. Henry Bieler, author of *Food Is Your Best Medicine*, but instead, he went to the arthritis specialist who took him off yoga and put him on more steroids. I'd been against this, but to no avail. Now was my opportunity to get him to Bieler.

Dr. Bieler was no longer taking new patients, but after much persistence on our part, he agreed to see us at his house in Capistrano Beach. We were greeted by his assistant, who explained, "Six weeks ago, Dr. Bieler, while walking, was hit by a car and his pelvis was broken. He is taking few callers." As we followed her to the living room, the smell of cooking zucchini wafted past our noses.

Dr. Bieler was lying on his couch; a wiry Scotsman nearly eighty years old, but still with a shock of brown hair. He had a dry, crusty personality. His opening comment to Tony was, "Your adrenals have probably atrophied from cortisone; it will take years to repair the damage."

I spoke up, "My husband has determination and discipline. If anyone can do it, he can."

He examined Tony in the light from the large picture window overlooking the sea. "Even if the Scripps Clinic did tell you it would be impossible for you to get off cortisone, I say we can do it, if you have the determination. It won't be much fun, there will be a lot of pain, and your sex life will disappear for awhile."

When Bieler came to me, he pronounced, "You have strong adrenals. If you take care of yourself, you will last forever."

From that meeting on, the eating habits of our household changed drastically. Tony's diet consisted mainly of steamed vegetables, meat, dairy products and baked fruits. No more salt, sugar, white breads, or fried foods. If we did go to a restaurant, I took Bieler Broth with me. With Dr. Bieler's guidance, I experimented until I created a very nice soup that helps eliminate acid from the body:

BIELER BROTH
4 medium zucchinis (equal amount string beans optional)
1 large white onion

1 large baking potato, peeled
1/2 head of celery
1/2 bunch parsley
1/4 lb. butter
water

Chop vegetables in large pieces, add water to just below the top of the vegetables—do not cover with water. Bring to a boil and cook for 20 minutes *only*. Add 1/4 lb. butter, put in blender and process until smooth. Keeps 4-5 days in refrigerator. Serve hot or cold. When serving, can add basil and oregano, or sour cream and chopped green onion. Curry powder is also nice.

The whole family supported Tony in his battle to get off the dreaded steroid. His pain level, masked by the cortisone, increased as he slowly withdrew from the drug. Several times Dr. Henshel, Bieler's associate, had to come in the middle of the night. The first few months were terrible, and poor Tony became a tyrant in the house. The children and Mercedes tiptoed around him. They tried to understand what he was going through, but it wasn't easy, and I was caught in the middle. As the boys were away at college most of the time, it was especially hard on María Luisa. Used to bringing friends home after school to visit, swim or watch television, all activities came to a halt when Tony came home from the office. The house had to be totally quiet—that is, until his music took over.

With a passionate love and knowledge of music, Tony helped to organize and support the Los Angeles Chamber Orchestra.

During this time, Tony was adamant that his clients not be aware of his illness. He saved every ounce of energy for the office. We cut back our social schedule almost completely, except for business connections and continued to entertain at home. If we had guests and he felt tired, Tony would quietly disappear to his room and leave me to carry on. I was happy to do this, but at the same time I was beginning to feel more like a business partner than a wife.

It was no one's fault, but our relationship changed totally. There was no longer any tenderness or touching. If I did embrace Tony, he was apt to wince; even the pressure of bed sheets bothered him. Our sexual relationship disappeared completely; it had worried Tony in the beginning, but I'd convinced him our love was not based just on sex. Maybe this was part of God's plan to put me on a spiritual track. But I did feel sad; the first five years of our marriage had been such fun—however, I was not complaining; it was Tony who had the ordeal, and I certainly was not one to run out on a sick husband.

Besides my periodic lecture tours, I threw my energies into meditation. My life became inundated with initiations and people coming for checking. One morning, my cousin, Phil Spalding, stood laughing at the front door. The taxi driver had just wished him, "Lots of luck, buddy." Having flown in from Honolulu with a few hours layover, he'd brought some fruit and flowers and come to me for initiation.

We howled, "Do you realize what grounds Tony would have for divorce?" I laughed, "Yes, men arrive after he's gone to his office. They bring flowers. I take them into my bedroom, and an hour later they leave, thanking me, saying they feel much better, and when will I need to see them again."

My schedule evolved into teaching one weekend a month at the Center in Brentwood, and I became more impressed with the benefits of meditation. The people I met there came from all walks of life, encompassing the gamut of life's dilemmas. Most of these strangers reported improvement in their lives after learning to meditate; this was very satisfying to me.

In my enthusiasm, I also made mistakes. I had been warned not to make it too easy for my friends to learn meditation by coming to my home; that they would appreciate it more if they had to struggle a bit. This was difficult for me; I was so anxious to share my knowledge with everyone. Eventually, however, I learned that when individuals had to go to the Center, attend two lectures, make an initiation date, and then come for three nights of checking, they got off to a more committed start. We now had a center we could be proud of.

The student movement was booming under the guidance of Jerry Jarvis. S.I.M.S. (Students' International Meditation Society) came into being, and a center was opened near U.C.L.A. Keith Wallace's Ph.D. dissertation on the physiological changes that take place during meditation caught the attention of Dr. Herbert Benson at Harvard University Medical School. The subsequent investigations carried out by Dr. Benson gave respectability to TM in the eyes of the medical world. How Tom Slick would have loved this phase—all the testing using machines "under scientifically controlled conditions."

The S.R.M. was branching out. During the following year, I helped open many centers, besides hitting the regular lecture circuit with my Costumes, Customs, and Cultures show, which now featured India, Pakistan and Afghanistan—an excellent opportunity to mention TM.

The demand for TM grew, in spite of the bad press Maharishi had received from the Beatles' rebellion. Unfortunately, some of the other celebrities who had been at the ashram kept quiet and said nothing. I wondered what Paul McCartney thought; had he forgotten the love in his heart the day he said goodbye to Maharishi? Never a word was heard from him, or Mia or Donovan—at least publicly. There were times when a word from them would have helped.

Shortly after returning to the U.S., Maharishi was asked to appear on the Johnny Carson Show. We were thrilled. His audience numbered in the millions each night. Helen, Charlie and I were among those who went to the studio with him. Just before going on stage, Helen took Maharishi aside. "Maharishi, we want you to be presented at your glorious best. May I comb your hair on the sides just a bit?" Maharishi laughed and gave her permission.

Johnny Carson was his usual sardonic self. He watched with raised eyebrows as Maharishi tucked his feet into the lotus position, but Johnny gave Maharishi an excellent opportunity to present his case for meditation. When he asked Maharishi about other gurus, Maharishi was the picture of benevolence. When asked about specific personalities, especially other gurus who were beginning to appear in the U.S., he had nothing but kind words—"If he is helping people then he must be a good man himself." He had always said to us, "Never speak against anyone else's way. Listen to the other man; he will then think to himself how intelligent you are, and then he will listen to you."

Johnny asked him about the Beatles, and Maharishi replied, "They are talented young men. Their time with me was very creative. I will always love them." Nothing more could be inveighed out of him. After the interview we were happy it had gone beautifully.

We were not so pleased in the months that followed. Carson took every opportunity to poke fun at Maharishi and imitate him in absurd ways. My mother, a loyal Carson fan, called to alert me to the final blow, "Honey, turn on your TV; they're talking about Maharishi on the Carson show."

A heavily made-up young woman was being questioned. She indicated that she knew the real reason for the Beatles' bolting the ashram. "It was because of a bird."

Johnny looked puzzled. "A bird, what's that?" He looked out to the audience, bewildered.

"You know," she insisted, "a chick, a tomato; as you say, a dame. Maharishi made a pass at one of the Beatles' chicks, and that did it. That was the final straw."

I couldn't believe my ears. How could anyone utter such a terrible lie! What karma, to attack a holy man in such a disgusting way. The phone rang. It was Mother again. She was almost as angry as I. "Honey, people like Johnny Carson don't care about hurting people. He knew what she would say, or he wouldn't have invited a nobody to be a guest. It's sensational; that makes news."

I called Helen. She couldn't believe what had been said. She agreed with me when I demanded, "Someone must get to Maharishi. A thing like that has to be retracted. It's one thing when the press writes about his imaginary Swiss accounts and Rolls Royces, but this is something different." I sputtered with indignation. Later Charlie called me. He had put in a call to Maharishi to explain what had happened on the Carson show.

"I've worried about this. After the Beatles left, one of the course participants who was close to the Beatles told me a disturbing story. Evidently, Magic Alex told John Lennon that one of the girls was having sex with Maharishi—that little blonde who shacked up with the actor, Tom, from California."

I wasn't surprised. I remembered warning Maharishi.

"But, Charlie, why do they tell such lies? That girl was never at Maharishi's—you know how often I was there, and I never once saw her near there."

"Well, maybe she wanted to ingratiate herself with the Beatles, at the same time discrediting Maharishi. She obviously was not going to be selected as an initiator. Maybe Magic Alex put her up to it; they seemed very chummy."

"Have you ever spoken to Maharishi about this, Charlie?"

"Yes, as a matter of fact, while I was still at the ashram, I repeated the story I'd heard to him. His reaction was, 'But, Charlie, I am a lifetime celibate; I don't know anything about sensual desires.' No, no—we must not even talk of such things." Charlie then added, "It's so hard to understand the malice some people feel when confronted by pureness."

Maharishi remained firm. He was saddened by what was happening, but stuck to his guns, "We do not recognize the negative. We just keep on working, putting one foot in front of the other. If we refuse to resist untruth, it will fall on its own. By resisting it, we give it support." It proved to be a great lesson for all of us. Maharishi was single-minded in his goal, and nothing was going to distract him.

Soon, the press moved on to newer, more sensational news. Maharishi had the opportunity then to turn his full attention and energy to organizing the movement. Centers were springing up all over the world; teachers were urgently needed. Transcendental Meditation had come to stay.

# PART THREE

## New Beginnings

## 23

# Politicians Versus Saints

THE LATE 60s AND EARLY 70s were good years for me and my family, with the exception of Tony's sickness. Although he had been off cortisone since 1969, the rigidity of his frame entered his personality. I continually cautioned the children to overlook his crankiness as he became more limited with his body movements.

Even though Tony and I now lived like brother and sister, we were a good team. I threw my energies into my family, the S.R.M., traveling, and entertaining for him. His energy went into music and the law. I continued with my lecture series and also was a judge for the Miss California beauty contest each year.

Occasionally, we took a month's vacation to Honolulu or some place where Tony could swim. He always returned vastly improved, but then he would return to his workaholic ways. Several doctors commented that his mind was killing his body, but Tony would not listen. He took in more partners, and the money rolled in. He didn't consider the personal cost to him and to his family life.

Maharishi taught, "You judge the effectiveness of your meditation by how your life flows." Life was flowing for us financially, if not in health. My children had come through the frantic sixties drug-free, happy, well-balanced young people with a sense of direction and joy in life. The boys missed Vietnam by flunking their health exams—two had extra vertebrae and one a heart murmur. Rik had graduated from UCLA and gone off to architecture school in Oregon; Starr was finishing Stanford; Brett still attended Yale; and María Luisa was happily at Westlake. I had so much to be grateful and thankful for. The only negative we had was Tony's delicate state of health.

I did a lot of traveling with the children. Brett, María Luisa and I visited Spain, Italy and Greece—Tony joined us in London. Another trip with Brett and María Luisa was to Berlin, where I was still working with German couture. With Brett's ability to pick up languages, he was a joy to travel with.

But no country pulled me back like India. I returned regularly to work on different secular projects—I helped design fashions that would be attractive to Western buyers; I originated itineraries for India's Minister of Tourism. The Indian travel industry had no idea of how to present their incredible country. In 1969, under the supervision of S.K. Roy, still the Director General of Tourism, I brought twenty friends and gave them a thirty-day "fairyland" tour of India. My Indian friends entertained us; we stayed in Maharajahs' palaces; we went from the untouched beaches of Trivandrum to the high peaks of Nepal. They all came back confirmed Indiaphiles.

Because of the success of my Indian trip, the airline gave me three free round-the-world passes. So, in 1970, Tony, Starr and I went to Rishikesh together. Brett and María Luisa were in school, so could not join us. The ashram had a new image. In order to accommodate the increasing numbers attending courses, the blocks had been closed in, and the porches made into rooms. Unfortunately, it was not well done. We were given the Beatles' old block. What luxury in comparison to what I'd experienced in '68. Now there was a new ashram kitchen and dining room complex—very nicely done, except it leaked in the rain. I was so happy to have Tony along and prayed he would enjoy the trip.

At the end of two weeks of resting and meditating, Tony looked like a different person; his aches and pains were gone. I began to hope I might get my "real husband" back, but once back in the highly competitive world of law and business, the advances soon disappeared.

It was the last time I saw Maharishi at the ashram; he was now giving most of his courses in Europe. Because of tax problems with the Indian government, he did not return to India for many years. I frequently told my Indian friends, "You have driven away your best export. You should attract Maharishi back to India. Think of the money India is losing. The thousands attending Maharishi's course would have, and should have, come here." I guess they felt TM was a flash in the pan.

Throughout this period India continued to intrigue me. No other country offers such a range of contrasts. It is a mosaic of not only people, but traditions, climates, cultures, and scenery.

Each time I went to India I returned to the ashram to see Satyanand. In spite of letters and phone calls advising of my arrival, the result was always the same. I would climb the hill, be greeted by peons, and nothing was ready for me. Everything was uncared for. New buildings had gone up instead of taking care of what was there. It had gone "Indian" in spite of Satyanand's supervision.

Several times returning home from India I called on Maharishi, who usually was in Italy, Spain, or Switzerland. I begged him to send a European couple to take over management of the ashram, but it fell on deaf ears. His courses grew in number and the organization became prosperous in spite of the press, who continued to print any scandalous rumor about Maharishi that came their way—no thought was given to authenticity.

One who did come to Maharishi's defense often was the world famous nutritionist, Dr. Gayelord Hauser. This vigorous, young seventy-year-old had sold over seventy million books and was responsible for bringing yogurt to the Western world. During the fifties when I first met him in Paris, he had his followers on the blackstrap molasses, wheat germ and yogurt kick. He had a huge following around the globe, but lived most of the year in Beverly Hills; we had become intimate friends.

He once said to me regarding lecturing, "Honey, just remember five little words, 'What's in it for me'—that's what an audience wants to hear." His six-foot-three physique was trim and tan, no fat on him. His thick, grey hair crowned a large head always held erect. His blue eyes were surrounded with laugh lines. "That little guy," he said, referring to Maharishi, "really has something. People in Germany (Gayelord's place of birth) were prepared to laugh at him, instead they started to follow him." He paused and said in a soothing voice, "Girls and boys," as he loved to address his audience, "he knows that tension is one of the worst sicknesses of America. If you meditate, tension leaves you."

Once, during one of his lectures, he introduced me to the three thousand staring faces, "This is my friend, Nancy; she introduced me to

Swedish Life Magazine
Nancy as Ambassadress of Fashion, 1957

*Reviewing the Staebe-Seger collection in Berlin*

*Staebe-Seger's farewell party for Nancy Cooke in Berlin, 1958*
*Nancy with the "West Berlin Couturiers"*

*As the Ambassa-dress of Fashion in Rome with the Princess Marchella Borghese, 1958*

*Addressing the Moscow Chamber of Commerce, USSR, 1960. Mr. Nesterof, head of the Chamber and Dal Sherman, our tour leader*

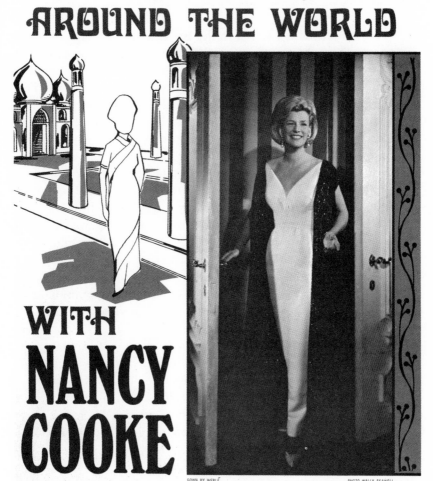

*Nancy's lecture brochure during the seventies*

Maharishi and then taught me meditation, one of the great gifts in my life." A nice plug from a world figure.

Slowly I reconciled myself to the fact that my marriage situation was not going to change or get much better. I rationalized, "I have a happy secure base for myself and the children; I've already had more romance in my life than most people; socially I belong to the best organizations and groups in the Beverly Hills/Los Angeles area—any outsider would think I lead a very glamorous life. I think so too, so what do I have to complain about?" If I were going to have a love affair, it would be with travel.

My friend, Carroll Righter, the astrologer, had advised me when I'd told him of my plans to marry Tony, "Well, take lots of trips. Cancer and Aries are not a good combination; water and fire getting together produce steam; you'll need an escape valve for sure." He was right; my trips were this valve. Tony encouraged our trips; he liked the quiet times when we were away. The house was well run, and he could have his beloved Bach blaring at ear-bursting levels.

My mother once asked, "How can you stand that continual loud sound all the time when Tony is home? It would drive me mad. House-guests often complained and asked that the music be turned down. Sir John Barbirolli, the well-known conductor, once provided ammunition when he said, "Tony, turn that music down! Music is to be listened to, not shouted over." Tony was Sir John's lawyer so he had to respond.

My solution was to wear earplugs, or I'd go into my bedroom and shut the door in order to concentrate on whatever I was doing. It seemed a sensible solution, now that our marriage had assumed the platonic level Dr. Bieler had predicted.

That Tony enjoyed having the house to himself was confirmed, when, against everyone else's advice, he encouraged me to go to India, just weeks after the Pak-Indian war came to an end in 1972. "Go and present the U.S. side to our Indian friends." He loaded me down with all sorts of information and data and practically pushed me out the door.

It wasn't a happy trip. None of the children could go with me, so this time I went alone. Once back in India, I did nothing for six weeks but argue that President Nixon had tried not to take sides in the war. Originally, Pakistan and India had been offered the same armaments deal. The former accepted, while the latter haughtily turned it down. U.S. columnists Leon Frankel and Jack Anderson, with their violently anti-Nixon views, had done much to erode friendship between India and the U.S. As the only U.S. journalists heard from in Indian newspapers, India judged the U.S. attitude by their writings.

My friend, Piloo Mody, tried to explain these attacks. "The Indians, having won what on a world scale was a small military battle, are now plumped up like proud pigeons. Don't let them get to you, Nancy." Then my Parsee friend added, "And don't forget, Nancy, arrogance comes easily to an Indian."

But, eventually, it did get to me. I couldn't understand why all of India seemed so anti-U.S. We did have a record of trying to help them over the years with a massive educational and agricultural aid program. Was this all forgotten, or was it just an illustration of this story: "One day, Confucius, walking with a friend, nodded in recognition to a man coming toward him. The other man defiantly ignored his acknowledgment. Confucius turned to his companion, 'What strange behavior; I don't remember having ever helped him.'"

However, one evening, while dining with Goodie and Bikki Oberoi in their penthouse suite at the Oberoi Intercontinental, an energetic, hawk-nosed, mustachioed man strode into the room, carrying a plastic bag full of greens. "Here, enjoy this lettuce. It was raised in my garden, and I can guarantee no bloke has ever peed on it." He was introduced to me as Uncle Sam, my escort for the evening. He had a forceful, outgoing personality. When he heard I was on my way to Israel, he asked me to get some information on solar heating and water collection methods. I agreed and asked his full name and address.

Goodie laughed, "All you have to put on the envelope is Field Marshall Sam Manikshaw, India. He's the general who won our war."

He had attended Sandhurst with the Pakistani President, General Yaya Khan and had psyched him out on every tactic, knowing exactly how the general's mind worked. At one moment, when Sam had Delhi practically surrounded by tanks, an anti-Ghandi sympathizer reportedly asked him, "Why don't you just take India?" Sam replied, "Who wants it?"

He was presently the only Indian Field Marshall. How different his attitude was. He spoke with warmth and admiration for the U.S. and excused the Indians' excessive pride over their "little skirmish." He even spoke well of Ali Bhutto, who, becoming Prime Minister of Pakistan, had the job of soothing the wounded national pride of his countrymen over the loss of Bangladesh—a loss which Bhutto later confessed to me had probably been a blessing. This was during a trip I made to Pakistan in '74.

Finally, getting fed up with politics in the capital city of India, I decided to travel south to check out some new potential tourist attractions and several holy men I'd been hearing about. In Madras, I had a delightful spiritual encounter. I sought out the Shankaracharya of that area. It reminded me of the quests Tom and I had made together.

Though advised that I'd never find him, and, even if I did, he wouldn't see me, I took a young Indian guide, Vigi, and we set out in an Indian-made Ambassador. Having no air conditioner, we had to leave the windows open, so we arrived at the marketplace of ancient Kanchipuram hot and covered with dust.

Crumbling sandstone temples surrounded a square filled with exotic colors, pungent smells and people hawking their wares. Southern Indians seem smaller and darker than Northern Indians, and in Madras they speak Tamil, not Hindi. Most of the young women had woven fragrant flowers in their hair. We bought bright orange flower garlands mixed with sweet narcissus, and asked for news of the aged sage whose only mode of travel was walking. If he were nearby, the people would know it, as he was one of the most revered saints in India.

"Yes, he is here. He arrived yesterday." So the tip we'd been given was correct. A skinny arm pointed the direction.

The Swami's place of refuge was a small building with a thatched roof. In front was a water well. A group of people stood waiting. A white-robed Indian explained to Vigi in Tamil, "Tell *Memsahib* Swami does not see Europeans."

I persisted, "Please explain to the Shankaracharya that I am a follower of Maharishi's and the wisdom of Shankara. I do my *puja* every day, and I have come to receive his *darshan.*"

He disappeared, then came back to say, "It is all right, *Memsahib*, please stand behind these people."

I felt so happy as we waited for the Swami to appear. I studied the group in front. All were men and, by the sacred threads around their shoulders, they were of the Brahmin caste. Many times I had seen Maharishi give deference to a Brahmin over another of a lesser caste.

A hush fell over the group as a white-haired old man slowly emerged and stood at the other side of the well. His skin was dry and parched from years of walking in the relentless sun of Southern India.

His hand grasped a staff. He looked at us with pale eyes and said nothing. His aide motioned to the first Brahmin. He prostrated himself on the ground and, rolling back and forth, wailed out his story.

"He has a very sick wife," Vigi explained.

Each came forward and repeated a similar tale.

Then my turn came. Vigi told me it was not expected for me to roll on the ground. I went toward the well and gave my flowers to the aide. Vigi explained who I was and what was in my heart as I spoke my words in English. The old Swami beckoned me closer to the well. He peered at me closely with seemingly blind eyes. Then his parched face cracked with a slight smile, which revealed toothless gums. He moved forward and put the garlands around our necks. Then he turned and slowly left us. A tremendous surge of love filled my being.

Vigi and I wordlessly got back into our taxi. Months later, he wrote, "I had not been to the temple for a long time, and my family was upset with me. Now I go regularly and am studying our scriptures. My family is happy and joyous over the change that has taken place in me since I had the good karma to go with you to Kanchipuram."

Before leaving Kanchipuram, I bought an exquisite sari—one typical of that place, so I would always have a material reminder of that experience with the old Shankaracharya. Experiences such as these were the jewels I gathered in India.

My love affair with India continued. Friends who consider me an expert on the "subcontinent" frequently ask to "tag along" on my next trip. They feel they will see India correctly with me.

Several times I took a group of friends to India; Rik went as my assistant. With one year of architectural school behind him, Rik became convinced that photography would be his profession, and architecture his hobby. These trips provided a good opportunity for selling photos to magazines.

In 1970, Shankar Bajpai wrote, suggesting we visit him in Gangtok, Sikkim. He had been the Indian Consul General in San Francisco in the 60's, and we'd met through B.K. Nehru. Now he was the Political Officer of Sikkim, which meant he ran the country, as India provided the small mountain country with its foreign policy, currency, and military presence. (Later, India swallowed it up as it did Goa, all the time criticizing the U.S. for expansionist policies in Vietnam.) His letter was provocative, "Two hours from Gangtok there is an exotic monastery in

Rumtek. The top boy is a very important Tibetan Lama. Rik will get dramatic pictures and you can have the thrill of knowing another saint." He loved to kid me about my holy friends.

We decided to do it and put a group of friends together. It was turning out to be a new hobby for me—taking people to India. Shankar and his wife, Meera, were delighted. He wrote again, "Before you leave Darjeeling, call me. It's always a frightful bore at the border. Just to be on the safe side, I'll have my men waiting for you. And by the way, do you suppose you could bring me about twelve pounds of fresh pork? If so, we'll have an authentic Tibetan dinner for you." He went on to name a few other items impossible to get in the tiny kingdom.

Months later, through the Tenduf-las, the owners of the old-fashioned, cozy Windemere Hotel in Darjeeling where we stayed, it was possible to find everything.

From our hotel on the highest part of Darjeeling, our group caravan dropped over the back side of the mountain on a winding road down to a turbulent river. Crossing the gorge, we started the climb up the next mountain to enter the Kingdom of Sikkim—about a four-hour scenic drive. Bajpai's men were there, and we passed through the official gate with no problems.

As we approached the official residence, we saw the Bajpais sitting in lawn furniture in front of the government house, having tea. Shankar's round face broke into a wide smile as he welcomed us to Gangtok in his flawless English. Light reflected off his bald pate; he looked like a Buddha in his warm, monk-like robe. Meera had a woolen shawl around her sari. The mountain air was cool. "Come join us. I'm sure you're all ready for a good hot cup of tea." We blessed the British. And what an enchanted tea it was. Good conversation was as available as good food when around the Bajpais. Oxford-educated Shankar was a popular diplomat for India. His next ambassadorial posts were to China and the United States.

The next morning, the sun back-lighted Katchenjunga, the huge mountain worshiped by the Sikkimese. Through the leaded windows of my room in Raj Bavan, another colonial gingerbread house, I watched the spectacular sunrise. Often the magnificent mountain was hidden by cloud cover, but not this morning. There it was, soaring twenty-nine thousand feet into the air, dwarfing the rest of the Himalayan chain. It was so cold as I stood there that I had my electric heater in my hand—luckily it had a long cord and went everywhere in the room with

*Ambassador and Mrs. Shankar Bajpai in Beijing, China, 1980*

me, including the bathroom. I set it next to the tub while I splashed hot water over myself from a bucket. The huge, marble bathtub would have taken a week to fill.

Starting out for Rumtek monastery, we were bundled in our coats as we bounced along in our Land Rovers. An hour later, coats were discarded. It had become a lovely, sunny day in the mountains. There was no way to alert the monks that we were coming; we'd just arrive, all eighteen of us.

We switchbacked over several mountains, until the driver of the front vehicle stopped and pointed to the top of a distant peak. "Monastery, *Memsahib.*" At that distance we could see nothing.

Swinging back and forth on the winding road, we passed between barley fields tended by farmers winnowing grain. Oxen walked slowly in circles, around and around, as they had for centuries. The tidiness of the land bespoke of their care. Bright-cheeked Sikkimese and Tibetan girls called out their traditional greeting, *"Jole."*

"Mom, stop the car—here—I *have* to take that picture!" Rik demanded. "Those fields with the girls' costumes are great."

There was the monastery—bright red, glistening in the sun. On both sides were rows of prayer flag trees, similar to those I'd seen at Govinda's in Almora on my first visit to India. Behind the monastery, providing a silent frame, were more mountains. My friends were filled with excitement; none had been to a Tibetan monastery.

As we drove to the entrance, the round wooden door, divided in the middle, stood open in welcome. Three burgundy-robed monks stood by to receive us. A high-cheekboned Tibetan introduced himself. "My name is Tashi. We are most happy to welcome you. It is very auspicious. You have arrived just in time for the Black Hat Ceremony. This event takes place once a month at the time of the full moon." We thought it a coincidence; the monks thought otherwise.

"Please follow me." We crossed the enclosed courtyard. Ahead stood the main building. Through the painted doors we could see a high-ceilinged room, filled with long benches on which sat monks of all ages—from ancients down to those of five or six years old. A huge, golden Buddha watched over all. The ceiling held bells of all descriptions. Long, brocaded panels, statues, butter lamps and old *thangkas* cluttered every available spot. Incense curled through the air.

We were led up a worn and uneven wooden staircase to a spacious, high-ceilinged room at the top of the monastery. Both ends of the room were opened to the temple below. We had no sooner seated ourselves on the floor than the ceremony began. We had arrived at curtain time.

Darkly clad monks slowly paraded in with long copper horns, at least eight feet in length. Standing to the side of a high, throne-like chair and platform, they blew long, discordant, sonorous notes. Soon another group arrived, escorting to the seat of honor a stocky young man, who wore a high-peaked, brocaded lama's hat. Adjusting his heavy, gold-embroidered cape, he beamed happiness down upon us. He nodded his head to the monks to proceed.

"That is His Holiness, the Gyalwa Karmapa," Tashi informed me, handing out some papers of explanation. The Karmapa was the sixteenth incarnation of a Tibetan saint, recognized as the embodiment of Avalokitesvara (the Buddha of compassion) who attained enlightenment in one lifetime. His followers are called the Karma Kagyus. The Black Hat, which was made of human hairs in the 11th century by devoted followers, was believed to have tremendous healing effects for viewers. "The Karmapa and the Dalai Lama are the two God-Kings of Tibet. Sikkim and Bhutan revere especially the Karmapa's line," explained Tashi.

An elaborate brocade box was carried in with much fanfare and presented to the God-King. After opening the box and putting the stiff, black, onion-shaped hat on his head, the Karmapa, with one hand holding the hat in place, closed his eyes in meditation. It was signaled that we follow suit. With my eyes shut I thought to myself, "a God-

King—how impressive for my friends. Shankar doesn't know this—how lucky we are to be here!" Later, as we were each introduced to His Holiness, we presented white prayer scarves, *khatas*, which Shankar had advised us to take along.

One of my friends could hardly contain himself. "Wait 'til you hear what happened to Winnie." It seemed while his wife was sitting with closed eyes, she had the cherished "golden sun" wash over her entire being. She was still in shock, but radiant.

After the Karmapa left, Tashi asked us, "Would you like to meet our sister?" We, of course, said yes and followed him along an outside ledge to a corner room. It was a breathtaking view as we looked down into the valley over the winding road we had followed. All we could see were brown mountains in all directions.

"You must come back again later, when the mountains are green." Following Tashi through a narrow frame door, I stepped into a small hall; to the left a larger room opened out. As I entered, I gasped in surprise. On a low platform sat an English woman in monk's robes. She appeared to be in her sixties—her large, pale blue eyes looked enormous because of her shaved head.

"Come in, I am Sister Palmo. It is a joy to welcome you." Recovering from our start, we formed a circle around her on the floor. As we gathered confidence, we asked questions about herself and the significance of the ceremony we had just witnessed. "What good fortune, coming here on this particular day. It was not accidental; every movement of even a grain of sand is planned." She gently explained some of the basic Buddhist beliefs and traditions to us.

Time flew by, and, unfortunately, being on a tight schedule, we could not remain long enough. Rik took me aside, "This place is sensational. We simply have to come back here and spend more time with Sister Palmo."

While the group had tea in another room and ate the picnic sandwiches we'd brought, we made our plans with the English nun.

"Yes, yes, do come back—I knew you would want to. We are meant to become friends. If you would be so kind as to bring me a few things from the Gangtok marketplace, I would be so happy. Then you can have lunch here with me."

We decided that Avi, who had joined us in Gangtok, could take the group to Calcutta the next morning, and we'd follow a day later. Shankar had suggested it earlier; "Take more time here; you can use my

*His Holiness the Sixteenth Gyalwa Karmapa performing the Ceremony of
the Vajra Crown (Black Hat) at Rumtek Monastery, Sikkim, 1972*

*Sister Palmo at*
*Rumtek Monastery,*
*1972*

*The seventeenth*
*Karmapa,*
*age 8,*
*enthroned in*
*Tsurphu Monastery*
*(the Karmapa's*
*original monastery*
*in Tibet),*
*June 1992*

car and driver to go to the Badogra airport any time." In the jeep returning to Gangtok, we chattered like magpies, awed by our experience at the monastery.

That evening, we celebrated with a Tibetan dinner. The table was heaped with all sorts of succulent, hotly-spiced vegetable and pork dishes. The Bajpais had outdone themselves, and they seemed proud of us as a group. We came from Argentina, Washington D.C., New York, Beverly Hills, Honolulu and Hamburg, Germany. Included were top social names, a former U.S. ambassador, a famous choreographer (Tony Duquette), the head of the Beverly Hills Testanant Chevalier (elite gourmet society) and a woman astrologer, the grandniece of the legendary flying ace of World War II, Baron Manfred Von Richthofen (the Red Baron). Yes, we were an interesting assortment. We, in turn, were honored to meet the Chogyal with his American wife, Hope Cooke, and the General who had accompanied the Dalai Lama on his escape from Lhasa. The Chogyal was charming, Her Highness was shy and aloof, and the General complimented me, "That turquoise amulet you are wearing is an extremely good one."

I had bought it the day before in Gangtok. A Tibetan in dusty robes, wearing one long turquoise and coral earring had tugged at Rik's shirt. We followed him down a little alley and up a broken staircase to a tiny little room where two elderly Tibetan women sat. From under their bed, they pulled out a trunk and carefully unwrapped their treasures wrapped in dirty clothes. The minute I saw the delicate amulet, I knew I wanted it. The price was reasonable, but Rik said, in Spanish, "Mom, you've taught me to bargain. Seventy dollars is a lot in Sikkim, you will get it for less." By bargaining, I got it for eighty dollars. We laughed at the reverse psychology of the Tibetans. The minute we started to bargain, they knew we wanted it and upped the price.

Our group left us early the next morning. Shortly afterward, I initiated Meera Bajpai into TM. Shankar scoffed, but added hastily, "I will not oppose anything that might interest her," remembering my criticism of years before. On his arrival in San Francisco as Consul General, he had been asked about Maharishi by the press. He had replied, "Oh, we laugh at all these holy men who come to the U.S. to make a fortune." I had jumped on him, "Shankar, you have never met Maharishi or taken his course. Why didn't you just say you knew nothing about him?"

By 8:00 a.m., the marketplace was open. Vegetables, eggs, spices, and all sorts of foodstuffs were spread out on canvasses in front of flimsy stalls. We laughed as we watched one owner beat a cow on the head as he tried to retrieve a bunch of carrots from its mouth. Succeeding, he brushed the orange roots and put them back in place—a sort of Julia Child attitude about a few teeth marks.

Soon we had our baskets filled with bread—a luxury in Rumtek—tomatoes, butter, cream, and all the requested vegetables and fruits. It was time for our return to the monastery. "How nice to be alone!" Rik said. Although we enjoyed our group, nearing the end of a thirty-day trip, we looked forward to being on our own. Now we were off on the kind of adventure we dearly loved. It was about 11:00 a.m. when we drove up to the monastery door, giving us at least eight hours of daylight for a nice long visit.

Anila, Sister Palmo's tiny attendant, took our parcels from us with joy and the quick, silent movements of a bird. Sister Palmo was sitting as she had been when we left her the day before. "Good morning, what a treat to get all those lovely foods. Come sit near me—are you sure you wouldn't like chairs brought in?" We assured her not.

She told us a bit about herself. She had been married to an Indian whom she had met while both were students at Oxford. They had three grown children. Their photos were beautiful. "This one, my son, Kabir Bedi, is a leading cinema star in Bombay. He's gone through a painful divorce, but is coming out of it. My husband was a businessman, but now has become a Hindu holy man and psychic healer. At present, he is touring Italy. We meet occasionally, when I go to see my children, and are good friends."

We asked how she had become a nun. "For years I followed Ghandi. One day I was attending a conference, and while walking with some friends, a voice from within spoke to me. It gave me instructions about what I was to do—that I was to renounce the world of activity and become a nun in a Buddhist monastery." Her full face glowed as she remembered. "My husband understood. He had felt the tug himself. It was a natural, happy parting, and we now travel different roads to the same destination.' She must have been a young beauty, I thought. Lovely white skin, but hard to tell what a woman with a shaved head would look like with hair.

We discussed her early years as a nun. Evidently, as the highest in the order, she was the confidential assistant to His Holiness. She even discussed the shaving of her head. "I guess that is the final commitment for a woman," her eyes twinkled. "You know vanity is gone when you see your hair on the floor."

We felt honored as she shared these intimacies with us. Then, abruptly, she changed the subject. "But tell me more about yourselves; what brought you here? How much do you know about Buddhism?"

I spoke first, "Well, I know that the Vedas inspired Gautama Buddha's 'seek out your own salvation,' but that he rejected the Brahmin's interpretation. Born as an Indian prince, he was horrified by what he saw outside the walls of his princely home. Needing to think, to rationalize the 'why's of creation,' he spent hours under the Bodhi tree contemplating. Occasionally he would slip into 'nothingness.' There he was free, free of worries, desires, emotions. There he experienced total release. Austerities didn't do it, worship didn't do it; contemplation and meditation did it. It brought about the nothingness—Nirvana!"

"Very good, that's all correct! Buddhism as explained by our Kagyu lineage also states that meditation, while unmasking our deceptions, helps us to know ourselves in the present situation, to face life, and to accept ourselves. It will bring transcendental common sense."

That struck a cord with us. Rik said, "Sister, that happens to be a word we are very aware of, but please go on."

She continued, "And from Buddha's illuminations, where he transcended the limitations of individuality, he replaced the idea of the immutable, eternal soul incapable of growth and development, with the conception of a spiritual consciousness yearning for freedom and enlightenment through the continuous process of becoming and dissolving." She spoke slowly and clearly.

"Those are almost Lama Govinda's words," I exclaimed.

"Yes, he will be known to the West as the first interpreter of Tibetan Buddhism into layman's terms. He helps one understand how we must abandon our thought habits in order to know the *real* nature of the Mind that encompasses both the individual and the Universe."

Agreeing with the Sister, I added, "The West will welcome his work. Many years ago, wanting to understand something about Buddhism, I read several books on the subject, but I gave up . . . to understand them, one had to learn a whole new vocabulary. "

"Indeed, and the whole idea was made easy by Buddha when he presented the eight basic rules to live by:

1. Right Thought

2. Right Understanding
3. Right Action
4. Right Speech
5. Right Livelihood
6. Right Effort
7. Right Mindfulness
8. Right Concentration."

By following these, one would become "enlightened"; no longer would life be directed by attachment. The goal, actually, was to be free from the pressure of the human race.

"But, Sister Palmo, what we don't understand is this: Gautama Buddha was against gods, priests, worship and dogma; he advised against building monasteries, as did the sages of the Upanishads, warning that, through the problems arising from household responsibilities and positions, jealousies would be born, and infighting would develop between superiors and inferiors. All that was important was pure thought; yet, when he died, they turned him into a god to worship.

"Not exactly—he's worshipped as Buddha, the Enlightened One, not as a god."

Rik and I couldn't see the difference. "Isn't it a shame that man always takes simplicity and complicates it?" mused Rik.

"Man feels more secure in clinging to traditions. He needs sets of commentaries, and philosophical principles that he can classify and put down in sacred texts—man clings to 'things.' He wants to possess and make his knowledge exclusive. Even the Karmapa once admitted to me, 'It took the Red Chinese to force Tibet into sharing its wisdom with the outside world.' That was our bad karma, trying to keep it to ourselves."

We admired the English nun for her honesty. What a rare treat this visit was for us. She went on to explain the symbolism found in Buddhist art and the importance it had to all meditative schools. We could have spent a week there sitting at her feet like enthusiastic little school children.

Soon it was time for lunch. Rik and I were hesitant to eat at the monastery, where sanitary conditions were uncertain, so we said we'd had a large breakfast. "Not at all; that was hours ago," insisted the nun. "Anila is cooking our meal in the next room; I have taught her to make crepes."

We couldn't believe it; I watched her cook over a little oil burner in the corner. Everything was spotless. The crepes, when served with

cream and honey whipped with butter, were delicious. I'd been afraid
we'd receive "buttered tea" and tsampa, made from roasted gingke, a
flour-like barley mixed with yak butter.

"What a treat for me," said Sister Palmo. "Our diet is sparse here.
One of the things I miss is toast with my tea—we often go weeks without
bread. We raise chickens and goats outside the monastery. So it's an eggs,
goats milk and grain menu." No wonder the foods we'd brought were
thought so dazzling.

Sister Palmo was interested in hearing about Maharishi and his
teachings. "He sounds like a wise man, and from the happiness you both
exude, one can see it's working." We then urged her to tell us more about
her life at the monastery.

She explained in detail her daily routine, how she counted hundreds of thousands of *Aum mani padme hum*, a Buddhist *mantra*, on her
rosary-type beads, her *mala*. She told us about visualization, very important in the practice of Buddhism, and the exaltation one felt when the
Buddha was seen sitting on a lotus with the honey of compassion
dripping down. Even though she detailed it carefully, it was foreign to
us and seemed laborious in comparison to our system.

Shortly after lunch, she announced, "Anila has brought a message
that His Holiness is ready to receive you." Gathering her robes, she stood
up. We had only seen her seated and were surprised to see that she was
as tall as I. She walked as an English woman, with good sturdy shoes,
taking long decisive steps.

From an outside door, the Karmapa's quarters were on the far side
of the monastery. The room was bare, but lighted by many windows. On
a small divan-like platform sat His Holiness. Without his hat and heavy
cape, he looked younger than he had the day before. Now he wore a
simple, wine-red robe. He smiled in welcome, indicating we should sit
on cushions near him.

Then we had a surprise. A beautiful Indian woman entered the
room. It was Goodie Oberoi. Sister Palmo was delighted to find we knew
each other, and left us with Goodie to interpret. "How is it that you are
here?" I asked. She had been one of the Indian friends I'd brought to
Maharishi for initiation while I was attending the 1969 course in
Kashmir. She hadn't mentioned the Karmapa to me.

"His Holiness is my treasured teacher now and has helped me more
than anyone in the world." I could understand her need of help. Her life

with Bikki, son of the hotel tycoon, had to be difficult. Bikki's love of drinking and women was well known among the social set of India.

"Sister comes to visit us and now we have one of her nuns with us at home. You have no idea, Nancy, what a wonderful change it has brought over the children. I will always love Maharishi," she continued, "but, for me, I need personal contact with my spiritual guide." Her handsome face looked more serene that I had ever seen it.

Interpreting was difficult. The Karmapa spoke rapidly. His man translated the Tibetan into Hindi; then Goodie put the Hindi into English. It discouraged any substantial penetration of his knowledge.

We were left with the simple enjoyment of sitting near him and receiving his serene vibrations.

"This is a most wonderful soul," Goodie explained. "You are fortunate to see him like this and share his *darshan*. He is revered as a God King by the Sikkimese, Bhutanese, and many Tibetans. He is the Supreme head of the Kagyu Order of Tibetan Buddhism, the embodiment of the power and compassion of Buddhist Tantra. They consider him a higher incarnation than the Dalai Lama. When the Chinese invaded Tibet, India offered the Dalai Lama asylum; likewise the Karmapa, but he came here to Sikkim at the invitation of the Chogyal."

The Karmapa radiated sunshine—and he was attentive when we spoke. He appeared to be in his thirties, but I heard later he was almost fifty.

"He would like to give you a special *mantra*," Goodie explained. It was an honor we couldn't refuse. We moved close to him. He had been knotting some cords while he spoke and with his expressive hands he now tied both a yellow and red cord around each of our necks. With a small pair of scissors, he cut a lock of hair from our heads.

"It is a great blessing," Goodie explained, "that he would knot the cords and put them around your necks with his own hands—it is unusual, and I'm so happy for you. You have taken refuge in the Buddha with this ceremony."

She wrote down our *mantras* on a piece of paper, handing it to us with some powder and pills. "Sister Palmo will explain these to you."

The good Sister was overjoyed when she heard what had transpired and clapped her hands. "When you walked into my room today and my *thangka* of Vajrasattva was exposed, I knew something auspicious would happen. Usually we keep that particular *thangka* covered."

We told her about the *mantras*, and she understood our dilemma. "You are right. Stick to what you are doing; but sometimes on a special full moon, or in a time of danger, you might use them."

She explained the healing qualities of the powder and pills, to which I reacted, "Oh, good, I'll take them to my husband." She agreed they might help. (Unfortunately, Tony never saw any apparent effects.)

Then she asked, "Now, may I ask you a favor?" We quickly nodded. "We have a convent in Tulokpur. You mentioned you were on your way to visit His Holiness the Dalai Lama in Dharamsala after your friends return to the U.S., to photograph the Tibetan New Year's celebration there. Tulokpur is between Dharamsala and Dalhousie. One takes a risk sending money by mail to India, but we need to get money to the monastery to feed the nuns and their cattle. Could we entrust the money to you to deliver?"

We agreed and got all the necessary instructions. We were happy we'd ordered five *thangkas* to be handpainted for us. We knew our money helped to fill the envelope given us.

Again the day came to an end, far too quickly. Sister Palmo escorted us to the jeep. "We will keep in touch through letters, and one day I will come to see you in the U.S. You will come back to Rumtek. It is written." In fact, the following year she stayed with us in Beverly Hills and made a lasting impression on my family. I felt my children were fortunate to meet such dedicated people.

As we wound down the hill, our minds relived our beautiful experience. "Where else could such a thing happen?" Rik said. "Here we are with the money for their convent's food, and they know nothing about us. We'll have to be *so* careful not to have anything happen to us, or those poor animals and people will starve!"

Later, we learned, the Karmapa, with his powers, probably knew more about us than we did ourselves! But we were complimented by their blind trust, and we did deliver the money safely.

My encounters with the world of Buddhism started with Lama Govinda, followed by the Dalai Lama, and now continued with the Karmapa. The more I was exposed to their spiritual leaders, the more attracted I became. There was no doubt that I felt a kindred spirit for the Tibetan race. They were bright, outgoing and friendly in spite of the terrible hardships their people and homeland had suffered; they were optimistic and determined to succeed. Maybe I had been a Tibetan in one of my past lives.

---

## 24

---

# *Doorway to Exotic Lands*

SOMETIMES, ON LEAVING INDIA, after ten or twelve trips there, I'd think to myself, "Now I've finally had enough. My next trip will be elsewhere." I'd almost deserted South America and my Argentine family and friends, as well as Europe, where I enjoyed many contacts made as the Ambassadress of Fashion.

But, once home, months would pass rapidly, and in a year's time I would long to go back to India. What was the reason? Was it because there I felt free, no longer confined to a rigid routine dictated by the needs of an ailing husband? Had I been an Indian in my last lifetime? Was this the reason I felt so at home in that faraway land?

In the summer of 1974, Avi wrote saying, "The door to Ladakh is open. If you can get an invitation from your friend, Governor Jha, under whose domain it falls, you could go. This is a special opportunity."

Rik and I had tried for years to get into Ladakh, the most northerly state of India, but it wasn't possible. Because of its strategic military position, Leh, the capital city, situated at twelve thousand feet, had been closed to all foreigners.

I had special reasons for trying to get to this remote area. A legend existed that a man named ISSA (Jesus) had journeyed there to learn his miraculous powers from the lamas. Was this where Jesus stayed during his "absent years"? It has been said the last words uttered by Jesus on the cross were spoken in Tibetan. Also, Rik had studied the monasteries of Ladakh at architecture school. The oldest was Himis—this would be our destination. It was rumored that some Tibetan scrolls existed at this monastery describing the time Saint Issa spent there. It was also the sometimes residence of Lama Kalu Rinpoche—one of the oldest living Buddhist monks. He supposedly knew of the location of Shambala, the residence place of the real earthly rulers of our planet. Jesus went to Ladakh. Was this the reason?

Another possibility was that maybe from Ladakh we could convince the authorities to allow us, as pilgrims, to cross the few miles of no-man's land into China in order to circumambulate Mount Kailash, the holy mountain of Tibet. Tibetans believe that anyone who does this stops the Wheel of Karma and has no need to return to this earthly plane again after death. It was a remote possibility, but why not try to get permission?

Ladakh is still referred to as "Little Tibet." Once belonging to Tibet and paying tribute to Lhasa, it was occupied by Mongols, then, luckily, taken back by the British. Now it is under Indian rule.

It is of special interest, as the Ladakhis are free to follow Tibetan traditions and customs outlawed by the communists in Tibet proper. It is divided from China by the Karakoram Mountains. Covered by wild leeks part of the year, they are referred to as the Onion Mountains. To the east is what used to be Tibet, and to the west, Pakistan. It is most easily approached from the southwest by jeep from Srinagar; one follows the Indus River to its headwaters in this most northern state of India.

For centuries, Leh has been an important trade center because of its unique location on the trade routes between Central Asia, India, Tibet and Western Asia. When reading about Ladakh, it is easy to conjure images of Genghis Khan, Marco Polo, and Kubla Khan. It was the meeting place for the caravans that carried wool, cotton, dyes, spices and general merchandise to Yarkand and Kashgar in China, bringing back silk, tea and carpets. One can only imagine the wealth that changed hands.

Because Ladakh was conquered by Moslems at one time, a combination of cultures exists there. It seems a contradiction in terms to describe a person as a Moslem Tibetan, but there are many to be found in Ladakh.

As it worked out, we received an invitation from the head of the Indian army, General Naveen Rawley, as well as the governor, so all was set. Our party, besides myself, included Rik, no longer with a crew cut; María Luisa— now a beautiful, curvaceous eighteen with Mother's large, grey-blue eyes and golden, highlighted auburn hair; and Dick Cooke's stunning blonde daughter, Cynthia, also eighteen. It was the first trip to India for both, and the girls were delighted to have each other for company.

Having a fear of heights, I had not been sure the trip was for me. However, María Luisa and Rik convinced me that if army trucks traveled the road, it could not be that bad, especially for a jeep. They suggested I sit in back, and when things got too scary, I could shut my eyes and meditate.

After it was all set to go, I had periods of doubt—especially when I dug up some old *National Geographics* and saw where we were going. I was beginning to wonder if I were not too old for this trip, now that I'd reached fifty, but Rik had me running a mile a day to get myself in condition. Letters arrived advising, "Be sure to bring alpine clothes, as you will go over high passes and the nights will be extremely cold. Most important is your car and driver—if you were to break down, it could be extremely dangerous." Were we going to the end of the world?

Just a week before take-off, I read a column by a journalist about his recent trip to Leh. He described the road as "a geologist's delight and a car passenger's horror." He went on to say that everyone in his Land Rover got carsick. I immediately ordered dramamine, as María Luisa had a history of carsickness. Also, I hid the articles from the rest of the party. It was too late to turn back.

When we finally got to New Delhi, it was the first of October, already a bit late to start. We would be in trouble if it snowed. Of course, the girls thought it would be fun to be snowbound with a whole Army garrison.

"Just think of the book we could write," María Luisa suggested. In the few days they had spent on Indian soil, they were wildly enthusiastic about everything they saw—especially the colorful bazaars and their bargain prices. "What a shame we brought any clothes at all; everything here is 'in'; we should have brought empty suitcases and filled them up."

There would be time to shop later. Now was the time to head north. In Srinagar we dined with the Jhas, who had just returned from Leh.

What a pleasure to meet people who had actually been there and survived. They commented, "You will be better acclimated by driving and arriving gradually in the altitude. It's too big a shock when you fly in to 12,000 feet."

A general's wife, who was an athletic-looking woman, warned us, "The altitude is severe. I had to have an EKG run on me after being there only two days. Because of the fear of pulmonary edema, the army keeps new men joining the garrison in their quarters for eight days."

There were approximately forty thousand men there, making it the largest army outpost at that height in the world. She pointed out, "The lack of foliage, related to the distance from the equator, makes the climactic conditions there far more severe than other places of similar altitude."

Governor Jha laughed, "Don't scare them to death. We had four days in Leh and felt it was far too short. However, there is a storm forecast for tomorrow afternoon, so you must get an early start, not only to get ahead of the big convoy that leaves Srinagar at 7:00 a.m., but before any water falls on the Zozila Pass."

The next morning, sitting in the back of the crowded jeep, as we approached Zozila Pass, I remembered the forecasted storm and began to pray.

"The mountains look as if a wrathful Nature threw millions of tons of jagged granite up in the air and let them fall at will," Rik exclaimed.

Encircling us were the most rugged, razor-sharp cliffs we had ever seen. This was Zozila Pass—we called it "Godzilla"—the pass I had been dreading since my friend Nita Thapar in New Delhi had described it.

"There are places so steep and narrow that if you were to get out of the jeep on the wrong side, you'd fall thousands of feet. Your driver has to have a 'vertigo pass' to go on that road."

This was the lowest of the passes we were to traverse—fourteen thousand, five hundred feet, but the most dramatic—a twenty-mile stretch of unpaved roads. Eight months of the year it is in a constant state of disrepair. Severe changes in temperatures and rarified, dry air grind the earth into a powdery dust. The traveler then has the choice of dust or slippery, melting snow.

The Indian Army, needing a supply road during the attempted Chinese invasion of India in 1962, had this road made by Tibetan labor, hand-carving it out of the sides of the cliffs. They had unsuccessfully tried to blacktop the surfaces, but water would slip under the tar, freeze, and the blacktop would slide off. Actually, the road is open only five months of the year.

Facing us across a huge chasm were perpendicular, granite walls. This was part of the road to Leh, Ladakh!

"If Jesus is supposed to have come here, how do you suppose he made it?" I ventured.

"He learned to levitate in order to get home," offered María Luisa.

"Look at all that dust in the distance—what causes that?" Rik asked our Kashmiri driver, Glom Cardiff. We later changed his name to "Glum," he was so grumpy.

"A convoy is coming from Leh."

It didn't seem possible—the road was hardly wide enough for one lane of traffic. We found a niche in the side of the mountain and waited. We beat the convoy from Srinagar, but hadn't been warned about this.

"How many trucks are usually in a convoy?"

"Sometimes as many as one hundred."

It was unbelievable. As we hugged the dust-covered mountainside, one huge monster after another crawled by us. Four trucks actually hit the canvas top of our jeep! There were weapons carriers, troop trucks and vehicles of all description. The air was so full of powdery dust we could hardly see anything. What nerve it took on the part of those drivers—driving practically blind, and there wasn't a pebble on the side of the road to keep them from going over. To think that I had asked in one of my early letters if there were guard rails! How would we ever get out of this alive? I opened a bottle of Scotch and fortified my courage.

Finally, the trucks started to thin out, and we moved forward, jockeying for position every time we met another vehicle. When the dust had settled, the sky was brilliant blue. We were above most vegetation except for occasional blazing orange-leafed trees hugging the steep slopes. When the traffic permitted, we stopped for Rik to photograph. (Later he became a photographer for National Geographic.) It was very quiet. In all directions we could see perpetually-snowcapped peaks, not even listed on maps, though they range from sixteen thousand to twenty thousand feet. Huge, blue glaciers hung ominously above us.

"What was that marker? I couldn't read it," asked María Luisa, about a plaque cemented into a mound of rocks on the cliffside.

"It says that twenty people were lost at that spot by an avalanche."

I was sorry she had asked, I remembered the General saying that this was dangerous avalanche country. We passed many more of these markers—commemorating people lost while trying to clear the road of snow. I took frequent sips from the bottle and kept silently repeating my *mantra*.

Suddenly Rik pointed, "Look at those beautiful wild horses on the cliff!" As we stopped to photograph, huge eagles flew by. When we reached the summit of fourteen thousand, five hundred seventy-five feet, we enjoyed spectacular scenery—all in shades of beige, brown, rust and maroon. The dimensions of the huge ranges reminded us of Katmai, in the Aleutian chain of Alaska. However, here the mountains looked younger, not having been worn smooth by age. The Himalayas are among the newest mountains in the world.

As we traveled on, the landscape kept changing dramatically. We followed the aqua blue glacial waters of the Indus River. The sand along the river banks was a pinkish-grey. This is the same river which caused a gigantic avalanche in the 1800s, when a huge glacier let go. It wiped out all the little mountain villages for hundreds of miles around, killing thousands and changing the course of the river. After Zozila Pass, we were astounded to see the river running in the opposite direction from before. At one point, we looked over the side and counted at least twenty-five switchbacks.

Later on, the land flattened out and looked like a desert plain full of rocks. There was almost no vegetation, only a brilliant grove of poplar trees now and then. As we passed through Dras, the second coldest place in the world, we were happy to have our alpine clothes. (The coldest place is somewhere in Siberia.) During winter, the strange rock formations and constant winds force the temperature down to 160 degrees below zero.

Rik muttered, "No wonder Tibetans always envision hell as a place of eternal cold."

We had been seeing yaks, indicating a fairly high altitude, before we arrived in Kharghil. Situated above the river, it is a town of houses stacked in rows within groves of poplar, apricot and apple trees. A main bazaar cut the town down the middle.

As we made our way to the tourist bungalow, people appeared out of nowhere, anxious to see new faces and hungry for news. Over a drink, the bungalow manager, Mr. Kaul, a young Indian, and his wife described life there. "After November 15th, the buses stop and start again June 15th. We are completely snowed in. It's a living hell for a man without a family." The Kauls smiled at each other. "Especially for the engineers, who do all their work in three months and then sit for the rest of the time. Here you will see the advantage of army discipline keeping men busy."

We asked about housekeeping and child rearing under these conditions. Mrs. Kaul flipped her long braid behind her shoulder as she replied, "We work all summer storing provisions, then while the men suffer from enforced idleness and play cards to break the monotony, we clean and cook. There is no TV—only bad Indian radio programs. In order to survive, it's very important to have hobbies. I paint and sew a lot."

We inquired about their diet.

"Well, it's dull; mainly dahl, rice, tinned vegetables, spices and a little dried meat. There is canned or dried milk only for the children."

She offered us dried apricots, adding that we would also find them in Leh, and pointed out, "You eat the almond that is inside the pit."

It reminded me of the craze in the U.S. health food stores for anything made out of the Hunza apricot. Hunza lies to the west of Leh and is not far as a bird flies. I asked her, "What happens if you fall ill and need an operation?"

Her dark eyes saddened, "There is no way out; that is a death sentence. There is no medical care available." She continued in her soft tones, "You met Mr. Mallik when you arrived. He is almost desperate; he has been here two-and-a-half years and was to be relieved this summer. His relief has fallen ill and can't come. There are only three weeks left to get another, otherwise, he will have to stay until next June. If he has to stay, I'm convinced he will lose his mind."

My thoughts went back to Govinda's words, "In Tibet, we live in silence." What for one man was bliss, was hell for another.

Our accommodations were dreary; the bathroom fixtures had been used frequently, but never connected—unbelievable! After a small supper, made up from our stores, and a couple of drinks, we felt better. Our packaged soup hit the spot. I went into the primitive kitchen to make sure the squatting chef boiled our water for ten minutes by my watch—always a must in India.

It had been a twelve-hour day; we spread out our sleeping bags and it was candles out early. Cynthia was awakened by a rat sitting on her chest, and there was a huge spider in the toilet. Otherwise, it was an uneventful night.

Early the next morning, once more in the jeep, we saw our first Tibetan village. (Kharghil had been a Kashmiri settlement.) The homes had whitewashed walls and exaggerated wooden windows. We also saw *chortens*, pagoda-like, whitewashed, sepulchral monuments, containing ashes and bone or relics of lamas and rajas, which some people refer to as "potted lamas." Big and small, they were everywhere.

We watched Tibetans in the fields, in their flowing robes and embroidered boots, winnowing the barley. Others led a combination of dzos (a cross between a yak and a cow), yaks and horses in a circle to thresh the barley—so primitive, but effective, and no need to depend on imported oil or parts. Huge Buddhas were carved in the mountainsides and, fluttering in the wind beside them by the hundreds, were the customary prayer flags.

We pleaded with the driver, "Slow down, Glum, don't go so fast. We've come all this way to see the scenery; you make us so nervous, all we see is the road." We were on a terrifyingly-steep grade.

The pavement on the hand-built road was made out of rock pounded into gravel by Tibetan women; they poured tar over it by hand. Sweeping the road with crude reed brooms, they called out *"Jole."* Often we stopped to give them candies. They had sunburned faces and cheeks rubbed bright pink with the juice of berries. Our general reaction was, "What a desolate life!"

As we rounded a precipitous corner, a scene from Shangri-La came into view. A monastery arose majestically, like a gothic cathedral atop a steep cliff. The mood of the setting was of complete solitude. Corn and wheat fields lay at its rocky base, and in the distance, huge mountains surrounded it. It was built like a Crusader's castle set for siege; the masonry seemed to grow out of the solid stone. Below, hundreds of *chortens* stood guard, lining the approach. This was the thousand-year-old Lama Yurru Monastery. It was reported to be filled with old frescoes and paintings depicting the life of Buddha.

We sat on the roadside wall and ate our lunch, while enjoying the view of Lama Yurru. We decided to visit the monastery on our return trip. It's lucky we had little to eat. By the time we got back to the jeep, we all had sunburned faces, the result of direct sun and rarified air. I was to use my umbrella a lot in the days to come.

It was 5:00 p.m., the second terrifying day of driving, when we saw the valley of Leh spread out before us. It looked like a moonscape—sand-colored mountains and rocks everywhere—a twelve-thousand-foot-high desert. The only signs of vegetation were barley and wheat fields. The houses in the distance were made of mud, and high on the precipice we saw the impressive monastery of Spituk, headquarters for the Yellow Hat order. As we sped by some Army jeeps, we happily returned their drivers' waves—we were so thrilled to have arrived.

It was only after crossing the military strip that a jeep cut in front of us and signalled us to stop. Three young Indian officers piled out of their car and one exclaimed, "What a chase you have given us. We were sent out to meet you—we've been trying to catch up with you for the last ten miles." He turned to Glum, "Are you trying to kill your passengers, driving like a madman?" We answered in chorus, "Yes!" He suggested we follow them to the Army Guest Bungalow, where we were staying, and have some tea.

What a joy to have a cup of Darjeeling tea, cookies and all the trimmings—the best part was the fact that we were alive to enjoy them.

It didn't take long for the word to get around that three American women had arrived—of special interest, two beautiful young ones. It is a land without women for Indian soldiers—no wives allowed. Ladakhi women would be hard to identify with, as it is customary for them to bathe only at birth, before marriage, and at death. One officer described them as "dirty, greasy-looking people." Rather cruel, but this probably didn't apply to the wealthier families, who maybe had bathrooms. After a few cold nights in Leh, I was more sympathetic to the customs of the area.

Colonel Aurora, who seemed to be in charge of us, advised, "It would be wise for you to have an early night and take oxygen before retiring—the biggest danger is the altitude. You will do better to take most of your meals with us, as conditions are very primitive in Leh. Tomorrow do all the sightseeing you can, but remember, if at any time you don't feel well, let us know at once—pulmonary edema is a major threat to newcomers." The Colonel was right. We were tired, dirty, and ached all over. What a joy to have a bathroom, working fixtures and all. Hot water was carried in by bucket. What a luxury—beds, blankets, heaters—the Leh Hilton!

Before sleeping, we each inhaled a few minutes of oxygen, as Colonel Aurora explained, "In sleep, the breathing gets shallow and one doesn't get enough oxygen. This results in insomnia; then the next day there is a feeling of fatigue—it becomes a vicious circle."

Early next morning, thoroughly refreshed, we set out for the city of Leh. The huge, snow-covered mountains of the Karakoram range stood before us in the distance, protecting Ladakh from the aggression of China. Alongside were the neighboring ranges of the Hindu Kush and the Pamirs. From the Leh Valley it is possible to see Mount Kailash. It is eternally snowcapped and hovers over the holy lake of Manasarovara. This was a thrill for me, as I had read many Tibetan books describing Mount Kailash. Almost all Tibetan *thangkas* depict it. Could this be the location of *Shambala?*

We were told that snow leopards and ibex populate the forbidding heights of these mountains. Also found in the lofty highlands and in the deep ravines were red bear, wild horses, Tibetan antelope and gazelle. It is one of the few areas that produces the pashmina goat, from whose coat comes the finest wool in the world. We passed many shepherds with large flocks of sheep and goats.

As we approached the town, we saw our first *"mani* wall." These prayer walls are about six feet high, five feet wide, and anywhere from ten feet to a mile long. The tops of the walls are covered with stones exquisitely carved with the Buddhist mantra, *Aum mani padme hum.* Devotees buy these stones from the lamas who carve them. The tradition is to keep these walls on one's right—as one does with the numerous *chortens*.

The surrounding fields were beginning to turn brown with the approach of winter. The city had no pavement, and the main street was one block long. Mud and clay buildings were two stories high, and open plumbing ran down the street. A group of women were sitting in the corner of the main intersection selling vegetables. They wore black velvet hats shaped like top hats. Their robes were black or mauve, cotton or velvet, and were tied in the middle by bright pink sashes. Married women were distinguished by ratty-looking sheepskin capes hanging from their shoulders. Many wore Chinese good luck symbols on their stovepipe hats. Single women wore the cobra-like *peyrak*, a broad leather strap studded with turquoise, shells and silver.

*Nancy's eldest son, Richard A. Cooke III,
as a* National Geographic *photographer*

*Nancy in Leh, Ladakh*

*Leh woman's robes*

*Nancy and Leh woman in
bridal clothes*

*Ladakhi women in market*

*Nancy and monk at
Spituk Monastery*

*Nancy with monks and Korshak Bakula in Leh*

"Suitors can immediately estimate a girl's dowry by this headdress," our driver said.

Under the loving guidance of Riaz Ahmed, a Tibetan Moslem and owner of the general store, to whom we had a letter of introduction, and the Indian army, the following five days were filled with visits to Ladakhi's homes, my drinking endless cups of Tibetan tea accented with yak butter and salt, (the young people refused it and drank *chang*, a beer made from barley) and sightseeing throughout the Leh Valley.

The ancient monasteries we visited were filled with beautiful *thangkas*, tapestries, statues, Buddhist relics, and old treasures that had been hidden from the eyes of the world for centuries. No attempt is being made to preserve them, and time is slowly causing them to disintegrate into dust. They have lasted this long probably because of the lack of moisture and mildew. We wished we understood more about Buddhism and all the symbolism. None of the monks spoke English, and our army guides could not speak Ladakhi. One visit was memorable. An old monk insisted we visit the highest *gompa* above the Spituk Monastery. He kept urging us on and then proudly opened the aged door to show us his treasure—it was a large colored poster of Peter Fonda on a motorcycle advertising *Easy Rider!*

Our trip to the Himis Monastery was special but disappointing; it lies in a hidden valley about twenty-five miles from Leh. Its location is undoubtedly what saved it from destruction at the hands of the conquering hordes that swept across the land. The valley is in a half-bowl of rugged mountains. At the far end, perched high on a crag, was the lamasery, surrounded by a grove of startling poplar trees at the height of their golden glory.

What a picture it made—the ancient stones of the monastery, the *gompas*, tiny retreats, high above, the impressively long "*mani* walls," and the glorious trees. We were now above fourteen thousand feet. There was no *Shushok* (Head Lama) for this monastery, the headquarters of the Red Sect, as he had been taken captive by the Chinese while visiting Tibet. (There is little difference in doctrine between the two sects of Buddhism; the Yellow Hats are a bit more austere and predominate in Tibet, the Red Hats in Ladakh.) An old monk told us we'd just missed Kalu Rinpoche; he was in Bhutan. He also said he knew of no evidence of a man named Issa ever having visited there.

"You mean we've come all this way for nothing!" moaned the girls.

"What do you mean, nothing—how many people ever have an experience like this? This only means now we must go to Bhutan." The girls quickly agreed. We also had no luck in getting to Mount Kailash.*

Our days were filled with contrasts. We played a few holes of golf on the army course. One had to tee up for all shots or get a face full of dirt. The greens were called "browns" as they were made of combed-dust heavily covered with dark brown oil. Traps were the many *chortens* scattered about the course. If one connected well with the ball, it really traveled in that thin air.

One morning, before the sun got too high, we traveled by horseback to visit the army's experimental farm that we had been hearing about. We rode along an irrigation canal lined by willows. With one five-hundredth of Ladakh's land arable, the Indian government built several canals as an experiment to bring water from the snowcapped mountains. Since the success of the farm, more irrigation is being planned. When water is available, the combination of strong sun and mineral-rich soil makes it possible to produce two crops in the time usually needed for one.

The Ministry of Defense is in charge of the agricultural experiment, and it was thrilling for us to see soldiers turned farmers. The results of this challenge may change the culture of high-altitude populations around the world.

We saw over twenty-six varieties of flowers growing at once—summer, fall and spring flowers. In beds dug six inches deep, they grew all sorts of crops—tomatoes, cabbages, carrots, radishes, sweet turnips,

---

*At the end of the nineteenth century, a Russian explorer visited the Himis Monastery. In the library he discovered the ancient Tibetan scrolls telling about the extraordinary saint whom the Buddhists called Issa.

Taken from Chapter 5:1-5, Tibetan scrolls:

"The fame of this wonderful youth spread throughout Northern Sindh; when he crossed the country of the five rivers and Rajputana, the worshippers of the Jaina God implored him to dwell with them.

"But he left them and went to Jagannath, in the country of Orissa, where lie the mortal remains of Vyasa-Krishna. Here the white priests of Brahma received him joyfully.

"They taught him to read and understand the Vedas, to cure with the aid of prayers, to teach and explain the holy scriptures to the people, to drive away the evil spirit from the body of man, and to restore to him the human form.

"He spent six years in Jagannath, Rajagriha, Benares and other holy cities. Everyone loved Issa, for he lived in peace with the Vaishyas and Shudras, to whom he taught the holy scripture."

(*The Forgotten Pilgrimage of Jesus*, compiled by James F. Forcucci, 1989. Lincoln, Nebraska: Sosana Press.)

cauliflower, corn, barley, tobacco, garlic, onions, potatoes, and many herbs and spices. The cabbages were bigger than watermelons, a Tibetan woman could carry only two on her back at one time.

We chewed on a crisp carrot that was at least nine inches around and three feet long—delicious. Pumpkins, eggplants, kale, brussel sprouts, turmeric and ginger grew alongside sweet peas, snapdragons, daisies and petunias. Strawberry plants spread out over the ground and wandered into the orchard, where apricots and apples were just fading out.

No wonder the local Ladakhis thought it was the product of magicians—to grow all this in a land that had been considered unproductive. Also, because of the low humidity, it was possible to dry the fruit and vegetables directly in the sun, dehydrating them for use during the winter months.

"It has improved the variety of diet that is now available for the army and the Ladahkis," our guide told us proudly. "In the past, after the snow began, everything had to be brought in by air."

One evening, on returning to the army bungalow, we were met by an agitated threesome, "Where have you been until so late? You have been gone nine hours. We warned you of the dangers of pulmonary edema from overdoing." The Major was plainly upset. He was accountable to their General to take care of us.

Rik asked, "How do we know if we've overdone? I do have a small headache." Carrying his heavy camera equipment up and down the mountainside to the various *gompas* we had visited, Rik had exerted himself more than the rest of us.

A new face stepped forward. "I am Colonel Kumar, the regiment doctor. Put oxygen on this man first." His curt manner indicated thoughts about "foolish foreigners."

"What happens if we get pulmonary edema?" I asked.

"You have three choices, Ma'am. Oxygen, get the hell out of here, or TM," he answered.

"Do you mean Transcendental Meditation? Are you a meditator?"

"Yes, Ma'am, I have been for twelve years." He was emphatic. "It is very effective in overcoming problems related to drastic change in altitude."

"Well, you will be glad to hear that we are meditators also," I announced with pride.

His manner changed abruptly. Now friendly, he explained, "During meditation, one's breathing becomes refined and the oxygen in the body is used more efficiently."

Maybe this was why we had felt so little effect from the high altitude everyone had warned us about.

It was a heart tug when we said goodbye to Leh—it's not a place we're likely to visit again—at least not me, over that road. We would never forget the hospitality of the Indian Army. Two years later, Rik flew back to Ladakh and spent ten weeks during the winter, living in various monasteries. He returned with an incredible slide show—photographs of scenes never before captured by the camera of a Westerner. Before leaving for Leh, he took an intensive course in Hindi; otherwise, he would not have been able to communicate with the Ladakhis.

On returning to Kashmir, María Luisa made a comment that said a lot. "I'm so tired of our adjectives—fabulous, breathtaking, awe inspiring, over-powering, fantastic, beautiful, stupendous—this country simply defies our vocabularies. How will we ever describe this trip to others?"

We all felt the same. After brown bear-hunting in the Arctic Circle with the Laplanders, tiger-shooting from the back of an elephant and crossing the Andes by bus, I can freely say to those who are strong in body—if you are looking for adventure and the unusual, put this trip on your itinerary.

We were travel weary, cramped and dirty when we arrived back in Srinagar, but we didn't care—we had been to Ladakh!

---
## 25
---

# Adventure Becomes Addictive

O N ARRIVAL IN DELHI, with the relief of having made it to Ladakh and back alive, Avi's call came like a bombshell. "You are going to be thrilled; I've got permission for us to go to Badrinath." He poured on the sales pitch. "We have to take off as soon as possible; winter is coming and soon the roads will be closed." As if we didn't know. One of the worries had been that we might get stuck in Leh. "I've got all the papers in order."

There seemed no getting out of it, but I tried. "Avi, you have never made that trip to Ladakh, it's a killer. The idea of more mountain travel, at this point, is not for me."

But he was persuasive. "Come on, where is that great spirit of adventure? I never thought I'd hear you say no." He went on selling. "We can stop over for a night in Rishikesh, where you can visit with Satyanand. Also, we'll go to Jyotir Math, where Guru Dev lived. You will be going into the heart of the Shankara tradition." He knew my weak points. Being the eldest, I was the hardest to convince; youth recovers quickly, and my other three companions were soon talked into "working on Mom."

"At least this time we won't be in a jeep, which is a plus. The Ambassador can make it—in fact, we'll take two cars."

344

Finally, I relented. "Okay, but you have those cars gone over by a good mechanic." Breaking down on the road was standard procedure for Indian travel, and Avi's record was not the best. We had been his "advance men" in many of the places he later developed into areas of tourist interest. Now we would be counted among the first sixty foreigners to go to Badrinath, the source of the Ganges. A new road recently had been built by the Indian Army. Until then, only the hardiest of pilgrims had made it there by foot or on animal back.

Years before, Jerry Jarvis, Charlie Lutes and Maharishi had gone to Jyotir Math, but were not allowed any further. For this trip, we decided to visit the ashram but not stay there. I didn't want to go through all that cleaning up for just two nights. It was easier to stay in a government DAK bungalow.

The Valley of the Saints was an exotic place for the girls to see. The *sadhus*, the temples, the boat to cross the Ganges, the walk up the hill to the ashram. First they wanted to see the "Beatles' block" and the one I'd lived in. On seeing the two dark little rooms, María Luisa exclaimed, "This is where you spent three months, Mom?"

The ashram looked as though the Indians were taking over. Little temples and *lingams* (phallic symbols often done in stone, worshipped by some Hindu sects) had appeared; it was acquiring a junky look and losing the serene, simple atmosphere it originally conveyed. Indian courses were in session, and many permanent families lived at the ashram.

Satyanand, however, was delighted to greet us and catch up on our news. He always asked, "How is my friend, Helen Lutes?" And then, "The last time I saw her was when I had Thanksgiving dinner at your home in Beverly Hills." His beard was longer and filled with gray, but he bustled with enthusiasm. "So," he turned to Rik, "you want me to initiate your sister into meditation; fine, you go off to see Tatwala Baba and leave Cynthia with me." We had arranged all this from Delhi by phone.

Wishing Cynthia, "Happy Initiation," we left the ashram and followed the trail toward the cave where Tatwala Baba lived; forty minutes later we climbed up the hill to the dirt platform where the holy man received his callers. Shaded by trees, the dirt floor was cool; half of the area was sheltered by a makeshift wooden shed.

Under the lean-to, sat the *sadhu*. Sitting in the lotus position, hands on his knees, his long coils of solid black hair covered his shoulders

and slithered to the ground. Around Tatwala Baba time seemed to stop
. . . all was serene. His luminous eyes were warm as he acknowledged our
presence. An elderly Indian served as his interpreter. Four others sat on
a mat covering the ground. We joined them and became part of the
general discussion of universal truth. Questions were asked to initiate
his discourse. As he spoke, he gestured with his beautifully-formed,
long-fingered hands. Eventually, I asked a personal question. His eyes
looked directly into mine—the whites of his eyes seemed to give out
light, and it was difficult to continue looking into them.

"I will be seeing Maharishi soon in the U.S.," I said. It felt as if he
knew exactly what I would say next—he was inside my head. "Would
you like me to give him a message from you?"

Tatwala Baba smiled and gently answered, "No, that will not be
necessary. We are in constant communication with each other." The
others chuckled at their guru's words. He didn't need the mail or a
telephone in order to communicate.

After a polite interval, Rik asked the interpreter, "Would it be
possible to take some photographs of Tatwala Baba? I am a photographer
and have brought my equipment with me—visiting on other occasions
I've had nothing but a hand camera."

The elderly gentleman was enthusiastic, "That would be very nice;
then we devotees will have a good picture of Swamiji."

Rik wandered around seeking the best background. He asked to go
up to the next level, where the saint actually lived. Following behind
him, I caught a glimpse of a simple opening into the rocky cliff. A bowl
of dahl and rice and a blanket lay on the cave floor. Suddenly Rik jumped
back, almost knocking me down the stairs carved into the steep path.
"My God, there's a snake moving under his blanket. The way it's coiled,
it's a big one." Rumor had it that a cobra lived with the aged saint. We
decided not to introduce ourselves.

Rik settled for one pose under the saint's favorite tree and another
in front of the cliff sitting on a large round cushion. Scrutinizing this
man, it was hard to believe his age.

Tatwala Baba accepted no gifts of money, fruit, or flowers. If a
person arrived with such, it was given away to people in the village. The
saint ate only rice and dahl; this way he would not develop a new desire,
opening himself to expectations that one day might not be fulfilled.

Over the years, each time we visited Rishikesh, we looked forward
to paying our respects to this incredible holy man. But this was to be our

last visit. Two weeks later, a devotee shot the saint five times. He was convinced that Tatwala Baba was indestructible and was going to prove it. Unfortunately, his aim was good and he killed the master. Satyanand told me later that many saints die a violent death, "Otherwise they would live on forever." We wished he could have, he was so special. It was sad news for us.

After leaving Rishikesh, it took two twelve-hour days of driving to reach the Valley of Badrinath, about the same distance as Leh. Both cars took turns breaking down, but the Ambassador, like a Model A Ford, was so simply constructed, it proved easy to repair. In many ways it was a repetition of the road to Ladakh—steep, treacherous, winding. Some corners were so precipitous that little metal bridge-like platforms had been fitted in to allow the passage of one small car. On some of these, we got out and walked.

It was midnight when Badri, one of Avi's men, announced, "*Sahib*, from here we go into the Valley of Badrinath." It was now downhill. The silence was ominous when we stopped to notice it. We could see nothing; there was not a light anywhere.

"How do we find a place to sleep?" we asked.

To pacify us, Avi blithely said, "Something always turns up. Don't worry, we'll start knocking on doors." If we could find a door. We seemed to be in a primitive sort of village, but all was closed up tightly against cold and drop-ins. "There has to be a government bungalow somewhere," Avi insisted.

Just then, María Luisa, with her young eyes, said, "Look over there, isn't that candlelight?" It was a hostelry—of a kind.

It wasn't fancy, but within a short time we had our sleeping bags spread out on cots and were fast asleep. Each of us, I'm sure, said a special prayer of thanks for being there instead of on the side of a mountain. However, we were not to sleep long. At dawn, a strange, wailing sound echoed throughout the small, bowl-shaped valley.

"It is a record of pundits chanting the Vedas," explained Avi. "They must have hooked it up to a public address system."

After an improvised breakfast, we went to the Badrinath Temple, the number one in India, as it is the closest to the headwaters of the Ganges. It was built into a mountainside overlooking a small waterfall.

"The water is sacred here. All pilgrims strip off their clothes and bathe in the fall," Badri explained.

It didn't sound appealing to me. "I think I'll settle for halfway measures and just wade in." It was cold and the water did not look inviting. "I can always say I went in."

I felt the same way about the temple. It had a lovely silver statue of Vishnu, but otherwise, it was dirty and damp. Further on, a rocky cave was much more attractive. This was the actual spring from which the Mother Ganga was born—now we could claim we'd been to the source!

On the way home, our car gave up. No more gas. Rik was incredulous. "But Avi, how can that possibly happen? Surely the drivers knew how many miles we had to drive."

Avi took it in stride. "No problem (the universal *mantra* of India). I'll go ahead and get some petrol." It was always the same, no matter how often one stresses that the car, tires and gasoline be carefully checked—it's never done!

Shaking our head in exasperation, as we knew it would be hours, we spread out peanut butter, guava jelly, biscuits, canned cheese, and a bottle of Scotch on a rock wall overlooking a vast canyon, and had a picnic.

"Would you have ever guessed a week ago when we were worried about the trip back from Leh, that we'd be here, stranded on this mountainside?" asked María Luisa. Her words were cut off by a tremendous roar.

"My God, what was that?"

Rik volunteered, as though it were nothing, "An avalanche. The Himalayas are the most avalanche-prone mountains in the world, being the youngest range, and they are constantly moving." It seemed to me we'd heard all that just two weeks before.

Every hour a vehicle would pass but could not help us, as we needed gas, not diesel fuel. We had been there for about four hours when a Citroen approached. "Say a prayer," someone murmured.

We waited and the car stopped. "I say, do you need help?" The two occupants were bearded young Sikhs. They introduced themselves as geologists trained at UCLA. What a reunion. They shared their fuel with us and suggested we follow them into the next town. "You'd be better off to spend the night there, as our driver will have to go on to the next town to buy petrol and bring it back." They assured us there would be tent space available, as there was an Avalanche Conference taking place.

Less than an hour down the road, we came upon Avi and his car; it had broken down. His driver had walked ahead, hoping to return with a mechanic. He greeted us sheepishly.

We eventually got back to Delhi in one piece, but our adventures were not over. Piloo and Vina, who got a vicarious thrill out of our wanderings, had set up an invitation to visit Pakistan as guests of Prime Minister Ali Bhutto, a friend from school days of the Modys. Tony had called and Piloo cleared it with him. Tony's reaction was, "Great, I'll interview Nancy on my program. Tell her to ask lots of questions when she meets Bhutto." It was too tempting to resist, even though we were a bit "battle fatigued."

As no communication or transportation existed between the two countries, we would have to walk across the border at Amritsar, the Sikh capital and one of India's poorest cities, to Lahore, which before partition had been known as the "Jewel of the Punjab." In spite of the affluence of the Sikh society, Amritsar was depressing. Lying halfway between Delhi and Kashmir, I usually flew through without stopping over.

I had been there once to visit the Sikhs' beloved Golden Temple, which is surrounded by water in a small lake, but once was enough. I found it badly taken care of and depressing. So we flew in, got into a filthy taxi with broken seat springs, and went straight to the border.

Conversation was out; it wasn't possible to hear over the noise of the taxi as it creaked and clunked its way to the exit from India.

Regarding us with suspicion, Indian customs and border officials were in no hurry to give us permission to leave; anyway, they enjoyed looking at the two pretty girls. Finally, coolies packed our luggage on their heads—they wrap long cloths around their heads to make a platform for the bags, then another coolie stacks them.

"Look at that poor man," protested María Luisa. "Don't let them put another bag on top; he's got too much already!" We were happy to pay a few rupees more and spread out the load.

Then we started the walk across the quarter mile of no-man's-land. Passing us from the Pakistani side were bearers carrying contraband tobacco and all sorts of foodstuffs. From the Indian side came boxes marked "ghee" (clarified butter) and "betel nut," not obtainable in Pakistan.

When we reached the mid-point, Pakistani bearers appeared and our baggage went on their heads. It took us five minutes to be welcomed into Pakistan, given a cold 7-Up, never seen in India, and escorted to a sparkling clean mini-bus, provided by the waiting travel agent.

There were no wandering cows to leave a mess or eat the foliage. The hedges and bushes were green with leaves and bright flowers. The border city, Lahore, is beautiful. Surrounded by Mogul gardens with geometric designs, many of its monuments were built by Shah Jahan, the creator of the Taj Mahal. It was also the scene of a ghastly massacre on the eve of partition.

As we checked into the Intercontinental Hotel, new, small and modern, there was a message asking us to "Please contact the Prime Minister's aide, Mr. Ali Khan."

"An easy name to remember," chorused the two girls. It seemed, after talking to Mr. Ali Khan, that a complete itinerary had been planned for us, to visit Peshawar and Swat besides the capital city of Islamabad, adjacent to Rawalpindi. It started that evening, but the dinner at the Prime Minister's was not until two nights later in the capital. The aide would accompany us throughout Pakistan. What a luxury to have all travel plans taken care of.

Dinner with the Prime Minister and his wife was the highlight of the trip. On arrival, in the official car which had been sent for us, we stepped out to the smart salutes of the Prime Minister's private guards and were ushered into a side waiting room, where we were immediately welcomed by Bhutto's wife, Begum Nusrat.

She held out her hand, "What a pleasure to meet friends of Piloo and Vina (the Modys)." Her soft blue-grey sari matched the walls of the room. Her grey eyes looked directly into mine; we were the same height. "I can't wait to get all sorts of firsthand news." She shook her coiffed head, "It is absurd that we can't write to each other; I have to send letters to friends in England or Afghanistan and ask them to forward them. Half the time, the letters never arrive."

She spoke in a modulated voice. Everything about her was graceful. "Come into the next room; Zulfi will join us, but because of a busy schedule, he may not be able to stay long." She made us feel like intimate friends by using the Prime Minister's first name. Piloo had attended school, both at the Dun School in Dehra Dun and the University of California, with Bhutto. The book Piloo wrote about him was entitled, "My friend Zulfi," (Zulfikar Ali Bhutto), in spite of the hatred which existed between the two countries.

We were now in a large reception room. The walls were the same grey-blue. Pale Persian carpets covered the floor. The chairs and sofas were upholstered in complimentary soft brocades.

A door opened and Bhutto briskly walked up to us. "It is a joy to meet you. Have you been taken care of properly? Are you getting all caught up on Pakistan, so you can go back and give a good report to Piloo?" I felt his animal charisma at once. Not a large man, he conveyed strength—also, sex appeal.

"So that you will learn a bit more about our country, we have invited several ministers to join us. One who will be of particular interest to you, Mrs. Cooke, will be the Minister of Tourism. Ali Khan tells me you often bring groups of friends to India. I hope we can encourage you to bring your next group here." He was a super salesman.

We were complimented. Instead of ducking out, after being provided with a logical excuse, he stayed for the entire evening. Afterward, back at the hotel, Rik commented, "I think he was thrilled to have intelligent people to question. Wasn't it interesting when he asked if anyone used the mosques in India?" Even after partition, there are many Moslems still living in India.

"And how about the way he laughed when I described the smuggling activities. I hope I didn't speak out of turn," said María Luisa.

"Not at all, and I thought it was amusing when you pointed out how nice the hedges looked with no cows to eat all the leaves."

She chuckled, "I liked it when he said Pakistan would be glad to help India with the cow problem; all they had to do was drive them across the border. They would be happy to eat them. Wasn't it nice to have beef for a change?"

"What did you think of Begum Nusrat, Nancy?" asked Cynthia.

"I thought she was stunning. Not beautiful, but that bit of grey in her hair, her few exquisite jewels—everything was done in such good taste," I said. "She could not have been more charming."

"Did you see that gorgeous sari the Minister of Tourism's wife was wearing? Imagine tie-dye done in stripes on chiffon. She said it came from an area near the Rajasthan border." Our European dress looked quite drab next to their silks, satins and brocades.

The other guests had proved to be intelligent and well-traveled. It was pleasant to find them all pro-United States. One man had invited Rik to go to a carpet factory with his son so that Rik would not be taken advantage of in the bazaar. Evidently, Pakistan is the place for carpet buys, not India.

"We were bound to be the most interesting tourists Bhutto's met for a while. He couldn't believe that we had just been to Ladakh and how many of the same people we knew. Isn't it remarkable that he knew General Rawley," María Luisa added.

"Yes, and I'm glad none of you mentioned the fact that there are forty thousand Indian troops in Ladakh. Bhutto was far too polite to ask, but I bet he would have found it interesting."

"Isn't it sad to think that this was all one country; that Mr. Bhutto, for instance, lived part of his youth across the street from Piloo in Bombay and hasn't been able to go back there for twenty-seven years," said Cynthia.

"Well, what about Avi?" I replied. "You saw the house where he was raised in Lahore. Being Hindus, he and his family had to leave everything behind and enter India as refugees. They were the lucky ones, when you consider the millions who were slaughtered."

We had mixed emotions during our days in Pakistan, but we came away impressed and hoped that Mr. Bhutto was correct in saying that there would soon be a large tourist business between the two countries. He had pointed out that Pakistan would be an appealing point of destination for Indian nationals, as Pakistan was close, cheaper than India, and shared a common language and culture with many. He was optimistic that this exchange would help to create better relations.

Other friends of the Modys, to be our next hosts, were Prince Miangul Aurangzeb and his family. Actually, he was the Wali (King) of Swat and a member of parliament. Swat is a mountain state bordered by Afghanistan, the Hindu Kush, and the Karakorum Range. To get there, we flew to Peshawar and then continued by car. The twisting road was nothing compared with what we had recently been on. Soon we were enjoying the groves of apple trees as we descended into the Valley of Swat and the town of Saidu Sharif.

We had agreed to meet Mr. Ali Khan back in Peshawar after our three days with Aurangzeb. It was a welcome change of pace, to stay in a private home, surrounded by this wonderful family. Aurangzeb was enthusiastic about Americans.

"Come here, sit down, you must see the scrapbook I have from the trip Nazeem (his wife) and I made with her father to the U.S. as guests

*Piloo Mody and Prince
Miangul Aurangzeb,
the Wali of Swat*

of President Kennedy." Nazeem's father was Ayub Khan, one of the respected founding fathers of Pakistan and at that time Prime Minister.

María Luisa and Cynthia were captivated by the three beautiful daughters, Fahkri, Mumtaz, and Ishrat. They couldn't believe the girls had never visited the bazaar where we went to shop.

"No, we are not seen by the people of Swat. If a local person other than family comes here, we go to the private part of the house. However, when we are away from Swat, we no longer cover our faces," said Fahkri, a tall, slim, dark-eyed beauty, swathed in glimmering silk harem-type pants and a long chemise. Completing her costume was a full scarf of the same material, which could be used as a veil, both ends falling over her shoulders to the back.

The girls talked about their sister's forthcoming engagement. I asked if Mumtaz knew her fiancé.

"Oh yes, they are lucky. They have met and they liked each other." Several years later, Fahkri became engaged to her first cousin. She'd known him since birth, but, once engaged, they never looked at each other and hardly spoke. Two of the girls and their brother, Hassan, were our houseguests years later in Beverly Hills.

A few days later, days packed with sightseeing, *tandori* barbecues, ghandara art, *mullahs* calling out at prayer times, and friendly people, it was time to leave Pakistan. As we crossed over the border into Afghanistan, at the top of the Khyber Pass, we said goodbye to Mr. Ali Khan. "We will miss you. You have spoiled us completely."

The next four days were spent in Kabul, where we were captivated by the fiercely handsome Afghans and their amusing Chicken Street Bazaar. Here a shopper could find all sorts of treasures, from old cutlasses, muskets and oriental samovars, to lapis lazuli. We noticed many Russians buying in depth. Several times I was asked, "Are you a Russki?" to which I replied, "No, an Amerikanski."

Piloo was delighted when we returned to Delhi from Kabul to tell what we had seen; the prosperity of Pakistan in comparison with India, the common sense approach by Bhutto toward healing the wounds of the two countries. "Tell them; they won't believe it from me." Piloo encouraged us to talk to his Member of Parliament friends from the rival Congress Party.

"Tell them about the lack of beggars, the people all wearing shoes and hats, the cleanliness of the cities, the big crops they are raising. They prefer to think of Pakistan as a broken country. Tell them what Bhutto said about being relieved of the burden of Bangladesh."

He was so earnest in his attempt to make them open their closed ears and minds, but we had to be careful not to tread too harshly—we were guests in India.

Only a few months later, in 1975, Mrs. Ghandi declared a state of emergency and police arrived to take Piloo, a member of the opposition, off to jail, where he joined many friends. There he stayed for fifteen months. When finally released, he announced, "I'd become too expensive to feed, so they had to let me out."

On several other occasions, I was to see the Bhuttos again. One time while I was driving with Bhutto in Lahore, we heard the radio announcer say, "News from India indicates that today Piloo Mody was released from jail." Then, after an army coup, Bhutto was imprisoned by Zia Al Hag, then the president of Pakistan. In spite of pleas from the U.S. and many other governments, including India, Zia, afraid of the popularity of Bhutto, charged him with a political murder and had him hanged. It shocked the entire world.

As Piloo put it, after studying all the evidence presented, "The facts just don't add up. Maybe Bhutto made mistakes, but there was no excuse for his execution."

In November of 1982, I visited Begum Nusrat Bhutto at her home in Karachi, where she was under semi-house arrest. After the loss of her husband and five months of solitary confinement, she had aged considerably. Her spirit was strong, however, and her prime worry was for her daughter, Benezir, who was just completing her ninth month of solitary confinement. It was hard to understand what the Pakistani government had to gain from such harsh treatment of two women.

Later, when I saw news photos of the ailing, aged Begum Nusrat, my heart was sad for this brave woman, who is also fighting lung cancer. In the meantime, Benezir had become a rallying force for those opposed to Zia's dictatorial methods. What a thrill it was when Benezir won the election in 1988 and became the first woman Prime Minister of a Moslem country! We wished her well in governing a male-oriented country such as Pakistan.

And so, over the years, India continues to call me back. Occasionally I'll visit parts of Europe, especially England, and every two years I'll return to Argentina with my daughter, but no area seems to attract me as much as India/Pakistan. No other country seems to provide the contrasts which are evident there, from the teeming cities to the quiet solitude of the mountains; from the poverty of Calcutta to the dazzling splendor of the Maharajahs; from the callousness of the Indian merchant to the lofty ideals of their spiritual heritage.

---
## 26
---

# Karmic Bull's-eye

I N 1972 MY SON, STARR, AND CATHY WERE MARRIED. It was a happy event for both sides of the family and our week in San Antonio was filled with bridal parties. Avi Kohli had joined us after a few days in Beverly Hills, and reported all was well at home. However, he added, "I felt badly about your other houseguest. I tried to get him to come along with me several times, but he refused."

I hadn't realized anyone else was at the house, so, puzzled, I asked Tony who was there. "Oh, just a friend from Thailand," was his answer, and I forgot all about it.

Home again several weeks later, planning on working in the garden, I asked Mercedes to bring me my rubber gloves. Her reply surprised me. "They aren't here anymore; the man who stayed in the guesthouse used them to dye his hair."

Now I was curious, so I demanded from Tony, "Who was that mysterious friend from Bangkok?"

"It was Howard Hunt. He needed a place to hide out after the Watergate break-in."

I was thunderstruck. My mind went back to Avi's remark about the other houseguest being so reclusive. "No wonder he refused to go out with Avi!"

*E. Howard Hunt of Watergate fame.*
*"He hid out at our house."*

Then it had started. Our house was bugged by the FBI and Tony, as Howie's lawyer, was up to his ears in Watergate. He also represented Howie during the Ellsberg break-in trial.

During previous years, Howie and his friend, J. Gordon Liddy, used to drop by occasionally for dinner. While Howie and Tony, who had been in the OSS together, swapped stories, I had an opportunity to get to know Gordon, a man content to listen, but when he did speak, it was about something of substance. I liked this quiet man. Little did I know then what roles these two men would play in the bringing down of a president.

Howie's trial and subsequent imprisonment added to Tony's heavy work load. So, between his law practice, his health problems, and his music, during the fall of '74 he was delighted to have me off travelling. He had the house to himself and Mercedes made it easy for him to entertain at home. In his letters, his remarks were always complimentary, "Everyone asks about you," ". . . you are usually the source of conversation; we admire you for your adventurous spirit," or, ". . . the telephone seems to know when you are away. You are missed by one and all." Our intimacy seemed greater in our letters than when face to face.

For this trip, returning for Thanksgiving was my ETA. The Lutes and Gayelord Hauser would join us for our yearly feast. Rik, María Luisa and Cynthia decided to stay on for the Pushkar Camel Fair in Rajasthan. Vina tried to talk me into staying; "This is a must for you. It is easily one of the most colorful festivals of India. When you see those thousands of camels out on the sand dunes in the desert, at night under a full moon, attended by Rajasthani women all decked out in their saris, jewels and bangles, and the men in their brilliant turbans, you won't believe it." (Since then I have attended the fair and it's all she said it was.)

But it would be seven weeks that I'd been away by the time I stopped over in Thailand. Besides, I loved Thanksgiving. I'd find some "lonely strays" to fill the children's chairs. I decided to stay on schedule.

My stopover in Bangkok was a looked-forward-to ritual. Arriving at the custom's desk, I peered around for Maxine North. She was like a third sister, and had introduced me to Tony. It was easy to pick her out of a crowd as she was slim, beautiful and elegant. She never aged from year to year, and, as she put it, "I don't intend to."

With Maxine's help it was only a matter of minutes before I was cleared by customs and my bags were stored in the trunk of her car. Her business partner, Rak, laughed as we started "at it." He knew we had a lot of catching up to do. "Nancy, I hope you are here for at least a week. It will take that long to answer our questions about your trip," he said as we headed for home.

Maxine broke in, "Just a moment, sweethearts, I want to call Ampah and tell her we are a few minutes away." I knew the routine: Ampah would then go out to the driveway and shoo away the frogs that might otherwise be run over.

Maxine has several industries but her bottled drinking water, Polaris, was her main concern. Her product was used all over Thailand, especially in the major hotels.

Because of increasing crime and violence, Maxine had built a home on the property behind her plant, thus sharing the twenty-four-hour guard. Her compound was separated from the factory by high walls enclosing a small lake and lush tropical gardens.

The compound came alive when the car rolled in; her staff was out to welcome me back, and some of the stray dogs and cats she had fallen heir to also came running. I could hear the myna bird calling. He and I were old friends. With his large cage situated outside my bathroom, I tried to teach him a new tune each time I came to Maxine's.

Later, curled up on a sofa in a comfortable caftan, I thought to myself, "Boy, looking at Maxine no one would ever guess this glamorous creature is an industrialist." Her thick hair was piled high—it was sometimes blonde, sometimes brown. Her hands sparkled with brilliant jewels, her long, shapely legs were always seen at their best in delicately made, high-heeled shoes. Her eyes, deep brown, were exquisitely made up. Slightly slanted, they express humor, excitement and intelligence.

After the death of her husband, Bob, in 1954, instead of leaving Thailand, Maxine stayed on, feeling she was meant to be there for a special reason. "I haven't found out exactly what it is yet, but I'm getting closer." Living so much of her time alone at night within her compound, her thoughts turned to metaphysical matters.

As a spiritual babe-in-the-woods, I met her in 1957 while passing through Thailand on my Ambassadress trek. One of her first remarks to me was, "We were sisters in our last lifetime." She introduced me to the writings of Edgar Cayce and then to the books by Gina Geminara. Through the years, we have carried on a voluminous correspondence, often suggesting spiritual and occult books to each other.

Now she was relating some local news. "There is a great Chinese seer at the Dusitani Hotel. Would you like to go?" I agreed. Actually, over a period of years, several astrologers and numerologists had told me astounding things which have come about. I was game.

"Good, I'll make an appointment on Monday. This will give us the quiet weekend to ourselves."

After India, I usually needed a few days at Maxine's "fountain of youth" to disintoxicate myself from all the hot, spicy food I'd eaten. What a pleasure to practically drown myself in her pure, sparkling water after limiting myself to tea and beer, two safe fluids, while traveling through the subcontinent.

Her cuisine, prepared with loving care by Ampah, featured the wide variety of fruits and vegetables only found in Thailand. While we were munching on a delicate dish of chopped dates, nuts and assorted tropical fruits by the swimming pool, a cable arrived from Tony: "BIG CHIEF ROARING WATER AWAITS ARRIVAL SQUAW LEAPING FLAME." It referred to our astrological signs.

So, after lunch, we called Los Angeles. Almost immediately, Tony's cheerful voice came over the line. "Maxine, how are you? How is my

*Maxine North and her partner, Dr. Rak Panyarachun*
*(his brother became Foreign Minister of Thailand in June, 1992)*

girl? I'd like to be a fly on that wall!" It made me feel wonderful to know all was well at home.

But then, after hanging up, Maxine asked me, "Are you happy with Tony, Nancy? You don't seem to laugh as much as you used to. Is it from living with a semi-invalid?"

"Oh, no, we have a very nice marriage—in spite of his illness. He has his firm and I have the freedom to do the things I'm drawn to. We're interested in each other. We respect and love each other." I sought more things to say.

"But I take it, there's not much romance left."

"We haven't had sex together for over five years."

"Five years, that's terrible! Was that Tony's decision, or was it mutual?"

"Dr. Bieler said his sexual urge would disappear when he stopped taking cortisone. Since then we have never discussed it."

"Did you have a good relationship before that?"

"Yes, it was one of his best events. Sex was important to Tony."

"And then it's just cut off completely. You aren't ill, you still have needs. Have you supplemented on the outside a bit?"

"Oh no, sex is not that necessary to me."

"My God, that must be difficult for you. You're not on a monk's path, are you?"

"No, but what are you going to do with a sick husband?"

Maxine looked directly at me. "Is Tony still affectionate with you, even if the sex part is out?"

I had to be honest. "No, not at all, but that is all part of his sickness. How can I expect him to feel tender when he is in constant pain?"

Maxine agreed, "Yes, that's true. What a shame, but maybe you can still get him to Sai Baba. You certainly were impressed with him when you finally found him."

Maxine and I had shared an unusual experience in relation to Sai Baba during my 1962 expedition with Tom Slick, when Maxine had joined us at the Mody's in Bombay.

During breakfast one morning, Piloo had mentioned, "You should go see the saint our cook visits. He's supposed to be a great healer. His name is Shirdi Sai Baba, and he lives on top of a mountain near Poona. It takes an hour by train. If you'd like, the cook will draw a map for you. Seems the fellow is revered by Hindus and Moslems alike."

It was enough to intrigue us. The next morning Tom; Cathy McLean, the Mody's houseguest; Maxine; Peter Byrne, a white hunter from Nepal; and I set off for Poona. Arriving there by train we picked

*The search for Shirdi Sai Baba in 1962.*
*Maxine North, Cathy McLean, Tom Slick and Nancy*

up a broken-down taxi whose driver seemed to know exactly where to take us. It was a dusty, hot twenty minutes with the six of us squashed into the small vehicle. The driver never took his hand off the old-fashioned bulb-type horn, which gave out a constant "aaa-oooooo-gaaah!"

In the middle of the desert-like scenery, a small mountain jutted up from the flat terrain. "Looks like about a two-thousand-foot climb," said Peter.

Several old buses were parked next to a cold drink stand. "There must be quite a few people there already," said Tom. "Let's have a drink—it'll be a hot climb."

Maxine was delighted with her orangeade. "Look, there's a fly baked in the glass!"

Peter had gone off to inspect the path. Now he returned and advised us, "Change some rupees into coins; there are a lot of beggars on the way."

He underestimated the situation. On both sides of the steep, rocky path were ledges where lepers sat in front of the small caves they lived in. These unfortunate beings used their grotesque appearance to scare strangers into giving *baksheesh*. They held long feathers poised to touch the passersby, unless coins were thrown into their little metal cups. As we filed by, we each hastily dropped our donations, trying not to see these poor creatures too clearly. Soon we were above them.

It was noon, and, as we climbed, the sun beat down mercilessly. My heart thumped in my chest, "Tom, are you sure we're on the right mountain? If the Mody's cook had a bad heart, he'd be dead before he got to Sai Baba!"

Tom took one look at my beet-colored face. "Maybe we'd better rest and ask someone how much further it is."

Peter came back laughing. "It seems Shirdi Sai Baba has been dead for over thirty years, but there is a temple at the top, which is reported to have great healing powers from the saint who formerly lived and died there." He was in fantastic shape; his handsome Irish face showed hardly any perspiration—but then, hunting tigers required stamina.

We took a vote; Cathy and I decided to stay where we were. Maxine, trim from years of yoga and acclimated to the heat of Thailand, joined the men.

While we waited for their return, we observed bearers with grain sacks on their heads struggling up the mountainside. "There must be people living up there," said Cathy.

Soon our curiosity was satisfied. Our companions returned to describe the sight they had encountered. "There is a small temple, nothing impressive, in honor of Shirdi Sai Baba," said Tom. "But the real scene is the people kept there. Evidently families bring mad people to have the demons driven out of them. Most of them are naked, dirty, and have long matted hair. From their expression, one can see they are not normal."

"Are they lepers?" I asked.

"Oh, no," Peter explained, "the keepers of the temple would never let lepers come near; they are considered damned. You will see lepers near holy places, but not next to the temple itself."

I reminded Maxine of that day in 1962. "You went up that mountain like a billy goat. Everybody was exhausted by the time we returned to Bombay, but not you!"

Now, ten years later, she pursued the subject of healers, "Well, Tony did go to Taipei for a month of acupuncture with Dr. Wai Wo Ping, last year, and it helped."

"Yes, but once home again the benefits didn't seem to last."

"So now get him to Sai Baba."

About 1969, we started hearing stories about Satya Sai Baba, who claimed to be the incarnation of Shirdi Sai Baba, the saint we'd gone in search of. Several Indian friends had gone to him for cures, such as Avi's cousin, Moni Kohli, who assured me, "Nancy, I would have been blind except for Baba—he worked a miracle for me."

The now-famous swami was considered by many to be the most revered saint of India. Originally I had been skeptical of this holy man, who produced all sorts of trinkets for his followers, demonstrating the art of materialization.

Satyanand and I had discussed these tricks. "This leads to expectation. One day, when this ability is gone, his followers will lose their faith," declared the Bramachari.

"Yes," I countered, "but Jesus resorted to some pretty good tricks, didn't he? Maybe it is a way to help his followers have faith."

Finally, on the advice of my spiritually-wise friend, the Maharajah of Mysore, who thought highly of Sai Baba, I decided to go see for myself. Several times I had missed him in Mysore, his home state, as he had been "out of station," but eventually, in 1972, I caught up with him at his ashram in Puttaparthi.

I flew to Bangalore, rented a battered taxi driven by two wild-looking young Indians, and, six hours later—after a hot, dusty drive out into the desert and into the neighboring state of Andhra Pradesh (and two flat tires)—I arrived, thirsty and elated to find Sai Baba was in residence. I was not expected and had nowhere to stay.

No one paid the least attention to me. There were reportedly about five thousand people staying at the ashram, but seeing two young women who looked like Westerners, I asked their assistance. "I'm Nancy Cooke; do you know where the office is, or anyone who could tell me where to go?"

They took me to their primitive quarters, let me freshen up and then suggested, "Come with us. It is time for *bhajans* (their traditional chanting), and Baba will be coming to the temple."

In the middle of a bare, sandy landscape stood the temple of Satya Sai Baba. The temple looked like an oversized gingerbread pudding topped with whipped cream. The stone structure was beige, decorated with balconies and white elephant statues. Thousands had gathered and were sitting quietly on the sand waiting for their master to appear. On one side were men and on the other were the women; a fountain separated the two groups.

We were as far away as we could be. While we waited, my two new acquaintances advised me, "You haven't a chance of seeing Baba; we've been here six months and have never had a private audience with him. Some have been here a year and have never seen him except for his daily appearances. If you need help for your husband, you'd better write a letter."

I refused to be dismayed; at least I'd see the famous holy man from a distance. The girls asked, "Where are you going to stay? People are sleeping on the ground, it is so crowded." I didn't know, but I was glad I'd borrowed a pillow and a blanket at the hotel where I'd rented the taxi.

All of a sudden a hush fell over the crowd; my friends whispered, "Sai Baba must be coming. Oh yes, here come his advance people." They were young men wearing orange handkerchiefs around their throats. They lined up on both sides of the wide temple steps.

All faces were turned front stage. Then came Satya Sai Baba. He walked briskly to the front of the steps and raised his arms in a wide salutation. I felt a tremendous wave of exultation flow over me—then another, and another—it was better than an orgasm. But why was this happening? Why would I have this reaction to a complete stranger? It had never happened on seeing Maharishi. Now my focus was really on Sai Baba. He looked more refined than in his photographs; his Afro hair-do looked appropriate. His slight frame was covered in a light-weight orange cotton chemise ending just above his bare feet. Bell-shaped sleeves hung wide and loose above his wrists. There was an electric quality about him. His movements were quick and bird-like.

The sick and crippled had been placed to one side of the steps and he moved to them, touching each with his hand, while from his palm flowed gray ash. "Is that the *vibuthi* I've heard about?" I asked. It had been described to me as a sacred powder with healing powers.

"Yes. He will touch a thousand people and everyone will receive some. He manifests it from the Divine Source."

"Is it true that he considers himself an Avatar?"

"Yes, as the reincarnation of Shirdi Sai Baba. He is accepted as *the* Avatar of this present age."

As we talked, the swami moved from person to person; some held up photos for him to touch or bless. He was reported to heal the ill even from a distance.

"He won't come to the women's side today. Yesterday a woman, overcome by emotion, rushed up to him and embraced him. That is not allowed."

As Sai Baba moved, the *vibuthi* continued to flow. If he'd had a tank on his back, it could not have held all that powder. There was nothing concealed on him. His cotton chemise was almost see-through.

While I watched this display, my eyes suddenly recognized a face in the crowd. "How amazing; there is Mrs. Rajgopal!"

My friends asked, "Do you know her and her daughter? They are very close to Baba. Maybe she could help you." They urged me to make myself known.

The Rajgopals and I had called on an old swami together in Hollywood many years ago. Her husband edited and published Krishna-murti's early books. Would they even remember me? Not only did they, they were most cordial when I approached them after *bhajans*. Ana Lisa helped me get a room. It even had a western toilet!

While chatting over an orangeade, Ana Lisa suggested, "Baba is meeting a group from Delhi tomorrow. Why don't you get up before it's light, go over to the temple, sit with your eyes shut meditating so no one will bother you, and stay there until Baba comes out on the temple steps.

Then everyone's attention will be on him and they won't worry about you. They are very jealous about who gets near him; this will be your only chance to see him up close. Later, write a letter requesting help for your husband, and mention you were here today."

The next morning, I followed her advice to the letter. I was in position before the five o'clock bell rang out. It wasn't as though I melted into the background; instead of a sari, which was required of the women, I was completely covered by a long *pherron* (a Moslem overblouse), worn over slacks. My blonde hair shown like a sunburst, but no one disturbed me. By eight o'clock everyone was in place. I peeked out from almost closed lids to see how things were developing. From the chattering voices around me, I knew I was surrounded by many women. Then there was a dramatic quiet . . . not a voice was heard. The Master was coming! Feeling safe, I opened my eyes and waited.

Again, the quick arrival and warm salutation. Then, with penetrating eyes, the brown face turned from side to side, surveying his audience. His eyes stopped on me, "Hello, White Face, what is your name? Where are you from?"

I felt nothing unusual this time as my voice rang out. "I am Nancy Cooke, from California."

He nodded and moved out among the crowd. It was a repetition of the day before, but this time he did not shun the women. After blessing many individually, he walked up to me and, beckoning, said, "Come in, come in." He also nodded to several other ladies and invited them in. I couldn't believe it. I had wanted to see him and hear him speak, but I'd given up hope of an interview.

We entered a tiny square room about ten-by-ten feet. There was no furniture except for one large chair for Sai Baba. We crowded together on the floor mat. He looked pleased and asked us if we were happy; we answered in one voice, "Yes!" His English was rough, but he asked me if I were married, if I had any problems, where my husband was. I described Tony's condition—he nodded his head. Then he spoke half Hindi and half English, so that I would not be left out. His message was, "In order to bring mankind into an era of worldwide peace, security, happiness and heartfelt devotion to God, we have established an educational program that begins with kindergarten and develops through the university level. The program is called Education in Human Values."

As I smiled in agreement, he turned to me and said, "Hold out your hands." He reached over and *vibuthi* poured from his palm into mine! A woman gave me a paper envelope to put it in. "Take this at night before going to bed," the swami instructed.

"Would this help my husband?" I asked.

"We will give you more for him, but are you sure he is so ill?" It seemed a strange question, but more *vibuthi* was produced. Resuming his conversation, he spoke to the women for a few more minutes and then came back to me.

Again the command was, "Hold out your hands." This time a small medal dropped into my palm from his. I had been watching his hands carefully. He had been speaking with empty palms held up, his loose bell sleeves falling back to his elbows. Where had the coin come from? It had a raised engraving of Sai Baba's face. I carefully pulled my gold chain from inside my shirt. The coin was the exact dimension of my St. Christopher; a jeweler could not have cut it closer to size!

After more than an hour of stressing truth, right action, peace, love and non-violence, Sai Baba got up to leave. My shoulder was almost touching his as we all gave the sign of *namaste*. Glimpsing a tin ring on the hand of a young woman in front of him, he reached out and slid it off her finger. Holding it up for us to see, he asked, "What is this?"

We answered, "It's a picture of Baba." It was a cheap tin ring with a photograph stuck on it. He closed his hands over the ring for maybe three seconds and then put it back on the woman's hand. "Now it is much nicer." It had changed into a gold ring with an engraved face on it! We stared in amazement.

Stepping outside, I was a *cause celebré*. Everyone wanted to see my coin and touch it. "It is different from others he has made," explained Ana Lisa. "It is a copy of a bust of himself which was shown to him last week by an Italian sculptor." I was still in a state of euphoria over the unexpected interview.

Before leaving that afternoon, I saw Sai Baba once more. At *bhajans* he passed in front of me, paused, asked me if I were happy. He knew I was, after having such a special meeting with him. Then from the step of the temple he threw me a wave of farewell. My karma was good that day. It was an unforgettable meeting for me. He had approved when I told him of my involvement with Maharishi, and had also said, "You will come back here again." The big question was, would he help Tony. This he had not answered, except with a smile.

Two women requested a ride back to Bangalore, and, having an empty taxi, I was delighted with their company. It turned out that one

*Maharajah of Mysore during "Dassera," a religious ceremony*

had been with Sai Baba for years. She recited story after story of his curing people—but only if he felt it was a test they no longer needed. I felt encouraged.

What a shame I was never able to share my happy experience with the Maharajah of Mysore. He had recently died under what some referred to as "mysterious circumstances." Unfortunately, they were not so to me. I was convinced that he had been poisoned by his daughter and son-in-law. A few weeks prior to his death, he had been with us in Beverly Hills. He had confided, "It is very sad for me, but I have indisputable evidence that Laksmikan and Minakshi have tried to poison me. I went to Mrs. Gandhi for help and she advised me to leave India for at least six months, during which time an investigation could take place."

One night he repeated this story in front of Vina Mody and others who were having dinner with us. We all asked him about the motive. He answered, "They feel I have given too many of my properties away. Now, to end their avarice, I have divided my estate up and given it to them." At one time he had been one of the wealthiest Maharajahs in India.

Several days after telling us of his suspicions, he received word that his eldest daughter (not Minakshi) was fatally ill and he had to return to India. Rik and I put him on the plane; one week later he was dead. The family ignored tradition and had his body cremated before anyone had time to come to Bangalore and pay respects. There was great dismay on the part of his former subjects—he had been a beloved leader of his people. I had visited him several times at the palace in Bangalore—what fun it would have been to go there now and describe my meeting with Sai Baba.

At the airport I bought a book about Satya Sai Baba and settled down into my plane seat for the flight back to Delhi. A tall, grey-haired man squeezed past me. I got up and made room. He thanked me and I went back to my reading.

"Are you enjoying your book?" he inquired. I politely said yes and continued reading, discouraging conversation.

"I'm glad you like it. I wrote it."

"Oh, Dr. Gokak, I'm so delighted to meet you. I was invited by Richard Bock to have dinner with you in Los Angeles, but I was going to be here in India."

For the next two hours, this man, who had been president of Bangalore University before becoming the head of the Satya Sai Baba Education System, filled me in on the background of his beloved master. I returned to Delhi impressed with the legend of Satya Sai Baba, and hopeful that this might be the answer for Tony.

However, Tony's reaction had been, "Very impressive. One day I'll go see him, but India is out of the question just now."

The arrival of Ampah's coconut dessert brought me back to the present and Maxine's home in Thailand.

"Well, if I were ill I'd certainly go see Sai Baba, so keep trying. Miracles happen all the time," stated my hostess.

"The doctors say Tony's brain is killing his body. What do you think of that?" I asked.

"Then he'd better start thinking differently."

Saturday and Sunday streaked by. On Monday, Maxine called from her office. "Bring your tape recorder when we visit the Chinese seer. It's hard to remember what they tell you."

The seer was a bit hard to understand. Mainly what he said was, "The new year brings big changes for you; changes of everything. In fact, you won't have to wait until the new year: big news awaits you when you get home." That didn't mean anything to me. Otherwise, it was the same old things; that I was energetic, adventuresome and bossy—that I would become the General if I were in the army; if a crook, the top gangster.

"Guess he got your number," said Maxine.

My stop-over in Hong Kong was delightful. In the company of friends, I ate my way through mounds of hot, steaming Chinese food. Another cable from Tony awaited there to welcome me on my way.

In Honolulu, I placed a call home. Tony didn't get back to me until after 1:00 a.m., California time. "He must be feeling much better to stay up this late," I thought.

During our conversation, Tony suggested, "Stay with the Harris's for Thanksgiving. I've called it off here, as I have a big case and will be in conference for the whole holiday. It will be less distracting for me if you'll come on Saturday—as much as I'm looking forward to seeing you." I reluctantly agreed, but was disappointed not to enjoy the holiday at home. Also a bit puzzled . . . it seemed strange that Tony would cancel out this very special day. I hoped he wasn't ill.

Tony met me at the airport. He looked better; his color was good. How wonderful it was to get home. Mercedes had the house glistening; Rama, my black labrador, almost turned himself inside out, he was so happy to see me. Traveling was nice, but it was so pleasant to be home.

The next night, before going to a chamber orchestra concert, I brought out a package for Tony; it was an antique Buddha hand I'd bought in Bangkok. Maxine felt it had great healing powers, after testing it with the divining rod with which she had found her water springs. I waited to see his joy on seeing what it was; instead, a look of shock registered on his face.

"What's the matter? Don't you like it?"

He immediately recovered and said, "Oh, I love it; it is just such a surprise. Honey, you shouldn't have brought me such a present." He raved on about its form and beauty, but I felt strange about his initial reaction.

Later, as we approached the Dorothy Chandler Pavilion, a complex of three theaters, Tony said, "Come over here, I'd like you to meet some new friends." He introduced me first to two youngsters, about twelve and fourteen—whose reaction of "Oh, so you are Tony's wife," made me feel like an orangutan, then to a woman of about forty, who stared at me with bulging eyes. I felt ice water go through my veins. It was such a strange reaction. I did not put out my hand.

I asked Tony afterward, "Who is that woman? Have I met her before?"

"Oh no, she's just someone who sings in the Bach Chorale. Come, it's curtain time."

The next morning Tony came into my room. "Darling, how would you like a luncheon date? "

I was still jet-lagged and sleeping late. "Great, come home for lunch," I mumbled.

"No, let' s make it a real date. Let's meet at Señor Pico's."

I agreed, thinking he'd probably surprise me with some friend from out of town. Before he left, I related a strange nightmare I 'd had that night. I dreamed that Tony had gone to my safe deposit box and taken all my things. He laughed when I told him this.

"What fun to have a luncheon date," I mused as I took special care to look well. It was a nice change to get into a fall suit after the cottons and pale colors worn in India and the Orient.

It was a clear, December day—good football weather; Thanksgiving had been very late this year, just twenty-three days before Christmas. "How lucky, I've done all my shopping in India. This holiday I'll just enjoy the parties instead of the hassle."

The parking boy took my car in front of the adobe building nestled in the heart of Century City. Trader Vic was the first to build on this location. The restaurant was now surrounded by high-rise office buildings on all sides.

"*Buenos Días, Señora* Nancy." It was Ivan, the *maitre d'hotel*. As Tony had not yet arrived, he guided me across the inner court, which was a busy, boutique area filled with colorful Mexican items. The place was full, but I was glad to see we had our favorite spot, a little alcove just large enough to hold one table. It was set for two. "Guess there's to be no surprise, but how nice; it really is a date."

At that moment Tony arrived. He looked smart in his pin-striped suit; he was very particular about his clothes and always was well groomed.

After sliding into the banquette and giving me a casual kiss on the cheek, Tony asked if I'd like a cocktail. "No, I don't think so. This is a special occasion, but I am still tired from my trip; you go ahead."

After studying the menu, we both decided on Spanish omelettes. It took a while to get the waiter's eye—Tony became exasperated.

"Are you in a hurry to get back to the office?"

"No."

"You seem nervous about the time, what is it?" I asked.

"I have something to discuss with you and don't know quite where to start."

"Why not start in the middle." I thought I was going to get a lecture on my personal checkbook, which didn't always balance.

"I'm going to leave you," he stated.

"Where are you going? I thought you weren't going to Denmark for the cure until January." He had written about this possibility while I was still in India. I had encouraged him to go.

"No," he replied, "I don't mean that. I'm leaving you. I want to live by myself and have more time for my music."

"But you've just had seven whole weeks to enjoy your music." I felt confused. Was I missing something?

He went on to say he'd done a lot of thinking, that maybe he didn't have a whole lot of time left. He wanted to do the things he wanted to do. I asked, "Is there something medically wrong that you aren't telling me?"

He answered, "No, as a matter of fact, since I made this decision, I've been feeling great."

I asked how long ago he'd made the decision. It had been a month. I was beginning to feel bewildered. "I just don't understand; why didn't you give me some warning in a letter?" I stared at him. "Surely we can talk this thing out before you come to any definite decisions. Why did you bring me to a public restaurant to tell me this?" I was so puzzled.

His answer shocked me. "I thought it was better to meet on neutral territory. I didn't want a scene."

"Oh, Tony, please—let's discuss this at home this evening!" The shock was getting to me. I felt sick.

"No, it's decided. I'm leaving today; my bags are packed."

"Are you talking about a separation or a divorce?"

"I guess ultimately a divorce. I'll help you for a few months until you get working again. Before you know it, you'll be doing just fine."

I couldn't believe it—twelve-and-a-half years ago I had closed my PR office in San Francisco! Now I had almost no income of my own. When my father had died the year before, Tony invested my inheritance, largely in tax shelters. Something wasn't right. Suddenly I heard myself asking, "Tony, are you having an affair with the woman I met last night?"

My question startled him so, he answered, "Yes."

Now I understood my reaction when I met her. "Are you planning on marrying her?"

"Yes, but not for a while."

I picked up on that. "She's not free. She's still married?"

"Yes."

"And you are her lawyer helping her get a divorce?"

"Yes."

"But Tony, this is all so unexpected. You may change your mind. I can be understanding about it. Keep her as a girlfriend for a while."

He seemed offended. "She would never agree to that arrangement."

"Oh, I see. But she doesn't mind breaking up our marriage."

I was on the point of tears. He was responsive to nothing I said. I had honestly thought his home and our family meant everything in the world to him. I had to get out of there. I was not going to cry in a public place—especially in a restaurant where all the waiters and *maitre d'hotel* knew me.

"I have to leave," I said and started to stand. At that moment, the waiter appeared with our order.

"But aren't you going to eat your omelette first?" inquired the callous man who had been my husband. (I've often wondered if he ate both omelettes!)

On seeing my face when entering the house, Mercedes gasped, "Oh, *Señora, qué pasa?*" Rama came to my room and licked my tear-stained face.

That night I sent a cable to Maxine, "Well, I got The Big News. Tony has left me for another woman." The Chinese seer had scored a bullseye!

## 27

# *Come Into My Parlor*

EVIDENTLY MY KARMA HAD BEEN OUT IN THE WINGS accumulating and now my nightmare began. Mercedes cried constantly, worried about me. With his tail down, Rama was my shadow—his instinct telling him something was amiss, and he was there to comfort me. My mind was traumatized. I couldn't stop asking, "But why, and why in this brutal, unfeeling way? Why no warning? Why the loving letters and the welcoming cables?" Sleep was impossible. I now understood the expression ". . . to walk the walls." I felt violated—my sense of loyalty bruised. How could someone who meditated behave this way?

All of my children were away; there was no one to comfort me except by phone. Besides my family in San Francisco, many friends called, all in shock.

Before I left the famous Señor Pico's lunch, Tony had reminded me that our good friend, George Frelinghuysen, was coming to dinner that same night. I had reacted bitterly. "You call him and tell the truth. Tell him you are leaving me for another woman."

"Now, honey, you don't have to tell people that," was his ingratiating answer.

"Oh yes. Tell them the truth. I would rather they know that, than to think I'd walk out on a sick husband." My character was of more importance than my vanity at that point.

A huge bunch of yellow roses arrived from George after Tony called him. Then he telephoned me. "Just sit tight. This whole thing will probably blow over. I must say, I still find the whole affair unbelievable." What a friend. Every morning he'd call to see how I was doing. One day he commented, "If Cobina were still alive, she'd kill him."

My reply had been, "He probably would have never tried it." Cobina had died almost two years before, about the same time as Daddy's death.

My mother and sisters were incredulous about Tony's departure. "It can't be true; he's mad . . . after all you've done for him. If you had been the one to leave, maybe we'd understand. How cowardly to do it in that manner. When he was here visiting us last week, he was talking about how happy he'd be to have you back. What a liar!"

Tony hadn't wanted to, but I had insisted that he call and tell Mother. "You owe her that courtesy, at least."

When he did call, he presented it as, "Just one of those things that has been coming on for years, with nobody at fault."

Mother caught him up short, "Come on, Tony, I may be a bit of an old goat, but I know human nature—who is the woman?"

He insensitively answered, "She's really a lovely person, Marie. I hope you will meet her one day."

Some calls brought me a laugh, such as the call that came from Linley Sanchez Elia, my great friend from Buenos Aires. We had lived next to each other when our husbands were still alive. As a widow, she now lived in New York. Tony was impressed by her, not only because she was attractive, amusing and had a quick brain, but because her uncle was the Chairman of the Board of Montgomery Ward. Tony loved success. "Nancy, it's unbelievable that Tony, the snob, would leave you for a little brown wren from Arcadia . . . Arcadia! If it had been for a Maria Callas, that would be different." Linley had enjoyed Tony while staying with us on various occasions, "I know how the house revolved around his every little wish. He's going to miss that. It's hard to believe he's in good enough shape to carry on an affair!"

Gayelord called from New York. "Darling, after the lengths you have gone to help him with his illness, it's a shocker." He hesitated and then went on, "I might as well tell you; Tony called, he is anxious to stay a friend of mine. I told him it would depend on his treatment of you." Then he added, "I was not overly friendly." He went on, "But darling, God is being good to you. He is releasing you from a terrible burden."

Helen Lutes called several times a day. "I feel like a part of my own family has been shattered. I just can't understand what has happened to Tony. He must be going through male menopause. Before you returned, he called to tell me what he was going to do. His girlfriend, Mrs. Savage, wanted him to tell you as soon as you got off the plane. I begged him not to—that was too cruel," her voice was incredulous, "but that tells you something about her, doesn't it? She's well named." She continued, "He's called several times; he wants to bring her over to meet me, but I've said, 'No, I'm too good a friend of Nancy's.' Don't you think that's dumb?" I certainly did.

Tony's former secretary of nine years was dumbfounded. "Oh, I've seen him use people for years and just toss them away when he didn't need them any longer, but I never thought it would happen to you. You've lent him money, helped him get loans on your credit, introduced him to clients, entertained the whole office," her soft Texan voice drawled on. "He treated me so badly, I had to leave. You'll be better off without him."

It was one hundred percent that I "would be better off without him." This should have made me feel better, but it didn't. To live with a man for twelve years and not know him shook me. Had the whole thing been a set-up from the beginning? Did Tony marry me only because of what I could do for him? One of the big attractions for me had been his spiritual interests. Later, Maxine scoffed, "All during the years in Thailand, I never heard a thing about anything spiritual, unless it came out of a bottle. Dear, that interest originated with you."

In the beginning of our marriage I had not been anxious to get back into the "entertaining game" again, but I did it for him—I knew Tony was ambitious—nothing wrong with that. The first parties we gave were for his old law school professors, members of the firm he was with, and several judges. Any loving wife would have done the same.

I reminded myself of all the fun we'd had the first five years. He'd been a bright, supportive companion when we started TM together and I did have the freedom to come and go as I pleased. I would miss this man I'd shared my life with. Maybe it wasn't ideal, but I was satisfied. I mustn't forget some of the positive aspects.

Tony's sister, Jeannie, leveled with me, "All of his life, he's run over people. He has no loyalty to them. When he met you, I hoped that at last he was getting what he really wanted; you had money, social position, and he appeared to be in love with you. Everything seemed to go well, except for his health. I don't think he'd be alive today if it weren't for all the care you've given him." Her eyes were sad. "I'm ashamed of my brother, but it mustn't change our relationship." We hugged each other, promising a loyalty that has lasted.

Only one person tried to be conciliatory—Tony's partner, Mac. He came in person. "Please hang in there; don't do anything. It's a sex thing, and it'll blow over. I know he's been sick, and there's probably been nothing doing. This gal comes along and gets it up for him. I can't tell you how many times I've seen this happen." His kindly face showed concern. "I've pleaded with him, 'Where will you get another Nancy, who has been wife, partner and nurse? You know she'll stick by you, and not everyone will. Man, if Marilyn Monroe got into bed with me and it meant I might lose my wife, I'd roll over and go to sleep.'"

In spite of all the support I was receiving, I was having a terrible time. Nights were the worst. Alternating between sadness and anger, I couldn't sleep. What was the matter with me? Where was my strength? Why couldn't I take the advice I'd so glibly dished out to others when they'd come to me with their problems? Where was my spiritual strength? Meditation was hopeless. My mind just went around in circles. I seemed rudderless in the midst of a violent storm.

Tony had meditated for twelve years. I asked Helen, "Where is that softening of the heart that comes with meditation?" Maharishi had always referred to this.

Her answer was, "Don't forget, Maharishi said you would be better at whatever you did. Maharishi must always have suspected something. You notice he never made him the lawyer for the S.R.M."

Finally, Dr. Henschel, Dr. Bieler's disciple, came to the house. "I've been worried about you. How are you doing? Tony told me what he was planning. I figured you would need some help." It seemed that everyone had known before me.

His face showed concern, "You know I don't like sleeping pills or sedatives, but there are times when you need to take them to keep from doing more damage to yourself." He held out two bottles. "You are a strong woman. In six months you will be fine again. Unfortunately, I see a lot of this, and six months is about average." He confided, "I was very surprised. I thought you guys had a good thing going."

It could have been so different. It hurt my feelings that Tony didn't have enough confidence in me as a person to say, "Look, Sweetheart, I love you, but I'm not happy. With my state of health, I'd like to make a change ... please try to understand." I think I would have understood—I probably would have gone apartment-hunting with him. After all, we'd both been through a divorce before; it wasn't anything unusual for two intelligent people to decide they wanted to split up.

Ten days passed and not a word from Tony.

A letter arrived from Maxine, "What an idiot! And how unsophisticated. Rak is furious with Tony. A gentleman does not rub his family's nose in his sordid little love affair—especially when it's been of such short duration. You'd think he would have stashed her away quietly for awhile. When sex rears its ugly head, these men go crazy." She closed with, "How about that seer . . . incredible!"

Finally, it was too much. I called María Luisa in Paris. She had planned on being there until the first of the year, but I asked her to come home for Christmas. I needed help. She was almost speechless when I told her the news, and said she'd come at once.

At the end of two weeks, I'd lost a lot of weight due to sleepless nights. George informed me, "You are not staying in that house any longer." He'd come several times for dinner but now said, "You are going to Perino's (one of L.A.'s best restaurants) with me tomorrow night and I won't take no for an answer."

The next night I pulled myself together to go out for the first time since the bomb dropped. George was right, it was good for my morale to get away from the forest. We were no sooner seated in a banquette at Perino's when Carroll Righter walked by. "Ah, the beautiful Aries and the royal Leo," he said, referring to George, "But where is Moon Child?" His cherub face crinkled with pleasure.

"Moon Child done left," I answered, and suggested he sit down. He did, in shocked surprise. He was a true Philadelphia gentleman, always dressed in suit, vest and tie.

"You know, Nancy, I shouldn't be surprised. A twelve-year period closed for Aries this month. How long have you and Tony been mar-

*Carroll Righter, the astrologer, Nancy and Dr. Gayelord Hauser, the health food czar, in 1968 at my home*

ried?" The answer was twelve-and-a-half years. I also told him about the seer in Bangkok.

I loved this dear man and treasured his advice. Syndicated in many parts of the Western world, Carroll was considered the dean of U.S. astrologers, and the astrologer of the movie stars. He had been the Ronald Reagan family's astrologer for years. He had cautioned me against marrying Tony. Now he reminded me, "Remember, every problem is an opportunity to learn." Then he added, "and nothing keeps Aries down for long."

But, even with the support of loving friends and family, my insecurities took over—the future threatened and robbed me of the present. I felt ineffective and helpless. Tony was completely in control of the family's finances. He had a power of attorney for everything I owned. The days dragged on—more problems and more bills arrived at my doorstep. Not a word was heard from Tony.

December 20, eighteen days after Tony's leaving, María Luisa came home. As I stood at the airport waiting, a thought drifted through my

*María Luisa at seventeen*

*Our housekeeper of twenty-eight years,
Mercedes de Chavez*

mind, "How different things were the last time I saw her. She and Rik were off to the Camel Fair, and I was returning to celebrate Thanksgiving with my husband." Suddenly I saw her dear face and she was giving me a big hug—my heart nearly burst with happiness.

"Don't you recognize your own son, Mom?" There stood Brett. In my concentration on María Luisa, I had seen no one else.

"What are you doing here? You're supposed to be in Poland with Olga." I couldn't believe it—how welcome his loving face was to me.

Brett and the Russian girl he was in love with were spending a year at Warsaw University on a Stanford fellowship. They were both working towards their Ph.D.'s in slavic languages. On our way to India we had stopped over to visit them.

"We arrived in France for Christmas vacation just the day after you called María Luisa. I figured you could use a little extra support."

Could I. I was so lucky to have such children. Brett is a beautiful soul. Gifted with a tremendous IQ, he is in love with knowledge, an enthusiastic sportsman, and a gentle person in every way. He had been the closest to Tony, as they shared a love of music. Now he was giving up his vacation with Olga to help me.

"We called Rik in India as soon as we heard the news, but he's trekking in Nepal and unreachable; he'll be checking in soon."

How like them, our family unit was hard to beat. Back home, as I caught the children up on my news, Mercedes bustled around us, her face happy for the first time in weeks. She'd been practically spoon-feeding me, insisting I was *"demasiado flaca,"* too thin. Rama's tail was up. There was joy and laughter and happiness in the house again. Starr's wife had also joined us. She had given me great moral support while Starr finished up a job in New York.

"Mom, you're going to be so much better off without him," from my daughter. "He hasn't been very nice the last couple of years. I think he's used his illness to hold you. At the office, he's a completely different personality." She had worked there one summer. "None of us are going to miss his crabbiness."

I slept for the first night in weeks without a sleeping pill. How different the house seemed with my son and daughter home. But the sleepless nights had taken their toll—I was beginning to have serious problems with my eyesight. My eyes seemed to be my Achilles heel.

One day, George McLean, Genie's husband, came for tea. I was delighted—he had always been a favorite of mine since the days we worked with MRA (Moral Rearmament) together. "Nancy, you're going to have a terrible time with Tony." He had been a client of Tony's for years and Starr had once worked in his architectural office. "He will take every legal advantage of you that he can, so be prepared." This was my Newborn Christian friend speaking.

"It's funny," I answered. "Carroll Righter said more or less the same thing, that Tony would try to get every nickel he could lay his hands on—that the cancer crab would scuttle around and attack from all sides, with greedy pincers out."

George suggested we get on our knees and pray for guidance.

"Are you still meditating?" he asked.

"Yes, but my meditation has been a big disappointment to me; it hasn't given the support I'd expected. How can Tony behave this way after so many years of meditating?" I'd lost a bit of faith in TM.

He smiled, "Why don't you turn to Jesus, Nancy, you have only to ask for His help."

I confessed I'd done a lot of praying for understanding and strength since December 2nd, but I reminded George, "I don't feel I've ever left Jesus. Maharishi has taught me so much about His teachings. He says, as Westerners, Jesus is the prophet for us to follow!" He let that go. I knew he was thinking, "He is *the* only Prophet."

Feeling calmer after George left, I wrote a letter to Tony, suggesting that we meet. We had unfinished business to settle; there would be no recriminations and there were his personal things he'd probably like to have. His partner, Mac, had suggested it, saying, "I'll work from my end."

A few days later, Tony drove into the driveway. Mercedes called to me, "Look, *Señora!*"—Rama, who had always put his feet up on the railing overlooking the drive and would go into a little jig as we arrived, was sitting with his back to the drive. As Tony walked to the house, Rama, who had grown into a large, powerful dog, did not even turn to look at him. It was as though he knew this person, his former master, had caused hurt.

We talked as two polite strangers. He didn't ask what I was doing for money, even though he knew I had almost no income at that time. He had invested large sums of my money in tax shelters—he got the tax break, but I got no income. After a cup of herb tea, he went to get the things he'd need in Denmark.

As he left, he threw a sheaf of papers on the coffee table—the iron hand was out of the velvet glove. He pointed to the papers, "This will show you what you have, so maybe you'll feel better."

I picked them up and quickly scanned a list of trumped-up figures, almost doubling my net worth. "But where is the house—I did pay for it with my own money?"

"That's not yours. It's half mine and don't ever forget it. I have paid the mortgage." His face was set; eyes narrowed, all charm had fled.

I pointed out he'd have had to pay rent somewhere if I hadn't bought the house. I'd sold my San Francisco house and used that money. I had a "quit claim" that clearly established my ownership.

"Then we will let a court decide. Here's a copy of the note you signed giving me the house." The "lawyer" threw another paper down and stomped out of the house. I was stunned and burst into tears.

It was during the first year of our marriage that I'd signed that note. I had been packing to go to New York to present a German fashion show, and he'd called from the library, "Honey, will you sign this? It's just a precaution in case something happened to you, your heirs couldn't throw me out of the house overnight. It would never be used otherwise and in no way changes the title of the house, which is naturally in your name." It seemed logical to me—he had all my other legal powers and, as my husband, I trusted him one hundred percent. For eleven years, nothing was ever said about this little slip of paper again.

Brett and María Luisa arrived as he was leaving. He hardly spoke to them. Rama continued to sit with his back to Tony.

Soon Rik was home. He had called from Avi's on receiving the news to say, "I'm catching the next flight, Mom, and I'll come straight through."

I convinced him to spend at least one night with his father in Honolulu, which he did. Later it amused me to hear Dick Cooke's reaction, "How could Tony behave in such an ungentlemanly way— Nancy made him what he is today."

What a joy to have Rik on board. He and Brett were so unflappable. They went together and confronted Tony, not that they felt it did much good. Rik tried to reason with me. "Mom, what is it that is causing you to do yourself so much harm? Tony has not been an easy man to live with. What worries you now are material things. Even if worse comes to worse and you have to sell this house, you'd still be okay."

I knew he was right, but I couldn't let go. I'd worked like mad to help Tony build a firm and a future to enjoy together. Rik and Brett couldn't reach me, although I knew their words were correct. I was too full of fear and bitterness.

Starr finished his month's work in New York and was home for New Year's. As he was working in land development for Tony's top client, he was in a delicate position—Tony came to his office regularly. We decided to keep him out of my legal problems. However, he was always there to give me business advice, especially later on.

Then things started to move. Mac came back a month after his first visit. "Well, you better get a lawyer, Nancy. There is nothing I can do to change Tony's mind. You'll need protection."

The minute I went to a lawyer, the axe fell. I was still asleep when the phone rang at 8:30 one morning. "This is Mr. Battersill at the bank. You have five checks that were returned—your account is closed. It was at your husband's request."

I agreed to get there as soon as possible. Thank God I had my own personal account in San Francisco in my name of Cooke de Herrera. Tony had suggested I change it, but I liked it that way. By the end of the week, I'd been notified that my three joint accounts were closed, and all my charge accounts had been canceled—even accounts such as Gumps in San Francisco, Saks, I. Magnin—accounts I'd had for years before I ever met Tony. The pool man had received notice, even the milk man.

I had been so stupid. Whenever construction or major improvements were made on the house, I'd use money from my private account—after all, it was improving my property. Then we had a joint account into which I put a certain sum each month—for my children's expenses, most of my clothes, and all of my travel costs. I had never heard of the dangers of "co-mingling."

I would have been wiser to pay the mortgage and other expenses directly and let Tony take care of my expenses as most husbands do. But I looked on us as a team—what I had was his and vice versa. When we married, I had much more than he did, but I was confident, with Tony's ability, that it would all even out.

After Brett returned to Poland, Rik and I interviewed lawyers. Looking back, I can say that's a waste of time. A layman can't pick a lawyer. I would have done better representing myself. When the going gets tough, most lawyers think of their own skin, not their clients'. They want the "fast buck." Tony knew this—it was all a matter of stalling and using up time. His time was free, my time had a meter attached to it.

Winter quarter at UCSB had started for María Luisa in Santa Barbara, and Rik had to go back to Oregon. He would pick up his architectural assignments and tools at school so he could return to spend the next few months with me.

During the time alone, I spent long hours working on records the lawyer needed. Finally, this strain and the worry caused by insecurity and indecision took its toll. My eyesight got so bad I could not drive at night—spots floated through my vision. I kept seeing things which were not actually there, which added to my nervousness.

One day I answered the phone. "Nancy, this is Jules Stein. Doris (his wife) heard from a friend that you were having severe eye problems. I want you to see Dr. Robert Hepler at the clinic (the clinic which the Steins had founded at UCLA). With your permission I will make your appointment."

What a friend. With his busy schedule as president of the Music Corporation of America (MCA), he had time to worry about my eyes.

Dr. Hepler, in his calm, reassuring way, treated me with gentleness. "The tests done here at the Stein Clinic show a case of severe uveitis complicated by retinal hemorrhage. We don't know very much about uveitis, what causes it or what cures it. It is an inflammation of the tissues behind the eyes. I'd like you to go to the Scripps Clinic and undergo a complete checkup. You may have picked up some exotic bug in your travels."

"Is there any chance of my going blind, Doctor?" I asked.

"I would say it is remote." But that "remote" scared me.

Scripps confirmed Dr. Hepler's diagnosis and suggested cortisone to avert the possibility of another retinal hemorrhage. Now I was really scared; my reaction to the idea of cortisone was violent—we'd worked so hard to withdraw Tony from that terrible drug. I was all too familiar with its ghastly aftereffects.

My house seemed to be caving in like a deck of cards. My sense of security plummeted to the depths. If I were to lose my eyesight, what would I do? How would I start another career with my eyes even the way they were? I'd always felt confident that in an emergency, I'd be able to do something. Now I was really frightened.

From the Scripps Clinic in La Jolla, it wasn't far to Capistrano Beach—I'd go to Dr. Bieler. Not reaching anyone by phone, I decided to drive there directly. What luck, a woman answered the door; the smell of zucchini floated past my nose. I was told Dr. Bieler was home.

It was a shock to see Dr. Bieler, who'd been having complications with his own health ever since his broken pelvis. His color looked bad; he had aged in the two years since I'd last seen him. He did not rise, but sat in a chair with a scarf wrapped around him. However, his spunk was still there. After hearing my tale of woe, he remarked, "Here, give me that report. We can use it to write on—that's about all it's worth."

He snorted at the suggestion of cortisone. "When they don't know what to do, they use cortisone." He gave me a strict diet to follow, "No nuts or seeds of any kind; they will aggravate the inflammation. Just raw milk, fresh fruit, fresh vegetables, and a little bit of beef and lamb." His advice included, "Get out of Los Angeles basin to some clean air—sulphur in food or in the air will be an aggravation." He added, "You are a strong woman, don't let a weaker person than you ruin your health. Get your nerves in shape and your eyes will heal themselves." That was the last time I saw Dr. Bieler; he died shortly afterwards. He lost his battle, but helped me win mine.

Later Rik and I talked it over. "Mom, why not rent the house?"

I answered, "The lawyer told me not to."

"I don't care what the lawyer said; he doesn't see the look on your face when bills come in. You have a perfect excuse, Dr. Bieler has told you to get out of here."

Fate stepped in to help me. The Michael Yorks came for tea one afternoon. "Poor Michael has been so nervous after that awful fire involving the Rolls Royce," said his wife, Pat. They were visiting friends. "How we'd love to rent a quiet place like this and be alone." Before tea was over, we'd made a deal. If I could find a place to go to, they would take the house.

That evening, George McLean called to check on my well-being. "Nancy, come use our little guest house in Palm Springs; we're only there on weekends, and it's nice and quiet now that the winter season is over." He finally agreed to let me pay a token rent; he even invited me to bring Rama—that did it.

So the Yorks moved in to be taken care of by dear Mercedes, Rik went back to Oregon, and I went to Palm Springs. The weight of the house and all the memories and expenses were off my shoulders, for a few months at least. My whole family breathed a sigh of relief—they had felt so powerless to help me.

---

28

---

# Action-Reaction

THE LITTLE GUEST HOUSE WAS ABOUT AS BIG AS A MINUTE, but it held all my old BMW could hold (Tony had helped himself to the new one I'd just bought). It was surrounded by lawn, a swimming pool, and a high hedge, giving me complete privacy. Genie left a bicycle for me to use. I was there for April and May.

Riding out on the desert roads, with Rama running alongside, my problems took on a new dimension. I talked to myself sternly about self-pity; hadn't I made the remark many times, "If I were to drop dead today, I couldn't complain; I've had so much more in life than most." I was not *that* old, and I still had more security than most people, due to my father's and grandfather's estates. My new financial advisor, an old friend in San Francisco, assured me that in time he would straighten out my affairs in order to provide me with an adequate income. Now, my health was up to me.

Didn't I believe in karma? If I did, then I *must* accept whatever came and get through the test as best I could—my past actions had caused the present tests. Hadn't Maharishi said, "Forget the messenger, get on with the message"?

I started to discipline my mind, making it turn away from troubling thoughts. It was hard. How the mind loves to feed on problems, to roll in the negative. But self-pity and doubt had almost cost me my sight. Stress had brought on a retinal hemorrhage in my left eye. Now I looked through a field of floaters—it almost drove me crazy at first, but I was becoming used to it.

Two of my disciplines were eye exercises and typing, so, between shopping, cooking, bicycling, swimming and playing with Rama, my days passed quickly. I began to feel a renewal of optimism and strength.

During the winter months, my meditation had given me little comfort; when I most needed it, it had failed me. Helen Lutes kept trying to encourage me, but deep inside I was skeptical—where was that strength I'd been promised? Instead, I found myself more attracted to prayer; prayer had helped me through the crisis of Luis's death.

The McLean house was the center of Newborn Christian activity in the area. A Christian Help House was located nearby, and George employed Christians to do his remodeling—he hoped the sound of hammers wouldn't disturb me, and it didn't. The carpenters were lovely, happy, young people—every time they hit a nail, they said, "Hallelujah" or "Thanks to God." They sat around the pool eating their bag lunches, throwing a ball in the water for Rama to retrieve and talking about God. It was a perfect atmosphere for my shattered senses. I began to look at what had affected me so deeply; it wasn't only losing a husband and feeling financially insecure, it was also the testing of my spiritual beliefs.

Did I really have the faith I proclaimed to have found in Nature, God, Creation? Was this all a test to find out? If my faith were complete, wouldn't I then allow events to happen without resisting to such extremes that I almost ruined my health? I'd already affected my eyesight, a gift far more precious than my house or any worldly goods. Was I flunking Maharishi's yardstick of discrimination as to what is important and what is not?

Tony did not have the qualities I admired in a friend or a husband. It was a blessing to have him out of my life. So why did I feel so much pain? Was it because I was thrown out of control? Most of my life I'd been able to manage things—organizing, directing, controlling, bossing. Tony was in balance with me until he became ill. Maybe with my Florence Nightingale act, I'd robbed him of his muscles. I thought I'd acted out of love; was it the love of being needed? When Tony could no longer dominate me sexually, maybe the trouble began. Maxine had pointed out that I was usually the center of attention (she was prejudiced); this would be hard for an insecure person to live with. But in fairness, it was a role often pushed on me, as Tony found it more restful to sit back and make little effort.

Tony's sister, Jeannie's previous description of her brother's drive to succeed illustrated something. Life hadn't been as easy for him as it had been for me. Mother had raised my sisters and me with love and support, she gave us a wonderful inward security; had it made me insensitive to other people's insecurities? When Maharishi asked me what lessons I needed to learn, I'd answered, "humility and patience." Had I become a "stupid know-it-all" in my teaching of TM? Had I invited Nature to step in and show me otherwise? I had a lot of thinking to do and it was time to be honest with myself.

George saw an opportunity to bring me into the Newborn Christian fold, but I'd protest, "I believe in the basic message of Jesus. I just don't believe in man's interpretation of what he was supposed to have said."

George insisted, "You either believe the Bible in every way or you deny it. There is no middle ground. Why don't you slowly re-read and study the New Testament. I've brought you a copy in large print." He was leaving me no excuse.

"Give up reading all this stuff your friends are sending—they mean well, but it's all trash."

He was referring to books such as *Three Magic Words*, by my friend U.S. Anderson, *The Daily Word* (Unity), and lectures from a minister of a Mind Science Church.

George pointed out, "You admit meditation hasn't helped you. Has Maharishi sent word to you of any kind? Why not turn to Jesus for help—he helped you before. But don't do it half-heartedly—it's all or nothing. You can't negotiate with Jesus."

That statement pushed a button. Maybe I should give up questioning and just give over. TM certainly hadn't done a very good job with Tony or me. I would listen to George.

We made a deal; for one month I would read the Bible, listen to tapes, and pray to Jesus. Then he added, "I think you need to be rebaptized." He'd been disturbed by the fact that at my Christening, I'd merely been sprinkled. "Only by being submerged can you receive the Holy Spirit."

As George was a new minister and weekly baptized friends in his swimming pool, I agreed. After all, what was the big difference? I went into the pool every day anyway; a few words read from the "good book" over my head couldn't hurt—and it would make George happy.

My sisters were hysterical. "You character! Would you like us to arrive in long white robes?"

Mother was bemused, but didn't care what I did as long as I was happy. She was critical of Maharishi. "I don't care what you say, he should call you, after all you did for him." This had come up before, but I knew that Maharishi had given me the tools to help myself.

On the big day, to my surprise, a group of young people appeared. The McLeans had invited them to sing and play their musical instruments. It was a special occasion and I tried to feel uplifted and holy—but it didn't work.

The time came for the immersion. I dropped my beach jacket and walked into the pool to join George and his book. After the singing stopped, he read, putting his hand on my head saying, "I baptize you, Nancy, in the name of The Father, The Son, and The Holy Ghost."

Then with pressure from his hand, he pushed my head underwater. At that moment, Rama, who had been quietly watching the festivities, decided to join me and jumped into the pool. We had a double baptism.

Another woman declared the day had come for her baptism and rushed to join us. Her actions inspired another. The pool was getting full.

When it was all over, I heard the husband of a newly-baptized lady saying, "It's a miracle. I've been praying for this day." People were talking about acquaintances who had come out of the water speaking "many tongues."

Everyone congratulated me—I had become a member of the club. They were dear in their love and enthusiasm. I understood how their warmth could save a lost soul. But, I honestly felt no different. I was just happy to satisfy my friends, the McLeans. Rama was the hit of the show—in spite of being black—more fitting for Satan—he was fussed over as a redeemed soul. It was a joyful afternoon.

As the weeks passed quietly, I knew that the McLean's house was the perfect setting for me. I thanked God for their friendship. It was also proving a point to Dr. Hepler, my eye doctor. Whenever I drove into town and had an appointment with my lawyer first, I showed no improvement, *but*, if I went to Dr. Hepler first, he saw progress. The inflammation responded that quickly to the condition of my nerves.

For months, we waged a legal battle trying to get Tony to agree to some sort of settlement. It had been five months since he'd paid a cent to me, and my capital was dwindling. I fretted over the mounting legal fees. It seemed so unfair—as a lawyer, Tony could stall indefinitely as he was in control of our income. He was now on his second lawyer, which probably cost him almost nothing in comparison to my ticking meter. So, while the legal haggling went on, I commuted back and forth from my desert refuge.

One night early in May the telephone rang. A soft but masculine voice asked, "Is that you, Nancy?"

I immediately recognized the caller, "Willy! How wonderful to hear your voice! It's been too long—several times my sisters and I tried to reach you—we left messages, but you never called back."

"But I have called back. I spoke to your husband; didn't he tell you?" Obviously not. Willy was a great love from my past. He was just checking in; he didn't know I was single again. We arranged to meet.

A flood of memories came back. With the exception of Luis, no man had been as important in my life as Willy Schaeffler. We met at Squaw Valley when he was in charge of the '60 Winter Olympics. For two years we had a strange love affair—strange because he was always on a mountaintop somewhere. At least we never got tired of each other. We discussed marriage, but Willy felt his lifestyle was not conducive. He'd already been through one bitter divorce.

For me, his just being Willy was enough. He had an extraordinary history and the strength of ten men. In the early forties, as one of Germany's top skiers, he was called on by Adolf Hitler to rescue two skiers off the face of a mountain. They were carrying the Nazi flag to the top. Succeeding where others failed, Willy was presented with a medal by the *Fuehrer* himself.

Later, recounting the scene in a letter to a cousin in the U.S., Willy noted, "I'm afraid the little guy with the mustache is going to get us into war."

The letter was intercepted and Willy spent the next year in a detention camp digging trenches. Later he was "rehabilitated" and sent to the Russian front. This was the army that watched Moscow burn in the winter of '42, while they froze in their summer uniforms. Eventually, routed by the Russians, most of the fifty-thousand-man German force were either killed or frozen to death. Willy was one of the few survivors;

in spite of being bayoneted through the neck and carrying a bullet in his heart, he lived to become the greatest ski coach in the U.S.

But Willy was not finished with tragedy. One night he called with the tragic news that his eldest son had drowned while at camp. Heartbroken, I wanted to go to him, to help in some way, but he needed to be alone with his grief. The mountains would be his source of strength and healing. Three months passed with no word; then he came for a couple of days. I felt so shut out; was it possible that Willy was too strong for his own good?

More months passed; I went on the Yeti hunt with Tom Slick, then Tony appeared on the scene. Soon it was time for my departure for Iran and then on to India. Months later, when I got to Honolulu, Willy called from Juneau, Alaska, but it was too late. Tony was sitting in my room, so not much was said. Before getting married, and not being able to reach him by phone, I sent a letter to his home in Denver. Willy brought that up at our first re-connection, "That was a hell of a way to let me know."

Now Nature was truly supporting me. Willy and I picked up where we left off. My problems became small in comparison to those he had surmounted. He chuckled at my religious fervor. "I think what you need in your life is a man, not the Bible." He was right. Maybe if he'd spent less time on the peaks, I never would have married Tony.

Willy put it differently. "Maybe if you had stayed home more, I would have known where to find you and kept you out of trouble."

So, after living as brother and sister with my husband for seven years, my body came to life again. Only Willy could begin to arouse the passion in me that Luis had unleashed and developed. It was a healing relationship, and by June, the six months Dr. Henshel had forecast, I was feeling more like myself again. For two of those months, I had prayed to be shown whether or not meditation was as counterproductive as George had said. But nothing was received except my *mantra's* insistence to be there.

Mentally I now spoke to it. "You are like an old and dear friend and I have doubted you. You, however, have never deserted me; you are now part of my nervous system's need. Please excuse my lack of faith." It seemed natural to return to my routine of meditation, closing with a prayer to Jesus.

How blind I had been. I'd let the messenger of my test assume importance, instead of getting on with my test. Now, when I saw Tony across a lawyer's table, I would thank God for my release from that sour-looking man. Helen Lutes informed me that Maharishi had sent instructions through the Olsen daughter, ". . . no one is to contact Tony. He has dishonored my teachings." He evidently was kept up on my news by Charlie, and his response was, "Nancy will know what to do—she has a great opportunity to learn."

Before leaving the McLean's, I had leveled with George. "I just can't buy it; the Bible has been through too many hands. How can Christians claim to have the complete corner on the market? There have to have been prophets for all times, and Jesus was never jealous of His knowledge. I believe in Jesus, the Christ, but my image of Him comes from the East, not from the West." George expressed his disappointment at my confusion, but listened as I went on.

"My meditation seems a more clear channel to God than studying the written word of man—this is my path." We hugged and kissed and parted dear friends. They accepted my heartfelt thanks for all they had done for me.

My day in court arrived finally—almost nine months after Tony left. Gayelord volunteered to join María Luisa and give me moral support. We were sitting on the hard corridor benches when Tony came down the hall. He looked pulled over, his neck rigid. He seemed much older. I startled him by saying hello.

Gayelord said again, "Nancy dear, God has been good to you— what a burden he has taken off your shoulders."

I agreed. I thought about the relationship I'd settled for during the past six years; then I thought of Willy. "Yes, Savage is turning out to be an angel in disguise."

Maxine believed she'd been heaven sent. "You'd passed your tests with Tony; you didn't need him anymore. If Savage had been green with black spots, he couldn't have resisted her—she was the bait to take him out of your life. That poor sucker will never know how he muffed his chances. Here he was, living with a golden goddess (my prejudiced pal), and he flunks his test over a mere woman."

For seven hours, the lawyers scuttled back and forth down that hallway, wearing me down. What I'd originally agreed to got chiseled down, down. But Gayelord and John Renshaw, my financial advisor who'd flown in from San Francisco, advised me, "Get out of this—it's a sick situation. Get out and forget it."

At 4:30 we went into court and announced to the judge that we'd come to an agreement. She asked, "Will you read the agreement into the court record?"

Tony's lawyer announced, "Your honor, our papers are so crossed out and filled with corrections, could we have a couple of days to clean them up and then submit them to the court?"

The unsmiling judge replied, "It's against my better judgment, but with three lawyers involved, if you all agree, I will."

I didn't understand the procedure, but stated my desire for a divorce and asked to take back my previous name. I wanted no lingering connection of any kind. Originally, I had refused to be the instigator—I thought spiritually it made a difference, but Maharishi told Charlie, "The technicality is not important. It is what is in the heart that goes on record."

Even though it was an unfair settlement, I was glad it was over. Now I could pull my life together and go forward. That evening, I checked Gayelord's meditation and, after our spiritual cleansing, getting rid of the court's negative vibrations, we went out for a big Chinese dinner. At the table I raised my glass to toast, "To getting away from Tony and all those terrible lawyers." I will never understand why Tony's lawyers—both of them—had to treat me so brutally, both in court and out. They were professionals. Did they have to avenge themselves on helpless women? I made a vow to Gayelord, "If I meet the most attractive man in the world, and he's a lawyer, I'll walk the other direction."

The next day I took off for San Francisco—it was time to put all this behind me. Later, Willy joined me up at Lake Tahoe, where I stayed at my sister's house. My house was still rented, luckily. It was like old times; my sisters and children were delighted—they all adored Willy. As before, he appeared only occasionally, but I didn't care, I had lots of matters to attend to.

My relief, however, was short-lived. On returning from San Francisco a month later, a letter awaited me from my lawyer, who'd gone to Europe. It seemed that when Tony's lawyer presented the "cleaned up" settlement papers, they had added another bill that I was to pay Tony out of the sum agreed to. In a fit of fury, my lawyer called the whole thing off—without even notifying me!

My reaction was dramatic—"How could he! Why hadn't he at least called me?" My fury changed to despair when I realized the whole mess would start all over again. I would have gladly paid the extra bill! I just couldn't believe what my lawyer had done, and little did I know then how much that gaff would cost me.

Going back into court months later, I found I'd been "bifurcated." Tony knew that in California it is possible to get a dissolution of marriage without a financial agreement, and, through trickery, I had agreed to just such a condition. Now Tony was free to remarry, which he did almost immediately, and I'd lost my leverage—he could string out making a financial settlement with me for as long as he wished!

Asking my lawyer what "bifurcation" meant, he explained, "It could be described as 'being screwed without intercourse.'" He then went on, swearing, "I'll litigate that son-of-a-bitch 'til my dying day to get even for this doublecross." Sure, he would, but he didn't add that it would cost me $85.00 an hour. That is where I made my second big mistake. Under misguided loyalty, I stuck with him.

"Bifurcation" was not the only new legal term I learned in the following nine months. A paper war descended on me—interrogations, depositions, pleadings, cross-claims, and countersuits. My files filled up two Bekins packing boxes.

I will never understand Tony's malice. He changed lawyers again, this time retaining a man with a reputation of absolute brutality toward his opponent. Hardly a week passed that legal papers and legal bills didn't arrive. Now it was a struggle in another dimension. I was trying to survive and hang on to what was mine before I married.

My lawyer had given me a big pep talk when Rik and I had first gone to him. "You have an excellent case. The law is cut and dried. You are entitled to one-half of what you and Tony built up together. Don't worry about that scrap of paper regarding your house. It is highly unethical for a lawyer husband to have his wife sign away her own property. Did he ever file a gift tax on receiving such a gift?" We had left his office reassured.

Now he was telling me, "When a woman has money of her own, it goes very heavily against her. That paper regarding your house is dangerous. The court may very well make you sell it and give Tony half. With his physical disability, the judge may feel his future is bleak and put no value on his practice."

The meter kept running. On several occasions my lawyer and I sat in court "trailing"—waiting for a judge. Once we waited for five days; during this time, I was charged $750 a day in legal fees even though during the waiting time my lawyer went to the court's law library and did research on another case. I listened to the "boilerplating" of the lawyers—their excessive verbiage in the courtroom—all designed to baffle the layman. I watched callous judges cut down individuals trying to represent themselves, and gradually came to the conclusion that most judges were impatient, lacking in compassion, and lucky they no longer had to earn a living as lawyers.

My health was being affected by the indecision and delays. I had increasing back problems. Luckily, my eyes didn't get worse. My lawyer's interest dwindled. He pointed out, "With my new clients, I'm charging $95.00 an hour."

One week I had a serious bout with the flu—this time I caused a court delay; other days it was almost impossible to sit in the courtroom, my back hurt so, and I began to pace the corridors. My lawyer wanted me to throw my hat into the ring—Brett, who was back from Poland, was disgusted with his performance and suggested I change lawyers. But it had gone on too long—both my will and my back gave up.

My mother, a semi-invalid, sat fuming in her Piedmont home, "If I had a gun and I could get to L.A., I'd gladly give the rest of my life and shoot Tony for what he's doing to you."

My family was dismayed at the viciousness of his tactics. "He has a big practice, his new wife, and a new life; why can't he show some compassion for you?"

Jeannie, Tony's sister said, "It's because you dared to oppose him."

Finally, I gave up and accepted a pittance. It didn't even amount to what Tony had borrowed from me. What a laugh. Tony kept my car, didn't have to pay my lawyer, or repay any of the monies he'd borrowed from me, for which he'd given notes.

If I had paid a dollar for *How To Handle Your Own Divorce*, I would have been money ahead. If I'd just said, "Adios, thanks for the ride, of course you owe me nothing," I'd have still been better off.

I had not only lost a husband, suffered a severe spiritual shock, injured my eyes, been taken to the cleaners financially, but had now lost all respect for the California court system.

"I think I could sit in a witness box, lie straight out, and no lie-detector would ever pick it up," I told my family. "It's a farce for a layman to try to find justice when opposed by a lawyer." After the false sworn statements, the blown-up figures and facts, and the lawyers who battled against each other in court and then walked out arm-around-

*Uell Anderson, author of* Three Magic Words

the-shoulder with each other afterward, I was completely disillusioned and bitter.

Brett had been my constant support those last bleak days. One hour spent in the final court convinced him the judge was a man with a grievance against women. I never even got to testify. He dismissed the whole thing, saying, "Let the parties get together and settle this themselves." I simply came to the end of my strength.

After dropping Brett at the airport to return to Berkeley where he was now living, I could not face the prospect of the house alone. Uell Andersen, who lived in Beaumont, California, near Palm Springs, had asked that I let him know how things went. He suggested I come out for the night, and I accepted. During some of my down periods, Uell had come in and taken me for long walks on the beach. He believed, "a troubled mind can't keep up with walking feet."

While at the McLean's in Palm Springs, we had caught up with each other after a break of several years. Two friends sent me copies of his spiritual book, *Three Magic Words*, thinking it would help me. It was one of the books George had objected to. After reading it, I dropped him a note, saying there were some points I disagreed with him about.

His short answer put me in my place, "Because I wrote it, does that mean I believe it?" Our friendship bloomed through the correspondence, and then he moved to Beaumont.

As captain of the Stanford football team, Uell had been a campus hero. After several years as a professional football player, he became a successful businessman in Southern California. One day, he decided he had had it, and walked away from it all. For the past five years, he'd been living as a hermit on Maui. An alchemist at heart, he had put himself through all sorts of drug tests, long fasts, and occult experiences. He also became a celibate, so there was no relationship to get in the way of genuine friendship. Friendship was what I needed after those brutal days in court.

With a genius IQ, he looked at the world in his own unique way. When I arrived, he greeted me with, "So you got screwed, did you? Well, baby, you are now learning about the big, bad world."

There was barely enough light to see by. Uell was sitting on his broken-down couch—his furniture had come from the Salvation Army shop down the street—plucking out tunes on a guitar. "Okay, now what can I do for you? Do you want a joint or a stiff drink? You look like you need something."

I didn't know. There was so much tension inside me, I thought I'd explode. "Which would be best? I have to do something. I've never been this uptight in my life."

He shrugged, "That's a choice for you to make." He got up to throw some more wood into the fireplace. As the flames shot up, the one-eyed bandit in the painting hanging over the mantel grinned down on me.

"Okay, give me a joint." I'd only tried hashish in Nepal once and hadn't liked it. Sitting in the rocking chair, I rocked and puffed furiously, "It's not doing a thing for me."

As I came to the end of the joint he handed me another. "Take it easy on the second one." But it was too late.

Suddenly, lights shot through my head. It felt as though a hand were squeezing my brain, and it was running between the fingers.

Uell spoke to me, "What's the . . ." I couldn't hear the end of his sentences. When I spoke, I could hardly hear my voice. It came from far away. Movies flashed across my vision, but they went so fast I couldn't focus on anything. "Oh, Uell, I feel terrible, so cold, so sick . . . is this what you do for kicks?"

He felt my head. "Hey, you're like ice. You're supposed to get a nice glow on. You'd better get into bed." My bed for the night was a double mattress on the floor inside a large painted circle. An altar was at the head, and a metal triangle hung from the ceiling. I'd have lots of help.

He piled blankets over me and brought a hot water bottle. It took four hours before this seizure let go. All the time, the lights and pictures continued.

Uell shook his head, "I've never seen anyone have that kind of experience on just marijuana. You really went on a bummer."

Once it started, recovery was equally fast. "Boy, that's the last time ever for me. At least with liquor, you know what to expect."

"Well, it did get your mind off your problems, didn't it?"

With the whole dreary scene behind me, I knew I had to leave the Los Angeles area—at least for awhile. Maybe Fate decided I needed a break. Richard Burton appeared on the scene and rented my house for six months. I went off to Sonoma to my friend Ruth's summer house on a wooded hill, with my faithful Rama, to pull myself together and lick my wounds. The "big roaring wave" had almost drowned the "leaping flame."

## 29

# *Garbo and Gayelord*

B UT DARLING, WHY MUST YOU LIVE LIKE A HERMIT IN THE WOODS? It's not
safe. Your sisters are worried also." Mother's voice was full of
concern. "You can come here or stay at one of their houses with
all the privacy you want."

"Honey, it's something I have to do alone," I explained. "I have so
much garbage inside me to get rid of. I'm safe here with Rama, and we'll
talk every day by phone. Please don't worry."

For the two months of May and June, 1976, I stayed at Ruth
Dillingham's house and saw no one, except the people in the market
where I bought food. The house was small, needing little effort to
maintain. Rama and I walked by the hour. We took long swims in the
pool. Night and day became one. Remembering Maharishi's advice, I
broke up my periods of meditation every half hour with his technique
of rounding (*pranayama*—yogic breathing, *asanas*, meditation, and then
ten minutes of rest). Knowing my system was full of tension, I wasn't
taking any chances of "blowing out" while alone. I meditated four or five
times a day in small doses.

Many nights I awakened dripping with perspiration, filled with
bitterness and resentment. I argued with my subconscious mind, "I don't
want to be tied to this through hatred—go away with all your negativity."

*Willy Schaeffler on the cover of* Sports Illustrated
Robert Riger/*Sports Illustrated*

*Willy Schaeffler as head of the 1960 Winter Olympics at Squaw Valley*
Margaret Durrance/*Sports Illustrated*

I reminded myself of all I had, wonderful memories, health, a beloved family, friends . . . so much more than most people. Why did this come out in my sleep?

By day, I could rationalize everything. Finally, with pencil and paper handy, I started putting the bitter sensations down in written form. Soon they left me, and stayed on paper. As I started to feel better, I thought about writing a book. Maybe I could encourage other women to have faith, to hang on; it was all a test and things would get better once the lesson was understood.

Sometimes I wondered about the actions of my last lifetime which had brought this recent trial to me. "But it was your resistance that brought the pain," my inner voice would remind me. "Did you continually thank God for all the pleasures you've had? Or have you taken many of them for granted? Can't you take the medicine you have coming to you? Do you really believe in karma, or don't you? Isn't it just action and reaction? Haven't you let the personality of the messenger get in the way of understanding?"

My hours were filled with squabbling with myself. I was all alone. There was no one to fool, but how hard I resisted the truth. Rama and I walked on.

One night during my second month of solitude, a wave of pity for Tony poured over me—he had that terrible sickness to deal with, that was certainly a heavy sentence for some past actions. It was not for me to judge him, another court would take care of that. If I believed that you get back what you give out, he'd need plenty of sympathy one day.

No doubt about it, I was healing. I could think back on many of the good aspects of our marriage; all the freedom I had had to follow my spiritual path, a home and father figure for María Luisa, lots of positive aspects; wasn't it lucky we never had any fights in the house to upset all the lovely vibrations there, and, better it came now rather than ten years later. I'd had my time to mourn, which was necessary, but now negativity was being replaced by positive thinking.

Life was definitely picking up. All I had to do was get my house in order after being in limbo for seventeen months. In the Fall of '76 I'd agreed to take another group to India—that would be fun. All sorts of opportunities were opening up, and I'd have to make up for lost time. Mother reported that several old beaus from my Stanford days had called—word was getting out. Seems that people were being constantly recycled in and out of relationships. Yes, soon I'd be ready, but first I had to come to some conclusion about my relationship with Willy. We had kept in touch by phone, but he understood my need to fight out my internal battle. I loved him dearly, but I'd been burned deeply. Also, his life style, his love of the mountains, and his ski activities around the world, precluded a permanent relationship for us.

Then about the time I was becoming whole again fate stepped in and dealt Willy a terrible blow. The artificial mitral valve Dr. Denton Cooley had put in Willy's heart broke. Luckily, he was at the Mark Hopkins Hotel on Nob Hill, just a few blocks from the Presbyterian Hospital, or he wouldn't have had a chance. Dr. Gerbodi, who performed the emergency surgery said he barely had minutes to live, and only a person of Willy's strength and determination would have survived. The news jolted me out of my problems. I immediately left Sonoma and went to San Francisco to be near Willy.

I prayed and prayed with all my heart that my valiant friend could fight his way back to health. God answered my prayers; as before, Willy defied the odds and won. A few weeks later María Luisa and I took him to a home on a beautiful sea cove on the island of Kauai to fully recuperate. Within weeks, lying in the sun and floating in the healing Hawaiian waters, Willy gradually came back. The whole experience was dismaying for him—both physically and psychologically.

While on Kauai I also got myself back into better shape. With Willy barking out instructions (once a coach, always a coach), María Luisa and I exercised, ate well and meditated, all with a sense of joy. Willy made plans to return to Denver, but I had no desire to return to Los Angeles for awhile. Nature responded with a call from Rik. "Mom, come to Oregon. You can work on your writing while I'm building my house."

It was a great idea. So, three months after arriving in the Napa Valley area, battered and bruised, I left feeling reborn—much more so than I did after the baptism in Palm Springs. I left my tensions and bitterness behind. I felt whole again. Not that some memories wouldn't remain as a warning to be more careful in the future. No more marriage contracts for me.

The lot in Eugene where Rik was building looked out over a valley full of firs, spruce, maple, dogwood, and the Oregon pest, wild blackberries. It seemed miles from civilization, rather than a five-minute drive from the University of Oregon campus, where he had received his architectural degree. He was now putting those years of schooling to practical use by building his own house. He knew how to do everything—plumbing, electrical wiring, framing, roofing. I envied the freedom that comes with having all those skills.

The house grew up the hill. We called it "couture architecture" (like the Winchester Mystery house in San Jose, California, for which my grandfather was the architect/contractor). Decisions were made on the moment; a window would appear to take advantage of a particular view or to outline a tree. Rik had bought over one hundred windows of various sizes and shapes from an old house that was being torn down. The house developed an airiness from the many different light exposures. On one side it opened into the cool forest, while the other side had a wide porch overlooking the valley. Many architectural students came to admire his work.

My room was at the top of the stairs; it had been designed to be a large closet under the steeply slanting roof. Now, with two windows added, it became my little space. There was room for my suitcase, a bed, a tiny bedside table, and a hook on the wall for hanging my towel. All I wore were jeans or shorts, so closet space wasn't needed. As I knew no one in Eugene, I spent my days writing and cooking. What a joy it was to cook for those hungry young workmen. Most of them had degrees of some sort, but they were helping Rik with cement pouring, brickwork, bulldozing, felling trees, and all sorts of odd jobs. I had never lived in such a community. None of them had a bean, but all were full of confidence.

It made me think back on how I had almost let material possessions rob me of my true gifts. When friends wrote, saying, "What a pity you have to have strangers living in your home, using all your lovely things," I'd think, funny, it doesn't bother me at all. I just hope they are enjoying them. Naturally, I was pleased when Mercedes wrote saying how much she liked Richard Burton and his friend, Susy. She described him as *"muy grave"*; he was studying for his part in *The Heretic,* and he spent much of the day to himself. At night, she recounted, he and Susy sometimes went out, "the Señora all decked out in jewels and beautiful clothes." My financial advisor was slowly straightening out my affairs, and brought in more income. If I rented the house half the year, I would be in good shape. (As it has turned out, the house, with the addition of Mercedes' service, has attracted many celebrities over the years.)

In October I returned home, a whole person again. Friends welcomed me, and the pendulum made a full swing back. Escorts wined and dined me, and my writing was put aside for another day. I saw a lot of Gayelord Hauser. He was often my escort for social events. We laughed at life together. Although he was in his eighties by this time, he was younger than most of my friends in their fifties. He was truly a modern man, with a completely open mind—even to facts which have sometimes proved him wrong.

Recognized as the Czar of the health food world, he was always generous with newcomers in the field of holistic health. After coming back from a month at the Nathan Pritikin Clinic, he confided to my guests and me at dinner one night, "Children (we were all in our fifties), I must rewrite my books. I've told my followers to use refined oils such as sunflower and safflower oils. Now it's proved wrong—the more refined the oil, the easier it gets into the bloodstream to do damage. The best oil is butter or olive oil."

I thought to myself, that is what Dr. Bieler always taught, but how honest of Gayelord to make such an admission. He went on to add, "Pritikin may know the chemical facts, but he sure doesn't know how to serve appealing food." He straightened his paisley cravat and ran a hand over his thick, gray hair. "You and I, Nancy, could put together an enticing menu with the same raw materials."

In the 1930s Gayelord introduced yeast, blackstrap molasses, and yogurt to the Western world. His slogans "What you eat today walks tomorrow," and "You are what you Eat," revolutionized global eating habits. Celebrities such as Greta Garbo, Gloria Swanson, Marlena Dietrich, and the Duke and Duchess of Windsor flocked to his salon in Paris. His books were snatched up by millions of hungry readers anxious to *Live Longer and Look Better.*"

Thinking of Gayelord, my mind went back to 1969, when he called with some exciting news. "The Girlfriend is here and I've convinced her to allow me to invite you for dinner." I was thrilled; I knew the Girlfriend, as he called Garbo, was visiting him at his Coldwater Canyon home. Every spring she came for six weeks. I remembered his joking about the customary ritual of her arrival.

"I go with the car and driver to pick her up at the airport; she travels as Miss Brown. When we get to my house and drive through the gates, she gets down on the car floor. We stop directly in front of the guest cottage, she crawls out and dashes in the door as though pursued by crowds, and there is not a soul around, not even the Japanese gardener." His expressive hands went up in a gesture of surprise. Sun lines closed around his merry eyes, strong white teeth were revealed by the generous smile; he clearly enjoyed his description.

We agreed on a date, but Gayelord warned me, "She may not show, so don't be disappointed. You and I can catch up—it will be her loss. And, oh yes, how about bringing some of your delicious zucchini soup? I've told her about it, and she'll love it."

As Tony was out of town I planned to go alone. He would be so disappointed. Actually, I'd met Garbo in 1949 at the beach home of a friend. I remembered my surprise when I first saw her, her languorous eyes were framed by "frownies." My mother used to stick on the paper triangles before going to bed;, they were designed to ward off frown lines while sleeping. I had tried hard not to stare at the patches.

A few nights later, as I drove up the winding side road off Coldwater and entered the eucalyptus-lined courtyard, both apprehensive and excited, I doubted that Garbo would remember me from twenty years before.

The single-storied country house looked more French than Californian, with its elaborate, black wrought iron gates. Hedges, shrubs and magnolia trees complimented the white exterior trimmed with yellow. Tom, the bright-eyed Irish butler, opened the door.

"Dr. Hauser and Miss G. are waiting in the sunroom. Also, his nephew is there." That was good news; Dieter Schmidt was an easy, outgoing personality.

I knew the sunroom well. Floor-to-ceiling, wooden-paned windows looked out to the pool area surrounded by lawn, rose bushes and flowering fruit trees, now heavy with blossoms. Black-and-white checked floors added a crispness to the room; white cane furniture was covered in flowered chintz. Couches and chairs formed a U around a long, wicker coffee table, covered with magazines and tempting cocktail nibbles, such as freshly roasted pecans and jumbo black olives.

As I entered, the tall, handsome uncle and nephew stood up to greet me. Both shared the same expansive foreheads and high, teutonic cheekbones. Their proud heads were held with authority and confidence. Gayelord came forward to give me a warm embrace.

"Come meet Miss Garbo." Miss Garbo, in camel-colored slacks and turtle-necked sweater, was curled up in the corner of a couch, sipping on a drink. The atmosphere was casual and informal as I slipped into it. On being introduced I omitted to mention that we had met before. I could see the changes in her. Time and smoking had taken its toll on the lower part of her face. Her mouth was lined by wrinkles, as Gayelord pointed out, "from all that puffing on those damned cigarillos you love so much." The memorable eyes were still recognizable, however, and her silky hair hung naturally about her unforgettable face. Playful and talkative, she had just finished entertaining the men with an off-color story.

"Nancy is a patient of Dr. Henry Bieler, author of *Food Is Your Best Medicine.*" He knew that would get his houseguest's attention.

"The soup we are having tonight was created by Nancy with the OK of Bieler."

"The famous Bieler broth?"

"Yes, but she vastly improved it. It's now like a lovely green Vichyssoise, not the unattractive-looking boiled vegetables he prescribed before. If I ever write another cookbook, this will be the first recipe in it." I was flattered. Dining with Gayelord was always memorable, a treat for the eyes as well as the palate.

Tom announced that dinner was served. Garbo preceded me. Her shoulders were square, the figure still slim. She seemed shorter than I remembered her. It flashed through my mind that a bra would be an improvement.

The dining room welcomed us with candlelight and enticing aromas. One wall featured the food *trompe-l'oeils* given to Gayelord by Lady Elsie Mendel. Four antique, cane chairs encircled the round table draped with red damask and set with silver candelabra, flower-decorated china, and tall, delicate wine glasses.

Once seated it was easier to observe her. With hands unadorned by jewelry and nails unpainted, she ate with delicacy, but with gusto,

"Yes, I approve of the soup; please teach me and I'll make it myself."

Next came a crisp, green salad. Defying European custom, Gayelord served it before the main course, saying it stimulated the digestive process. Our *entré* was chicken breasts pounded flat and sautéed in wine, herbs and butter. Grated carrots and beets, barely cooked, added color and interest along with the braised celery. Our plates brimmed over with enzymes and vitamins. "A little Poully Fuissé?" asked our host as he poured the chilled wine into the glasses. As a European, born in Germany, Gayelord felt wine, in moderation, was a food. A diet expert, but not a food fanatic, he often said,

"If you get all the essentials, you can then play around a little."

Dessert was irresistible—fresh blueberries mixed with raspberries, accompanied with thick Devonshire cream. When I moaned about my waist, Garbo spoke, "You don't have to worry. That long top covers everything. Where is it from? The embroidery is very nice."

"It's a Kashmiri *pherran*; the Moslem men wear them. I had several made in silk, cotton and wool. My ethnic clothes have saved me a fortune, and they never go out of style."

"Nancy goes to India every year; we should go with her and stay on one of those marvelous houseboats."

She nodded in agreement and then asked, "Why do you keep going back to India? Doesn't the poverty bother you?"

"Actually most of the poverty exists in Calcutta and Bombay; in the villages people are productive and happy."

"She is a teacher of meditation for Maharishi, that is one reason she goes back so often; also, as a good-will fashion authority for the state department, she collects things for her show, *Costumes, Customs, and Cultures.*"

Our conversation took off. Garbo asked many questions about meditation and reincarnation; she wasn't interested in the fashion part. Soon it was time to leave. At the door, G.G., as she asked me to call her, rubbed my back affectionately and remarked, "You must come back; I like you. I am sometimes jealous of Gayelord's women friends, but I approve of you." I was thrilled with the evening and floated home.

Soon the phone rang. It was Gayelord. "Mushka (another pet name for her) adored you. Come sit in the outdoor jacuzzi with us tomorrow."

So started an intimate friendship with the world's most famous recluse. Each year she arrived in April and we would pick up where we'd left off. She was happy and secure during those weeks. It was hard to visualize her as cool and aloof. During my long legal ordeal she was warm and sympathetic, as well as indignant that Tony would treat me in such a brutal fashion. She would rub my tense shoulders; even though the media had hinted at her being a lesbian, I never saw any indications. She was an affectionate woman, reaching out with tenderness. Her love was gardening. She cut, trimmed and cleaned up Gayelord's entire garden.

One day she met me at the car, hidden by the huge fern she was carrying. "Here, take this home; we have no place for it." Then, looking at her hands, "They look like they belong to the Japanese gardener. Come see what I have done."

A torn, wide-brimmed straw hat shielded the famous face from the sun. Her outfit of old khaki pants and a man's shirt with the tails hanging out thoroughly disguised her. I followed her to the pool area. It looked as though a cyclone had struck, debris and trimmings were scattered everywhere.

"I've cut all the roses and trimmed every geranium. That gardener never sees a dead leaf. He should be fired." At that moment Gayelord joined us.

"I won't have to fire him, he's threatening to quit as you do all his work." It was hard to believe that this man, with his tan, trim figure, was in his late seventies. There was not an ounce of fat on him. His posture was inspiring; with a long stride he approached the pool, dropped his towel and went for a swim. Floating leisurely on his back, he had more to say. "Yesterday, we couldn't sit out here; Mushka was painting the garden chairs."

Another afternoon I arrived to observe a domestic scene. G.G., seated on the ground, was giving Gayelord a pedicure. "May I be next?" I asked.

"Look at these feet. He doesn't have a single callous or bunion; is that what you call them? He has the feet of a young boy." She got up with agility to take her manicuring things into the house.

Gayelord loved her babying him, but now registered a protest. "Mushka, why don't you sit down and talk to us? You have to be fussing around doing something all day." He looked at me. "She's already washed the deck and the umbrellas. I think you must teach her to meditate and relax."

G.G. put down her tray and came over to give me a hug. "That is a very good idea. I am ready any time you are; just tell me what to do."

Often when I came to the house I would check Gayelord's meditation, and she respected this. She knew it had brought him solace when his beloved, life-long companion and manager, Frey Brown, died. That sad event propelled him into reading volumes about the religions of the world, and on several occasions we went together to hear Maharishi speak. As a world-renowned speaker himself, Gayelord was impressed. "How these people love Maharishi. I've never seen such large crowds be so quiet and attentive. That is a great sign of respect."

Often he would talk to his audience of several thousand people about Transcendental Meditation, "It is the best health and beauty treatment of them all."

Another time he confided, "I think I must have accumulated some bad karma when I left Brownie for Garbo. We lived together for several years, and it almost broke his heart. But I was besotted with her beauty. I can still remember one night at Lake Tahoe—we went skinny-dipping in the lake. Afterwards we laid out on a huge rock in the moonlight—I will never forget her perfect body and the beauty of her skin. Later, when we went our own ways, I tried to make it up to Brownie; without him I would never have accomplished what I have." He mourned for Brownie the rest of his life and kept his ashes in the Buddha head near his bed.

So G.G. wanted to learn to meditate. It was now 1976. I had been a TM initiator for eight years, and realized what a responsibility I was taking on. Her unusual behavior patterns over the years indicated large amounts of stress on her nervous system. I would have to stay close at hand the first few weeks in case she had any traumatic reactions.

For her initiation it was all set to use the small, secluded library. Airy and light, the walls were covered with flower prints as well as bookshelves. On the desk was a fragrant bouquet of fresh roses cut from the garden. On greeting me, Gayelord pointed out, "She has been up since dawn getting everything ready, the roses are from her. Last night she washed her hair, and later she had me select which shirt to wear. She has so few clothes. She certainly has enough money to buy what she wants, but she won't go shopping. Meditation may do a lot for her—at least I'm praying it will. She is so lonesome when she is away from here. She lives in a huge apartment filled with millions of dollars worth of paintings that no one ever sees."

At that moment Garbo arrived. She exuded the excitement of a young girl about to receive a diploma. There was a radiance about her, her hair smelled of fresh pine and she wore a heavy, white, silk tailored blouse.

"Oh, Nancy, I feel this is an important day in my life. Here is my tray of offerings; is it all right?" There was the required linen handkerchief, more gorgeous roses and, for fruit, a papaya, a pear and two peaches.

"It is perfect, and you look glorious in your beautiful blouse. Maharishi would approve. Now, Gayelord, out you go; we have matters to attend to."

I gestured to the yellow and white couch. "Let's talk a bit before I give you your *mantra*." Taking more time than usual, I explained in detail the principle of meditation, stressing that it would bring a "drop by drop" improvement in the quality of her life. I didn't want her to be over-expectant.

"Will it help me to be less afraid of life?" That was her big question. "I feel such panic when people come up to me suddenly. How I envy you your natural friendliness."

Her face was full of rapture as she stood alongside me while I performed the *puja*. We knelt together when I gave her the *mantra*. Wisps of spicy incense drifted around us as she carefully practiced her now special sound. She returned to the couch, I to a chair, and I led her into her first meditation. Then I left her, returning twenty minutes later.

"How do you feel?"

"The most relaxed I've ever felt in my life. I have no feeling in my hands or feet, my body seems jointless. It's like a dream. May I please just stay here and never leave?" Ten years had dropped from her face. The lines around her mouth were softened, her gaze was dreamlike.

"Well, I'd say you've had a good beginning. Now it will depend on your consistency. You will have your ups and downs, but remember, there is no such thing as a bad meditation."

She took to meditation like the proverbial duck to water. We talked daily, and she was religious about her half-hour practice time. She often asked Gayelord if he had done his meditation. When Gayelord's financial associate, Tony Palermo, arrived from Milwaukee, where the Gayelord Hauser Modern Products were located, G.G. met him with, "This is now a house of meditators; maybe Nancy will teach you."

"Oh no, you are not going to get this crazy Italian to clean up his act." Tony was comic relief for G.G. and Gayelord. He overflowed with wisecracks, suggestive stories and outrageous behavior. He would offer himself, "How would you girls like a real man—you can have me bald or with hair." With that he would lift his hairpiece and roar with laughter.

Gayelord had trained Tony from youth; he was part of the family. Luckily he amused Miss Garbo. She recognized his intelligence and also used him as a financial advisor. She was astute and down to earth about money matters. She and Gayelord owned the best block on Rodeo Drive in Beverly Hills. Amongst their renters were Hermes, Gucci, and Wally

Findley Galleries. Once, when G.G. asked Gayelord about some business matter, he replied, "Oh, I leave that all up to Tony."

G.G. reprimanded him, "That is not right. You must know what you have at all times. You ask Tony to give you an accounting."

He promised he would, but nothing was done, so one day Garbo said to Tony, "Maybe Gayelord doesn't ask you, but if you don't give him an accounting, I'll start to doubt you." It was said lightly, but the information came immediately.

On receiving it, Gayelord exclaimed, "How nice. I'm worth much more than I thought."

Garbo's coy reply was, "Now that you are such a wealthy man, don't you think it's time we got married and you made an honest woman of me?"

One day when I came to check her meditation, G.G. greeted me, "I have a lot to talk about. Let's take a walk over the hill." Looking at my high heels she added, "I'll lend you some tennis shoes." I thought of the legend, the wide-brimmed Garbo, sneaking around New York in large tennis shoes, but they were not big, maybe a seven and a half. Mine were a seven and her shoes were fine for me. One more myth shot down, and walking in HER SHOES was exciting in itself.

"How is everything going? Are you enjoying meditation? The time going by quickly?" These were the essentials for me to know.

"Yes, yes, I like it very much, and usually the time rushes by, but last night something strange happened." Her brows were pulled together, I thought back on that first day at the beach when she was wearing "frownies."

"All of a sudden I was looking down at myself meditating. I had gone out of my body and it scared me. What do you think of that?"

"Wonderful, it shows your mantra is doing its work. Remember, as I said before, nothing can harm you in meditation. Just take it easy and take it as it comes. Don't start expecting things to happen now. What is important is how you feel in your every day life. Experiences within meditation are usually a result of some impurity or stress on your nervous system."

"Then I should have a lot of strange things happen. I have been full of stress all my life, especially when I stopped acting." Branches and pine needles crunched under our feet, and our shadows were getting longer. We were oblivious to the forest around us.

As she had brought the forbidden subject up, I pursued it, "That is an unusual statement. I thought it would have been the reverse."

"As an actress, I could escape myself into another world. It is the real world I'm terrified of." She looked like the pitiful little matchstick girl. "Sometimes I wish I were invisible; then I could watch people but they would not see me."

"You better go to India and become a Yogi; that is one of their tricks." We laughed, but then she added, "I wonder how I have survived all these years without meditation." The statement was followed by a deep sigh. Later Gayelord did say he felt she had become more outgoing and less neurotic about people since she started TM.

Often Gayelord would call, "She wants to come to your house for dinner again. She has already decided on the menu. She'd like that boiled leg of lamb with the white caper sauce and Mercedes' wonderful 'smashed potatoes' (as Garbo called the mashed potatoes). For dessert, how about that *crème brûlée*? Your cook's recipe is the best."

Once, mentioning this to my sisters on the telephone, I immediately received a return call. "We are inviting ourselves for dinner. Wait 'til the bridge club hears we had dinner with Gayelord and Garbo!"

What characters, but they were so welcome. "Just make sure you are here before she arrives. If you are staying with me it seems more natural."

I had my sisters stay in their rooms until G.G. was settled in a chair with a scotch and water in her hand. As soon as she was happy and secure, I'd signal my other guests to appear; the format was always the same for the many nights G.G. came to the house in the future. This particular night it was fun bringing my sisters out. They already knew Gayelord, but when I introduced them to G.G., it brought the response, "I think I'm seeing things, it is not fair . . . three look-alikes. Are you triplets?"

"No, but we're within three years of each other," answered Doryce, the youngest.

Ardagh Marie, the eldest, then jumped in. "One day in San Francisco I was standing in Gumps, when an elderly man came up to me and said, 'Nancy dear, don't shed a tear, always cheer and drink your beer.' I looked at him with amazement and said, 'I believe you must think I'm my sister, Nancy.' He stared at me and said, 'You are not!'"

I cut in. "It was Carroll Righter, the astrologer. I've had lunch with him every month for the last 15 years . . . he'll never forget that." That

*Woody (C.V. Wood, Jr.) and Joanne (Dru),
my neighbors. He bought the London Bridge and
made a river to put it over in Havasu, Arizona*

got the party going. It was an animated evening and Garbo gave each sister a big hug as she left.

The consensus was, "She is divine . . . not snobbish at all . . . so basic, such fun . . . like the person next door . . . doesn't appear sophisticated or glamorous . . . pretty hair . . . lovely nose . . . her eyes are still fabulous." They had a lot to report to their friends.

Later Gayelord reported in. "The evening was most successful. Mushka loved the sisters. In the car she commented, 'Look at what joy they have together. Why couldn't I have that kind of happiness?' I wasn't going to let her get away with that self-pity, so I let her have it, 'Because you give nothing of yourself to anyone. In life you get back what you give out.'" He was indignant. "She is always saying she's had nothing in life. She had the world at her feet."

On May 17, 1976, Gayelord was to celebrate his eightieth birthday. For this special occasion G.G. agreed to attend, even though there was a large guest list. George Frelinghuysen, now one of the area's most prominent hosts, called me. "I'm thrilled; I'm going to finally meet Garbo. I'm invited to the party on the 17th."

I hastened to say, "Don't get your hopes too high; she is likely to change her mind at the last second, especially when she sees the courtyard full of cars."

Having to drive in from Palm Springs that day, I arrived after the guests had assembled, including George. I quickly asked him. "Has she appeared?"

"Yes, and I've never been so disappointed." This from a man who so admired beauty. He pointed out the window to the garden. "There she is."

I couldn't believe my eyes. She had on a dirndl skirt—where she got that I couldn't guess—her hair was pulled back in a ponytail, and her beautiful eyes were covered by dark glasses. Hardly recognizable, she was playing a part, hopping around and offering everyone iced-tea, like some barmaid. I laughed at her perversity.

I stayed on after the party to dine with Gayelord, Dieter, Tony and G.G. When the guests left, Garbo went to her room, combed out her silky hair, put on well-tailored slacks and a matching turtle-neck, and came out looking terrific. She certainly gave the guests something to talk about. Gayelord said nothing. She had kept her promise—and maybe she actually had a good time.

She was very animated at the Black Forest Restaurant that night. She cautioned Gayelord, "You must check your caterers. They were serving white sugar with the coffee. I took it away and said, 'Go to the kitchen for brown sugar. White sugar is poison to Dr. Hauser!'"

Another evening was memorable. Gayelord had met Joanne (Dru) and her husband, C.V. Wood, at my home many times and simply adored Joanne. The Woods said they would love to meet Garbo, so I asked Gayelord, "What about it?"

His reply was, "Fine, but tell Woody to go a bit slow."

My reaction was, "That will be the day, when anyone gets Woody to go slow." An outspoken Texan, he is one of the world's greatest promoters, as well as a brilliant business man. I decided to take a chance with Garbo.

When the Woods arrived, Garbo was sitting on my antique cane couch, her pale cream blouse blending with the light yellow, velvet cushion cover. With the large, Coromanel screen behind her, it made an appealing scene. The pungent smoke from her cigarillo tickled my nose.

"G.G., this is the Joanne you have heard Gayelord and me talk about."

"Yes, and now I know why." Joanne is the essence of femininity—slim, pretty and soft-spoken. Woody is a total contrast, with his wide girth, circus barker's voice and mischievous face; he comes on strong. It didn't take him long. He sat down beside G.G., patted her knee and asked, "Pretty lady, I see you don't have a drink in your hand yet. Have you ever had a mint julep? I'm famous for making the best." I held my breath.

"Why no, I never have; do you think I would like it?" Garbo lowered her eyelids seductively and flirted right back.

"Ma'am, I can guarantee it; give me two minutes while I pop across the street to my house . . . I have them all frozen, ready to go."

Woody loves to tell the story, "I had that Garbo drunk in thirty minutes, and she and me got along just fine." It's true; G.G. asked to see them again, something she had never done before.

Garbo even accepted an offer to go to their house after Woody promised, "I'll cook you the best little ole Mexican dinner with my own hands." He then added, "And this boy of yours," pointing at Gayelord, "should know that chili peppers are full of everything that's good for you. Hey, I have an idea, Gayelord; how about y'all being a judge at my next chili contest?"

In shock Gayelord responded, "My dear Woody, could you really imagine Gayelord Hauser at a chili contest?"

"Why sure, man, you need to prove you have an open mind."

A few days later, true to his word, Woody whipped up a delicious Mexican dinner. He was in his newly-remodeled kitchen when we arrived. Fifteen-foot ceilings, red tile floors and natural wood cabinets provided an appropriate setting for his culinary efforts. Multiple pots were boiling; spicy aromas seduced our salivary glands. Woody placed flowers made from carrots on each pottery plate. He was not going to be outdone by Gayelord.

"This here is my famous chili con carne; no beans, man, and I make my own suet." Did I notice Gayelord wince?

G.G. ate every bite of her enchilada, taco, chili, tamale and tortilla, "Woody, you are an artist. If I stayed here I would gain fifty pounds."

As *flan*, Mexican custard, was served, the Wood's houseguest, Don Kendall, came in. President of Pepsi Cola and a director of Arco, Don came to L.A. for the Arco meetings. A lifelong friend, he always stayed with Woody. This night his Western hat made him look more like a cowboy than an industrial genius. When Joanne introduced him around, he was noticeably cold to Gayelord. As the conversation progressed, the coolness turned to rudeness.

Garbo's face was taut, her eyes wide open with anger. When Kendall excused himself, she exploded, "What a terrible man!"

Gayelord soothed her as he explained to us, "Years ago I took on both Coca Cola and Pepsi Cola. I exposed the amounts of sugar in their products. It was a national campaign; he has not forgotten me." The tension broke as we enjoyed the irony of the situation, but Garbo was unforgiving. No one was going to be rude to her friend. As we left, Don Kendall came to say goodbye. Gayelord gently patted his shoulder, "Goodbye, mine enemy." We all laughed about it the next day. The only ones still disturbed were Joanne and Garbo.*

Occasionally I would rent my house when I was going on a two-month trip. Mercedes didn't like being alone, and I liked the income. I had made my garage into a two-story studio apartment that I could move my things into in case our times overlapped. During the spring of 1983 Frank Perry and his wife, Barbara Goldsmith, took up residence in my house. Frank was directing *Mommy Dearest*, and Barbara was starting a new book after having finished *Poor Little Gloria, Happy Again*. On my return from India I was in my studio with them and happened to mention that Garbo would be coming for dinner a few nights later.

"Nancy, that is the one star I have always wanted to meet," Frank implored. "Isn't there some way we could arrange it? Could you give the dinner in the mainhouse and pretend we are your houseguests?" Laughingly I admitted I'd done that once before.

"But it's not necessary; we'll just make it seven instead of five. However, you can't say you have anything to do with the movies. That's a subject she is pathological about. I called Gayelord the other night and asked him if he'd seen any of the Garbo Film Festival that's playing. His

---

* In March 1992, Woody suddenly died of lung cancer. It was a shock—such a vibrant man to disappear so quickly. At Woody's request, Warner Bros. Studio had a "big bash" for 700 intimate friends to celebrate having known Woody. Featured were a Dixieland band and his famous chili.

reply was, 'Are you kidding? We are not allowed to even turn the TV on. I knew about it because Tom had it on in his quarters, and I warned him to keep it very low.'"

Frank persisted, "I'll be anything; how about a painter?"

"Fine, house or portrait?" Barbara spoke up. "What about me? Can she know about my book?"

"Yes, I think some of the Vanderbilts were her friends. She's perfectly happy to talk about people other than actors. She has a good sense of humor once she's in a secure position. In fact, she was amusing the other day. She said to me when I'd just returned, 'Well, here I am again. For someone who shuns society, I sure come around a lot, don't I?'"

Nancy Oakes actually was my houseguest at the time, so she joined us. She and Gayelord shared the same birthdate and were old friends. Jack Warnecke, the architect who had just finished the U.S. Senate building, was also in town and would come. It was a good group. G.G. knew Nancy and could easily relate. After Nancy's father, Sir Harry Oakes, was brutally murdered, Nancy was hounded by the press unrelentingly.

Mercedes' lamb shanks were perfection, as were the "smashed potatoes." G.G. made a trip to the kitchen to say thank you in Spanish, "*Grácias,*" with a slight Swedish accent. She always showed her affection for Mercedes by patting her shoulder. G.G. was a sensual woman and liked to touch her friends. This was picked up by Frank Perry. "She is still fabulous; she eyeballed me all through dinner and even played a bit of footsie." Garbo had just left and he was still under her spell; his pleasant face was flushed and happy.

"You have no idea what this evening has meant to me. She never asked me what I do in life." Later I heard she asked one question, "Does he have a lot of money?" Barbara then added, "I was pleased she liked my book; she was very open about talking of her friendship with several of the Vanderbilts."

"Listen, that woman still has plenty of sex appeal when she wants to turn it on." This from Jack, who at one time had been romantically linked with Jackie Kennedy.

"And, incidently, wasn't a Vanderbilt married to Stowkowski, one of Garbo's old lovers?"

"Frank, you can now claim that Garbo stood up the King of Sweden in order to be your dinner partner," I threw out.

"What are you talking about?"

"Actually, in some ways it's true. A few days ago a Mr. Svenson called. George White, the manager of the Beverly Wilshire Hotel suggested he contact me, as he knew I was a friend of Gayelord Hauser and Greta Garbo. Mr. Svenson was anxious to know if Miss Garbo was in town and, if so, could an invitation be sent to her to attend a party being given by the Swedish community to honor His Royal Highness, the King of Sweden (who was staying at the hotel). Mr. Svenson assured me that Miss Garbo would be seated on the right hand of the king, the place of honor. I told him I would contact Dr. Hauser and get back to him. When I mentioned the invitation to Gayelord, he responded with a loud 'No way. She has been asked this before and always refuses. It's better not to even mention it.'"

"Even though it is the king of her own country?"

"Absolutely not. It amazed me, too."

"The Swedish party was given tonight! So, you see, it would not be all fabrication." We had a good laugh; it had been a happy evening, and G.G. had captivated my guests once again.

Another time, my sister and I were talking on the phone. As she chatted on, I heard the interrupt signal, so I cut in, "Wait a minute; there's another call."

"OK, but don't hang me out to dry."

I was back in half a minute, "It was Gayelord. I'm going to pick him and the Girlfriend up and go shopping at Trader Joe's in the Valley. I'll get back to you later."

By my driving, Tom, the butler, could stay home and do his work. Besides, I had a station wagon we could load up.

As we entered Trader Joe's, Gayelord instructed us, "I know just what I want, so you two wander and buy what you please."

He sped off to select his nuts, cheese, olives, and wines. They had a good selection of imported wines at good prices. The first thing to attract our eye was a woman offering samples of baba au rum.

"Let's try that," suggested my companion. We both took one. "It's delicious; maybe I can have another?" asked my now not-too-shy friend. After polishing off the second sample, G.G. announced, "I will leave here drunk."

The saleswoman joined in with the fun. "Enjoy yourself; you have such a pretty smile, and your teeth are lovely." Garbo had spent the day before at the dentist's while he worked on a back bridge. Now she opened her mouth to show the woman the work he'd done.

As the salesgirl strained to see the bridgework, Gayelord rejoined us, "If that young woman knew whose throat she was peering down, she would faint."

Another time a salesperson commented to me, "Has anyone ever told you that you look like Ginger Rogers?" She hadn't even looked at Garbo who was standing next to me.

Another time, my son Brett and his wife Olga came into town from Riverside, where they were both professors of Russian and Polish at the University of California. As a fan of Tolstoy, Brett was eager to meet the incarnation of Anna Karenina. It was arranged on the agreement that he would not mention the name, Tolstoy, yes, but Anna, no. Olga, a native-born Russian, was shy about the meeting. She was afraid Garbo would be cold and unapproachable. We convinced her to come. I knew G.G. would like them; they are such warm, loveable, bright young people.

Imagine Olga's amazement when Garbo, shortly after they met, asked, "How many months pregnant are you?"

"Almost seven months." Olga was caught off guard by the question. Her lovely, wide-eyed slavic face showed surprise.

"Then you can feel the heartbeat."

"Oh yes, it's been quite a while now."

"Do you suppose I could put my hand on your stomach and feel it?" When Olga laughingly agreed, G.G. shyly placed her hand on Olga's bulging abdomen. "Yes, I can feel it. It is very clear. This is thrilling. What are you going to do with your baby when it is born?" Olga didn't know exactly what she meant, so she said she would stop teaching for several months and take care of the baby. That seemed satisfactory. For some reason it made me feel sad. Here was a woman who had so much and had experienced so little.

My middle son, Starr, and his wife also joined the party. Starr played bartender and watched my guests' glasses closely,

"OK, Miss G., your drink is finished; time for a refresher."

"Oh, no, I've already had two."

"Nobody's counting. You can always take it to the table." I never saw Garbo take too much, and Mercedes had just given us five minutes notice.

The menu consisted of what G.G. had ordered—more farm food. This time it was corned beef and cabbage, and "those good boiled potatoes served with vinegar and chopped onions." As it was Easter time, the table was decorated with colored eggs.

Always interested in games, Brett had one to suggest. "Have you ever played egg-knocking?" It was a new one to all of us, but his enthusiasm was catching. "You take turns challenging each other to an egg knock . . . you each hit the other's egg on its tip; the one that does not break stays in the game."

Before long the contest came down to the eggs of G.G. and Gayelord, all the others lay broken on the table. G.G. was determined to win. She took a ribbon from the centerpiece, stuck it on the top of her head and approached Gayelord like a matador. "Now for the final thrust!" She deftly knocked the tip of his egg into pieces, and we all roared with approval.

As she was being congratulated, Gayelord quietly said, "This is the one time you could have taken a picture if you'd had a camera ready." I had never even dared to think of having a camera around. Damn it!

When it came time to return to New York, G.G. seemed particularly sad to leave California. "I've had such a happy time; now I go back to lonesomeness."

"That is your choice," answered Gayelord, never letting her get away with feeling sorry for herself.

"Why not join us in Taormina? Dieter and I will be there in July." He had a wonderful villa in Sicily. While Brownie was alive, Gayelord and he spent many months there enjoying the sea, their gardens, and the perfectly trained staff of Italians who cooked and attended to their every desire.

Several weeks after her departure, a stunning lucite coffee table arrived, a present from Garbo to Gayelord.

"This is most unusual. She hates to spend money, and this is an expensive table. I'm thrilled with it; it is a beauty. She must have noticed that the old wicker table was looking tired." He was touched by the unexpected gift.

Every Sunday morning, whether she was in Klosters, where she went each summer, or in New York, Gayelord would call G.G. for a long chat. Often he would then call me. "I need to talk to someone who is happy and optimistic. That woman is so pessimistic, she has nothing in her life. I talk about everything I can think of, but she always brings it back to her own gloom and doom." He was exasperated and needed to let it out.

"We've all had tragedy in our lives; I lost Brownie, your husband died when your daughter was a baby, but we don't moan about it continually. Life has to go on."

"Yes, but what does she have in her life? You are her father, friend and family all in one. What would she do without you?"

"I've thought about that; it is a big responsibility. I will simply have to outlive her." I was to remind him of that statement in the coming year, 1985, which was to be the last year of his life.

For some reason, G.G. came in March of that year and stayed for a full two months. Her early arrival coincided with the presentation of the Academy Awards.

"I just announced to her that you and a beau were going to join us for dinner and watch the show together as we have in the past," Gayelord informed me. My friend, Ash Haile, was staying at my house. He was a friend from Stanford days, had been at the Hauser house on several occasions and was the type G.G. would take to—tall, broad shouldered, Texas handsome and an avid admirer of the ladies. It proved to be a natural.

"You have an army of good-looking men, Nancy; I thoroughly approve." Over the years I'd invited an assortment of interesting men for dinner when I knew she was coming. No one ever refused when he heard the guest list.

The show began; we took our places in the sunroom's comfortable chairs and couches. G.G. and I commented on the women's gowns. She smoked a cigarillo and enjoyed herself. An elderly star made a presentation.

"My God, what a dreadful face-lift she had," came from Gayelord.

"I've been meaning to ask you if you think I should have one." Garbo lifted her cheeks up, pulling her mouth back to smooth out the lines.

"No, you've waited too long, and it wouldn't do any good as long as you continue smoking those awful things," answered our host. That seemed to finish the conversation. I felt he was a bit hard on her, but she shrugged it off.

A commercial was on; they were showing scenes from old movies. All of a sudden, the screen was filled by a picture of Garbo's exquisite young face. No one said a word, the moment passed, another scene took

*A young Dr. Gayelord Hauser at age seventy-five.
He died in 1985 at age ninety.*

its place and Gayelord picked up the conversation as though nothing unusual had happened. In the car going home, Ash commented, "That sure was strange when Miss Garbo's picture was shown and nobody said a word."

During his stay in Taormina the summer of '85, Gayelord took a bad fall. I knew nothing about it until he called on his return in September, "Come see me, Nancy. I'm not getting around very well. Luckily, I didn't break anything, but tendons and sprains often take more time to heal than breaks."

I didn't add, "Especially for a man almost ninety." He used a cane, but still looked vibrant and strong, maybe a bit thinner. I felt reassured.

During that autumn we dined together often, but he refused most invitations. "How can I, Gayelord Hauser, the health authority, go out walking with a cane," was his excuse, but I noticed other changes that worried me. Gayelord knew that several years before I had taken the *Phowa,* the Tibetan course in death. The ancient teachings not only taught a person how to prepare himself for death but also to help a friend or pet die in what the Buddhists considered the best way. Gayelord was intrigued by this, his mind was very much on death. Tom would drop him off at my house for dinner, and even though I often suggested including another person, Gayelord would say, "No, let's keep it the two of us."

I knew what he wanted to discuss and I tried to change his mood, "You are such an inspiration to everyone, dear Gayelord. You are the living example of what eating and thinking well does for one. You have so many friends who adore you and need you—what would Garbo do without you? You've always promised to outlive her." I searched for more. "You told us to plan on living until 100, then we'd still feel young in our eighties." This came as a reaction to his statement, "I'm tired of life. I've done everything. All my family is gone, and most of my friends of many years."

I reminded him of his newer friends, like myself, a friend of only thirty-four years. He still had a sense of humor and laughed. We'd met at a cocktail party in Paris, given for him by Marian Preminger, in 1951. That was before she joined Schweitzer in Africa. Gayelord loved to tell stories about the famous doctor.

We often reminisced about many mutual friends who had gone on.

"I think of the last time we saw Cobina, it was after the memorial service for Brownie, back at the house. She went from table to table, toasting everyone with champagne."

"Delmar Daves gave a beautiful toast also . . . now they are both gone."

When Colette Cachin, his associate and head of the Gayelord Hauser Foundation in Paris, came to visit, I brought the subject up.

"Do you notice a change in Gayelord?"

"Definitely. It has me worried. When I'm talking to him, he seems as though his mind is somewhere else. It's not that he's forgetful. If I question him on a detail, his mind is as acute as ever."

"He has lost his interest in life; he talks about the 'other side' a lot. He refers to it as 'his next adventure.'"

"Oh dear, how sad . . ."

"I've been taught by my Eastern spiritual friends that this life on the mortal plane is grade school; when we die, it's like graduation. It means we have passed all our tests and it's time to go on."

"But what about *our* desires? We don't want him to leave us!"

I agreed, and continued to pray that it was a momentary mood caused by his injury.

Christmas decorations went up the day after Thanksgiving; the holiday season was in full swing. Mary Robling, the famous astrologer Carroll Righter's cousin and only woman bank president in the U.S., was in town from New Jersey to celebrate, "Nancy, Carroll and I want a repeat of that glorious lunch we had last year at Jimmy's. Will you and Gayelord join us again?" It took persuasion, but finally Gayelord agreed to go.

Jimmy always made sure Carroll had his special table. One by one the waiters filed by to say hello and ask what the old astrologer saw in the stars for them. Four years younger than Hauser, Carroll appeared ten years older; with his long Buddha ears, he looked like a wrinkled cupie doll. What a difference a year made. During the previous luncheon, Gayelord commanded the conversation and amused us all, this time he was quiet and reserved. Later I talked with Carroll. "I'm worried about my friend. Did you notice the tremendous change in him?"

"Yes, his aspects are not good just now. December will be a dangerous month; he could go over to the other side."

Carroll had been right on target with me many times, so I did not discount what he said.

Just before Christmas, Gayelord went to the hospital with a prostate problem. Tony and Dieter assured me, "It is nothing, just a mechanical matter. We're getting the house decorated, and he'll be home for Christmas."

Not satisfied, I called Dr. Julian, the person who had given Gayelord his series of chelation and who would see him in the hospital. His words alarmed me, "He's almost comatose."

"Please, Dr. Julian, the family doesn't want anyone to visit the hospital; would you do me a favor? Please remind Gayelord to keep mentally saying his *mantra*." To be certain I told Julian the word to whisper in our friend's ear.

Two days before Christmas, Gayelord came home. "He was on a stretcher, but we carried him through the house to see the tree and all the decoration. He is so happy to be home and sends you his greetings," Dieter assured me, but I was not convinced.

"I am very worried; he has lost all interest in living. If he is given a choice I think he will choose to die and start his next trip."

Tony came on the line. "No, no, he is not that sick; there is nothing seriously wrong with him. Go to La Jolla with your son and his family; have your Christmas as planned. We'll keep in touch by phone."

Three days later when I was called to the phone, I didn't want to answer it. I knew, but didn't want to know. It was Dieter. "Gayelord died peacefully several hours ago." I didn't want to believe it; he'd made the choice. How I'd prayed to be wrong, but intuitively I knew it was his time. I would perform a special *puja* and say goodbye to my beloved friend. Then my thoughts turned to Garbo.

"She will be here tomorrow; the service will be two days later. She does not want to see anyone before then," was the message Dieter passed along.

After the memorial service, attended by hundreds, but not Garbo, we went back to Gayelord's house for lunch. A tent was erected by the pool to take care of the sixty people expected.

As we filed through the house, out to the garden, there stood Greta Garbo. Dressed in grey slacks and sweater, she received each person intimately. She quietly embraced every friend, offering her condolence. All I could say, as I put my arms around her, was, "Gayelord is watching, and he is very proud of you." That day her love for him was stronger than her fear of people.

Later, Tony announced that the house would be kept the same. It would be there for Miss Garbo to use; those were Gayelord's wishes. I kept in touch, but stayed out of the way while people were coming and going. One night G.G. came for a quiet dinner with the Cachins, who were there from Paris. She barely said a word while Colette and I chatted on, promising that we would stay close, as our old friend would have desired. His death would leave a sad void for all of us. Already I missed his late night calls, a time to share a bit of amusing gossip.

A short while later, Garbo called to say she would like to come see me. Tom dropped her off. She was stoic; little effort was made to seem other than sad. Over a teacup she spoke in a low, husky voice,

"Gayelord loved you very much, Nancy. I also. These have been some of my happiest times in this house. I will continue to meditate, but I feel my life is almost over. . . ."

"I will always be as close as the phone, dear G.G. If you feel like calling on a Sunday morning, please do so." I was thinking of Gayelord's calls and the vacuum that would exist.

We reminisced, we talked of death and its meaning. She was comforted by this thought: "In the East, they teach that the departed soul stays close to the loved ones left behind for the first three months or so. What that soul wants to know is that you understand all is well with him. If Gayelord could speak to you now, he would probably say, 'Hey, it's great over here; I now have the total picture in view.' The way to help free his soul from this plane is to understand this and wish him well on his next adventure."

"I will try, but it is very hard to do; he was everything to me."

"When you feel sad, think back on some specific time you enjoyed together." Her classic face was pensive as she listened attentively. When we said goodbye, she rubbed my back affectionately, "Goodbye, dear Nancy."

The curtain came down and I never saw or spoke to her again.

On May 17th, a year later, Jack Warnecke and I were taking a walk in New York. We passed Garbo's apartment. I told the aged doorman that I was a close friend of Miss Garbo's. "If I were to write a note, would you pass it along?" He encouraged me to write it. All I said was, "Today is Gayelord's birthday; I am in New York and thinking of you. Call me if you wish." I included my telephone number. The phone never rang.

---
### 30
---

# *Without the Magic Carpet*

G OING BACK IN TIME, 1977 is remembered for a sad event. Our wonderful, supportive mother died, and what a terrible vacuum that left. Born July 17th, her astrological sign was Cancer and, as Carroll Righter always said, "Moonchildren love to be around food." This was true for Mother and it was her undoing. As a superb cook, it was easy for her to gain weight in her latter years. This put an extra strain on a heart already weakened by childhood rheumatic fever, and one night she quietly left us as her nurse sat nearby watching television. Her treasured miniature schnauzers were sleeping beside her as she peacefully slipped away.

Even though she was bedridden, her death came as a shock. She still seemed young and beautiful. God gave us three sisters the best mother possible, and never will a day pass that we won't remember her and thank her. With her unlimited love she gave each of us that all-important good self-image and inner strength.

We were comforted by Maharishi's comment. "She had good karma. One doesn't get that easy death by chance; you earn it."

She had seemed quiet and pensive the last days of her life. We feel she was preparing herself to go and left willingly. I realized then how much more I understood about life and death because of the teachings of Maharishi. He would tell us, "Don't think of her last days when she was ill; she is rid of that body now and would want you to know that all is well with her. Happy thoughts will be with you always. This way you will release her to her next journey. Once she knows you are all right, she will be free."

We all felt this and let her go.

But one thing I did insist on was that Mother not be cremated until a full three days after her death. "It takes three days for the *prana,* the life force, to leave the body. It is a great shock to the soul if the body is destroyed before then."

This was espoused by Maharishi and all my holy friends. Also, they were totally set against burial, "If one could see the spirits hanging over a cemetery, waiting to be free of the body, you'd never bury anyone." Embalming was barbaric to them.

But then, some of their practices would be a bit hard for us to understand. The Parsees take their dead to the top of the "Tower of Silence," where the birds carry off the remains. The Tibetans do much the same, dismembering the male corpses first. Women and children are thrown into rivers, and the lowest of the low, a criminal, is buried in the ground. Only a holy person's bones and ashes are put in a *chorten* (a *stupa*).

A few months after Mother's death, my children came to me and said, "Mom, why don't you take the Siddhi (pure truth) course? Maharishi would want you to come. You've gone this far with him; why not do the whole thing?" They were really serious! "You go, learn to levitate and come home and teach us."

The idea did fascinate me, as did the prospect of four quiet months in Switzerland. I had been completely out in the world for the past few years. Mother had been so vicariously caught up with all my social doings—the flowers, the gifts, the special attentions being showered on me. Now, she was no longer there to share in my adventures, and a bit of withdrawal was needed.

I told my family I would seriously consider it. I started asking questions about the course and reinvolving myself with friends in the movement. Maybe it was time to take another big step forward on the path.

A few weeks later Maharishi came to Los Angeles to appear on the Merv Griffin Show. Helen called, "If you want to go, tell me now. Only a special few will be allowed in during the taping of the program. It should be interesting. Besides Doug Henning, the magician, and Dr. Glueck, a prominent Connecticut psychiatrist, Clint Eastwood will be on."

"I didn't know he was meditating. That's great!"

"Yes, and he's got his friend, Burt Reynolds, started. Isn't that something!" I accepted with delight.

The small studio was packed. Everyone carried a flower to give to the guest of honor. The atmosphere was full of love as Maharishi arrived and settled himself in his chair. Then the stars were presented. We were especially amused when Clint Eastwood brought his hand from behind himself holding a rose, which he presented to the guru. Merv quipped, "Maharishi, this is very special. That hand usually holds a gun." The audience loved it.

When the program ended, Merv came to the lip of the stage and announced, "We are now inviting all those standing outside the theater to come in to greet Maharishi, so if you in front will come forward, we can make more room."

Helen whispered, "Isn't he a darling. He is so devoted to Maharishi." Merv had become a meditator a few months before.

Maharishi came forward to receive our flowers. In the three years since I'd seen him at a lecture in Los Angeles (in 1974), more grey had appeared in his hair and beard. As I presented a rose, he exclaimed, "Ah, Nancy, how is everything?" He reached back and selected a creamy gardenia from a bouquet nearby, handing it to me with a big, "Jai Guru Dev." Then he asked, "Are you coming to the Siddhi course?" When I indicated that I was thinking about it, he turned to one of his "ministers." "See that Nancy gets the forms to fill out." Turning back to me, he said, "The course in Switzerland starts in January. I hope to see you there." I felt so special. Everyone heard the personal invitation.

Back in the car, Helen pressed me. "You have to go, Nancy. It's such an opportunity to go this way. Later they will give courses in the U.S.A., but it won't be the same. Even today, we can tell the difference between initiators who took their training in India and those who didn't. The India-trained teachers have a better record with their pupils."

Helen and I went back to her house in the San Fernando valley, while Charlie hurried down to the hotel to have a chat with Maharishi. Sitting in the tranquil atmosphere of Helen's blue living room, we were on our third cup of tea, an hour later, when Charlie came stomping in. "How come you're home? I thought you were going to stay at the hotel for awhile," Helen inquired.

"Those idiots who surround him wouldn't let me in. They had me wait in the hallway." This came from the man who had been the head of Maharishi's movement in the U.S. for years. "Finally I got fed up and decided to come home." He took off his tweed jacket and threw it over a chair in disgust.

As he finished his sentence, the telephone rang. Helen answered and turned to Charlie. "It's Maharishi, he wants to speak to you."

Evidently, Maharishi apologized to Charlie for his being treated so rudely, but it still evoked, "God damn it, Maharishi, I wouldn't wait more than an hour for Jesus Christ!" Charlie refused to go back to the hotel, but he did agree to accompany Maharishi in the car to the airport the next morning. "I'd like to talk to you in private, so don't have any of those jerks along." Charlie wasn't one of the growing group of "yes men" who were beginning to surround Maharishi.

I hadn't had much contact with the organization since my legal troubles had begun. I dropped out of initiating at the center, and mainly kept up on the activities of the S.R.M. through Helen and Charlie. Maharishi didn't need me; he'd become respected and acceptable, and the Students' International Meditation Society (S.I.M.S.) now over-shadowed the older organization. Maharishi spent most of his time in Switzerland. His TV shows were filmed in Seelisberg, in the Capitol of the Age of Enlightenment. I was delighted with his success.

Then came the news about Maharishi teaching levitation.

Originally, I agreed with Charlie about the publicity which greeted the Siddhi Course and the flying classes. "Just when he gets respectable, he comes out with something like this. The press will eat him up." The Lutes and I were at Casa Escobar, eating Mexican food and having our monthly catch-up on the news. This we had done for years.

"Why do you suppose he's done this, Charlie?"

"They've got a huge overhead with all the real estate they own these days. They'd better do something to bring in more money. Our initiations are way down."

"Why is that?"

"People are fickle, and there are lots of other gurus teaching here now. They needed to come up with something new."

None of us were convinced it was a smart move, but my skepticism weakened when pictures appeared in the newspapers, showing meditators up in the air while sitting in the lotus position. It was intriguing.

Then came another call from Richard Burton. "We're hoping we can have your house for three months. Susy and I are very much looking forward to being spoiled by Mercedes again." He had sent her roses at Christmas time. "Also, I miss Rama. Are you sure you wouldn't let me buy him from you? You know that dog understands Gaelic."

I was so pleased to have them for a second time and surprised he enjoyed my unpretentious house so much. I made my travel plans.

March 1978, the delayed starting date of the course, I arrived at Zurich Airport, not knowing where to go, but trusting that someone would be there to direct me. Nobody was around. Finally I reached someone by phone in Seelisberg. "Just wait there for a couple of hours; the charter plane will arrive from New York. We are sending buses to pick you up."

When the charter was announced, I saw an efficient-looking young man and explained who I was. He didn't offer, "How nice to meet you," "Welcome to Switzerland," or anything. He acknowledged that he was from Seelisberg, in charge of transportation, but too busy to talk to me. Eventually the group arrived. We were directed to buses.

It was 10:00 in the evening when we arrived at our hotel in Brunnen, a small town across Lake Lucerne from Seelisberg, where Maharishi had his headquarters. We were fifty-two women from all parts of the world—all ages, all sizes. The men had been sent to another hotel and couples to yet another. It looked as though our bulk would be getting smaller soon. On arrival we were offered a glass of orange juice, with the announcement, "The first five days will be an orange juice fast."

A friendly young English woman, named Daf, suggested, "Please be patient, ladies. We will give you your room assignments as quickly as possible." It was the royal we; she didn't seem to have any helpers.

My turn came. "You will be on the third floor. You don't mind steps, do you? You will share a bath with two other rooms." It was okay with me. I had promised Rik that I would not expect special treatment, I would not volunteer for anything, and I would keep a low profile.

He had cautioned me, "This time, don't get involved with the organization. Just be selfish and get all the benefit for yourself. If you volunteer, you'll end up doing all the work, like you did in Rishikesh."

My room was certainly an improvement over the ashram. It was large, square, high-ceilinged, clean and friendly. Soon the crisp sheets enveloped me and I was sound asleep.

The next morning, winter sun poured in from windows on two sides. Mine was a corner room overlooking the lake in the distance. A large fir tree nodded to me. "I think I'm going to like this place." On the lawn below, a covey of ducks waddled among grazing sheep. Snow-capped mountains showed in the distance, like Switzerland on a post-card.

Everything was wonderful except the orange juice. "What a crazy fast. If it has to be fruit juice, there should be a choice. People will get sick on this. Neither Dr. Bieler nor Gayelord Hauser would have approved," I thought to myself.

Now that I could see it by daylight, the hotel was an old-fashioned, wooden Victorian structure, complete with gables and all the ginger-bread trimmings. It was a popular resort hotel during the tourist seasons, winter and summer. By taking it off season, Maharishi paid less than the going rate.

Assembled in the large conference room, we met Rindi, a slim, red-haired girl in a rust-colored sari. She introduced herself as one of the Ministers of the Age of Enlightenment (one became a minister by taking the course following our governor's course), welcomed us to the AEGTC (Age of Enlightenment Governors' Training Course), gave us instructions and outlined our diet. It was worse than India. We were to have no flesh, spices, onions, garlic, tea, coffee, or anything which might "excite our senses." This included no books, TV, radio, newspapers or music. All this was aimed at purifying our nervous systems.

"From now on, you will receive all instructions by phone. There is to be no head of your course. We only need a person to act as a liaison between you and Seelisberg—would someone like to volunteer?" A hand shot up. Rindi seemed to know the girl. "All right, Karen will be the liaison. Now, Karen, select two women to be your aides." My reaction was, "How can this selection be made when we're all strangers to each other?" But I kept quiet.

We were told we could go into the village, a few blocks away, to buy necessities, but from that day on it would be permissible only on Thursday afternoons between 2:00 and 4:00. "Also, we have a 'buddy system' here. At no time are you to be without your 'buddy' unless you are in your room. Will you please select your 'buddy' now."

I was lucky. Margareta Kaindl, a pretty young Austrian from Salsburg, asked me, with quiet dignity, to be her "buddy." Not until later did I realize she was the best possible choice in the entire course. Fate was good to us both; nothing happens by chance. In her late thirties, Margareta had black hair, green eyes, and her white wool costume was obviously couture. She told me later, knowing of the pairing off, she deliberately sat next to me to make sure we'd end up together. I had to like her immediately.

Walking into town later, I confessed to my buddy, "I'm about to break a rule already. I'm going to buy some apple juice. If I stay on orange juice for five days, I will have cystitis in no time."

On our way back to the hotel I heard my name called, "Nancy, I've been looking for you. Maharishi told me you were here." It was Eilene Leroyd, now one of the heads of the movement in Canada. We'd met at Catalina. How nice to see her smiling face in a strange town. "Come, let's have tea." We agreed and, continuing down the cobbled street, found a quaint little tea room.

As we sipped the steaming brew, I asked her how she had liked the course she'd just completed. "It's been the worst four months of my life. The knowledge is incredible, but the people in charge are just terrible." She went on to warn Margareta and me, "They will treat you like prisoners, encouraging others to rat on you. If they find out you are important to Maharishi, they will be even worse. They have made my life hell." Her face looked sad.

Margareta then spoke up, "I've known Karen, the one who is our liaison, from before. She's a bitch. We'll have problems with her."

The one bit of good news Eilene passed on was, "Jerry Jarvis is here; he is looking forward to seeing you. He's been put out to pasture for awhile. I think it's jealousy within the organization. I don't understand why Maharishi stands for it—not after all Jerry has done for the movement."

Eilene was leaving the next day. Her parting remark was, "Sneak out and buy yourself a decent meal once in awhile. We 'old timers' did."

Our first days were spent rounding, again and again, from 6:30 in the morning until noon. We met a half hour for lunch, then had "walk and talk" for another half hour. At 1:00, we were broken up into three smaller groups of eighteen and assembled in separate rooms to read the Vedas for two hours. This was tedious. We sat on sheet-covered mattresses—all the furniture having been removed—and tried to stay awake while reading words that had little meaning for us. Finally, after days of my back aching, I laid down. Immediately Karen announced, "We do not lie down in class."

I answered as nicely as possible, "Karen, I can hear better this way, rather than trying to concentrate over the pain in my back. I'm sure Maharishi is more interested in exposing us to knowledge than to torture." The class agreed, and from that day on we made ourselves comfortable, and only sat up when it came our turn to read.

At 3:00, we took a thirty-minute nap. Then more rounding until 6:00; then dinner, another walk and talk—rain, snow, or shine—and into class for more Vedic reading. At 9:00, we returned to our rooms, with one hour before lights out at 10:00. I suppose it was like being at boarding school. It was so boring!

The first days I paced my room, not knowing what to do with my energy. In Rishikesh we'd spent energy fixing up our rooms the first week. Mealtimes were the highlight of the day—at least we had conversation. Several women became regulars at the table where Margareta and I ate. One was Ruth, from Rio de Janeiro, a funny, jaunty woman who told us about her love affairs; she was fortyish, with wide, cat eyes that never missed a thing. The other was Jenny, from South Africa. She was gorgeous; young and tall, with a strong athletic figure, honey-colored hair, green eyes and the rosiest cheeks I've ever seen. She was like a ray of sunshine, exuding health, vitality and happiness. What a fabulous example of what meditation could do for one.

Places were not assigned, just eight chairs to a table. Ours was always filled. Knowing of my longtime friendship with Maharishi, I was plied with questions. We laughed and had a good time; maybe we generated jealousy by our obvious enjoyment. Sometimes our table companions changed, as it was first-come, first-serve.

One lunch time, about two weeks into the course, the mood at the table was different. Ruth, Muff, an American from San Diego, and Margareta were fuming. It seems they had been called up in front of the three-woman board. Muff exploded. "I'll be damned if they are going to criticize my every move; so I did walk over to the post office during rounding time. Big deal!" She was the head of her center at home. Ruth's complaint was the same.

Margareta warned me, "You're next. I was chastised for going to the village with you yesterday."

Rather than wait, I walked over to Karen's table where she sat with her council members, Marian and Diane. They greeted me pleasantly. I came right to the point, "I understand there are things you'd like to discuss with me? Good, there are matters I'd like to take up with you. Why don't we meet this afternoon?" We agreed on an hour.

Back at the table, I heard more disquieting news. First was Jenny, "I'm on probation. It was reported from another course that I'd broken the rules."

Julie offered, "My boyfriend was thrown off the course for nothing. If you cross some of these people, they really go for you."

Margareta seconded their statements. "Nancy, you don't know how vindictive this organization can be; you must be careful. Remember what your friend Eilene told you."

That afternoon I appeared before the council of three. I suggested they speak first, that I understood they had a grievance to air. Karen took charge, pursing her thin mouth. "Nancy, we have strict rules to enforce here. You are allowed to go into the village only on Thursdays. You and Margareta went on Monday."

"Yes, because of all the orange juice, I needed medicine to treat cystitis. Daf told me where to go; Margareta came to interpret."

Karen sat playing with her blonde curls, which were coiffed differently each day. She was very ingratiating, in a cool way. "You know we are just doing the job given to us."

"No, you have volunteered to be liaisons, not prison guards. In two weeks, you have alienated half the women here. We are all teachers. We came here on our own. We cheat only ourselves, if we don't get what we came for." I could see I got nowhere with her, but continued to state my case. "When we asked about getting permission to go to church on Easter Sunday, you said, 'No, you cannot go.' We didn't ask your opinion, only for you, as liaison, to get the okay.

"Karen," I insisted, "we want you to ask. Maharishi won't keep us from going to church. If he did, I'd go anyway." We looked at each other eye to eye. By the glint in hers, I knew I'd made an enemy.

After the first period of restlessness disappeared, the days settled into a routine. We had the luxury of being one-hundred-percent selfish. In the beginning it was difficult to tear the senses away from all the lovely objects of activity they were used to. With no books, radio, television or newspapers, there was little diversion. In India we had had Maharishi's lectures to anticipate.

On one occasion, summoned downstairs to the phone, I heard ghastly sounds coming from the large conference room. It was as though cats, dogs, pigs, chickens, and a cow or two were fighting.

"*Diós mio, qué es este ruído horrible?*" (My God, what is that horrible sound?) I asked the Spanish cleaning woman standing nearby.

In Spanish, she explained, "This goes on all the time. Sometimes we see heads go up and down—this is what they call their 'flying room.'" This is where the Minister's course took place; they were more advanced than we, and didn't want people looking in.

It took awhile to get over those sounds. "I'm beginning to have a few doubts about this whole thing. This rigid diet, those strange sounds; all this hierarchy business," I confided to Margareta.

Each evening we'd stroll past Lake Lucerne, where ducks paddled around in the chilly water. Snow still continued to fall on occasion.

One bright light was Daf, our one-woman staff. She was always helpful and in good humor, except one day when we met her down at the lake where the ferry boat returned from its crossing to Seelisberg. She was in a rage. "Those bloody fools, they behave like the Gestapo! I went over for the Spring Equinox Celebration . . . I had so looked forward to it." We knew that; she'd been so happy to get some time off. "I forgot my identification card. They all know me over there, but do you think they could be just a bit humane and look the other way? Oh no, it was identification or nothing."

Her curly, dark head shook with anger. "They knew there was no other boat to go back and forth on." After having said all this, she calmed down, became resigned and went on to explain, "There is a group, made up of young Germans mainly; we call them Maharishi's gestapo. They see that no one gets in, but sometimes they carry it to extremes." I thought of Charlie Lutes's experience. She did have some good news, however. "Maharishi will fly over here before you leave Brunnen."

I ran into Jerry Jarvis one Thursday in town. We embraced and enthused about how happy we were to see each other. What a joy to see his kind, beaming face. We had lots to catch up on. "Margareta, be a good 'buddy' and walk back with the others. I'm going to have a coffee *hag* (decaffeinated) with Jerry." He was living in the couples' hotel and was hoping Debbie would join him before long. He'd been there for ten months.

When I asked about Maharishi, his reply verified what Helen had heard. "I haven't seen or talked to him for almost three months." This from the man who had been Maharishi's confidante, meditation leader and workhorse for eighteen years. Things certainly had changed.

We agreed to meet each Thursday. How wonderful to have him there to discuss aspects of the course that puzzled me. Not that he would ever criticize his Master, but when I asked him his opinion of the course, he was honest with me. "The knowledge is profound, but I don't think some of those being taught the Siddhis are ready." I had wondered how some of the would-be governors had even become teachers. He lent me several books. "The last course used them as textbooks." As he had been in charge of setting up the original course, I was thrilled to get something to read.

"Don't mention them to any body, Nancy," Margareta warned me. "There already is obvious envy over your meeting with Jerry." I agreed and we shared them secretly. They were books on *Patanjali's Sutras* (Patanjali, the father of Yoga, and his aphorisms). I had read parts of them at Maxine's, but hadn't understood them.

Then, one day, Maharishi's tiny, white helicopter flew in, landed on the front lawn and our little bearded saint stepped out. He waved his flowers at us as we stood in a reception line waiting to welcome him. My heart felt full. I hadn't seen him since the Merv Griffin show. As he passed me, he commented, "You are working hard, Nancy? Very good, continue and the rewards will be yours."

Sitting at the foot of the flower-bedecked platform where he sat, we waited in anticipation. Maybe something was going to begin at last. All the conditioning we had been doing had been a bit boring. "I have good reports on your progress, so we will move on to the next step. Today we will start with the Siddhis. Today you will learn the Sanyama technique." At last.

Giving us instructions, he warned us, "You needed these weeks to get your nervous systems purified; now you will be introduced to the computer of universal knowledge. You will acquire knowledge without knowing it. This is a powerful program and we will need to go step by step." He asked that all phases of the teachings be kept strictly to ourselves. "Later, if you wish to share some experiences with your family,

*Annie Wehrens and Margareta Kaindl at the Siddha Course in Switzerland, 1978*

*AEGTC (Age of Enlightenment Governors' Training Course), 1978*

*Disney artist, Herbie Rhineland, sent this to me*
*at the Siddha Course in Switzerland*

you may do so, but we keep the technique to ourselves." By the time Maharishi left, we were filled with anticipation—morale was up again.

Later, mentally practicing Sanyama alone in my room, it seemed simple—but pleasant things started to happen to all of us. During this time, Mother "visited" me often in my thoughts. She seemed very close. Scenes of my youth floated across my consciousness. One was the day my sisters, Mother and I had returned to Honolulu; I could smell the fragrance of the flower leis hanging around our necks. I became very attracted to that particular set of *sutras*, aphorisms.

After one month in Brunnen we had to move on to the next place; the tourist season was starting. We would go to a ski resort hotel which was closing down, but before leaving the area we were to lunch in Seelisberg. It was with excitement we boarded the ferryboat. What fun to be out on an excursion. The small island was covered with winding roads and charming old houses with blooming flower gardens; hardly a car passed us. "No wonder Maharishi likes this place. It's quiet, private and in the middle of Europe. He can hop off in his helicopter and be in a major capital in minutes," I commented.

Margareta added, "And now you'll see the Capitol of the Age of Enlightenment." There stood the large, old hotel which served as headquarters. The official crest was etched on the large lobby windows. I remembered Charlie's comment, "If you knew the amount of money being spent on that place, you'd drop dead. Maharishi even has a royal crest for the movement. With all his ministers and governors, one would think he was establishing a monarchy." It flashed through my mind; Maharishi was raised in India under the British Raj; maybe this was his inspiration.

Lunch was served cafeteria-style and was a welcome change to the food provided for us the past month. It had been fresh, wholesome, and dull.

Soon we were assembled in the main meeting hall of the "Capitol." It looked like the setting for a small U.N. Golden cloth hung from the ceiling and covered the walls behind the dais on which Maharishi's chair was placed. For the benefit of the TV series he made in this location, lavish artificial flower arrangements decorated the platform. A world globe sat on Maharishi's right. Flags of all nations fluttered from standards. Placed in a semi-circle, with the focus on the dais, were approximately eight rows of chairs. Writing platforms ran in front of each row. Everything was upholstered in gold fabric. The carpet was bright red. How happy Maharishi must be with this room. Also, how much this must have cost!

We were enjoying ourselves. We didn't know where we were going, but we liked where we were. When Maharishi met with us, it was an intimate time for personal matters. "Even the Ministers are friendly today," I said in an aside to Margareta.

He encouraged us to ask questions, so I waited with hand held high, until I was recognized. "Yes, Nancy, you have a question?"

"Maharishi, this chamber for government conferences is like a miniature United Nations; is it all a *yagnyag?*"

Smiling broadly and nodding his head, he replied, "Very good, very good . . . yes, this is our architectural plan for the universe."

During the early days, we in the movement used to chuckle when Maharishi would plan, "When we have our first center, we will have so many rooms, and in each room we'll have a window, a carpet, two chairs, an altar for Guru Dev," and he'd list all the details. Charlie would scoff, "We don't have a pot to pee in, and he's doing the decorating."

But later Maharishi had explained to us about *yagnyags*. "You must visualize the scene of what you want to come about in detail. This becomes an architectural plan for the universe to aide you in bringing it to fruition. Remember, Jesus said, if you ask the Father for something, you must visualize it as granted."

So all of this was a grand *yagnyag*. Now it made more sense. Maharishi invited delegates from all nations to come to conferences held here. Mainly representatives of the Third World accepted.

My mind wandered until I heard Maharishi's voice announce, "Now we will go to a more suitable area, and I will give you the flying *sutra.*"

We couldn't believe it! What an unexpected surprise. Other classes had waited into the third month to get this *sutra*. The atmosphere became electrified—Rindi appeared to lead us to a flying room.

It was a long, train-like room. We spread out in four rows of thirteen and sat on sheet-covered mattresses. Each of us had our own earphones. Rindi was in charge of the tape from which Maharishi's voice would be piped into each of our ears. It was a clever system; every few feet from the main cord was a six-foot extension ending in individual earpieces. We could each hear the Master speak his words clearly.

"Now we will use a new formula . . ." As his words gave directions, I felt a whirling sensation, as though I were losing my sense of balance. My body started to rock back and forth, everything seemed weightless. I felt a total loss of direction. At the same moment, I heard Doris, a heavy-set, Jewish girl from Los Angeles, let out a scream that brought everybody to. Her body rose up and flipped about the mattress. She looked comical bouncing around. We broke up. Rindi looked surprised at our reaction.

"Did you feel something?" I asked Margareta.

"I certainly did. If Doris hadn't let out that scream, I might have taken off myself."

By the time buses came to take us to an unpronounceable place called Sonnenmauzer, the sun had set, but we didn't care if we went to the moon. We were so excited, we traveled cheerfully throughout the night.

The Sports and Golf Hotel in Sonnenmauzer, sat in a small, snowcovered valley, enclosed by mountains. Less pretentious than the previous hotel, it was a friendly, old wooden building. All the rooms were airy and light, with outside porches running around each story. The large, front veranda looked across to the ski slopes. "What fun this must be during the ski season."

Daf came up to us. "Nancy, this is Annie Wehrens, the manager of the hotel." Annie's suntanned face radiated friendliness, health, and athletic ability. Her trim figure was sheathed in smart ski pants. She welcomed us and immediately volunteered to help me with the rooming list Daf had asked me to make up. She made sure I got a bathroom.

The first morning we met in the flying room, which during the season was a high-ceilinged discotheque. Sheet-covered mattresses completely covered the floor, and the windows were masked with paper. It was all set for action.

We sat around the four walls in a square facing each other. There was a sense of expectancy in the air. Ingrid, a Swede with a whiplashed neck, volunteered, "I'll call out the time signals; with this collar, I'm not likely to do much."

Maharishi had stressed, "For the first week you must not 'fly' for more than five minutes at a time. Then you can work it up to ten minutes." The rest periods were of utmost importance.

By now it was easy to sit in a lotus position. I closed my eyes and mentally repeated my *sutra*. A loud scream from Doris opened my eyes. She was off again, scooting along like a frog. A young German girl started to move; she burst into song, and continued to sing as she hopped along the floor. There was no way I was going to close my eyes for this period.

Ruth started to laugh uncontrollably. Julie, the plump Dutch girl, let out, "Whoop, oh, whoopee!" She collided with another flyer. It was a weird scene. Some were hopping around, others seemed to be jerking and moving in their place.

"The five minutes are up, ladies," announced Ingrid. Everyone lay down where she was and rested for the prescribed time, then we read the Vedas out loud.

"Oh, dear, I can't stop!" Doris hopped past me; evidently the Vedic sound triggered her. It was amazing.

We repeated the program several times during the two hours. By the end of the session, about one-fourth of the class was hopping up and down. It was such a sideshow, I couldn't keep my attention within. I was in no hurry. I'd promised Helen and my family, "I'm not moving off this pad unless something pushes me. I am not going to get carried away by group dynamics."

The second day, Margareta shot up in the air and landed about three feet in front of herself, then made another hop of the same distance, and another. During the rest period, I whispered, "How did it feel?"

She was exuberant, "It's very strange. You feel so light and full of energy. You just *have* to hop!"

"But was it you who hopped, or did some force enter you?"

"I don't know. When it happens again, maybe I'll be able to tell. This time it was so unexpected." Her reserve had dropped, "Nancy, this is fun!"

At dinner Annie remarked, "Everyone is so exhilarated, what's happening? We heard peculiar sounds from the downstairs room."

We explained as best we could. "How extraordinary! Do you suppose you could sneak me in sometime and I could watch?" We made no promises.

Each day more women "took off," and so did the sound. The shrill screams hurt my head. Ingrid was amazing; when she started to move, her head went around and around. How was it possible with a whiplash? Later she explained, "I don't even feel it while I'm using the *sutra*. I think I'm actually better."

It was on the fifth day that I got my wings. On other occasions when repeating the *sutra*, I had experienced dizziness, a loss of direction, and other unusual sensations, but no urge to rise up. Now, into the five-minute period, I began to feel strange. My body started to shake uncontrollably; it started in my bottom and worked up to my head in spasms. Next came a real shock of Kundalini, a shaft of heat shot up my spine, it was scary. I'd had some experience with Kundalini in Rishikesh, but not like this. I thought of stopping the repetition of the *sutra*, but no, Maharishi assured us we'd be all right if we obeyed instructions. These thoughts flickered through my mind as my head seemed to be held in a vice—the vice became tighter. Suddenly, it was as though someone reached down and pulled me up into the air!

I went up and down, and up and down—not forward or sideways, just up and down. What fun! It was so easy. My legs slipped out of the lotus position; I went up about two feet in the air just touching the pad with the outsides of my baby toes. Time was called. "I'm so excited for you," gushed Ruth. "It really is fun, isn't it?"

During the rest period, I could hardly believe it myself. "I wasn't hypnotized, and I couldn't will my muscles to do that. It really is amazing!"

Each day, we reported to the flying room for two hours in the morning and another two hours in the afternoon. It was fatiguing—the noise as well as the exercise. During one rest period, Doris took off and landed on my head; for days afterward I felt my neck was out of joint. Then my lower back started to give me trouble. It was those landings! Two mattresses weren't enough. A lot of us had back problems and had to go to a chiropractor in the village. The chiropractor became so intrigued with the structural changes taking place in our bodies, he came to the hotel to be initiated into meditation.

Finally the noise became too much for me. It was like descending into hell. People howled like animals, chattered like monkeys, let out piercing screams, grunted in pain, moaned as in orgasm—it was pandemonium. Finally, we pulled mattresses into the side barroom and made an area for about twelve of us who were more conservative in our "flying." "Don't you think it should be called the 'hopping room'?" we suggested. Now it was more pleasant. Ruth still laughed from time to time, and a *wheee*, or a *whoop* would be heard, but not the paralyzing screams.

One evening, I was called to the phone to be told I had become a grandmother. "We have a baby girl, named Caroline," Starr announced. "Some day, she will be told that her grandmother was flying around Switzerland when she was born." I was thrilled, but it did make me feel far away. "If you don't need that return ticket for flying home, Mom, we can always use it," joked my son, whose hobby was working on and racing dune buggies. It was a joy to get his news and hear his voice. So, I had a granddaughter! I was thrilled and felt impatient to see her. Starr promised to send a photo.

I had an association with a travel agency in Los Angeles, and one day my travel business associate, Gerhard Muller from Germany, came to see me, or rather, I sneaked out to see him. Weeks before, Annie had said, "Here is a key to the hotel. If you ever want to get out, use the cellar door, it's hidden from view by bushes; and you can walk right up to the road."

So, taking Margareta with me, we sneaked out just before lunch; we'd get back before flying class. Gerhard was delighted to have caused such a conspiracy. "You mean you could not even get away for lunch? It is like living in a convent." He insisted that we try the specialty of the house, raclette, and, with eyes twinkling, announced, "no raclette can be eaten without wine." Two full bottles of wine later, Margareta and I joined our companions in the quiet room. We also distributed the brandy-filled chocolates Gerhard had brought. It was not a very quiet room for long; Margareta and I flew higher than ever!

---
31
---

# The Eye of the Storm

I T WAS A LATE WINTER; the snow continued to the end of April. We had been visited once by the "Ministers" from Seelisberg and given another *sutra,* but otherwise we seemed forgotten by the outside world.

My birthday was special. Sitting in my room, lighted only by the greyness of a snowy day, I was practicing the *sutras* as instructed. Then, slowly, I felt the never-to-be-forgotten golden glow begin to envelop my consciousness. It spread out inside me and all around the room. With my eyes open, everything was lighted by golden sunshine, even while I could see the snow falling outside. "What pure bliss; don't go away just yet." It stayed and stayed. I opened and closed my eyes, all the time repeating my magic formula. Then it slowly receded; I sat there stunned—I didn't want to move—to disturb the aftermath of the exaltation. Later, I floated down to the flying room and shared my ecstasy with the others.

But all was not bliss with the group. One woman had left the course. Irma, who spoke only Spanish, in her frustration would also occasionally pack up and disappear on the electric train into Gestaad, only eleven miles away. Lorraine, now our group liaison, would come and request that we go after her, as I also spoke Spanish. Several times

Margareta and I went; we'd find Irma and then treat ourselves to a Napoleon pastry and a coffee *hag*. Sometimes I'd bring a dozen eggs and a can of tuna back with me. I had an electric coffee warmer and a pan, so I could boil eggs. With a tube of mayonnaise and the tuna, I'd have a treat. I rationalized that my body needed this added protein.

In May several couples and Jerry moved into our hotel. I was delighted; I hadn't seen him since we'd started with the flying *sutra*. Now I wanted to pick his brains. Also, I needed his advice. "We're worried about one of the women, Diane. She's been nauseous for days, and is deeply depressed." When Jerry asked if we'd called the doctor, I replied, "Oh, that dumbbell, all he ever suggests are cold showers! There is no one to talk to at Seelisberg. They're all in the States setting up new courses."

Jerry's council scared me. "You'd better keep an eye on her; we had one governor injure herself by jumping out the window. Which floor is she on?"

Margareta and I guessed the problem. Karen and Diane had been inseparable. While Karen was the fairy princess, in her dainty dresses and saris, Diane was strictly masculine, and undoubtedly had a heavy crush on Karen. Then, when the couples moved in and some were friends of Karen's, she cut Diane dead, and asked her to stop pestering her. Poor Diane went into a complete decline and refused to eat or attend class.

Margareta and I tried to help her. After a long talk, Diane agreed to follow our strategy. She wrote a note to Karen saying, "I've come to my senses, please excuse me. I'm fine now, so don't worry about a thing." She ate her meals at our table, joined us for walk and talk, and sat next to us in class at night. This dealt with her loneliness, at the same time preserving her pride. Within a week, we had her back to normal, once again attending classes. She hadn't needed cold showers, just warm hearts.

Days filled with snow continued and passed without interruption. Finally, in June, spring arrived and wildflowers started to appear. Cows were herded past the hotel on their way to the lush mountainsides. At first they were allowed out for one hour, then two, and so on until we heard their bells early morning and again in the evening as they were led back to their wooden huts. If I have to come back as a cow one day, I hope it will be in Switzerland.

Sometimes Annie would come to my room. "During your rest period why don't you meet me; I'll take you to a place where the bluebells are just coming out." Annie had a deep love of her country and enjoyed showing us the vivid fields of flowers. One day we picked armfuls of jonquils and brought them back to the hotel. As the snow receded, each field had its special days of glory. Because of this new friend, Margareta and I, and sometimes Jerry, saw the real splendor of Switzerland. Looking deep into the fields, one could see countless varieties of dainty flowers. Putting wet moss into small tart pans, we made bouquets which lasted for days in our rooms.

Another improvement was reflected in our menu—delicious tropical fruits appeared. We gorged ourselves on pineapple, mangoes and bananas. We made sinful combinations of berries with thick cream or cream cheeses. No one was losing weight. When Jerry arrived, he brought his cook with him, a young student, Michael, who was working for course credits. Michael took over our kitchen. Now we looked forward to mealtime as the highlight of the day—he had the makings of a French chef.

With the slow approach of summer, we often took our lunch outside. We spread out blankets and took sunbaths. Our lily-white bodies soon turned golden. Occasionally, Annie, Margareta, and I went to a swimming club nearby—always careful to get back in time for class. It was good therapy to get outside, after being cloistered. Besides a few emergencies and personality clashes, all proceeded serenely.

Weeks passed and we heard nothing from Seelisberg; we felt abandoned. Then one day we were notified that ministers would arrive to teach us our next set of *sutras*.

The hotel came alive. We got busy moving furniture and getting the *puja* room ready for our coming initiation. We carried armloads of flowers from the fields to the hotel. We washed our hair, pressed our clothes, and got ready for the big day. The hotel and its fifty-two ladies were sparkling when the Ministers arrived. The atmosphere was filled with happiness and expectancy.

The phone in my room rang. It was Daf. "Nancy, one of the Ministers would like to see you and Margareta."

As we ran down the three flights, Margareta commented, "She is probably going to thank you for the help you have been, especially with Irma and Diane. They would not still be here except for you."

Barbara Woods sat in the side lobby waiting for us. We had met before in Seelisberg, but briefly. She greeted us warmly, her orange sari was in nice contrast to her heavy black hair. "Why don't we just stay in this quiet corner?"

She started the conversation, "Tell me, how are you enjoying the course?" We both expressed our enthusiasm. "Are there any criticisms you have to offer?"

She waited, and I started, "Yes, there are a few. I've kept notes on some of the facets that I feel could be improved on."

However, she didn't seem interested and indicated that we would get to them another time. She shifted around, running her hand down the pleats of her sari, "There is a small problem that has come up regarding the two of you."

My eyebrows went up, "Really, what is that?" I felt confident and happy.

"It has been reported that you have consistently left the course without permission, that you have been seen in Gestaad, and that you have been generally uncooperative." We were stunned. "Because of these reports, we are putting you both on probation. You will not be initiated today. If you can convince us of your sincerity, we will reconsider the possibility of initiating you in Seelisberg before you leave." What a bomb.

I fought to stay calm, "Who reported us?"

She gave me a saccharin smile, "This we are not free to divulge."

My next question was, "Where did we supposedly go when we left the course?" Margareta sat quietly in shock.

"It was reported that you went swimming three times."

Now I could feel the heat of my anger rising, "Yes, and at the Catalina course, I went swimming every day under Maharishi's hotel window with Mother Olsen. I have never heard a rule against this."

"You should know the rules from the Science of Creative Intelligence Courses," came her haughty answer.

To which I replied, "I have never been to an SCI course."

"Then you should not be on this one."

"Even though it was through a personal invitation from Maharishi?" Now it was my turn to attack. "Listen to me well; you have made a big mistake. First of all, Margareta is the only one here who has not missed a single session, especially the early ones, while half the class sleeps in." I spoke slowly but clearly. "I have been in Gestaad on behalf of one of the class participants, Irma. She was totally fed up with the arrogant handling of this course and being badgered for more money. She only speaks Spanish and has been very lonesome. She was leaving and going home. The original mistake came from Seelisberg, but the organization wouldn't give her credit. Oh no, it took two strangers to step forward and give her the money."

She tried to stop me, "This is not the time to go into that," but I went on.

"No, you are going to hear me out. I know exactly who reported us. Has she also told you about some of the problems we've had here while you were in the States?"

She stared at me coldly; how could a course member challenge a Minister!

I was furious. My voice got lower. "Unless we have an apology from Seelisberg, I will leave the course. And when I leave, I leave the movement. I have been a friend to this organization and Maharishi for seventeen years. I have initiated thousands of people; I've opened centers all over the world. I was a friend at a time when there were no others. Do you think my loyalty is going to be repaid like this?" I was so angry now, I got up to leave.

At that moment, Jerry walked past—Barbara tried to keep me from calling out to him. "We should keep this between ourselves."

"Jerry, please come over here."

He turned at the sound of my voice and, seeing my face, exclaimed, "What is the matter?"

I started to explain, but couldn't finish. "I can't talk. I'm so angry that I can't stay here. Margareta, please fill Jerry in." With that, I left.

Once back in my room, I stalked the floor like a caged animal, trying to get rid of my anger. An hour later Margareta arrived, her eyes swollen with tears. She was furious, "How dare they do this to you! You have held this course together. Everyone has come to you with their problems." She went on to say that Jerry had said those exact words to Barbara.

Evidently, Rindi, the senior Minister, had joined them and Jerry cautioned the two women, "You have made a serious error. You should have checked those reports before acting upon them. It's a pure case of jealousy because Nancy and Margareta have been so happy and well liked."

Shortly after, Jerry arrived at my room. His face looked sad. "Why do they behave this way? They have driven all the intelligent older people away from the organization." He tried to console us. "I will call Seelisberg tonight, and make sure the truth is known. There will be an apology."

Not for years could I remember being in such a rage. It especially infuriated me that Margareta should suffer so. "It's not fair; you are not the one they are after. I'm the target, and you get punished for my actions." Her lovely gold and white sari, especially pressed for the much looked-forward-to initiation, was now crushed and wilted.

"Nancy, may I come in?" It was Daf. "I know what has happened. Jerry asked me to tell you what I've just related to him." Dear Daf, she was indignant. "You know in the lobby, where the window opens out on the porch? Well, this morning, just after the Ministers arrived, I over-heard Karen speaking to Rindi. She handed Rindi a paper and said that the two of you were hardly ever here, that you were troublemakers, that you lorded it over everyone because you knew Maharishi, and all sorts of lies. She asked Rindi to keep this confidential, but as a liaison she felt it her duty to report you." Then Daf's expression changed to disgust, "You know how she can put on that sweet little girl act when she wants to."

Later, one by one, our friends came creeping to my door—it was quiet time, and the rules said we were to be in our rooms. They were terribly upset. Ruth spoke for the others, "We all gathered in the big room and, just before we started with the *puja*, Jenny suggested we wait, that 'Nancy and Margareta are not here.' Rindi announced that you would not be there, and went on with the initiation." The concern showed on her face. "What happened, Nancy? Someone said you are on probation. We are all in shock."

Irma arrived—she was livid; her Spanish eyes flashed. "*Bueno, si Vsds. saldrán, yo voy también.*" (Good, if you leave, I go too.)

Soon both our rooms were filled with angry friends. Jenny announced, "We should go to Seelisberg and have a mass protest."

I tried to calm them. "We will wait; now go to your rooms, or you too will be reported. We'll let you know what happens. How dear you are!"

The phone rang; it was Rindi. "Nancy, can you meet me down-stairs? I'd like to talk to you."

My answer came easily, "If you want to talk to me, Rindi, come up here." She readily agreed.

When she arrived, I was not overly cordial. "We are sorry to have caused such a fuss," she began. "There seems to be some doubt as to the authenticity of the report we received."

"Don't you think you got a bit carried away being hatchet men for the organization? Wouldn't it have been wiser to have confronted us and let us defend ourselves? Is this the compassion the course stresses?" Then I restated, "If I do not have a full apology, and special arrangements made for Margareta and me to receive our *sutras*, I will leave." I was the haughty one now. "And, Rindi, you will not keep me from Maharishi. He will hear about this before I leave Switzerland." She left, promising to get back to me in three days—Maharishi was away until then.

The next night, Jerry came to my room, as I had skipped another meal. "What are you doing?" he asked, looking at my suitcase.

"I'm packing. I'm leaving. Margareta is destroyed by this. When the course started she was withdrawn; then her heart softened and she became more trusting. Now she has retreated back into a defiant shell. Have you seen her face?" He nodded; he had. I continued folding and packing.

He pleaded with me, "You can't give up. They win that way. You have to hang on and eventually get to Maharishi. If you leave the course, they will block your getting to him. I know!" I thought for a minute—I'll bet he did.

"If you complete the course, you will go to Seelisberg to be made a governor; then you lay it all out in front of Maharishi."

He had also suffered at their hands. I had to listen to him. I agreed to wait for the apology, adding, "If that doesn't come through, nothing in the world will keep me here," but I did stop packing.

Two days later, we were sitting in class. It was amusing, the class had divided itself. Our close friends sat around Margareta and me, the neutrals were in the middle, and Karen and her few cronies sat on the other side.

Nobody's mind was really on the closed-circuit screen from which Maharishi was speaking with a physicist about quantum mechanics. We listened, but we didn't hear; today was the deadline for Margareta and me.

Daf came to the entrance of the flying room, which was also used for evening class. "I'm sorry to intrude, but Maharishi is on the phone and wants to speak to Nancy." I beckoned Margareta to join me.

"Jai Guru Dev," came the soft voice. "I am sorry for what happened to you; you know you are very precious to me, like a member of my family. Please forget the past days, finish your course, and then come to see me; please tell this to Margareta also." What could I say; all the tension from the sleepless nights drained out of me.

Walking back into the classroom, Margareta made the announcement about the apology; then she went to Karen, who was lounging on the mattress-covered floor. Giving her a shove with her foot, Margareta asked, "How do you like it now, you bitch?"

With only two weeks more to go, we settled back into the course. The charm had gone for me, but, thank God, I stayed. It was not my nature to be a quitter, but I had come close. I was grateful Jerry made me stick it out.

Examining my reaction several days following the incident, I felt confused about the anger I had experienced. Why had such a rage enveloped me? Wasn't meditation supposed to teach one to remain calm in the eye of the storm? Another test flunked; I guessed I still had a long way to go before I could qualify as being spiritually evolved. It was an obvious lack of discrimination on my part to allow such shallow personalities to upset me. As I took it apart I realized it was the injustice that got to me. Wasn't it a search for justice that had originally brought me to Maharishi? Didn't I believe that everything that happened brought a lesson with it—the individuals involved were unimportant—it was the test itself that had significance.

Pushing the negativity of the past few days away, I thought back on the benefits we had received. This Siddhi course had presented the most profound knowledge of my life; all of a sudden I knew things I had never learned. Advanced Yoga one day would be the path I would follow; several of the books Jerry had provided really excited me.

The flying sutra was sensational, but several of the other sutras also brought exciting results. We were requested not to identify the sutras. Sitting quietly in my room one day, practicing the full program of sutras, I suddenly found myself on a trip. It was as though I were traveling into the universe; I could see from the back of my head, stars and planets whizzed by . . . there was the Pole Star. I got mixed up in the Milky Way, but I could see the earth far below. Eventually I returned to my room. Whether my body had moved or not, I don't know, but the experience was as real as any other I've had while being fully conscious. All I could say was, "WOW . . . I'd like to do that again!"

When I went downstairs to share my trip with my lunch mates, I found that Karen's pal, Marian, had gone on her own trip. She'd taken the dinner plates, and one by one, before she was stopped, had thrown them against the wall of the dining room. As we walked in, the floor was strewn with broken crockery.

Jerry explained, "Using the *sutras* is a strain on the nervous system and some people flip out." Maybe that explained why he'd said, "I don't think some people are ready for the Siddhi Course." Once he confided, "In the last course, we worked on invisibility. Several of us accomplished it on occasion, but Maharishi decided it took too much concentration." Undoubtedly, Maharishi was still experimenting, as he had done with us in Rishikesh.

Finally the day came—the course was over. I had been counting the minutes. Granted, the knowledge we received made it worthwhile, but it could have been handled differently and achieved the same results.

Once again we were taken to Seelisberg. When we arrived, Rindi took Margareta and me aside, and initiated us with our next *sutras*. We received the ritual like "zombies"; there was no thrill to the formality—we already knew the *sutras* from our classmates and our wounds were far from healed. How different our mood was from the last time we were here, filled with anticipation.

Later, gathered in the main hall, I murmured to Margareta. "They'd better clean up their own act if they are going to enlighten the rest of the world." Maharishi arrived and we were made "governors." With a sigh of relief, we watched Irma get her acknowledgment. Her radiant face made all our efforts worthwhile. She was profuse in her thanks to us.

Maharishi's advice to us was, "Be careful with your desires. Your minds are powerful now, and you are likely to get what you wish for."

Others joined us as Maharishi threw the meeting open. He asked for ideas of how to get financial support; he wanted to send *siddhus*, in teams of two, to the major U.S. capitals. "Their higher states of consciousness will help diffuse the negativity existing in those cities." He played with his beads and puzzled, "Why are the businessmen not more receptive to the young people who have approached them?" He called on me, "Nancy, what is your idea on this?"

Feeling very much detached from the action taking place, I stood up and tried to participate. "Why don't you send an engineer to talk to an engineer, a lawyer to a lawyer, a doctor to a doctor; when young men who have never worked in their lives come into a businessman's office, they already have two strikes against them; the businessman doesn't take them seriously."

Nodding his head with approval, he suggested, "Nancy, you have influential friends in all parts of the world; why don't you organize this drive; if you put your mind to it, you can accomplish anything."

How happy those words would have made me two weeks before; but now I was not a part of it. Before coming to Switzerland, I had thought that maybe this would be the time for me to work for Maharishi full time. When he'd asked me before to take a prominent role in the organization, I declined with regret, knowing my obligations were still with my family and a sick husband. Now, free to give my full attention and energies to him, I no longer had the desire. It was satisfying to hear Maharishi's complimentary words spoken in front of the whole assembly, but my mind was made up.

"I can't do it, Maharishi. I don't want to work with your organization." It was out.

"Oh, Nancy, you must not judge people during periods of unstressing."

"No, Maharishi, that is not what I'm referring to; I'm talking about your ministers, the leaders of your organization. They have no compassion or friendliness—two qualities stressed by the course. They are arrogant with the public; they spit on the people below them in the movement. I have a letter for you, in which I go into more detail." I had kept a diary during the course.

All eyes were on me as I stood there. Maharishi stroked his beard before answering, "You will work directly with me."

"But it's impossible to get to you if those around you don't want you to be reached." Might as well tell the whole truth now.

"You can always reach me through Rindi or Ma (Jemima Pittman was one of his trusted followers). They will be alerted that if you need to speak to me, I will be available." He wouldn't let me off the hook. "Who would you like to work with as your team? You can have anyone in the organization."

My answer was undoubtedly a surprise, "The only person I will work with is Jerry Jarvis."

Maharishi agreed and then motioned to me, "Come here, come here, so we can talk in private." Gathering up my purse, I slid past the others and made my way to the platform. Sitting at Maharishi's feet, with my back to the audience, I listened while he told me of the urgency which existed in the world, that we must move with bold strokes.

I tried to explain that my primary interest lay in building up initiations and concentrating on what he had stressed during the early days of the movement. I had no faith in the *siddhus* coming out of these courses. *Siddhu* means perfected one—I had seen none of these.

He convinced me to come up with new ideas and work with Jerry. He said, "You can be of great value to the world, Nancy." The ice around my heart began to melt—how could I resist him?

I began to worry about my schedule, not wishing to miss my plane. Mentioning this to Maharishi, he called to one of his aides. "Call my pilot; he will fly Nancy to Zurich." A murmur went through the crowd. "Get your things out of the bus, Nancy. Ma is waiting to see you. I will finish here and join you before you take off."

Margareta was the most thrilled of all—it was a total vindication for both of us. As I embraced her, I added, "I'll call you in Salsburg from London in a couple of days." Many of the women hugged and kissed me as I passed by; it was a happy ending.

Thanking Maharishi profusely, I promised, "I'll wait to hear from Jerry, and then we'll get to work."

As the helicopter rose from the ground, I could see the Capitol of the Age of Enlightenment fade into the forest surrounding it. Soon the island was a small speck in the middle of Lake Lucerne. It was a tiny place in the world, but it had big ideas.

---

32

---

# Keeping an Open Mind

A T FIRST, RETURNING TO WORLDLY ACTIVITY AFTER FOUR MONTHS of comparative solitude was traumatic. The noise and crush of people on busy streets assaulted me. Sometimes a chord in the musak at a store or supermarket would trigger me—an arm would shoot out, or my head would swing around as though I were spastic. My family and friends loved to tell everyone where I'd been and what I'd been doing. Naturally, everyone wanted to see me "levitate." It was a big joke, and I provided lots of provocative cocktail conversation.

While traveling through Europe, I meditated but did not use my flying *sutra*—no sense in breaking hotel bed springs and encouraging lewd remarks. However, once home, I placed large pillows strategically and managed quite well. For several months all went smoothly, but it was difficult to preserve the full hour in the morning and again in the evening. After awhile, I resigned myself to my regular twenty-minute meditations, putting away the *sutras* for another day.

For me, it was time for activity and I plunged into it with great enthusiasm. Hearing nothing from Maharishi regarding working with Jerry, I felt no obligation to Seelisberg—they could contact me.

I picked up life where I had left off before Mother died. My three sons were happily married and María Luisa was attending graduate

*His Eminence Kalu Rinpoche (photo: Naomi Schmidt)*

school, getting her masters in art history. Their lives were busy, so, being
free and unattached, I came and went as I pleased.

Renting my house frequently helped subsidize some wonderful
trips. In the early eighties, Maxine North and I went to Bhutan as guests
of the royal family. From Bangkok we flew to Calcutta where we boarded
a small plane, piloted by a big, turbanned Sikh, to fly to Paro. We felt
like characters out of *Lost Horizons*, going off to Shangri-la. Another
reason for our excitement was the news that Kalu Rinpoche was also in
Bhutan.

Of the fourteen passengers on the plane, three were ambassadors
going to Bhutan to present their credentials to the king. That meant

*Maxine North and Nancy with the royal family of Bhutan in Thimpu, 1985*

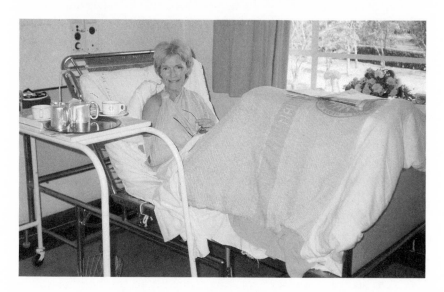

*Nancy's sister, Doryce, in Nairobi hospital after being injured
by a Cape buffalo*

that all sorts of special festivities would be offered. Our plane flew in and out of the mountains, skimming through narrow valleys as we followed a winding river. The countryside below was wild and showed few signs of civilization.

In nine days we fell in love with this beautiful kingdom and its handsome people. The Bhutanese worship the Karmapa as their spiritual leader, and, at the Punnakka Monastery, we finally found the old lama we had sought in Ladakh.

Replying to our questions, "Is the world coming to an end?," "Is there such a place as Shambala?," tiny, skull-faced, toothless Kalu Rinpoche stated, "Yes, there is such a place, but only the highly-evolved can find it. It is ruled by kings who rule for one hundred years. The twenty-fourth king has now ruled for fifty-six years. The twenty-fifth king will find a world with no organized religion, and all will be chaos and turmoil. A ring will encircle the planet and will neutralize all existing electrical forces. This king will institute military methods to reestablish order."

"Boy, that just gives us forty-four years," we commented, "but at least the planet will survive."

Later, in 1990, I visited the old lama's body resting in his monastery in Sonada, near Darjeeling, waiting for his gold and silver *stupa* to be finished. It will be his final refuge for eternity.

Another trip was not as pleasant, but it reinforced my belief in the power of meditation, which undoubtedly saved my younger sister's life.

What precipitated the trip was a call from my sister, Ardagh Marie. Her news hit me straight in the solar plexus. "Honey, Doryce is alive, but she's been badly injured in Kenya. She is in the Nairobi hospital; her friend, Barbara Wells, is dead—both hit by a cape buffalo."

With my travel experience and passport ready, Ardagh Marie felt I was the logical family member to go to Africa. With record speed I had my visa, tickets and all, and was on the plane the following evening. It was a long flight, but twenty-four hours later I arrived at Nairobi Airport.

A constant prayer went through my mind. "Hang on, Honey. You're going to be all right. Please, dear God, watch over her." Having done a lot of hospital work in Honolulu during the war, I worried about the deadly after-effects of shock.

On arrival, I was met and taken directly to the hospital where Doryce was about to undergo a second operation on her shoulder. As we walked down the corridors a sense of dread formed around my heart. It was such a plain, scrubbed, old-fashioned place. A nurse directed me to the room. As I quietly opened the door and looked in, a tired, small voice said, "Boy, am I happy to see you, Sister Dear."

Doryce looked so frail lying there. One eye was blackened; her hair was covered by a surgical cap. A raised tent held the sheets off her legs. Her speech was slurred. Morphine had been administered and soon she was asleep.

After the surgery, when she was again in her room, I went to see the doctor. Dr. Beecher was a plain-spoken Scotsman who inspired confidence. "I had to try what I did. Every day that arm stays out of the shoulder socket, the less her chances are for a good recovery. Your sister is lucky to be alive. When she was brought in, it wasn't her shoulder we were worried about, it was the gore wound. That could send her home in a box." I wished he'd spared me those words. Sensing my worry and fatigue he assured me, "We have her on a wide spectrum antibiotic; I think she'll make it. We'll keep her here for about ten days and hope no unexpected fever appears." I knew a lot of praying would be necessary also.

After checking into the Norfolk Hotel and a quick nap, I met with Doryce's traveling companions, who were returning to the United States that evening. I pieced together what had happened:

It was their last day at Masai Mara Park. In the late afternoon, invited by their guide, Dennis, eight of them took a walk out in the park to take pictures. Contrary to usual precautions, no cars accompanied them. Suddenly, a cape buffalo, hidden by the brush, charged the group. He first hit Barbara Wells three times, then turned on Doryce, who, on hearing Dennis's shout, "Hit the ground," had dropped. The first charge broke her shoulder in four places, the second gored her deep in the groin, the third charge was stopped by Dennis throwing himself on the animal. Only then did the gun go off (carried by the black hunter) and the enraged buffalo thundered back into the brush.

It took ten hours to get to medical help in Nairobi—a nightmare of no doctor, no medical supplies, and difficulty with the emergency plane landing at the camp. Barbara died before the plane arrived. Dennis, who had a concussion, lay next to Doryce in the Landrover for hours. Doryce told me later, "If I had not known how to meditate, I would not be alive." She also helped Dennis by telling him how to breathe and "feel the body." The doctors were incredulous that she never went into shock throughout the whole ordeal. She explained, "When I felt my life ebbing away, I started my *mantra* and never stopped until I got to the hospital. The thought of the *mantra* kept other terrible thoughts away; it was my connection with life—I knew my life depended on it."

On our return to San Francisco, many of Doryce's friends asked me to teach them to meditate, knowing the role it had played in saving my sister. Doryce's reaction has been, "Maybe that is why I was saved; maybe I'm meant to tell what meditation did for me."

My sister's story is only one of the dramatic events involving the supportive effects of TM that I could recite. People continue to appear in my life with special problems resulting from stress. They come by word of mouth, sometimes from psychiatrists I know. Some have problems that could be eased simply by having a better understanding of what life is all about. Many are successful leaders depleted of energy and health because of the demands of their positions.

After a reorganization by Maharishi's Board of Directors, the S.R.M. no longer exists, so I don't check in with anyone. I just teach meditation at home or wherever I am. I am very careful to adhere absolutely to the instructions I learned as a teacher, but do not charge for my teaching. I feel it is an honor to share this knowledge and frequently remind myself how lucky I was to find a teacher such as Maharishi. He definitely deserves credit for introducing meditation to the Western world. He exposed us to the idea of bringing the mind within. When meditation was still a foreign word, he described it as a technique for practical people, saying, "If you want to enjoy the fruit, you must water the root."

Whenever I have contact with the newly-inspired spiritual groups in the U.S., whether it be Sai Baba, Muktananda (now led by Gurumai), or different Buddhist factions, I find former followers of Maharishi. He opened the door to a new path for many of us.

As for Maharishi himself, I last saw him as I flew off in his helicopter in 1978. As I heard nothing from him as to what I should do, I went about my own life. I kept up on his activities and whereabouts through friends, but I missed seeing him and decided to visit his new ashram in 1988, while in India. Knowing how difficult it was to get past "the gestapo," I carefully followed instructions and went through the correct channels . . . several "old timers" had been turned away.

When arriving at Avi's house in Delhi, I gushed with enthusiasm, "I've arranged for a car and driver to take me out to Maharishinagar. I'm really looking forward to seeing Maharishi after so long a time. I'm told his hair is very grey now."

Avi put his hand on my arm, "I don't want you to have your feelings hurt by being turned away; maybe it's best you don't go."

"Why do you say this? Of course I'm going; I'm not going to let those idiots keep me away."

"Nancy, I've avoided telling you this. Our mutual friend, Mishra, told Maharishi you were coming, and he said he did not want to see you, that you are with the CIA."

I reacted with laughter, "That is ridiculous! I am a governor of his movement. I've never been or ever will be CIA, but if I had been, it didn't keep Maharishi from accepting my help in those early days. Maybe they got me mixed up with Tony." Such a stupid statement was not going to keep me from seeing my old friend. "Besides, he promised he would always be available to me. I am going."

Arriving at ten the next morning I was refused entry by the peons at the main gate until a visiting military officer drove up and volunteered to take me to the entrance to Maharishi's private house. Once there I sent a note in, "Jai Guru Dev, dear Maharishi, I know how busy you are but may I have five minutes to say hello and give you my love. It has been such a long time," and then my signature.

The Brahmachari returned to report, "He is too busy to see anyone."

I countered with, "I have a book. I'll just sit here and wait."

His answer surprised me, "You will have to wait outside the ashram in your car."

"But surely I can walk around a bit. I'd like to see what they've done here."

Again the answer was "No."

So, we waited in the sun, the day growing warmer. There was no shade, so I sat on the ground in the shadow of the car. We were surrounded by a dusty field full of dry weeds. How could they do this to us? I thought back to the day I had asked Doris Duke to give money to Maharishi to help him build his ashram in Rishikesh—she did, one hundred thousand dollars! My stock had been pretty high that day.

A young European man dressed in white approached us about 1:00 p.m. "You asked about Rindi and Ma. They are in deep meditation and cannot be disturbed." So much for "always being available." "I don't think you should wait any longer." The fact that we were here from California didn't make an impression.

"Go back to Delhi and we'll call you. Maybe it will be possible tomorrow."

When I arrived back at Avi's, Vydia Shukla and Vina Mody were there. "Well, how did your meeting with Maharishi go?" They were incredulous at my answer. "After all you have done for him just in India alone! Nobody can be that busy." (This from the man who would soon become the Foreign Minister of India.)

Vydia reminded me of the time I'd asked him to help Maharishi obtain a landing field in Rishikesh, and Vina added, "How about the time Piloo defended him in front of Parliament as a favor to you? He can't forget the people who helped him when he needed it most."

I could not convince them that it was all right, that I understood how busy he was. "Maharishi never stops working for the good of the world; he never has time for himself. He is single-minded about his mission; it was not important to the universe that he see me."

"But you went as an old friend." They shook their heads; they remained unconvinced.

Later, I tried to be honest with myself and put the matter in perspective. It was disappointing; I'd had such expectations, but Jerry Jarvis and Charlie Lutes had been shunted aside also, and they still loved Maharishi. Nothing had actually changed; I still had all the knowledge he had taught me. My mind went back again to 1962 and Lama Govinda's words, "Your guru will be in a mortal body and will be only a certain percent divine, so forgive his weaknesses and keep your eye on the divine."

I realized it was the mortal man who had disappointed me—his lack of loyalty to old friends—but was a Maharishi an ordinary man? No. And maybe he did not have friends, just people who could help or serve him. I was not going to judge him.

He always said he was not a personal guru, but a world teacher, and that his ultimate work would be to help India and bring about world peace.

He continues to attract brilliant young thinkers such as Harvard Ph.D., John Hagelin, who left Stanford to head the physics department at Maharishi International University. Recently on tour, he startled an erudite Oxford crowd of scientists and academics with his latest news on Einstein's dream, the discovery of a single theory explaining all the physical laws of nature—the Theory of Everything. He gives credit in his paper, "Restructuring Physics from its Foundation in Light of Maharishi's Vedic Science," to the influence the tiny guru has had on his thinking process. He calls Maharishi today's "Einstein in the field of consciousness." In its 1991 cover story, *Discover Magazine*, poses the possibility of Dr. Hagelin and his three collaborators being awarded a Nobel Prize.

Maharishi is also expanding his teaching through his disciple, Dr. Deepak Chopra, an Indian endocrinologist, who became dismayed by the side effects of much of Western medicine. He could not have selected a more impressive person. His books *Quantum Healing, Unconditional Life* and others are reaching millions. Instilling hope and confidence on his lecture tours, his audiences rarely fail to give him a standing ovation.

While attending a seminar on Ayurvedic Healing with him several years ago, I asked Dr. Chopra if he believed in Manav Mootra (auto urine therapy). He looked surprised, but answered, "Oh yes, it is part of Ayurvedic teaching."

I had heard of Manav Mootra through Maxine North. She wrote to Moraji Desai's office while he was the Prime Minister of India, requesting information as to how this octogenarian remained so young and energetic. Back came the book, *Manav Mootra*, which she then passed on to me. The theory is that urine is not a waste product but a healing "Golden Elixir," and the daily drinking of a small amount of one's own urine keeps the immune system healthy. Considered a sterile solution for the first twenty minutes, urine can be used in many ways. I had an occasion to try the theory out.

As a result of incorrect eye medicine prescribed for me in India after a bout with conjunctivitis, I started having severe problems with my corneas, the "dry eye syndrome." I became totally dependent on drops my U.S. doctor subsequently gave me; as long as I used them several times an hour, I was comfortable.

On returning to India in 1989, I carried enough ampuls to see me through the six weeks there. On the flight to Kashmir my medicine/cosmetic bag disappeared and with it my eye drops. I was in a panic as it was impossible to even buy "Tears" in India. So what was I to do? The American Embassy could not help me in time. So, remembering *Manav Mootra*, I bought an eye cup and used my urine three times a day—it worked!

Six weeks later, back in the U.S., I checked in with my corneal specialist.

"Dr. Levine, how do you find my corneas? I've been in India; there's been lots of heat and dust, besides flying."

"Well, frankly, I've never seen your eyes looking better. How often are you using your drops?"

"I don't need them any more." Then I told him what I'd been doing. He almost had a fit and said I was crazy. His mind was completely closed to learning something of value, even though the evidence was supported by his own examination.

Maharishi's life has been a wonderful example for me—to see how one person could make such an impact on the world. Thirty years ago he was a penniless holy man arriving in the U.S. with nothing but an idea. Now, in the '90s, Maharishi has moved his headquarters to Holland. Since the Berlin Wall came down he has taught over 40,000 Eastern Europeans to meditate, and at this writing he has 7,000 Siddhas gathered there, trying to combat the negative vibrations caused by the Gulf War. Maharishi maintains, "Peace will never exist until people become full within themselves."

Another example of the power of a strong belief was brought to me in the '80s by Tom Green and Terry Pearce, two successful business men in their forties. We met at a gathering of peace organization leaders in Los Angeles. It was a disappointing meeting—so much ego displayed, but after several hours of exposure to each other, Tom and Terry approached me.

"We would like two days of uninterrupted time with you to present our peace plan."

As they were the only ones to impress me at the meeting, they had my attention. "Fine, come stay at the house and we'll lock the doors and disconnect the phone."

"Ask your daughter also; she's a clear thinker." It was agreed.

The plan they laid out was simple but impressive. "We have taken an amateur poll across the state. We find everyone wants peace, but nobody thinks it's possible."

"So where do you go from there?"

"A person can't even pick up a glass unless he *knows* it's possible."

"Then peace is impossible?"

"No, what we need is a massive mind switch. Every idea has its time; that is evolution. We feel the time is now."

"No small job, how do you start?"

"We convince the leaders of China, the U.S.A. and Russia that it can be done. Each will think it's his idea and he will go down in history as the leader who brought peace to this planet."

"Well, that's thinking big, but how can I help with such a plan?"

"This will be done through networking. We must convince these leaders that they have the support of the business community—politicians, opinion makers, and even the military. Can you imagine what would happen if Dun Xiao Peng, Gorbachev and Reagan all spoke over a simulcast to their respective countries and presented a Peace Initiative? After the broadcast is finished, what happens when maybe a billion people say to each other, 'maybe peace is possible after all'—that starts evolution rolling and you can't go back."

"Wow, what an idea."

"You know a lot of important people we will need to get to—here is your role—open those doors."

By the end of two days going over fine details and role playing, I began to feel the power in what originally had seemed naive and simple.

"Try it out on a few friends and see if you are comfortable with the idea." These were their parting words. I began to think. . . .

Within a week I was convinced. I called Holmes Tuttle, the man responsible for getting Reagan to first run for Governor of California and then for President of the United States. "Holmes, may I have an hour of your time? I want to bring two men to meet you."

On the date agreed, I drove Tom and Terry to Montecito to meet Holmes. What a dear friend—his friendly, intelligent face beamed with pleasure as I introduced the two clean-cut, handsome young businessmen.

"Tom was an executive with General Mills, while Terry was likewise with IBM. They now own their own businesses. They both have families, and because of them feel a deep commitment to work towards a peaceful world."

At the end of the hour, Holmes burst forth. "You guys remind me of myself thirty-five years ago! Yes, I will help you," and he named key people to contact first. So, it started.

Four years later we saw the climax of our work. When Gorbachev and Reagan met in Geneva, each carried in his briefcase a one-page memo made out by Tom and Terry—Reagan's at the request of National Security Chief Bud McFarlane, and Gorbachev's at the request of Dobrynin. Both leaders had an image of a peace plan orchestrated by two unknown men, Tom and Terry, who spent hundreds of hours and thousands of dollars on continuous travel while networking. Theirs was a give-away idea with no egos involved.

We formed no committee, but reached out to power brokers from all walks of life, while concentrating on the three superpowers. It began as an idea with just a few committed players. The lesson was, never say, "I am only one person; what can I do to make a difference?"

Over the years I have become increasingly attracted to my Buddhist friends. Sister Palmo and the Karmapa, with his entourage, came to Los Angeles several times. Many of the monks stayed with me. Mostly they are simple, natural and unspoiled by civilization.

One year, the Karmapa's lama, Ayang Rinpoche, came and gave twenty-five of us the *Phowa*—the Tibetan course in death. During eight intensive days of chanting and visualization, we learned how to approach death and deal with the process of dying. After the course I invited Ayang and his monks to visit me in Beverly Hills for a well-deserved bit of R and R. I took them to Disneyland, and what fun it was. While everyone else in the park stared at the lamas in their long wine and saffron robes, they went from ride to ride like excited children. Their favorite ride was in the small cars; they took turns bumping into Rinpoche. Another day, while picnicking at Malibu, they saw their first scuba diver emerge from the sea. They all ran down the beach to investigate this weird figure in black carrying a speargun in his hand.

Most of my spiritual friends from India and Tibet are filled with unshakable, absolute faith, the result of the unbounded bliss often experienced during periods of meditations. In contrast, I think of my friend, K.C. Castenedas, the late minister of one of Beverly Hills' most attended churches. He married and buried most of my Protestant friends here. One day as we sat on a boat, waiting to throw the ashes of a friend overboard, K.C. and I were discussing different religions. Suddenly he asked me, "Have you ever experienced 'exultation'? I have preached about it for all these years, but have never experienced it myself."

A few months later, he died. I felt sad about him and his doubts; I thought back on the moments of exultation I had experienced under the guidance of Maharishi.

*Ayang Rinpoche was so amazed at seeing snorklers emerge from the ocean.*

*Ayang Rinpoche who gave the Phowa, the course on death.
What fun he and his lamas had at Disneyland*

In 1982 I visited Lhasa, Tibet, on the second plane of tourists allowed in. What a thrill for me—from my earliest memories, I have had an attraction for anything Tibetan. Then, to enter that forbidden land and see firsthand their imposing citadel, the Potola! It was even more imposing than I expected. The trip was fascinating and fulfilling. In spite of the terrible genocide practiced against them by Mao's Peoples Liberation Army, the Tibetans have retained their individuality, sense of humor and toughness. Their devotion to their Lamas living in exile remains undiminished.

Later I heard from Tai Situ Rinpoche, a Regent of the Karmapa's, educated by Sister Palmo in Rumtek, that during his journey around Tibet in 1985, everywhere he stopped, thousands of people came across the snow-covered land to receive his blessings for their parents who had been killed or died in exile. It certainly enforces the supposition that people who believe in something can endure almost anything.

I was very taken with this young monk and accepted Tai Situ's invitation to be on his board of directors (as I had been with the Karmapa). He had a dream of bringing all the major religions in the world together. I smiled at his big ideas but in October of 1989, I was there when he inaugurated his Pilgrimage for Peace in San Francisco. His guest of honor was His Holiness, the Dalai Lama, who had the week before been awarded the Nobel Peace Prize. What a thrilling occasion it was to sit in the Grace Cathedral while Tai Situ introduced his speakers—a Moslem *mullah*, a Greek Orthodox priest, a Catholic priest, a Jewish rabbi, a Chinese Confucius Grand Master, and the Cathedral's own Episcopal minister. In the background were approximately twenty Tibetan monks sitting behind the altar.

Another miracle of faith and determination. Maybe the explanation is to expect miracles and they will come about. World Peace will be my number one request.

*Tai Situ Rinpoche, one of the four regents appointed by the Karmapa,*
*visiting Nancy in Beverly Hills, 1987*

*He even enjoyed cleaning the pool. At this time Tai Situ wore an*
*amulet on his body, a gift from the Karmapa. Only in March*
*1992, when the amulet fell apart, was a letter discovered within it*
*specifying the name and the whereabouts of the 17th Karmapa,*
*an eight-year-old boy residing in Tibet. In June of 1992 it was an-*
*nounced from Rumtek that the new Karmapa was found.*

*Lhasa, Tibet with Tensing Norgay Sherpa and Ash Haile.*
*Tensing climbed Mt. Everest with Sir Edmund Hillary*

*The Potala, former residence of His Holiness the Dalai Lama in Lhasa, Tibet*

---
## 33
---

# *Closing the Circle*

SO MIRACLES CONTINUE TO HAPPEN IN MY LIFE. It has been thirty years since I was introduced to India and a spiritual path. That path has made a full circle. It has been a path from "right here to right here." I went looking for answers, for an authority, a "father-figure-God" to give responsibility to, or to blame things on. But the road always came back to me—the here and now. I was there all the time. There is not a "path to God." We are a part of God, Creation or whatever you desire to call that force. There can be no separation. All humankind and matter are God-like. The atoms which make up our diversity of forms are simply manifestations of different energy levels and frequencies.

God is my friend, my companion—He, She or It is always there to hear me. I used to feel stilted in prayer; now it comes from my heart, not my tongue. I have continual conversations with God, my partner, the creative force within me. Recently, an acquaintance asked me if I prayed. My reaction was, "Constantly. I never feel out of touch with the Godhead within me—we are one." It was my ignorance which thought there was a separation. "Going within" establishes this truth.

I don't have to depend on the wisdom of some historical person-ality, or some God-substitute. Yes, my spiritual awakening was helped

475

by a "guru," but now I have gone beyond gurus. I have the tools and must learn to use them.

I continue to read spiritual writings and now know what to call myself. I am a *gnostic*, as was Tolstoy (whose book, *The Kingdom of God Within*, inspired Ghandi into pacifism), and Dr. Carl Jung (who helped finance the translation of the Gnostic Gospels). In the early years of Christianity, the Gnostics were persecuted by the orthodox church and driven underground. They claimed truth was to be found in "heart knowledge"—"gnosticism" means "knowingness," and the way to that "intuitive knowingness" was through meditation.

So, this is my belief system, and it seems to work for me; however, don't mistake me, I am not following the path of a monk. I am an active householder. The glamour of activity still attracts me, but now a better balance exists between quiet and action, and I bless both aspects of life. Being more discriminating as to where I spend my energies, I love the "now" and treasure solitude. Meditation has been a tool to "ground" me. If a negative mood tries to capture me, I recognize it, analyze it, and most times throw it off. Sometimes it requires stopping my activity and meditating.

I feel a serenity and security I never had except during my childhood. Isn't this what we are all seeking? Shouldn't religion help a person get through life with less fear and more understanding? Living in contentment brings better health; doctors now admit that stress seems to be the root of much sickness, because it breaks down the immune system.

My energy level stays high and my health is excellent. Besides my routine of meditation and daily exercise, I follow the advice of Dr. Bieler and Gayelord Hauser and eat lots of "living food."

With each passing year I am more convinced there are two methods of getting through life—the easy way and the hard way. If, by writing this book, I can help even one person put his or her life into the natural flow of evolution, it will have been worth the effort. I'm convinced there *is* justice in the Universe, but sometimes it requires a lot of "hanging in there."

I am attracted to individuals interested in metaphysics and spiritual probing; they don't have to agree with me, as long as they are concerned with what life is all about. My house is constantly used by groups working for good causes, and the law which is continually demonstrated in my life is, "What you give out, you get back."

When I do something wrong, it comes right back—like instant karma. It pleases me to know that no one gets away with anything—especially me! Nature sees all. If people are mean, they will pay for it; it has nothing to do with me. I have found the system of justice I was looking for.

As the decades roll by, I don't think much about aging and death. The East teaches there are three parts to a lifetime. The first is that of the child; the second is the householder, the parent, the supporter of the family; and the third is a period of reduced responsibility, with time to devote to one's soul. This pleases me. I like the idea of working for the good of my own evolution. So, instead of feeling unneeded, as so many older people do, I am looking forward to this final part of my life as the best time. Now is the time "to be," and often I see great value in doing nothing. This is a big lesson for me. It has been my nature that when I have not known what to do, I would run off in all directions in order to be doing "something." Now I wait for my intuition to guide me. Meditation feeds this intuition; then comes the comfort of that "intuitive knowing." When I go against this "knowing," Nature gives me a kick—a message, "Get your trolley back on the tracks."

Gradually becoming more centered in myself, I will increase in value to those around me rather than decreasing with age. Professor Heizenberg suspected that enlightenment was a highly ordered state. Lama Govinda confirmed that the unbounded man (the enlightened state) should know no limitations in time and space. Such individuals are capable of "extraordinary behavior." This is what our planet seems to need—maybe our Founding Fathers who created the Constitution were such spiritually-extraordinary men. I would not compare myself to them, but self-improvement should be a reasonable goal for everyone.

Carl Jung, after a long life of dealing with people's problems, came to the conclusion that it is near to impossible to live life happily without a spiritual belief. It has brought me happiness to be able to share some of my beliefs with others.

My symbol is the circle; it has no beginning and no ending. It just keeps revolving—meditation makes for orderly thinking, orderly thinking looks for practical solutions, practical solutions support Nature's Laws, and natural law supports man and his planet. Maybe it is as simple as that—a matter of "getting in tune."

Life flows as a never-ending series of new happenings and new opportunities. When death does close my eyes, it will be another "beginning"—this time into the unknown, which must be the greatest adventure of all. And so, as the soul seems to go from life to death, from the unmanifest to the manifest, and back to the unmanifest, a circle continues into eternity.

> Not shaken by adversity,
> Not hankering after happiness:
> Free from fear, free from anger,
> Free from the things of desire.
> I call him a seer, and illumined.
>
> *Bhagavad Gita*

*from*

*Friends and Family*

*album*

*Nancy's eldest son, Rik Cooke, and wife, Bronwyn James Cooke*

*Brett and Olga Cooke with daughters, Sonya and Sasha,*
*at home in College Station, Texas*

Nancy with grandaughter,
Caroline Cooke, 1992
"She's fourteen years old and two
inches taller than I!"
(Starr's daughter)

Starr Cooke with second wife, Joan

My beloved Eleanora de Herrera (who died in Dec. 1991), my step-daughter

*The three look-alike sisters, 1989*

*María Luisa and Nancy's birthday, April 12, 1992*
*Back row: Starr and Rik*
*Front row: Brett, Nancy and María Luisa*

*Nancy dune buggy racing with son, Starr—"It's thrilling!"*

*Sidney Butchkiss and Michael Oliver with Nancy, rafting on the Ganges*

*Arnold Schulman and Mrs. Aldous (Laura) Huxley having dinner at Nancy's house*

*Nancy and Madam Pandit (Nehru's sister), Michael Oliver, and Rita Dar (Madam Pandit's daughter)*

*Nancy with Ingrid Von Richthoven in front of Katchenchunga Mountain in Darjeeling, 1990*

*Nancy at Windamere Hotel in Darjeeling with owner, Mary Tenduf-la, 1990*

*Nancy about to ride a camel at the Pushkar camel fair, 1990*

*Nancy with Sir Edmund Hillary in November, 1990 on a camel trek in Rajasthan, India*

*The Maharajah (Bubbles), Nancy, Doryce, and Ruth in Jaipur*

*Tatwala Baba*

A SAN FRANCISCO BORN CALIFORNIAN, Nancy Cooke de Herrera left her studies at Stanford University during WWII, and crossed the Pacific in a military convoy to marry the scion of a famous missionary family of Hawaii. During the war years, she found herself involved with history-making events as hostess to Admirals Nimitz, Halsey and Towers, leaders on the Pacific front. After the war she gave birth to three sons, threw her energies into community service, and opened her home to the flood of visitors who descended upon Honolulu. Among her guests were famous actors, authors, and politicians. Nine years later the marriage ended in divorce.

In Paris, 1951, Nancy met Luis de Herrera, a member of the American team racing at Le Mans, and a year later married the dashing sportsman from Argentina. In Buenos Aires a daughter, María Luisa, was born to this glamorous couple, but tragically, due to atomic radiation exposure, Luis died when the baby was nine months old.

Upon returning to the U.S., Nancy turned away from her former life and pursued a career in the fashion world. Chosen by leading fashion czars to be the U.S. Ambassadress of Fashion, Nancy presented American couture around the world for twelve years.

Continually seeking the exciting and the meaningful, Nancy is captivated by India, its peoples, its spiritual heritage, and returns there yearly. At her home in Beverly Hills, one is apt to meet activists from all corners of the globe. To quote a syndicated columnist, "Dining with Nancy is like a visit to the United Nations."